SPORT, MIGRATION, AND GENDER IN THE NEOLIBERAL AGE

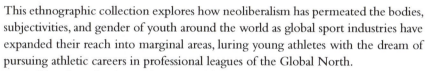

This ethnographic collection explores how neoliberalism has permeated the bodies, subjectivities, and gender of youth around the world as global sport industries have expanded their reach into marginal areas, luring young athletes with the dream of pursuing athletic careers in professional leagues of the Global North.

Neoliberalism has reconfigured sport since the 1980s, as sport clubs and federations have become for-profit businesses, in conjunction with television and corporate sponsors. Neoliberal sport has had other important effects, which are rarely the object of attention: as the national economies of the Global South and local economies of marginal areas of the Global North have collapsed under pressure from global capital, many young people dream of pursuing a sport career as an escape from poverty. But this elusive future is often located elsewhere, initially in regional centres, though ultimately in the wealthy centres of the Global North that can support a sport infrastructure. The pursuit of this future has transformed kinship relations, gender relations, and the subjectivities of people. This collection of rich ethnographies from diverse regions of the world, from Ghana to Finland and from China to Fiji, pulls the reader into the lives of men and women in the global sport industries, including aspiring athletes, their families, and the agents, coaches, and academy directors shaping athletes' dreams. It demonstrates that the ideals of neoliberalism spread in surprising ways, intermingling with categories like gender, religion, indigeneity, and kinship. Athletes' migrations provide a novel angle on the global workings of neoliberalism.

This book will be of key interest to scholars in Gender Studies, Anthropology, Sport Studies, and Migration Studies.

Niko Besnier is Professor of Cultural Anthropology at the University of Amsterdam. In 2012–17, he directed the ERC-funded project titled "Globalization, Sport, and the Precarity of Masculinity" (GLOBALSPORT), which inspired this edited volume. With Susan Brownell and Thomas F. Carter, he coauthored *The Anthropology of Sport: Bodies, Borders, Biopolitics* (2018), which has been translated into French, Spanish, and Japanese. His other works have focused on sexuality and gender, globalization, precarity, and language.

Domenica Gisella Calabrò holds a Ph.D. in Cultural Anthropology from the University of Messina, Italy, and is currently discipline coordinator and lecturer in Gender Studies at the University of the South Pacific in Suva, Fiji. She was a postdoctoral researcher in the GLOBALSPORT project. Her research has focused on indigeneity, sport and gender in Aotearoa New Zealand. She is now also involved in research on gender-based violence in the Pacific Islands.

Daniel Guinness holds a D.Phil. in Anthropology from the University of Oxford and was a postdoctoral researcher in the GLOBALSPORT project. His interests are in the changing social relations and performances of masculinities in the context of globalized neoliberal labour markets, particularly those involving sporting migration. He has undertaken ethnographic field research in Fiji, Argentina, and Europe.

SPORT, MIGRATION, AND GENDER IN THE NEOLIBERAL AGE

Edited by Niko Besnier,
Domenica Gisella Calabrò,
and Daniel Guinness

Routledge
Taylor & Francis Group

LONDON AND NEW YORK

First published 2021
by Routledge
2 Park Square, Milton Park, Abingdon, Oxon OX14 4RN

and by Routledge
52 Vanderbilt Avenue, New York, NY 10017

Routledge is an imprint of the Taylor & Francis Group, an informa business

British Library Cataloguing-in-Publication Data
A catalogue record for this book is available from the British Library

Library of Congress Cataloging-in-Publication Data
A catalog record has been requested for this book

ISBN: 978-1-138-39064-5 (hbk)
ISBN: 978-1-138-39065-2 (pbk)
ISBN: 978-0-429-42327-7 (ebk)

Typeset in Bembo
by Newgen Publishing UK

CONTENTS

FIGURES

CONTRIBUTORS

Niko Besnier is Professor of Cultural Anthropology at the University of Amsterdam. In 2012–17, he directed the ERC-funded project titled "Globalization, Sport, and the Precarity of Masculinity" (GLOBALSPORT), which inspired this edited volume. With Susan Brownell and Thomas F. Carter, he has coauthored *The Anthropology of Sport: Bodies, Borders, Biopolitics* (2018), which has been translated into French, Spanish, and Japanese. His other works have focused on sexuality and gender, globalization, precarity, and language.

Hannah Borenstein is a Ph.D. candidate in Cultural Anthropology at Duke University. Her dissertation is an ethnographic study about women long-distance runners in Ethiopia navigating a transnational athletics market of people, corporations, and capital. She has received support for her research from the Wenner Gren Foundation, the Olympic Studies Centre, and the Centre of French and Ethiopian Studies.

Susan Brownell is Professor of Anthropology at the University of Missouri-St. Louis. She is the author of *Training the Body for China: Sports in the Moral Order of the People's Republic* (1995) and *Beijing's Games: What the Olympics Mean to China* (2008). With Niko Besnier and Thomas F. Carter, she has coauthored *The Anthropology of Sport: Bodies, Borders, Biopolitics* (2018). She served as an adviser and mentor for the GLOBALSPORT project.

Domenica Gisella Calabrò holds a Ph.D. in Cultural Anthropology from the University of Messina, Italy, and is currently discipline coordinator and lecturer in Gender Studies at the University of the South Pacific in Suva, Fiji. She was a postdoctoral researcher in the GLOBALSPORT project. Her research has focused on indigeneity, sport, and gender in Aotearoa New Zealand. She is now also involved in research on gender-based violence in the Pacific Islands.

Michael Crawley is Assistant Professor in Social Anthropology at Durham University. Between 2015–2016 he conducted fifteen months of ethnographic fieldwork with Ethiopian runners, primarily in Addis Ababa. This research, as well as a subsequent Postdoctoral Fellowship, was funded by the Economic and Social Research Council. Alongside his academic work he has written for the Guardian newspaper and written a popular book on the culture of Ethiopian running entitled *Out of Thin Air: Running Wisdom and Magic from Above the Clouds in Ethiopia*, published by Bloomsbury.

Daniel Guinness holds a D.Phil. in Anthropology from the University of Oxford and was a postdoctoral researcher in the GLOBALSPORT project. His interests are in the changing social relations and performances of masculinities in the context of globalized neoliberal labour markets, particularly those involving sporting migration. He has undertaken ethnographic field research in Fiji, Argentina, and Europe.

Mark Hann holds a Ph.D. in Anthropology from the University of Amsterdam, where he was part of the GLOBALSPORT project. He has conducted long-term ethnographic fieldwork on sporting lifeworlds in Senegal, as well as having worked extensively in the field of sports, development, and human rights. He currently works as a programme officer for Human Security Collective, where his role involves both research and project implementation in conflict areas, currently including Cameroon, Tunisia, and Libya.

Matthew Haugen was a Fulbright Scholar in the Kinesiology Cultural, Interpretive, and Science Studies Program at the University of Illinois, Urbana-Champaign, from which he obtained a Ph.D. in 2020. His current research interest is sport development in China. He previously worked as the Head Tennis Coach in Hebei Province for the Chinese government Olympic development programme. While in China, he completed an M.Ed. in Education, Physical Education Pedagogy, from Boise State University.

Xandra Hecht holds a Master's degree in Social Policy at the University of the South Pacific, Fiji. Her academic interests are in social development and social policy issues, disabilities and other vulnerable groups in society. She has assisted in field research on rugby in Fiji as part of the GLOBALSPORT project.

Leo Hopkinson is LSE Fellow in Anthropology at the London School of Economics and Political Science. His research interests include the anthropology of violence, care, masculinity, belonging, and the body. He writes about how people make and maintain social relationships through violent sports, athletes' gendered aspirations and mobility strategies, and processes of racialization in sports industries and elsewhere. He has conducted research in the United Kingdom, Canada, and Ghana.

Adnan Hossain is a Research Fellow in the Department of Social and Cultural Anthropology at Vrije Universiteit Amsterdam. He was a postdoctoral researcher in the GLOBALSPORT project. His research interests concern gender and sexual diversity, race, nationalism, epistemology, postcoloniality, cricket, migration, and political economy. He has conducted fieldwork in Bangladesh, Trinidad, Guyana, and Greece.

Uroš Kovač is a postdoctoral researcher at the "Future Rural Africa" collaborative research centre at the University of Cologne and a teaching fellow at the University of Münster, Germany. He has conducted fieldwork in western Cameroon and northern Kenya on gender, migration, sports, and infrastructure. He completed his Ph.D. in Anthropology as a part of the GLOBALSPORT project.

John McManus is Honorary Research Fellow at the British Institute at Ankara, where he researches sport, media, and society in the Middle East, with a particular focus on Turkey and Qatar. He is the author of *Welcome to Hell? In Search of the Real Turkish Football* (2018).

Anna-Liisa Ojala holds a Ph.D. from the University of Jyväskylä, Finland. She worked as a postdoctoral research fellow in the research project Cold Rush, in which she examined youth ice hockey as an investment. She currently works as a Project and Research Specialist at the Jyväskylä University of Applied Sciences, where she also continues her research on youth sports.

Michael Kentaro Peters is an English instructor at the University of Shizuoka in Shizuoka, Japan, and an external Ph.D. candidate in Anthropology at the University of Amsterdam. He captained the Brandeis University cross-country and track teams and was nationally ranked in the marathon in Japan. He has worked in sport television production at ESPN and as a Japanese–English interpreter in Major League Baseball for the New York Mets. His research ranges between cultural anthropology and English education.

Sari Pietikäinen is Professor of Discourse Studies at the University of Jyväskylä, Finland. Her research interests include language and identity in emerging Arctic economies, including winter sports. She directed the Cold Rush project, which focuses on the political economy of identity and nature resources in the Finnish Arctic.

Introduction

1

SPORT, MIGRATION, AND GENDER IN THE NEOLIBERAL AGE

Niko Besnier, Domenica Gisella Calabrò, and Daniel Guinness

When Niko Besnier returned to Tonga in 2007, a small island country in the Southwest Pacific where he had been conducting fieldwork since the late 1970s, the society he encountered had experienced considerable change since he had last been there in the early 2000s. Particularly notable was the transformation of rugby from a form of leisure, in which boys and young men almost universally took part, to wage labour – in a context in which employment opportunities are very few and far between. But rugby labour was located elsewhere: many young men hoped to sign contracts in the sport labour markets in industrial countries such as New Zealand, Australia, Japan, France, and the United Kingdom, which promised scintillating careers, extraordinary salaries, and the ability to send remittances home and thus regain a productive masculinity that successive economic downturns had severely eroded. At home in Tonga, there is barely enough money to support the national team, whose members are for the most part employed by teams overseas, let alone a sport infrastructure. Whenever rugby recruiters were rumoured to visit from overseas to scout for new talent, a noticeable frisson ran over the neighbourhoods and villages of the country.

What young men hoped was to follow the example of some of their compatriots who had had successful rugby careers in foreign lands. Toetu'u Tāufa, for example, had won in the late 1990s a rugby scholarship at Nihon University, one of Japan's elite private universities, in the footsteps of other Tongan men who had followed similar routes since the mid-1980s. After graduation, he played for the Kintetsu Liners, a team in Japan's rugby Top League based at Hanazono Stadium in Osaka, until he retired from the game in 2018, and was picked for Japan's national team in 2011. He facilitated the recruitment of his younger brother Tafia by the Kintetsu Liners (another brother, Tēvita, was recruited in 2019 to play for a club in New Zealand, but was killed in a car accident on the eve of his departure from Tonga). A naturalized Japanese citizen, he still lives in Osaka with his Japanese wife and children, working as a coach. While playing, he estimated that the remittances he sent to Tonga supported over 70 relatives in Tonga, transfiguring him into an incarnation of male adult success.

But the success of Tāufa's trajectory is counterweighted by the fate of the many other Tongan rugby athletes who remain, literally and metaphorically, on the sidelines, waiting for their chance to shine or adjusting to realities that only vaguely match the dreams that led them far away from their island nation. In 2018, for example, the tribulations of former flanker Sione Vaiomoʻunga hit international sport headlines (*New Zealand Herald* 2017). After playing for Tonga in the 2011 World Cup in New Zealand and at the Hong Kong Sevens in the same year, Vaiomoʻunga secured contracts first with a British team and then with the rugby club of Baia Mare in the hinterlands of Romania, on the periphery of world rugby. Kidney failure suddenly interrupted what had already become a less-than-idyllic experience. No longer able to play, he and his family were close to losing their residence permit in Romania, but returning to Tonga was out of the question as the country lacks dialysis equipment. The player went from sending remittances back home to depending on the generosity of distant relatives, fellow players, and locals. A crowd-funding initiative gathered a large sum, and a few months later a kidney became available for transplant. Vaiomoʻunga was able to play again. He constantly tried to read his struggles in positive terms, helped by his strong Christian faith, the power of which was confirmed by the apparent happy ending.

While Toetuʻu Tāufa's and Sione Vaiomoʻunga's life trajectories can be thought of as representing two extremes, those of most migrant athletes from the Global South are closer to the latter than to the former. But Vaiomoʻunga's vicissitudes have not discouraged other young Tongan men from pursuing overseas rugby careers at all costs, or from families from encouraging similar endeavours for their sons. Dreams of success in the global sports industries since the last decades of the twentieth century have transformed Tongan society, restructuring its economy, reconfiguring gender roles and relations, and transforming the meaning of the future. Similar dynamics have taken place in many countries of the Global South and impoverished regions and marginalized communities of the Global North.

At the same time, the global circulation of high-level athletes has had a considerable impact on many sports, particularly those that command greatest visibility. For example, while prior to the 1980s expatriate footballers constituted a relatively small minority, and most moved between contiguous countries (McGovern 2002; Taylor 2006), by 2018 migrant athletes accounted for more than 41% of players in top-division European football squads, 34.5% of whom hailed from outside Europe (Poli, Ravenel, and Besson 2018; these numbers are much higher in lower-division clubs). Migrations today contribute to many sports a national, ethnic, and racial diversity that did not exist before the 1980s. However, this diversity has not democratized sports in any sense of the term, as those who govern sports structurally or practically continue to be, for the most part, older white men of elite background.

The new migratory trajectories link most visibly the Global South with the Global North, as aspiring athletes from destitute regions of the world attempt in increasing numbers to reap some of the fabulous wealth which sport in regions of the Global North was seemingly awash in. But they also take place within the Global South and within the Global North, and occasionally follow a reverse direction, from the North to the South. Athletes in some sports migrate from marginal locations to central locations within both the Global North and the Global South (Haugen, this volume; Pietikäinen and Ojala, this volume), or move from and to locations that are not easily characterizable with these vague labels (Calabrò, this volume). Guyanese men move to Trinidad to play cricket, but hope to make enough connections in Trinidad to then move to Canada or the United States, whether to play cricket or to work in other domains, while footballers from sub-Saharan Africa move to Istanbul in hope that it will only be a transit point to Europe (Hossain, this volume; McManus, this volume). While colonial relations of yesteryears continue to inform people's trajectories, other structures of global inequality have since emerged, adding new layers to the world map. Countries like the United States have their own "internal" Global South, namely urban neighbourhoods plagued with abject poverty, which feed some of their sports, particularly American football and basketball, with heavily racialized talent (Hoberman 1987; Smith 2014). In the absence of alternatives in marginalized areas of the world and disadvantaged neighbourhoods in wealthy countries, youth are increasingly orienting their futures to sport.

Contextualizing global sport migrations

In this book, we seek to embed these dynamics in a broad social, political, economic and ideological context. Media and other public representations typically frame migrant athletes' stories as individual endeavours, foregrounding the fact that they are a powerful expression of individual creativity and effort against all odds, a framing that only reflects the obsessive individualism that has become a signature feature of the contemporary moment, at the expense of the social (Giulianotti and Robertson 2007). Here, in contrast, we see them as unfolding in a much denser web of social relations. In addition to bearing witness to extraordinary talent and willpower, migrant athletes' careers are the result of the efforts and struggles of many individuals around them, who are in turn affected by their changing fortunes. Migration exposes these dynamics in whole new ways, nuancing our understanding of success, failure, and everything in between, as social relations, selfhood, and life perspectives are transformed by the hope and the reality of migrating for sport. In Tonga and other Pacific Island nations, why have young men sought to transform their rugby skills into migratory commodities only recently, even though they have been playing the sport with considerable talent and gusto for over a century? How and why have sport mobilities become such a visible aspect of the contemporary moment?

We can answer these questions by investigating how contemporary athlete migrations operate at the conjuncture of a number of dynamics taking place on different scales, which at first glance seem unrelated but which on closer inspection turn out to form an extraordinary web of interrelatedness. These include the collapse of many national economies of the Global South and local economies on the margins of the industrial world, and the havoc wreaked on economies and labour markets by the imposition or adoption of structural readjustment policies; the growth of South–North and rural–urban labour migrations; the transformation of major aspects of the world of sport into a corporate industry and of recruiting strategies that now encompass the entire globe; the widespread privatization of television in the 1980s in many parts of the Global North and the emergence of sport-only channels; the advent of satellite television technology, broadcasting images of sporting glory to the remotest corners of the world; and the growing importance of millenarian beliefs in miraculous economic success, cosmologies that echo the cruel optimism that the sport industries encourage. Athletes' mobility and attempted mobility complicate our understanding of the Global South and the Global North, as they both reinforce and challenge structures of global inequality.

At the core of these dynamics is the worldwide turn to neoliberalism, a reconfiguration of economies and lives that has gripped the world since the 1980s. In a nutshell, neoliberalism is constituted by the liberalization of economies, the deregulation of markets, and the withdrawal of the state from the responsibilities to the citizenry it had taken on in some countries in the second half of the twentieth century (Harvey 2005). Inspired by the economic theory of the early-twentieth-century Vienna School (Mirowski and Plehwe 2009), it was implemented in the Global North in the late 1970s and early 1980s as a fix to the economic crises of the early 1970s, which itself resulted from the unsustainability of maintaining both capitalist super-profit making and the welfare protection of workers (Bieler and Morton 2018, 165–166). In Western Europe, North America, Australia, and New Zealand, it resulted in the drastic rollback in the progressive welfare structures that the state had put in place after World War II to alleviate and prevent poverty.

While neoliberalism originated in the Global North, it has created a domino effect that now affects the entire world, and can only be understood in the context of global interconnections. In the Global South, starting in the 1980s, many economies collapsed as the result of the successive destructive power of colonialism and global neoliberalism. From roughly the mid-nineteenth to the mid-twentieth century, colonial powers had restructured the economies of many colonies around the production of single commodities to serve their metropolitan interests (e.g., groundnut in Senegal, coffee in Côte d'Ivoire, copra in the Pacific Islands), diverting ordinary people's energy away from more diversified and locally advantageous production activities. Starting in the 1970s, global commodity prices were increasingly determined by new forms of financial speculation in the financial centres of the world, such as futures and derivatives trading, a turn widely referred to as financialization, a central feature of neoliberalism, which introduced new forms of unpredictability and volatility. In the 1980s, countries in the Global North reduced or abolished preferential import tariffs on goods from their former colonies as part of the turn to neoliberalism. As a result, agricultural and other types of economies in the Global South were unable to compete on world markets and small produbers were particularly affected, while large corporations were better able to weather price fluctuations.

To rescue the economies of postcolonial countries from bankruptcy, the World Bank, the International Monetary Fund, and wealthy donor states stepped in with loans. But there were conditions: receiving governments had to implement structural adjustment policies, including wage freezes; the devaluation of currencies; the commoditization of government services such as education and healthcare; the radical reduction of bureaucracies, which had since independence served as a major source of employment; and the end of subsidies to small-scale producers of primary commodities. Unable to pay the interests on the loans, let alone their principals, many countries faced serious debt crises. This situation has led to what David Harvey (2003) has termed "accumulation by dispossession," whereby wealthy countries and wealthy elites in poorer countries deprive the poor of resources and of the means to generate them. In countries of the Global South, the real victims of the debt crisis are not the official debtors such as the states, banks, and corporations, but ordinary citizens (Federici 2018, 48). In the Global North, blue-collar work disappeared as corporations moved production to the Global South, where wages are cheaper and the state keeps labour under control, thus dramatically increasing the gap between the rich and the poor and between wealthy and destitute regions or neighbourhoods. These dynamics persist to this day.

Everywhere, ordinary citizens have had to develop new economic strategies that depended on their inventiveness, flexibility, and adaptability, precisely the qualities that are prized in the neoliberal order. Hustling, wheeling and dealing, and seizing every opportunity to extract meagre resources have become the norm, consuming all daylight hours and energies (e.g., Jeffrey 2010; Newell 2012; Thieme 2018). Young men, the group that was particularly affected by the shrinking of labour markets, were often the ones who were most likely to develop these new approaches. But these were rarely sufficient to provide for families and communities, and young men have been turning their attention in increasing numbers to the possibility of making it in the sport industries, even though the probability of success in this field is infinitesimal. Young men's dreams of sporting success are fuelled by their love of sport, but perhaps more urgently by their desire to fulfil what is expected of them, namely to provide for families and communities.

In the Global South, most countries are unable to support a sport infrastructure that could offer career opportunities to talented young men. This means that dreams of sporting success are always elsewhere, namely in the Global North, where one can actually make money as a professional athlete. Young men thus yearn to migrate to wealthy countries, but these yearnings are not limited to them. As countries of the Global South have experienced economic downturns, they have increasingly become labour-exporting countries, making "mobile and migrant labor the dominant form of labor" (Federici 2018, 29) in our times. People now see emigrating to seek employment in the Global North as the only way out of their predicaments and are prepared to take enormous risks to do so, such as crossing the Mediterranean in unseaworthy vessels piloted by untrustworthy people, with the tragic consequences that are chronicled almost daily in the media. In many cases, migrations across borders have been preceded by internal migrations, as rural people sought to move to cities when subsistence agriculture and fishing or employment in logging and mining were no longer able to provide for their livelihood, or as they seek sport careers for which opportunities are much more abundant in urban centres (Pietikäinen and Ojala, this volume). Young men's desires to migrate to pursue sports careers are thus part of much larger migratory trends.

Other transformations that have taken place since the 1980s are at the roots of the dramatic increase in athlete migrations. In the most popular global sports (e.g., football, rugby union, cricket, basketball, boxing, track and field), neoliberal policies have turned clubs, teams, and governing bodies into corporations driven by competition for resources and the struggle for survival, and the sports themselves into commodities sold to consumers in the form of televised programmes, logo-bearing merchandise, and other products. Like other forms of popular culture, sport acts as a powerful mechanism that injects the ideologies of neoliberalism into ordinary people's lives (Silk and Andrews 2012).

Pivotal to the neoliberal corporatization and commoditization of these sports was the privatization of television that started in many countries of the world in the 1980s, as states that until then had held a monopoly on television broadcasting (i.e., in most countries outside of North America) sold television broadcasting bands to private interests as part of the implementation of neoliberal policies. These private companies then had to fill airtime with the cheapest kind of unscripted programming possible, and sport fit that bill. Very soon, however, sport governing bodies and clubs in the most popular sports began charging increasingly large sums from broadcasting corporations for the right to broadcast and corporate sponsors for the right to advertise during sports events, leading to an exponential increase in revenues from sport, in top-level athletes' incomes, and in the cost of advertisements. The very practice of sport has been reshaped by neoliberal capitalist interests, as sport events have had to adapt to the requirements of television broadcasting (Barnett 1990; Whannel 1992; Giulianotti and Robertson 2009; Evens, Iosifidis, and Smith 2013).

These radical changes have had a number of consequences that are relevant to the topic of this book. One of these is that sports teams and clubs, locked in a cutthroat competition with one another, have been recruiting athletes much more widely than ever before, searching the world for the next brilliant young football player, rugby player, or marathon runner, and recruit him when he is still cheap and has little experience with contractual negotiations. Some of these efforts are undergirded by racialized discourses about the alleged "natural" talent of sportsmen from this or that continent, which frequently come together with not-so-flattering pronouncements about their limited intellectual capacity. Thus the push to emigrate from economically depressed regions of the world is matched by the pull that these agents exert on young athlete hopefuls in the Global South.

Television has played another role in encouraging young men in the Global South to think of sport as their ticket out of poverty. Satellite television, which became commercial in the early 1990s, now reaches even the most remote corners of the world (Williams 1994). It brings images of athletic glory to children and young people, who watch English Premier League and Australian rugby tournaments. People huddle around television sets in cafés, bars, and homes and no longer attend local games, which lack the spectacular qualities of sport made for global television (Akindes 2011), and dream of migrating, playing in front of global audiences, and earning enough money to support large numbers of people.

The neoliberal reorganization of the sport world has had important consequences for the lives of professional athletes, whether local or migrant. The vast majority of today's athletes (other than at the elite level) are expected to make do with short contracts, employment insecurity, and geographical uncertainty. More than ever before, they have to self-promote and "sell" their skills to agents and potential employers. These practices have trickled far from the centres of neoliberal economies, as in West and Central Africa, where young men seek every opportunity to upload videos of themselves playing football to YouTube and Facebook (Hann 2018, 139). These conditions echo those of workers in the neoliberal age in general, who are expected to be self-reliant and sovereign subjects on whose shoulders rests the responsibility of both success and failure (Rose and Miller 2008; Gershon 2011; Gershon and Alexy 2011; McGuigan 2014), but they are further compounded by the dramatic uncertainty of employment in the sports world even before the neoliberal turn.

Particular to sport, which showcases the body in salient fashion, is the increasingly biopolitical surveillance of athletes' bodies. Professional athletes' bodies are constantly measured, assessed, tested (for doping, as Henne [2015] documents, but in many other respects), and programmed through diet, exercise, sleep, and other minute features of the athlete's daily existence. These practices are controlled by physiotherapists, dieticians, coaches, medical professionals, and others with expertise in the "science" of sport, a vast cadre of specialists who today are as globally mobile as the athletes themselves. Daniel Guinness, who pursued a career in professional rugby for eight years prior to becoming an academic, experienced these dynamics firsthand, as well as the increasing self-surveillance of what one says, when one laughs, and how one presents oneself. Again, these new forms of biopolitical self-control trickle down to the Global South, where athletic hopefuls engage in personal projects of self-improvement that mirror the practices extant in professional sport, often with the help of local resources such as Pentecostalism or the mystical services of marabouts (Besnier, Guinness, Hann, and Kovač 2018; Guinness 2018; Hann, this volume; Kovač, this volume).

These dynamics also affect athletes who migrate within nation-states. For example, Finland is known as one of the world's major "hockey nations," where the sport is firmly rooted in regional towns for recruitment, infrastructure, and support. However, many Finnish boys and young men who harbour hopes of working as professional hockey players skate on thin ice. At a time of economic uncertainty for the peripheral regions of the country, local teams struggle financially, making professional career possibilities few and far between and fiercely competitive. There, neoliberal discourses of masculinity and disciplined and flexible sport subjects create pressure for development of not only hockey skills but also the skilling of the self, ready and apt for precarious yet potentially lucrative hockey markets.

Unlike the circulation of underclass workers, sports migrations evoke millenarian images of sudden success and unimagined prosperity, affording young men the fantasy of redistributing untold wealth, often in preference to keeping it for themselves, and thus reclaiming male productive citizenship. The resulting enchantment is illustrative of the magical emergence of wealth from nothing, which many see as a signature feature of the turn of the millennium (Comaroff and Comaroff 2000). While in reality only the lucky few from the Global South gain widespread recognition, the *possibility* of success in professional sports in the Global North informs the actions and haunts the dreams of countless others.

The increasing role of sport – notably football – in development projects targeting sub-Saharan Africa encourage youth to seek a future in the sport. European clubs and other entrepreneurial parties have opened numerous football academies (or "football farms") in West and Central Africa, designed to pre-select promising young athletes and offer varying levels of formal instruction in addition to football training. Boys, who rightly see little future in formal education, flock in large numbers to these institutions (Darby, Akindes, and Kirwin 2007; Esson 2013; Kovač, this volume). In the background, families, neighbourhoods, and communities also wager their hopes for a better life on the children, despite the misgiving that some may have about the boys turning away from education. In other contexts, countless nongovernmental organizations (NGOs) in the developing world and disadvantaged areas of the Global North promote sport with the promise that it will alleviate poverty, reduce violence, and build character, forming what has come to be called "sport for development and peace" (Collison 2016; Hartmann 2016; Besnier, Brownell, and Carter 2018, 234–239). These efforts are informed by underexamined neoliberal ideologies of self-reliance and "empowerment," and reinforce the illusion that sport will somehow solve structural problems.

Taken together, the constellation of macro-level changes has fundamentally transformed, at the micro-level, the lives of ordinary people all over the world. The chapters in this collection analyze and compare the transformations and their scalar dimension through a sustained ethnographic engagement in a broad variety of national contexts. As they pull the readers in the lives of athletes and people who surround them, the authors demonstrate how sport migrations can serve as a means to explore consequential questions about the world in the neoliberal age. These include local-global connections, the interconnections of dynamics on different scales, the changing meaning of the future and work, and the search for a better life in contexts where resources are more than ever lacking.

Sport migrations, gender, and social relations

The most immediate effect of the macro-level changes we have described is a reorganization of gender in general and of masculinity in particular. Women's increased participation and visibility in sports, including those stereotypically seen as strongholds of masculinity like football and rugby, suggest a progressive erosion of gender boundaries. In the volume's contributions focusing on boxing in Ghana or rugby in Fijian contexts, increased female participation is evident (Hopkinson, this volume; Guinness and Hecht, this volume). In running, the prize money is the same for female and male athletes, and people's perception is that it is actually easier for women to make money because it is less competitive (Crawley, this volume). Kenyan female runners find their way to Japan as easily as male runners, which enables them to achieve some forms of economic and social empowerment (Peters, this volume). In Chinese tennis, female athletes have been much more successful than their male compatriots on the international stage, enabling them to seek autonomy from state control over their careers, pushing the Chinese Tennis Association to implement reforms infused with neoliberal principles (Haugen, this volume).

However, in most other sports, women athletes systematically earn less. Inequalities are also manifest in the media's at best limited interest in women athletes and in the marketing of women's sports that pales in comparison to the marketing of men's sports. Female athletes often have to reconcile the pursuit of sport careers with social pressure to become wives and mothers, in contexts where their recognition as women is still largely contingent on their ability to perform such roles. Thanks to their overseas pursuits, Kenyan female runners have acquired economic productivity and leadership positions that would have been unavailable in their home country; still, they tend to retire earlier than their male counterparts, often at the peak of their career, so that they can return home to focus on motherhood and family (Peters, this volume). In the case of Ethiopian female runners, these tensions have strenuous emotional and physical effects, in that families and society at large expect them to simultaneously bear children and develop the skills to run in races overseas (Borenstein, this volume). In both domains, the women's bodies play a key role, but the demands that local understandings of motherhood and the international athletics industry place on the Ethiopian female bodies are incommensurable; the former demand fat bodies to guarantee a healthy child, while the latter is predicated on a thin body to win races. Yet this incommensurability is largely invisible to both the sporting industry and many Ethiopians, which, unlike the female athletes, do not perceive motherhood as work or fail to see the sacrifices required by sport.

Male athletes have greater opportunities to transform their sporting skills into sources of income, and sport has become a privileged site for the production and recognition of their identities in contexts where other avenues for achieving masculine adulthood previously available to their forefathers have now been challenged (e.g., marriage, reproduction, education, traditional economic activities). For young men from many poorer countries and disadvantaged areas of the industrial world who seek employment in the sport industries, sport looms large in the definition of the future. Dreams of sporting success provide them with the hope of achieving recognition and prestige, as well as the hope of providing for families and communities in ways still expected of them. In brief, while a few women manage to migrate to pursue athletic careers, the disproportionate number of athletic hopeful migrants are boys and young men, and expectations of men are being reconfigured around the realities of the sports industries.

In different contexts and sports, the male athletes may long for distinct forms of mobility. Some hope to migrate to specific areas, countries, or regions, others aim to become globally mobile, sometimes moving back and forward between local and international sporting scenes. However, all aspirations of mobility have a profound effect on the way masculinity is produced through the cultivation of a neoliberal subjectivity. This becomes particularly evident in the Senegalese young men's aspirations within two equally important sport industries, football and wrestling (Hann, this volume). These appear at first glance to be diametrically opposed in their orientations to mobility: while footballers aim to move to Europe to play in professional leagues, aspiring wrestlers focus on local competitions, with brief training sojourns overseas. The former engage with and respond to institutionalized disciplining practices, which sometimes contradict local Islamic understandings of their bodies. For the latter, "traditional" and "modern" means of investing in the body are hotly contested as neoliberal body projects are infused with magico-religious practices. Ultimately, both wrestlers and football players become neoliberal entrepreneurs of the self in their efforts to optimize their bodies for the demands of their respective sports.

As sport reshapes masculinities around dreams of mobility, new forms of relations between women and men on the one hand and men and men on the other develop. In Finland, young hockey players exclude their girlfriends from their hockey-related sociality, creating spaces for themselves only (Pietikäinen and Ojala, this volume). In Ethiopia, a common strategy for male runners who have not succeeded in securing a place in a race overseas is to work as a pacemaker for a more successful female athlete (Crawley, this volume). The relationships between Turkish agents and African footballers in Istanbul (McManus, this volume) or Trinidadian men and migrant Guyanese cricketers (Hossain, this volume) are characterized by tensions over recognition and productivity. Māori rugby players are ambivalent about Pacific Islander players: when they travel overseas, bonds of brotherhood may draw on constructions of shared kinship, but in New Zealand they compete with one another (Calabrò, this volume). In all instances, we encounter the production of hierarchies between and within migrant groups that also change over time and space, which mirror dynamics found among migrants in all contexts (Glick Schiller, Çağlar, and Guldbrandsen 2006; Çağlar 2016).

Yet new forms of cross-gender sociality can also emerge, as they do among female and male Kenyan runners, who develop non-gendered relations of "friendship," assisting each other to fulfil obligations back home and navigate immigration processes, although when male respect is at stake, male solidarity prevails, reproducing gender inequalities (Peters, this volume). The reorganization of gender coming into play in athletic migrations extends to social actors other than the athletes. For example, in their interactions with African footballers in Istanbul, Turkish agents reconfigure their own masculinities in the context of the football industry (McManus, this volume).

Boys, young men, and adult men are surrounded by women whose investment in athletes' dreams and careers is largely invisible. Such is the case of the wives and domestic partners of Fijian rugby players, whose unsung domestic and emotional labour plays an important role in underpinning the transnational sporting industries (Guinness and Hecht, this volume). They face consequential dilemmas: if they remain in Fiji to pursue sometimes successful professional careers of their own and bring children up, they worry about their husbands being surrounded with adoring female publics overseas; if in contrast they follow their husbands to countries like France, where their professional qualifications and symbolic capital is not be recognized and where they are not legally allowed to work, they end up spending their days staring at the walls of an apartment. They move between emerging gender norms in modern Fiji and an expectation that they will prioritize their husbands' careers, negotiating the demands of extended families while working to maintain new and old personal relationships, relying heavily on faith in their husbands and in God. The emerging transnational kinship system is profoundly influenced by the requirements and possibilities of the neoliberal global rugby industry, which offers men the hope of lucrative careers in exchange for uncertainty, mobility, and precarity, and which requires wives and partners to carry out most of the work of raising, caring for, and supporting men before, during, and after their careers. It is a system that challenges traditional family and gender norms of men and women even as it relies upon them.

The dramatic turn that Tongan player Sione Vaiomo'unga's life took highlights the importance of the role of spouses. When the athlete got the long-awaited kidney transplant, it was his wife Sala who interacted with journalists and described to the rugby world her husband's struggles and their urgency. Sala's arrival in Romania made a substantial difference to Sione's life, although that came at the cost of her ability to work. Smiling next to her ill husband prior to the transplant, she evoked the encouragement, warmth, and advice that silently sustains athletes' trajectories. Understanding migrant athletes' lives thus requires expanding one's focus to the social actors who surround them, sustaining as well as benefiting from the hope dynamics in which athletes and their aspirations for a better life are immersed. This expanded focus is only possible through sustained ethnography, which has rarely been the case in past works on the subject.

Indeed, the world of sport is rife with categories other than the athletes who labour on trails and fields and the people who watch them, such as agents, recruiters, traffickers, trainers, coaches, managers, and other kinds of specialists. In many sports, the equivocal figure of the agent looms large as a fundamental piece of the structure, acting as a broker between athletes' hopes and the sporting industries' promises (Klein 2014). Turkish football agents capitalize in symbolic and economic terms on the dreams of African footballers who have migrated to Istanbul as they mediate the aspirations of the footballers, deploying Islam-inflected discourses of "hospitality" that can easily be suffused with racial prejudices and justify structures of domination over the players (McManus, this volume). To survive in the world of running, Ethiopian athletes must cultivate a moral economy of deservingness by displaying submission to the authority of the sub-agent who decides who goes overseas, negotiating between the public realm (the state-owned clubs that pay their monthly salaries) and the private realm of sub-agents and managers who may be their route to great wealth (Crawley, this volume). The agent sometimes doubles as coach or as manager of an academy, juggling these various roles despite the potential conflicts of interest (Kovač, this volume).

Agents are often former players themselves who have walked the hope route and forged successful sport careers, which gives them stature in the eyes of prospective athletes who revere them as the embodiment of their own aspirations, while also criticizing them for having become mere businessmen and having turned away from "traditional" values (Peters, this volume). Sport-related institutions and intermediaries interacting with prospective talent on the socioeconomic peripheries also partake – or at least try to – in the promises of neoliberalism, as their own interests are entwined with those of the sport industries. Like the players, intermediaries are often waiting for their life-changing moment, when they will "discover" a talented athlete and partake in the wealth and social recognition promised by neoliberal sport. Like the players again, they are caught in competitive relations with one another as they search for the athlete that will make them rich. In both Ethiopia and Cameroon, intermediaries are self-proclaimed business people. In the neoliberal sporting industries, there is plenty of space for hope, but none for philanthropy.

A complex array of new social relations emerges around the transnational structures of the sport industries. For example, for Guyanese cricket players, Trinidad represents a migratory node that opens up various other career possibilities both in and beyond Trinidad, connecting them to a larger Caribbean migrant community in the United States and Canada (Hossain, this volume). Their lives are entangled with various dynamics of mobility that conjure the complex interplay of connections (social, economic, political, and ideological) between disparate locations and demand a rethinking of the readymade adoption of an "ethnic lens" in works on athlete migrations (Çağlar 2013; Glick Schiller, Çağlar, and Guldbrandsen 2006). These experiences are accompanied by a noticeable shift in preexisting social relations, reconfiguring cultural formations such as gender, marriage, age hierarchies, and state systems. Simultaneously, subjectivities are being reconstituted, reoriented to navigate industries governed by neoliberal logics, resulting in changes to religion, life projects, ways of conceptualizing the future, ideas about what a good life is, and ways of being in the world. All these projects take place in a particular setting, which demands attention to how place and time shape people's experiences and subjectivities.

These changes in relations and subjectivities are embedded in the complexities of local contexts. In different locales, they affect categories such as religion, ethnicity, indigeneity, kinship, and class, and they colour how athletes and their communities view, experience, and desire sport mobility. People's understanding of the future changes as economies become increasingly dependent on remittances, especially life-changing contributions that are so impressively large that they transform understandings of how society is structured. Social structures such as kin networks and religious communities are reconfigured to foster athletic migration, just as new hierarchies develop, especially as some athlete migrants access resources and renown outside of traditional political and social structures, exemplified by the growth of new churches, new concepts of personal prestige, and new approaches to family obligations. Gender informs the interactions between different localized systems and neoliberalism, revealing how the local mediates the global. Situated in the interface between sport, mobility, and gender, this volume aims to illustrate how neoliberalism transforms the life projects of individuals and communities, and to ask what it can teach about larger questions in the social sciences.

The future is now: new ways of being and relating

In Cameroon, the increasing number of young men who channel their aspirations into football prefer chasing the dream of a European contract over pursuing the possibility of securing a place in the national football league (Kovač, this volume). Ethiopian runners hire private agents to get them into a race in Europe at the same time as they take care not to jeopardize their place in the government-owned clubs on which their financial survival depends (Crawley, this volume). Kenyan runners enrolled in Japanese schools and universities train and study hard in hope of landing a contract in a Japanese corporation's team, but also do all they can to meet financial expectations back home (Peters, this volume). In Finland, boys devote their teen years to ice-hockey, moving from club to club within the country as they evaluate whether they will make it in the industry or be completely left out (Pietikäinen and Ojala, this volume). Chinese men submit themselves to complex negotiations in order to maintain a sense of cultural identity while attempting to achieve social and domestic mobility through tennis (Haugen, this volume). Situated in disparate parts of the world and diverse sociocultural and sporting contexts, all these examples illustrate athletes' struggles to invest in the possibility of a life-changing future in sports (Adams, Murphy, and Clarke 2009).

Hope strongly shapes the temporality and the structures in which people's daily lives unfold, acting as a catalyst for social action (Crapanzano 2003; Hage 2003; Appadurai 2004; Miyazaki 2004). On many occasions, hope of a better life translates into projects where the future is located elsewhere (Narotzky and Besnier 2014; Pine 2014). Sport is a particularly dramatic example of these dynamics, as individual and collective hopes for a good life construct geographical mobility to the epicentres of sport as the passage to grand opportunities. Athletes believe that if they commit to their passion and cultivate their talent, they will be rewarded with wealth, glory, and glamour within a short period of time. Framed within neo-liberalism and its millennial promises of miraculous success, sport promises make the actions of the athletes almost messianic, in a context where athleticism itself has a spiritual quality, as the growing importance of Pentecostalism and other charismatic and millennial faiths in the world of sport attests (Besnier, Guinness, Hann, and Kovač 2018).

Driven by these promises, athletes sometimes neglect less profitable but more secure opportunities at home, devoting their youth and early adult life instead to the pursuit of potentially life-changing projects, making multiple compromises and deploying diverse strategies to navigate the sport industries and the realities which they move to and through as they attempt to concretize these projects. Tears and sweat are no longer mere metaphors as they strive to become and remain professional athletes. Yet these struggles seem to become bearable as athletes are moulded into neoliberal subjects. Mental endurance and strategic approaches become distinctive features of the selves produced around the different sports. Materialized in muscles and actions on the field, they enable athletes to deal with challenges, such as honouring demands from relatives, paying off debts contracted to pursue their dreams, ensuring their own survival, dealing with financial, geographical, and contractual instability, negotiating identities, and navigating their relations of dependence with agents and other people. Cameroon football academies train budding athletes to deal with precarity to the extent that they enter into a logic of suffering (Kovač, this volume). Senegalese footballers and Ghanaian boxers cultivate "athlete selves" defined by their ability to set themselves into neoliberal practices and values while building upon their own localized practices and values (Hann, this volume; Hopkinson, this volume).

In neoliberal sport, work tends to lose its association with labour and duty and is redefined as a matter of passion and talent. While demanding entrepreneurship and creativity of its subjects, neoliberalism concurrently encourages them to cultivate their passions and gifts and to think that they can do what they enjoy if they have the "right" attitude, obscuring the enormous sacrifices that are needed to do so. For example, Māori rugby players and Finnish ice-hockey players both emphasize the fact that they are pursuing their passion as they discuss what motivates them to pursue a sport career (Calabrò, this volume; Pietikäinen and Ojala, this volume). While people around the athlete, particularly family members, may be ambivalent about the pursuit of athletic dreams, the athlete's perseverance is not simply a matter of hope but also an expression of desire. Athletes embrace a neoliberal understanding of the relationship between work and passion and of the achievement of one's dream as being desirable, profitable, and possible. However, this new understanding of work diverts attention from the economic conditions that underpin athletes' migration and from the physical and emotional price they have to pay.

As athletes chase their dreams, a whole structure of hope sustains and encourages them within and beyond the sporting arena. In places like Tonga, the whole nation has invested in rugby bodies as an export commodity (Besnier 2012). Among aspiring athletes in many places is a sense of "skipping" the present by being pro-active and strategic, working hard towards the future, thus essentially living in the future. Yet prospective athletes can end up in a protracted state of waiting, occasionally interrupted by feverish activity, as is the case of Ethiopian runners (Crawley, this volume).

Temporality plays another role in athletes' lives, in that athletic careers in virtually all sports (with a few exceptions like shooting and archery) place limits on age. People in their mid-twenties are no longer able to launch credible athletic careers, which means that most prospective athletes must decide on a sport career (and have access to relevant resources) when they are legally minors. In addition, professional sport careers are very short, as the deterioration of the body, injuries, and other factors render the ageing athlete become increasingly unemployable in a highly competitive neoliberal market. Many athletes whom contributors to this volume have encountered seemed oblivious to these limitations. A recurrent issue is the lack of a long-term vision as athletes neglect education and other resources to dedicate exclusively to sport, finding themselves at the end of sport careers with few marketable skills, a problem that is compounded in the case of migrant athletes, who often lack the social and cultural capital to fend for themselves at career's end.

The presentism of professional athletes' lives has other dimensions. Particularly when they are successful, many athletes have difficulties administering their material resources. Migrant athletes are often under extreme pressure to send remittances to relatives, whose expectations are often disproportionate to the athletes' actual income. The pressure to give is also self-generated, as athletes want to demonstrate their productivity in sociocultural contexts in which the gift plays a central role, but they must operate across different and often conflicting economic regimes. For example, Kenyan runners employed in Japanese corporations or on sport scholarships in educational institutions see their endeavours as an economic and sociocultural investment in a life back in Kenya (Peters, this volume). Families, friends, and many others expect them to deliver instant and miraculous social and economic transformations, while their supervisors and coaches in Japan encourage them to be frugal and focus on building a stable nuclear family.

The unfortunate fate of Rupeni Caucaunibuca, a top-level Fijian rugby player with a distinguished (if tortuous) career in French rugby and one of the first Fijians to gain global recognition, is chronicled in a documentary that showed him living in Fiji, unemployed and bankrupt (Pacific Rugby Players' Welfare 2019). In the film, the ageing athlete teaches a life lesson to his migrant compatriots, encouraging them to save money for post-rugby life rather than spending it on immediate pleasure or distributing it, and to seek better life-skills support during their careers.

In contrast, Māori rugby athletes distinguish themselves for their focus on long-term projects, which may involve coaching or business ventures that deploy the neoliberal logics and values with which they became familiar in the rugby scene, sometimes capitalizing on their indigeneity (Calabrò, this volume). However, when they move overseas, players have to negotiate new forms of Othering than those they face in their homeland, Aotearoa New Zealand, where their Indigenous status confer them *mana* but where they nevertheless suffer from discrimination and marginalization. Overseas, they have to engage with rugby industries and audiences whose understanding of the politics of indigeneity in Aotearoa New Zealand is limited at best.

In many other cases, the future materializes as desire and hope in the athletes' embodied sacrifices and efforts, but never actually becomes the present. Hope becomes the mother of precarity rather than a response to it. The story of Julius, one of the many Kenyan runners who obtained a sports scholarship to study in Japan, is a classic case of a missed future (Peters, this volume). His early achievements and his dreams are pitted against the ship containers that he has converted into a house and office for the small tourist company he now works for in Japan. Located in a parking lot in a new affluent residential neighbourhood, it offers a constant view onto a future that never eventuated. Julius' life also contrasts starkly with that of the Kenyan coach and agent who initially supported him and whom he blames for his predicament; unlike Julius, the coach was able to bargain his running achievements for a new career as coach and agent.

Yet Julius keeps foregrounding the positive. The good-mornings he exchanges with the Japanese inhabitants of the affluent neighbourhood, which Peters describes as the only bridge to the world he ran for, acquire distinct connotations if we think of them as bridges that still exist in Julius' mind. Similarly, Ghanaian boxer Daniel, who has never displayed the skills necessary for high-level competitions, keeps asserting that he can still make it and promotes himself with the self-selected moniker T.B.E. ("The Best Ever"), which he has appropriated from world champion Floyd Mayweather's nickname (Hopkinson, this volume). As athletes persevere in keeping the flame of hope alive, we are redirected to the notion of desire. Julius and Daniel seem aware that the splendid future promised by their sport industry will not materialize for them. But they remain attached to their hopes as their very identity is defined by the desires that have shaped their approach to their future. More than any other context, sport is a site of cruel optimism, where athletes and the people who surround them get sometimes so attached to fantasies of a splendid future that they in fact bypass the good life.

Conclusion: sport, migration, and gender in the neoliberal age

Many of the chapters in this book were written in the context of a five-year project titled "Globalization, Sport, and the Precarity of Masculinity" (2012–17) directed by the first author of this introduction. The project sought to understand the topics addressed in this book through long-term ethnographic fieldwork in a variety of locations around the world in five sports, namely football, rugby union, cricket, marathon running, and Senegalese wrestling. A few of the chapter authors who were not directly involved in the project (Hannah Borenstein, Michael Crawley, Matt Haugen, John McManus, Sari Pietikäinen, and Anna-Liisa Ojala) were invited to contribute chapters because their research provides valuable perspectives on the relationships among sport, mobility, and gender.

While the global mobility (or immobility) of athletes and prospective athletes involves very few people compared to the vast numbers who migrate to escape poverty, environmental degradation, or violence, it occurs at the conjuncture of consequential global phenomena and thus shed light on these phenomena. Ethnographic methods play a crucial role in this process, as they enabled the authors to go beyond simplistic explanations and to uncover the important role played by certain factors that have escaped the attention of other observers or have often been over-simplified. Through ethnography, the authors demonstrate how athlete migrations in the neoliberal age bring together micro-level factors, such as people's aspirations, their understanding of time, and their relationships to those who surround them, with macro-level factors, such as changes in global economies, the development of new technologies, and the large-scale mobility of people around the world. This book documents how people's lives in local settings are inextricably intertwined with the reconfiguration of the global in the neoliberal age.

Acknowledgements

The project titled "Globalization, Sport and the Precarity of Masculinity" (GLOBALSPORT, 2012–17), on which this introduction and several of the chapters are based, received funding from the European Research Council under Grant Agreement 295769. The ideas presented in this introduction and several of the chapters are the product of discussions held at several events, including one panel at the 2014 biennial conference of the European Association of Social Anthropologists in Milan, two panels at the 2016 annual meetings of the American Anthropological Association in Minneapolis, and the 2017 end-of-project conference in Prague. We thank the participants in these events and in particular Susan Brownell, who provided considerable feedback to all project members throughout the duration of the project. We also thank Andreas Bieler, Michael Crawley, Michael Goldsmith, and Adnan Hossain for their comments on earlier drafts. Niko Besnier's work on this book was supported by a fellowship at the Center for Advanced Study in the Behavioral Sciences at Stanford University.

References

Adams, Vincanne, Michelle Murphy, and Adele E. Clarke. 2009. "Anticipation: Technoscience, Life, Affect, Temporality." *Subjectivity* 28, no. 1: 246–265.

Akindes, Gerard A. 2011. "Football Bars: Urban Sub-Saharan Africa's Trans-local 'Stadiums.'" *International Journal of the History of Sport* 28, no. 15: 2176–2190.

Appadurai, Arjun. 2004. "The Capacity to Aspire: Culture and the Terms of Recognition." In *Culture and Public Action*, edited by Vijayendra Rao and Michael Walton, 59–84. Stanford, CA: Stanford University Press.

Barnett, Steven. 1990. *Games and Sets: The Changing Face of Sport on Television.* London: BFI.

Besnier, Niko. 2012. "The Athlete's Body and the Global Condition: Tongan Rugby Players in Japan." *American Ethnologist* 39, no. 3: 491–510.

Besnier, Niko, Susan Brownell, and Thomas F. Carter. 2018. *The Anthropology of Sport: Bodies, Borders, Biopolitics*. Oakland: University of California Press.

Besnier, Niko, Daniel Guinness, Mark Hann, and Uroš Kovač. 2018. "Rethinking Masculinity in the Neoliberal Age: Cameroonian Footballers, Fijian Rugby Players, Senegalese Wrestlers." *Comparative Studies in Society and History* 60, no. 4: 839–872.

Bieler, Andreas, and Adam David Morton. 2018. *Global Capitalism, Global War, Global Crisis*. Cambridge: Cambridge University Press.

Çağlar, Ayşe. 2013. "Locating Migrant Hometown Ties in Time and Space: Locality as a Blind Spot of Migration Scholarship." *Historische Anthropologie* 21, no. 1: 26–42.

Çağlar, Ayşe. 2016. "Still 'Migrants' after all those Years: Foundational Mobilities, Temporal Frames and Emplacement of Migrants." *Journal of Ethnic and Migration Studies* 42, no. 6: 952–969.

Collison, Holly. 2016. *Youth and Sport for Development: The Seduction of Football in Liberia*. Basingstoke, UK: Palgrave Macmillan.

Comaroff, Jean, and John L. Comaroff. 2000. "Millennial Capitalism: First Thoughts on a Second Coming." *Public Culture* 12, no. 2: 291–343.

Crapanzano, Vincent. 2003. "Reflections on Hope as a Category of Social and Psychological Analysis." *Cultural Anthropology* 18, no. 1: 3–32.

Darby, Paul, Gerard Akindes, and Matthew Kirwin. 2007. "Football Academies and the Migration of African Football Labour to Europe." *Journal of Sport & Social Issues* 3, no. 2: 143–161.

Esson, James. 2013. "A Body and a Dream at a Vital Conjuncture: Ghanaian Youth, Uncertainty and the Allure of Football." *Geoforum* 47: 84–89.

Evens, Tom, Petros Iosifidis, and Paul Smith. 2013. *The Political Economy of Television Sports Rights*. Basingstoke, UK: Palgrave Macmillan.

Federici, Silvia. 2018. *Re-enchanting the World: Feminism and the Politics of the Commons*. Toronto: Between the Lines.

Gershon, Ilana. 2011. "Neoliberal Agency." *Current Anthropology* 52, no. 4: 537–555.

Gershon, Ilana, and Allison Alexy. 2011. "The Ethics of Disconnection in a Neoliberal Age." *Anthropological Quarterly* 84, no. 4: 799–808.

Giulianotti, Richard, and Roland Robertson. 2007. "Recovering the Social: Globalization, Football and Transnationalism." *Global Networks* 7, no. 2: 144–186.

Giulianotti, Richard, and Roland Robertson. 2009. *Globalization and Football*. London: Sage.

Glick Schiller, Nina, Ayşe Çağlar, and Thaddeus C. Guldbrandsen. 2006. "Beyond the Ethnic Lens: Locality, Globality, and Born-Again Incorporation." *American Ethnologist* 33, no. 4: 612–633.

Guinness, Daniel. 2018. "Corporal Destinies: Faith, Ethno-Nationalism, and Raw Talent in Fijian Professional Rugby Aspirations." *HAU* 8, no. 1–2: 314–328.

Hage, Ghassan. 2003. *Against Paranoid Nationalism: Searching for Hope in a Shrinking Society*. Annandale, NSW: Pluto.

Hann, Mark. 2018. "Sporting Aspirations: Football, Wrestling, and Neoliberal Subjectivity in Urban Senegal." Ph.D. thesis, Amsterdam Institute for Social Science Research, University of Amsterdam.

Hartmann, Douglas. 2016. *Midnight Basketball: Race, Sports, and Neoliberal Social Policy*. Chicago: University of Chicago Press.

Harvey, David. 2003. *The New Imperialism*. Oxford: Oxford University Press.

Harvey, David. 2005. *A Brief History of Neoliberalism*. Oxford: Oxford University Press.

Henne, Kathryn E. 2015. *Testing for Athlete Citizenship: Regulating Doping and Sex in Sport*. New Brunswick, NJ: Rutgers University Press.

Hoberman, John. 1987. *Darwin's Athletes: How Sport Has Damaged Black America and Preserved the Myth of Race*. New York: Mariner.

Jeffrey, Craig. 2010. *Timepass: Youth, Class, and the Politics of Waiting in India*. Stanford, CA: Stanford University Press.

Klein, Alan. 2014. *Dominican Baseball: New Pride, Old Prejudice*. Philadelphia: Temple University Press.

McGovern, Patrick. 2002. "Globalization or Internationalization? Foreign Footballers in the English League, 1946–95." *Sociology* 36, no. 1: 23–42.

McGuigan, Jim. 2014. "The Neoliberal Self." *Culture Unbound* 6: 223–240.

Mirowski, Philip, and Dieter Plehwe, eds. 2009. *The Road from Mont Pèlerin: The Making of the Neoliberal Thought Collective*. Cambridge, MA: Harvard University Press.

Miyazaki, Hirokazu. 2004. *The Method of Hope: Anthropology, Philosophy, and Fijian Knowledge*. Stanford, CA: Stanford University Press.

Narotzky, Susana, and Niko Besnier. 2014. "Crisis, Value, and Hope: Rethinking the Economy." In *Crisis, Value, and Hope: Rethinking the Economy*, edited by Susana Narotzky and Niko Besnier. Supplement to *Current Anthropology* 55, no. S9: S4–S16.

Newell, Sasha. 2012. *The Modernity Bluff: Crime, Consumption, and Citizenship in Côte d'Ivoire*. Chicago: University of Chicago Press.

New Zealand Herald. 2017. "The Astonishing Story of Sione Vaiomounga, the Tongan Stranded in Romania." 20 December, www.nzherald.co.nz/rugby/news/article.cfm?c_id=80&objectid=11962990.

Pacific Rugby Players' Welfare. 2019. Oceans Apart #1: Rupeni Caucaunibuca. Presented by Dan Leo, produced by Callum Drummond. Accessed 1 November 2019. www.youtube.com/watch?v=lugT_TShU10.

Pine, Frances. 2014. "Migration as Hope: Space, Time, and Imagining the Future." In *Crisis, Value, and Hope: Rethinking the Economy*, edited by Susana Narotzky and Niko Besnier. Supplement to *Current Anthropology* 55, no. S9: S95–S104.

Poli, Raffaele, Loïc Ravenel, and Roger Besson. 2018. "Ten Years of Demographic Analysis of the Football Players' Labour Market in Europe." CIES Football Observatory Monthly Report, 39. Accessed 1 November 2019. https://football-observatory.com/IMG/sites/mr/mr39/en/.

Rose, Nikolas, and Peter Miller. 2008. *Governing the Present: Administering Economic, Social and Personal Life*. Cambridge: Polity.

Silk, Michael L., and David L. Andrews. 2012. "Sport and the Neoliberal Conjuncture: Complicating the Consensus." In *Sport and Neoliberalism: Politics, Consumption, and Culture*, edited by David L. Andrews and Michael L. Silk, 1–19. Philadelphia: Temple University Press.

Smith, Earl. 2014. *Race, Sport and the American Dream*. 3rd ed. Durham, NC: Carolina Academic Press. (First published 2007.)

Taylor, Matthew. 2006. "Global Players? Football, Migration and Globalization, c1930–2000." *Historical Social Research* 31, no. 1: 7–30.

Thieme, Tatiana Adeline. 2018. "The Hustle Economy: Informality, Uncertainty and the Geographies of Getting By." *Progress in Human Geography* 42, no. 4: 529–548.

Whannel, Garry. 1992. *Fields in Vision: Television Sport and Cultural Transformation*. London: Routledge.

Williams, John. 1994. "The Local and the Global in English Soccer and the Rise of Satellite Television." *Sociology of Sport Journal* 11, no. 4: 376–397.

PART I

Neoliberal sport and social relations

2

BENEVOLENT HOSTS, UNGRATEFUL GUESTS

African footballers, hospitality and the sports business in Istanbul

John McManus

It is a sunny Saturday in June, and Somalia are due to play Ghana in the quarter final of the Africa Cup (also called the "African Nations Cup"), a football tournament organized by African migrants living in Istanbul, Turkey. The cup is an annual fixture for Africans in the city, providing an opportunity to have fun and build communal solidarity. It also serves as an occasion for men who dream of playing professional football to possibly catch the eye of an agent or manager. First started by African migrants in 2004 or 2005 (the date is disputed), the tournament has been receiving support from the municipality of Fatih, one of the districts of greater Istanbul, since 2012. The players use a municipal stadium in the district, municipality-owned buses deliver them to the games, and the shiny kits that the Somalia team members wear as they warm up are also a gift of the municipality (Figure 2.1).

Twenty minutes after the scheduled kick-off time, there is still no sign of the Ghana team. The Turkish referee appears with his officials and then disappears back into the changing rooms. The Somalia players have been warming up for almost an hour. Engin, the organizer from the municipality, has been pacing around on his mobile phone. Finally, 90 minutes after the match was meant to begin, there is an influx of players who immediately disappear into the changing room.

I look at the pitch. People are milling around but, rather than preparing for the game, they seem to raise their voices. First speaks the referee: "This match is finished. Bring out the teams for the next one." The comment prompts an angry response from some of the African men present. "We will referee it ourselves!" replies one, producing a whistle. "What do they think? That we are black so we are – or that we are African so that we are stupid?" I then hear only snatches of the confusing melee of voices:

FIGURE 2.1 Players for Somalia warming up at the Fatih Mimar Sinan Stadı ahead of their match in the 2016 Africa Cup, Istanbul, 4 June 2016.
(Source: John McManus)

> You give us something, let us enjoy it! We are here, it's recreation … If you don't play this one you are not going to play the second one! … We are going to play or else we cancel the whole tournament!

I learn that the dispute is about the timing of the game. Two matches are scheduled for today, but it is now too late for two 90-minute games. The panoply of African actors – coaches and players, community leaders, a few who liaise with the municipality – want to play one game today, and move the second match to tomorrow. It's not apparent whether the Turkish authorities – the referee and the organizer from the municipality – are for or against this idea, as before they articulate their position the argument quickly changes course, no longer focusing on particulars but on more general frustrations about being treated as guests at what they feel is their own tournament.

"If you allow them to control the situation, tomorrow they could do something more than this!" says a portly middle-aged African man. He's wearing trendy glasses, a red New York Yankees cap and a white football top, which on closer inspection is for Manisaspor, a second-division club in Turkey's Aegean region (Figure 2.2).

"We are African," he continues. "We do it to enjoy our African solidarity not to impress them – do you understand? We're doing it for ourselves. They don't even

FIGURE 2.2 Dispute over the cancellation of the Ghana vs. Somalia Africa Cup match, Istanbul, June 2016.
(Source: John McManus)

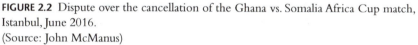

know the game, they referee it very *bad*" he lingers on the final word, drawing it out like a piece of chewing gum you trod on and are now picking off disgustedly. "They don't protect the players." "So they've cancelled the game?" I ask him. "They can't cancel the game, it's our game," he responds defiantly.

Who owns the Africa Cup? As the heated nature of the argument suggests, the question is charged with emotion. The tournament brings together African and Turkish, prospective football migrants and agents, those looking for fun and those seeking work and fame. It sits at the nexus of multiple geographic, political, social and economic worlds. The battle over ownership speaks to a deeper set of faultlines: what it means to be a male migrant in Turkey; the possibilities of making a living through sport; or how to navigate the slalom of obligations laid out for both "hosts" and "guests." It is this final point – the question of hospitality – that is the focus of this chapter.

With its historical focus on gift giving, reciprocity, and interactions with otherness, anthropology has long been concerned with ideas of hospitality (Pitt-Rivers 1972; Mauss 2002). Recent years have seen scholars argue for a "return" to the concept as an organizing heuristic, prompted by increased focus on alterity and difference brought on by current debates about immigration and multiculturalism

(Candea and da Col 2012). Anthropological attention is mirrored by philosophers and literary theorists, for whom hospitality's thematic can help fashion new "ethico-political frameworks" (Dikeç, Clark, and Barnett 2009, 2) to answer the challenge of coexisting in globalized social life (Derrida 2000). How categories of host and guest are assigned has consequences for contemporary social life – from who has access to material resources to who can claim different forms of belonging.

What Michael Herzfeld (1987) calls the "scalar slipperiness" of hospitality makes it a useful heuristic to explore the equally mercurial phenomenon of modern global sport. Driven by neoliberal interests, sports industries have since the 1980s exploded in wealth and prominence. Especially in the Global South, young men in increasing numbers aspire to an athletic career, as other work opportunities have declined as a result of the same dynamics of global neoliberalism (Besnier, Guinness, Hann, and Kovač 2018; Besnier, Calabrò, and Guinness, this volume;). Sport industries have come to act as a conduit for migration, as the imaginaries they evoke tempt many thousands into voyages around the globe. To understand how these global trends play out on the micro-level, this chapter focuses on one of the destinations for migrant athletes – Istanbul – and asks: who is playing host to those athletic hopefuls?

In the Turkish context, notions of "hosts" and "guests" are profoundly relevant categories of experience. The figure of the *misafir*, or guest, is emblematic of the Mediterranean region, albeit not devoid of problems (Herzfeld 1987; Friese 2009; Shryock 2012). It is deeply inscribed into Turkish social relations. Being subjected to hospitality is not only, or always, a positive experience. The category of "guest" can be used to black box difference, deny agency, and even suspend social and political rights. Of particular importance in the context of migration is how these cultural categories interact with the nation state's own mechanism for systemizing interaction with others, namely the ascription of the status of "citizen" and "foreigner." In Turkey, the recognition of migrants from Africa is only a new chapter in the century-long historical drama of the Turkish nation state and multiculturalism, one in which ethnic and religious minorities fight to be recognized as belonging on their own grounds, rather than those of the majoritarian "host" (Mango 1999; Clark 2007; de Bellaigue 2009; Brink-Denan 2010; King 2015, 121–131; Ekmekçioğlu 2016).

In many societies, dispensing hospitality is an inherently risky activity, one which can easily backfire if actors do not follow the script and play their roles effectively (Humphrey 2012; Shryock 2012). Those who can smooth out the ambivalences and mediate exchanges stand to accrue considerable power. In the context of the Africa Cup, these people are football agents, municipal council employees, and African community organizers who act as mediators between an unstable cadre of actors and a shifting array of resources. These "brokers" (who are all men, a point to which I will return shortly) compete for the benefits – both material and cultural – that they can gain by successfully playing the hospitality game.

A broker is "a human actor who gains something from the mediation of valued resources that he or she does not directly control" (Lindquist 2015, 870). In anthropology, the figure of the broker is particularly associated with the context of decolonization (Wolf 1956; Geertz 1960), as these new actors – or existing actors forced into novel roles – emerged in the context of rapid transition to new nation states. Boundary crossing and moral ambiguity loomed large as individuals balanced the distribution of new largess with preexisting obligations and social roles.

Subsequent waves in anthropology have washed away the unproblematic notions of "national" and "local" which these earlier works could speak of actors mediating. It seems important to reconsider brokerage in the light of two recent developments: twenty-first-century mobilities, which have served to scramble conceptions of place, scale, and time (Harvey 1989; Sheller 2014); and the increasing global ubiquity of neoliberal economic models, with their concomitant encouragement of entrepreneurialism, "self-help," and development of the individual (Harvey 2005; Gershon 2017). Both sets of dynamics have created new opportunities for those who wish to act as brokers, at the same time as they have made it harder to comprehend and operationalize the entities that are being mediated. Many figures in the world of global football work as brokers. The most obvious is the agent, the legal representative of a player who procures and negotiates employment in exchange for a cut of the player's income.

Brokerage does not simply involve mediating preexisting worldviews; rather, it involves actively constructing a social and moral universe in which the broker claims a place (James 2011, 319). As I conceptualize it, the relationship of hospitality to brokerage is of a wide philosophical and theological thematic providing individuals with idioms (such as reciprocity and receptiveness to the presence of an Other) which can be utilized for practices of mediation. Nevertheless, there is conceptual fuzziness between brokerage and hospitality – a broker who claims certain resources can act as a "host" but, as he or she forges new relationships, can alternatively take on the role of "guest."

One important element in the brokerage practices of the Africa Cup is masculinity. Players, coaches, referees, assistants, and council organizers are all men. The only women involved are a member of the ten-person African organizing committee, a couple of Turkish agents, and a few spectators. Consequently, entwined within the contest over who is hosting the tournament are struggles over different ideals of masculine success. Within these, the primary role of men as providers (Connell 2005; Jordan Smith 2017, 6) looms large – for both Africans and Turks. But the refashioning of "work" itself under conditions of neoliberalism complicates matters. Activities that carried little financial benefit historically, such as introducing an athlete to the right figure, now contain the potential of such significant financial reward that they can disrupt traditional circuits of male privilege. Claims of being in charge ("hosting") double up as existential claims of a particular ideal of masculinity. Understanding hospitality's gendered foundations is an important step in comprehending the strength of feeling that accompanies the denial of voice.

Here I focus less on the players than on those who position themselves as broker or host. I base my analysis on ethnographic fieldwork at the 2016 Africa Cup and follow-up visits and interviews with key figures, both African and Turkish. Divergences and contradictions emerged amongst those I spoke to in their narratives of the tournament's development and functioning. Rather than categorize or sift out the errors, I came to realize that these contradictions were key to understanding the idea of the hospitable broker, which required asserting his legitimacy in "owning" the tournament. What emerged most strongly were the issues that arise when the guests do not follow the script. Such scenarios will only increase in prevalence if Turkey continues to grow in desirability as a migration destination. Ultimately, African football migrants in Istanbul illustrates the astonishing increase in hustle surrounding sport in the neoliberal era, as well as the difficulties of balancing claims when everyone thinks they should be the host.

African migration to Turkey

Sub-Saharan Africans began to migrate to Turkey in the 1990s, first with small groups of students, many on Islamic Development Bank scholarships.[1] Following in their wake came other students and then traders attracted by Turkey's increasing role as a world hub of manufactured products such as clothing, plastic goods, and other consumer wares. By the early 2000s, enough sub-Saharan Africans had settled in Istanbul to form a "community," albeit one that is strongly divided by nationality and language. There are perhaps 35,000 migrants from West and Central Africa and the same from East Africa (Şaul 2014, 148–150, 2017, 134–135). Most are from Senegal and Nigeria. They represent Turkey's transformation from an emigrant to an immigrant society (Düvell 2014).

African migrants in Turkey are frequently viewed through the lens of migration waves that preceded and followed them. Since the 1980s, increasing numbers from Iraq, Iran, and Afghanistan have arrived in the country, driven by civil strife and war. Since 2011, 3.5 million Syrians have fled the civil war into Turkey. Many Turkish citizens and aid organizations now associate migrants from low-income countries with illegal border crossing, asylum, and poverty.

West and Central African migrants do not fit this profile. They are educated – most through high school and for a significant number to university. Unlike migrants from the Middle East and Central Asia, most of whom arrive illegally, nearly all African migrants travel to Turkey on valid visas (Şaul 2014, 157–162). The bookending of sub-Saharan migrants with other migrant groups says more about the inability of host populations (and sometimes researchers) to discern difference than the facts on the ground. Most of those who come to Turkey to play football are from this background.

African migrants in Istanbul enter a host of industries, from working in factories to starting their own entrepreneurial business ventures. Many are involved in shipping and import-export of goods between Turkey and their home country (Şaul 2014). Africans are associated with a few areas of the city dominated by new arrivals to Turkey, such as Kumkapı and Aksaray in Fatih, or Kurtuluş in Beyoğlu. These areas still act as hubs for African business, but as the city as a whole has expanded, Africans are increasingly found living and working in outer districts (Şaul 2017, 135–139).

Football-related migration is not drastically different from these wider labour migration patterns. African football migrants usually arrive in Turkey legally to study or, more frequently, on a short-term business or tourist visa. These footballers have various motivations for travelling to Turkey. Like other migrants (Yükseker and Brewer 2011; Suter 2012), many see the country as a transit point, a stepping-stone to a more high-profile position in the football leagues of Europe's sporting core, such as Germany, Spain, and the United Kingdom. Yet because of the growing wealth in Turkish football – the top division is now Europe's sixth largest league in terms of revenue (Deloitte 2018) – increasing numbers of sportsmen see Turkey as a destination in its own right.

Few if any footballers organize their own arrival. Instead, they rely on brokers who put them in touch with Turkish clubs. Both Turks and Africans operate in this role. Some take their job seriously but many operate unscrupulously. I heard stories of players arriving in Turkey with brokers' promises of a connection to professional football, only to realize there were no trials and no interested clubs. One player I spoke to, a Nigerian I will call Billy, was told by an African football agent that he was being sent to Iran.[2] Instead, he arrived on Kish Island – a territory of Iran in the Persian Gulf, but one with a visa policy that differs from the mainland. No agent arrived to meet him. "We hung on one week. No response. Two weeks, three weeks. No response. And the bills were going up," Billy explained. Realizing he was stuck, he was forced to fly to Dubai and then back to Nigeria, from where he subsequently made his way to Turkey. Billy's experience is not unique. African migrant footballers frequently report ill-treatment, both in Turkey (Tuvi 2010; Büdel 2013) and across Europe more broadly (Esson 2015; Agergaard and Ungruhe 2016). The experiences of these footballers speak to two important trends: the increasing mobility and internationalism of athletic hopefuls and the enduring importance of brokers to help them navigate the pinch points that still exist in the world system for those with the passport of a country in the Global South (Kelly and Chatziefstathiou 2018).

I began my research wanting to establish a brief history of the Africa Cup, the tournament that served as an anchor and context for my fieldwork. When I spoke to people, however, I found divergences and contradictions in the stories they gave. Overcoming my initial frustration, I realized that this lack of consensus was central to the wider question of ownership. The different casting of the cup by each actor revealed the varied narratives through which individuals position themselves as hosts of the event.

Brokerage revisited

My first port of call was David, a West African who is widely credited as co-founder of the Africa Cup. David used to be a semi-professional footballer, having played in Eastern Europe, North Africa and Turkey. He is married to a Turkish

FIGURE 2.3 African players at the Feriköy football school in Istanbul.
(Source: John McManus)

national, has two children and, in 2011, became a Turkish citizen. Three mornings a week, he runs a football school for African migrants at the Feriköy stadium, a small rundown ground with a capacity of approximately one thousand, located in Kurtuluş, a densely-populated central district of Istanbul that houses people of different ethnicities, social classes, and nationalities, including some Africans (Figure 2.3).

When he first arrived in Turkey in 2005, David and a Nigerian friend noticed that groups of Africans would organize casual matches among teams identified with their countries of origin. In David's telling, his friend proposed a more formalized event and called round the various national communities in Istanbul to ask them to form teams. The first Africa Cup in Feriköy stadium in 2005 involved teams from six countries: Ghana, Sudan, Congo, Nigeria, Guinea, and Senegal.[3] A Turkish friend of David refereed. David described the atmosphere:

> Oh, it was amazing. … When you came you felt like you were in Africa. People [were] playing drums the way we do it in Africa. People cooked some African food, sharing their things. People came here to have fun. … So I came to value this opportunity to unite Africa, to register an African community … that was my idea.

The tournament quickly grew. In 2007, the organizers secured sponsorship from *Finansbank,* a Turkish lender who agreed to contribute money in exchange for advertising at the event. By 2011, eight teams were taking part in the cup; the teams retained the names of African countries, but were often comprised of players who were from other countries, reflecting the uneven distribution of national-ities amongst sub-Saharan Africans in Istanbul.[4] As Mahir Şaul remarks, "it is the only instance I know of sub-Saharan migrant groups of different national origins working together to present a common image to the host nation in a pan-African spirit" (2014, 176).

David also works as a player agent. In 2018, he was representing five players in second and third divisions across Europe. Most agents, David included, hope to discover and represent a true world-class talent. "[If] I can transfer one player for a good team then that will be my successful life," he told me. "Maybe they can pay like ten million Euros. I will take a commission of ten percent." I asked David if he had ever done that. He laughed heartily: "Not yet. But I will!"

"I am Michael," another of my research participants told me, "I am UEFA[-affiliated] and also I am a football agent. I have my company. I have also my training centre. I have more than seventeen years in the football business." Michael chatted with me while overseeing the training of some of his charges on a warm June morning during Ramadan. A wiry man in his late thirties, Michael was invited to Turkey by a team in Izmir in 2011 after a long stint working in Latin America. Happy with the facilities that he encountered, he decided to stay. "I have discovered Turkey is the best country where you can make football business because more than 3000 teams come every year to have camps here in Turkey," he informed me, referring to the hosting of pre- and mid-season training camps of which, in recent years, Turkey had managed to capture the market.

Michael is from Central Africa and, along with David, is a member of the Africa Cup's ten-person organizing committee. Yet the cup is only one of a host of football-related activities in which he is involved. He spends most of his time arran-ging teams of Africans to scrimmage with foreign sides when they come to Turkey for their camps.[5] He also acts as an agent for a number of players.

"Brokers and mediators use assets furnished by the state and provide the means for others, less able, to gain access to these," writes Deborah James (2011, 318). While this is certainly true of many early examples of brokerage, it does not fully capture what people like Michael and David practice in Turkey. They rely on their resource-fulness rather than state assets. Their relationships to clubs and other agents are fre-quently more important than any connection to government: "When the team calls me [saying] 'Michael, I need a striker,' I send one boy to play. When he plays there, [if] they like him, they sign a contract, they give me my percentage and I go on."

In an era defined by economic individualism, free markets, and other hallmarks of a neoliberal politico-economic order, the defining characteristic of brokerage is its untethering from stable resources and capital. Football – one of the world's foremost transnational cultural phenomena – has long been in the vanguard of the movement of people and capital (Goldblatt 2007). As I see it, the pressing question is how practices of brokerage have been altered through interaction with global football. Or, put differently, how is it that a Cameroonian can come via Latin America to operate successfully as a football agent in Turkey?

The answer lies in the fact that these dynamics are embedded in large-scale processes, such as the growing wealth gap between Global North and Global South, the erosion of work opportunities at home and the increasing economic might of Turkish football and Turkey more generally. In the global sports system, however, not all places are equal. As a middle-income country trying to muscle in on the established system, Turkey is a whirligig of activity, from rapid stadium construction (McManus 2018, 75–79) to constantly bidding to host sporting mega-events (Polo 2015). This is part of a wider strategy to define the country as a global hub, exporting goods to new markets and establishing additional flight routes in and out of a new mega-airport by the partially state-backed carrier Turkish Airlines – a factor frequently mentioned by my African interlocutors (Öktem, Kadıoğlu, and Karlı 2012; Dursun et al. 2014). There has been a particular push by Turkey into Africa, which has seen increased trade, brand new embassies, and the opening of Turkish schools (Özkan and Akgün 2010; Angey 2012). This hunger for global importance brings new participants into Turkey's orbit, opening nooks and cracks for people like Michael to gain a foothold.

But to zoom in closer, the place where many African football brokers operate in Turkey is the sports pitch in Istanbul where the Africa Cup tournament takes place. For one month of the year, this rectangle of land, cut out from the dense urban framework of a global mega-city, becomes a market and a magnet, pulling in people – players, agents, journalists, researchers – all for different reasons.[6] Both Turkey in general and the pitch in particular operate as "contact zones" (Pratt 1991), places where difference is mediated and claims of ownership battled out. The key point about such zones is that no one controls them entirely. This means that they need to be continually managed, hence the importance of hospitality, a human strategy for managing the ever-present danger involved in contact with an Other (Pitt-Rivers 1977; Humphrey 2012).

Michael positioned himself as a football expert in his telling of the Africa Cup's history: "When I came here in 2010, those making the Africa Cup were not people involved in footballing matters," he told me.

> They were just people who were working in logistics. They had different jobs, they had a career. I saw the initiative was very good … so I have tried to bring my knowledge, my footballing knowledge, to bring to them to understand that, even if we are playing, we can make also our players get teams.

But he overlooks the footballing credentials of the other organizers, most notably David who, as an ex-professional, certainly does not fit Michael's depiction of football ignorance. Football brokers engage in competitive jostling, downplaying their potential rivals in order to stay on top amidst the restless churn of the football agent market.

Enjoyment or employment?

Michael's description of the Africa Cup invokes an ambiguity that was frequently raised when I spoke to participants: is the cup's purpose to generate pan-African solidarity or is it a marketplace for African players to find clubs? In other words, is it for enjoyment or employment? The question goes to the heart of two important dynamics underlying the tournament: how cultural notions of "host" and "guest" overlap with state categories of "citizen" and "foreigner"; and how masculine success is indexed to employment.

Many players at the Africa Cup dream of playing in one of Turkey's top professional leagues. In reality, the scouts and agents who come to watch represent amateur teams. Nonetheless, many of these teams pay their players. Salaries vary wildly. The top amateur teams can pay up to 100,000 lira (€16,500) a season. More common is a one-off payment of 8,000–10,000 lira a season (€1,323–1,654) with win bonuses of 200 lira (€33) a match.[7] If a side is moderately successful, the monthly amount can approach the minimum wage (1,404 lira or €232) – more than could be earned from the (black-market) manual labour that most migrants are forced to undertake. But it is not life-changing.

To earn money, however, foreign footballers need two state documents – a residence permit (*ikamet*) and a football licence (*lisans*). Many players in the Africa Cup arrived on tourist visas and let them expire, which makes them ineligible to apply for a residence permit. To become eligible, a player must return home, reapply for a visa and return to Turkey.[8] Some cannot afford this; others don't want to take the risk. The lack of a permit locks players out of opportunities. "I have taken part in three [Africa] cups, and I've had different managers asking for me. But there was no residence permit to sign a contract," promising footballer Kamal told me. "I didn't know the process before my visa expired."

Even with a valid residence permit, anyone who wishes to play for an established side in Turkey, whether professional or amateur, needs a licence from the Turkish Football Federation. Amateur teams can only have up to two foreign players in the squad. Moreover, the Federation makes the cost of the licence prohibitive for non-citizens: 3,000 lira for a new licence; 9,000 for converting a foreign licence. This is vastly more than it costs for a Turkish player (500 lira), so the clubs have to really want the player in question. The bureaucratic hurdles reveal how lower-league football in Turkey is ringfenced by formal laws on residence and citizenship.[9] Legislation thus mirrors the cultural logic of the "guest," whose welcome is only ever contingent and time-limited.

Sixteen teams took part in the 2016 Africa Cup tournament, each with a squad of 23, making 368 players in total. Of these, according to the organizers, about 35 were hired by a club. Even for the lucky 10 per cent who acquire the right documents, it's not a happy-ever-after story. Footballers are offered temporary contracts, sometimes as short as a few months. Many players only have verbal assurances of employment and complain about being paid late or not at all. Football labour reflects labour patterns more broadly for Africans in Istanbul – precarious, piecemeal, and forever shifting.

Not everyone taking part in the Africa Cup thinks that the tournament's primary goal should be as a market for employment. "We do it to enjoy our African solidarity, not to impress them," argued one participant. This view is more pronounced among older African migrants. Those who still enjoy playing football expect to feature in the starting line-up of teams. These are people who have nearly always given up the dream of earning from football – indeed, some did not come to Turkey for this reason. The Africa Cup thus reveals two divergent conceptions of how to achieve the masculine requirement of being the "head" – of a household, family, or group. African men long-established in Istanbul fulfil that role by playing for a team, through which they display their patriarchal authority and importance in the community. For younger migrants, it's the prospect of wealth and the ability to meet relatives' expectations of remittances that marks the successful performance of the role of provider.

Balancing viewpoints amongst Africans with different expectations can be a fraught process. For those like David, who work as both agent and coach, success is contingent on making the two aspects of the tournament cohere, keeping both financial reward and community status in play. Yet the zero-sum nature of the equation – every berth given to an established individual is one fewer existential shot at fame – generates pressure. Players often grumble and curse the broker for being either too community-focused or too commercially-minded.

The stance one adopts on whether the tournament is about work or play has a knock-on effect on who is "host" and who is "guest." Those who view it as a potential stepping-stone to employment need to interact with the Turkish state, its assets and bureaucracies. In this process, it is often the Turkish actors who hold the cards and thus claim the role of "host." In contrast, for those who see the tournament as being about pan-African solidarity, Turkish involvement and attempts at hosting make little sense. Since 2012, as the Africa Cup moved from Feriköy to Fatih and from a solely African-organized event to one organized in collaboration with the local municipality, the tension about the purpose of the tournament has become increasingly pronounced.

Benevolent hosts, ungrateful guests

Bilal is in charge of Youth and Sport activities at Fatih municipality (*belediyesi*). A portly man in his late 30s, like all Turkish citizens involved in the tournament's organizing, Bilal is keen to present himself as a consummate host to African migrant footballers. "Both as a state and as a nation we try to do what we can to make them feel they are not alone," he told me. Bilal's language was full of paternalistic flourishes ("there's a good reason we are looking after them") and much of our conversation was spent with him outlining the costs that the municipality absorbs to run the tournament. "We do the greater part of the work," Bilal concluded. "They just come out to matches and play."

In his claims of benevolence, Bilal positions himself as the "Big Man," a role which has long characterized Turkish political culture. As the anthropologist Jenny White explains, the Big Man is "envisioned both as a father figure and a hero" (White 2015), sitting at the top of a strict hierarchy of social relations. A key signifier of the Big Man is ownership of the levers of hospitality. Their authority rests on networks of followers whom they recruit and keep on side by doling out munificence. As the gendered nature of the term suggests, Big Men posture to express successful masculinity.

The Big Man is a "type" in many societies (Rosen 2011; Jordan Smith 2017, 5–6), suggesting a certain cross-cultural applicability – both of the primacy of the man-as-provider trope but also its manifestation in an intimate patron–client politics. In positing his claim to being the hospitable Big Man, Bilal stripped Africans of agency in what was originally an African-devised event. He did not appear to realize that preventing Africans from displaying their own masculinity might generate disquiet.

Bilal was helped in his role by Engin, who was responsible for the tournament's logistics, from organizing the African community members to arranging the transport. "It's a very good opportunity for them to advertise themselves," Engin told me. "Because there are managers coming and choosing footballers from here." Bilal also emphasized the important role played by Turkish clubs: "the way these Africans are being saved (*kurtuluş*) is actually these clubs. If the clubs decide to transfer them, they can get their residence and work permits."

Bilal and Engin's discourse positions Fatih municipality as yet another broker in the tournament. As a state entity, their relations are more in line with the "classic" broker controlling and doling out state assets. Yet they have tweaked the role. In their speech, both men shift the burden of success from the municipality to the players. Fatih municipality merely provides the platform, it is for the clubs to come in and "save" the players. In the new economic order, governmental institutions are not responsible for "saving" people but for providing the stage on which players can, in Engin's words, "advertise themselves" and be rescued by private entities. Viewing the migrants as guests, Bilal and Engin adopt a public discourse that has failed to wake up to the reality that the Turkish nation has, since the 1990s, shifted from a country of emigration to one of immigration.

Both men's representation of the realities of African migrant footballers were badly miscued. Bilal's description of their "salvation" by clubs misread the migrants' motivations. As mentioned earlier, most African football migrants in Turkey are educated and middle-class. Many don't plan on staying long; most are fully aware of the risks, and are constantly planning for the next stage. For example, Abdullah, a young Nigerian player, told me that he "need[ed] to go back to Nigeria. Maybe I can play in the premier league in Nigeria for one year, I think, to raise my profile. Then I can choose to come back to Turkey." Another footballer called Emmanuel, whom I interviewed at the same time, butted in: "Me, I have a different plan. ...

FIGURE 2.4 African footballers holding a banner praising Fatih mayor Mustafa Demir, Istanbul, 10 May 2016.
(Source: John McManus)

I have one of my uncles in England. I have somebody in Canada. My plan is to go to Canada if I have the opportunity." They cast mobility as a choice and refused to grumble or relinquish agency over their situation (compare Esson 2015).

The municipality are keen to ensure African footballers conform to a role that reinforces their benevolence. At the opening match in 2016, the players held a 15-foot banner that read in Turkish and poor English: "Thank you to Mr Mustafa Demir for his greatest heart" (*gönülünü açan sayın belediye başkanı Mustafa Demir'e teşekkürler*) (Figure 2.4). Mustafa Demir was the mayor of Fatih from 2004 to 2018. According to Bilal and Engin, it is Demir himself who has spearheaded Fatih's activities to help Africans in Istanbul. On the walls of the stadium are posters from previous activities. One sees Demir, paddle aloft, posing in a dragon boat racing competition on a boat with African migrants (Figure 2.5). The football banner had been produced by the municipality – I had seen it being unloaded out of a municipality van. The bilingual text confuses whether this display of munificence is aimed at the Africans (many of whom don't speak Turkish) or the Turkish public. It initially looked like a vote-winning ploy by Demir, until I recalled that all Turkish citizens I encountered were unhappy about the municipality spending money on foreigners.

FIGURE 2.5 Poster of Fatih mayor Mustafa Demir participating in a dragon boat race with African migrants, Istanbul, August 2016.
(Source: John McManus)

To me, the municipality came across as distasteful in how insistently they pushed the mayor and his benevolence. The display seemed to suggest that footballers' energies should be focused on catching the eye of a patron who, it is hoped, will "save" through his munificence. Playing such a role requires relinquishing the deep-seated idea of the man being the head of a household or institution.

But Africans involved in the tournament did not all share my reservations. "I tell them always 'thank you' for the things they are doing for we Africans," Michael told me. "When you come here [to Turkey] everybody always sees Africans as bad people… But if someone gives us an opportunity, we just tell him 'thank you' and we try to make everything [work]." "He *loves* blacks!" Kamal, a young footballer told me about the mayor. "One of his projects is to help blacks." I asked him if he preferred the tournament in African or Turkish hands. "With Turkey organising it, it's more better."

For Turkish actors, comments such as Michael's and Kamal's neatly adhere to the role of grateful guest. They give an impression of unmitigated appreciation that dampens self-awareness and reinforces notions of Turks as intrinsically benevolent hosts. "They are so happy and pleased with the support we give them that they thank me every time they come. It's like they are visiting family," said Bilal. The invocation of family relations is telling. As with the example of the Big Man as "father," tropes of family are commonly used in Turkey to personalize stranger relations: people address each other as "brother" (*ağabey*) and "sister" (*abla*); the state is nicknamed "father state" (*devlet baba*). But, in addition to closeness, family idioms convey hierarchy and deference. They potentially infantilize migrants, with Fatih indexed as munificent father/host, leaving Africans with the role of grateful child and guest.

Yet when Kamal and Michael adopt this role, we perhaps glimpse how concepts of masculine success morph with our neoliberal age. A man's identity as a provider is not solely tied to playing the Big Man host. Another route requires individuals to first accept the parameters of the situation, the imbalance in power relations between African and Turkish citizens, before making the most of the opportunity provided – be that playing well to attract attention or brokering well to make it a full time job. As structural limitations increase amidst rising global inequality, being a successful man will perhaps increasingly involve having the guile to slip through, take what one needs from the power brokers and move on.

When Africans involved in the tournament aren't content with playing their municipality-assigned role, difficulties arise. Some feel frustrated and annoyed at no longer having a say in a tournament that they themselves helped set up. "Fatih municipality have no right to take this tournament from us. We have 54 countries. We are not a small continent!" one player shouted in the argument that opened this chapter, laying out the stark inequalities between Global North and Global South: continents are forced to confront local government authorities.

Turkish participants generally view such complaints as the carping of an ungrateful guest who bungles his lines (Hage 2003; Shryock 2012). The response is frequently ill-tempered. "If they don't want to be here, let them go! The airport is just there," exploded one Turkish bystander when I filled him in on the argument. He interpreted what he saw as ingratitude as an affront to the nation as a whole and went on a racist diatribe:

> This is my country. This is heaven. I'm not talking about you, white people. It's the blacks. We give them a chance. If they don't value this chance, then let them piss off. ... This is Turkey. It's not some Congo Mongo.

"It's really very difficult to work with Africans and really they are very dirty people," Engin the municipality employee told me in our recorded interview. I tried to make him clarify, but he cut me off. "I want to say this very clearly, ok? They don't know how to eat, they don't know how to behave with the [Turkish] neighbours. They go outside with the shorts like this," here Engin pointed high on his thighs to indicate short shorts, "and, you know, it's not nice in Turkey these kinds of things." He then drew a distinction between the players and the organizers: "For the footballers I am very happy. But for the Africans who organise from their side, really they are very bad people."

It is hard not to conclude that his position is shaped by African footballers' relative lack of agency. It is the organizers, the brokers, with their attempts to take control or make a profit who threaten the host/guest dialectic. The entwining of racial, moral, and religious arguments in his response – from public displays of flesh to alleged eating habits – reveals yet again the extent and depth of feeling triggered by usurping guests, and the level to which people will go to in order to neutralize the threat by casting the stranger as having abused the hospitality to which they have been subjected.

Yet Engin's brokership involved having to support and defend the players in the eyes of Turkish people, many of whom feel annoyed that "their" money was being spent on a competition that does not benefit Turks. Engin found it hard to do this and ultimately he felt the same way. "[Turkish] people are right. They are right! What can you say?!" Nevertheless, I pushed him on the tactics he uses to try and defend the players. "We say: 'They are poor people, they are here. We have to host them. We have to give a place,' you know, you have to touch their hearts because you don't have anything [else] that you can touch." Once again, the discourse of poverty and help-lessness is invoked, the danger of the stranger mitigated by stripping him of agency. Some Africans try and work within the same logic to extract personal benefit ("I tell them always 'thank you' for the things they are doing for we Africans"). Others angrily reject the "help," seeing it as a way to deny them an opportunity to work. In both cases, the acceptance of the men making the comments *as* men involved in the workings of the tournament shows that conceptions of masculinity are flexible enough to sanctify both approaches as sufficiently "manly."

The drama of Turkish multiculturalism

"Africans and Fatih. We don't understand one another," concluded David at the end of our interview. He lamented how, in the absence of trust, both sides fell back on aggrandising claims of being in charge. "If you want to prove that you're right and I'll say 'no, I'm right', then we'll have an argument." These arguments seemed to have taken their toll. In 2017, Fatih municipality decided to end their involvement in the Africa Cup, citing the cost. That year, the tournament took place, but back in Feriköy stadium and under African control. "We [Africans] still want to do it with them. But we are waiting for them," David told me when we met again in early 2018. That year too, the tournament was again organized and hosted by Africans. David didn't seem too bothered. "We weren't [going] to go with Fatih Belediye for-ever. They [initially] came to us, you understand?" Yet he also confessed that finding money for the event was difficult without the municipality.

The guest/host model generates great tension in the football industry in Turkey. Shaped by deeply held values around the need to honour guests, buttressed by a state that does not acknowledge that Turkey is a country of immigration, the hosting lens means that African sporting migrants are misread and activities like the cup that aimed to help them are largely ineffective. They are not temporary guests who need to be shown a good time but active migrants who seek to work. While Turks and Africans alike see work and money as the sine qua non of a full adult masculinity, the fact that the former misread the latter infantilizes and emasculates them.

Across this fluid terrain, brokers are at work, shifting and scheming to try and extract individual benefit and keep both sides sweet. Some middlemen are willing to entertain the compromises to social position and ideas of manhood needed to access resources. Others refuse and, as a result, founder in frustration at the systemic blocks to fulfilling a typically successful performance of manhood. By showcasing the entrepreneurial individual, economic models and the political and social systems they co-constitute seem to create opportunities for Africans to succeed in Turkey, but when we peer more closely, the structural limitations shine through. One can flip the positions of "hosts" and "guests" between Turks and Africans, but the wider system of the sports industries doesn't change; Turkish football still commands enormous wealth but most Africans can access it only if they are Turkish citizens. Africans may now be unambiguously "in charge" of the Africa Cup, but they hold the reins of an enterprise with dwindling munificence to distribute.

To conclude, I wish to raise one final point about hospitality in the Turkish context. Even though the majority of players see their stay in Turkey as temporary, some settle in Istanbul. For these people, being seen as a guest is a barrier to proper integration. "It's not about football," David told me. "We have to come together and unite ourselves. Share ideas. Because our people are giving birth over here ... and the kid's gonna go to school, you understand?"

David is a case in point. Married to a Turkish national, he has become a Turkish citizen, removing many legal barriers to him operating as a broker in Turkey, if not the cultural and racial ones. Most Africans, however, are locked out of the process of formalizing residence and citizenship, hence David trying to use the tournament to raise awareness of their plight.

> He can't go to school and it's difficult to go to hospital – people don't have legal documents. Most of the people here are illegal. ... So, we are pleading to the government to recognise, to see our problems over here.

African recognition is part of a much wider issue in Turkey of the difficulty of non-Turks ever to be seen as belonging. Africans are trapped within the wider drama of the Turkish nation state and multiculturalism, one that has over the years affected Kurds, Greek-speakers and Armenians, often with disastrous consequences (Clark 2007; de Bellaigue 2009; Ekmekçioğlu 2016). Imprisoned in familial metaphors and hierarchies of hospitality, African arrivals in Istanbul find themselves following a well-trodden path, littered with the detritus of other minority attempts to be recognized on their own grounds rather than those of the "guest."

This drama looks like becoming only more pronounced. There are over 3.5 million Syrians based in Turkey, a small number of whom have already made the move from resident to citizen, but who in the minds of many Turks will not alter from fixed idea of "guest." In sport in general, and the African Cup in particular, we perhaps glimpse the increasingly unequal and fraught mediations that growing inequality in the world system is producing. Not only Turkey but the world as a whole will have to devise better strategies for "hosting" in the years to come.

Acknowledgements

My thanks to all research participants, without whose generosity I could not have undertaken this work. This chapter is based on research I conducted while Postdoctoral Research Fellow at the British Institute at Ankara (2016–18). I am grateful for its support. My thanks to the members of the GLOBALSPORT team, in particular Niko Besnier, for their encouragement and comments, from research through to publication.

Notes

1 Sub-Saharan Africans have long been present in Turkey and Istanbul in Ottoman times as slaves, traders, and scholars (Zalewski 2012), but this has no bearing on contemporary migrants' situation.
2 All names have been altered to protect the anonymity of my interlocutors.
3 Although David told me the first African Cup began in 2005, according to researcher Ricky Knight the first tournament was in 2004 (Knight 2011, 166–171). Either David and/or Knight have got dates wrong by a year, or David is claiming ownership for a tournament that begun before he arrived.
4 One year, South Africa was chosen as one of the teams despite there being few – if any – players from South Africa. When asked why, people explained that South Africa was "important" and should be represented (Şaul 2014, 199).
5 The next day he was to take a team to Bolu, a small city between Ankara and Istanbul, where an opposition was needed for an Azerbaijani side playing in the following season's Europa League, the second of UEFA's annual European football club competitions.
6 There has been much media attention on the tournament (Letsch 2011; Berlioux and Lecomte 2017).
7 All Euro figures taken from https://www.xe.com/currencyconverter/convert/?Amount=2000&From=TRY&To=EUR, accurate as of 31 December 2018.
8 Since my fieldwork, the Turkish state appears to be loosening the restrictions, making it easier for Africans in Turkey with lapsed visas to apply for residency permits. This is a protean phenomenon that may well affect lives in Turkey – and subsequent Africa cups.
9 This is in marked contrast to the two top divisions in Turkey, where teams will have dozens of foreign footballers – often fielding starting 11s that contain only a few Turkish players.

References

Agergaard, Sine, and Christian Ungruhe. 2016. "Ambivalent Precarity: Career Trajectories and Temporalities in Highly Skilled Sports Labor Migration from West Africa to Northern Europe." *Anthropology of Work Review* 37, no. 2: 67–78.
Angey, Gabrielle. 2012. "Turkish Islam in Africa: A Study of the Gülen Movement in Kenya." *Mambo!* 10, no. 3: 1–4.
Berlioux, Jeremie, and Thomas Lecomte. 2017. "Racism, Poverty: Istanbul's African Footballers Risk It All." *Middle East Eye*, 1 June 2017. www.middleeasteye.net/in-depth/features/racism-poverty-istanbul-s-african-footballers-risk-it-all-1870124243.
Besnier, Niko, Daniel Guinness, Mark Hann, and Uroš Kovač. 2018. "Rethinking Masculinity in the Neoliberal Order: Cameroonian Footballers, Fijian Rugby Players, Senegalese Wrestlers." *Comparative Studies in Society and History* 60, no. 4: 839–872.

Brink-Denan, Marcy. 2010. "Names That Show Time: Turkish Jews as 'Strangers' and the Semiotics of Reclassification." *American Anthropologist* 112, no. 3: 384–396.

Büdel, Martin. 2013. "An Ethnographic View on African Football Migrants in Istanbul." *Ankara Üniversitesi SBF Dergisi* 68, no. 1: 1–20.

Candea, Matei, and Giovanni da Col. 2012. "The Return to Hospitality." *Journal of the Royal Anthropological Institute* 18, no. S1: S1–S19.

Clark, Bruce. 2007. *Twice a Stranger: The Mass Expulsions That Forged Modern Greece and Turkey.* London: Granta.

Connell, Raewyn. 2005. *Masculinities.* Cambridge: Polity.

de Bellaigue, Christopher. 2009. *Rebel Land: Among Turkey's Forgotten Peoples.* London: Bloomsbury.

Deloitte. 2018. "Roar Power: Annual Review of Football Finance 2018." Accessed 9 July 2020. www2.deloitte.com/content/dam/Deloitte/uk/Documents/sports-business-group/deloitte-uk-sbg-annual-review-of-football-finance-2018.PDF.

Derrida, Jacques. 2000. *Of Hospitality.* Translated by Rachel Bowlby. Stanford, CA: Stanford University Press.

Dikeç, Mustafa, Nigel Clark, and Clive Barnett. 2009. "Extending Hospitality: Giving Space, Taking Time." *Paragraph* 32, no. 1: 1–14.

Dursun, Mehmet Erkan, John F. O'Connell, Zheng Lei, and David Warnock-Smith. 2014. "The Transformation of a Legacy Carrier: A Case Study of Turkish Airlines." *Journal of Air Transport Management* 40:106–118.

Düvell, Franck. 2014. "Turkey's Transition to an Immigration Country: A Paradigm Shift." *Insight Turkey* 16, no. 4: 87–104.

Ekmekçioğlu, Lerna. 2016. *Recovering Armenia: The Limits of Belonging in Post-Genocide Turkey.* Stanford, CA: Stanford University Press.

Esson, James. 2015. "Better Off at Home? Rethinking Responses to Trafficked West African Footballers in Europe." *Journal of Ethnic and Migration Studies* 41, no. 3: 512–530.

Friese, Heidrun. 2009. "The Limits of Hospitality." *Paragraph* 32, no. 1: 51–68.

Geertz, Clifford. 1960. "The Javanese Kijaji: The Changing Role of a Cultural Broker." *Comparative Studies in Society and History* 2, no. 2: 228–249.

Gershon, Ilana. 2017. *Down and Out in the New Economy: How People Find (or Don't Find) Work Today.* Chicago: University of Chicago Press.

Goldblatt, David. 2007. *The Ball Is Round: A Global History of Football.* London: Penguin.

Hage, Ghassan. 2003. *Against Paranoid Nationalism: Searching for Hope in a Shrinking Society.* Annandale, NSW: Pluto.

Harvey, David. 1989. *The Condition of Postmodernity.* Oxford: Blackwell.

Harvey, David. 2005. *A Brief History of Neoliberalism.* Oxford: Oxford University Press.

Herzfeld, Michael. 1987. "'As in Your Own House': Hospitality, Ethnography, and the Stereotypes of Mediterranean Society." In *Honor and Shame and the Unity of the Mediterranean,* edited by David Gilmore, 148–160. Washington, DC: American Anthropological Association.

Humphrey, Caroline. 2012. "Hospitality and Tone: Holding Patterns for Strangeness in Rural Mongolia." *Journal of the Royal Anthropological Institute* 18, no. S1: S63–S75.

James, Deborah. 2011. "The Return of the Broker: Consensus, Hierarchy, and Choice in South African Land Reform." *Journal of the Royal Anthropological Institute* 17, no. 2: 318–338.

Jordan Smith, Daniel. 2017. *To Be a Man Is Not a One Day Job: Masculinity, Money, and Intimacy in Nigeria.* Chicago: University of Chicago Press.

Kelly, Seamus, and Dikaia Chatziefstathiou. 2018. "'Trust Me I Am a Football Agent': The Discursive Practices of the Players' Agents in (Un)Professional Football." *Sport in Society* 21, no. 5: 800–814.

King, Charles. 2015. *Midnight at the Pera Palace: The Birth of Modern Istanbul*. London: W.W. Norton.

Knight, Ricky D. 2011. "The Long Wait: African Migrant Communities and the Production of Local Identity in Istanbul, Turkey." Ph.D. dissertation, Department of Anthropology, Washington State University.

Letsch, Constanze. 2011. "Waiting for Kick-off – Plight of African Footballers Left on Sidelines in Turkey." *Guardian* (Manchester), 18 September 2011. www.theguardian.com/world/2011/sep/18/african-footballers-turkey.

Lindquist, Johan. 2015. "Brokers and Brokerage, Anthropology of." *International Encyclopedia of Social and Behavioral Science*, edited by James D. Wright, 2nd ed., 870–874. Amsterdam: Elsevier.

Mango, Andrew. 1999. "Atatürk and the Kurds." *Middle Eastern Studies* 35, no. 4: 1–25.

Mauss, Marcel. 2002. *The Gift: The Form and Reason for Exchange in Archaic Societies*, translated by W. D. Halls. London: Routledge. (First published 1925.)

McManus, John. 2018. *Welcome to Hell? In Search of the Real Turkish Football*. London: Weidenfeld and Nicolson.

Öktem, Kerem, Ayşe Kadıoğlu, and Mehmet Karlı, eds. 2012. *Another Empire? A Decade of Turkey's Foreign Policy Under the Justice and Development Party*. Istanbul: Istanbul Bilgi University Press.

Özkan, Mehmet, and Birol Akgün. 2010. "Turkey's Opening to Africa." *Journal of Modern African Studies* 48, no. 4: 525–546.

Pitt-Rivers, Julian. 1972. *The People of the Sierra*. Chicago: University of Chicago Press. (First published 1954.)

Pitt-Rivers, Julian. 1977. "The Law of Hospitality." In *The Fate of Shechem or the Politics of Sex: Essays in the Anthropology of the Mediterranean*, 94–112. Cambridge: Cambridge University Press.

Polo, Jean-François. 2015. "Turkish Sports Diplomacy in the Service of Renewed Power? The Uses and Limits of Turkey's 'Sport Power.'" *European Journal of Turkish Studies* 21. https://journals.openedition.org/ejts/5241.

Pratt, Mary Louise. 1991. "Arts of the Contact Zone." *Profession* 1991: 33–40.

Rosen, Lawrence. 2011. *Varieties of Muslim Experience: Encounters with Arab Political and Cultural Life*. Chicago: University of Chicago Press.

Şaul, Mahir. 2014. "A Different Kargo: Sub-Saharan Migrants in Istanbul and African Commerce." *Urban Anthropology* 43, no. 1–3: 143–203.

Şaul, Mahir. 2017. "The Migrant in a Plotted Adventure: Self-Realisation and Moral Obligation in African Stories from Istanbul." *Journal of Modern African Studies* 55, no. 1: 129–153.

Sheller, Mimi. 2014. "The New Mobilities Paradigm for a Live Sociology." *Current Sociology Review* 62, no. 6: 789–811.

Shryock, Andrew. 2012. "Breaking Hospitality Apart: Bad Hosts, Bad Guests, and the Problem of Sovereignty." *Journal of the Royal Anthropological Institute* 18, no. S1: S20–S33.

Suter, Brigitte. 2012. "Tales of Transit: Sub-Saharan African Migrants' Experience in Istanbul." Ph.D. dissertation, Linköping University.

Tuvi, Reyan. 2010. *Ofsayt [Offside]*. Ominira Films & Altınsay Filmworks.

White, Jenny. 2015. "The Turkish Complex." *American Interest* 10, no. 4, 2 February 2015. www.the-american-interest.com/2015/02/02/the-turkish-complex/.

Wolf, Eric R. 1956. "Aspects of Group Relations in a Complex Society: Mexico." *American Anthropologist* 58, no. 6: 1065–1078.

Yükseker, Deniz, and Kelly Todd Brewer. 2011. "Astray and Stranded at the Gates of the European Union: African Transit Migrants in Istanbul." *New Perspectives on Turkey* 44: 135–166.

Zalewski, Piotr. 2012. "Turkish Descendants of African Slaves Begin to Discover Their Identity." *The National*, 1 September 2012. www.thenational.ae/world/mena/turkish-descendants-of-african-slaves-begin-to-discover-their-identity-1.364124.

3

"THIS IS BUSINESS!"

Ethiopian runners in a global marketplace

Michael Crawley

This is business! Think carefully, business has bankruptcy and profit. If the owner is a clever merchant, he can be profitable. If he is not a clever merchant, he will lose the gamble. Because the flow of water depends on the ground.

(Messeret, coach of Moyo Sports Athlete Management)

People do many different things to generate income, and the way they earn money is very different. When you get your income from running, you are proving what you have and what you have done in front of people. For instance, merchants are cheating someone and earning something that way, but in running you enjoy running, and you get what you deserve.

(Aseffa, marathon runner)

The ultimate aim of all Ethiopian runners is to create a "chance" to run in a race outside of Ethiopia, where they can potentially make a life-changing amount of money. Like professional sport elsewhere in the contemporary world (Besnier, Calabrò, and Guinness, this volume), professional long-distance running is both "neoliberal" and "millennial": deeply individualizing, wrought with insecurity and personal risk, and underpinned by speculation and casino capitalism. Elite-level professional running, in which athletes train in groups but compete alone, is an especially powerful site to explore the dynamics of communal work and individual responsibilization. As the epigraphs make clear, the disposition required of a runner is the subject of dispute. For Coach Messeret, it is important to cultivate the entrepreneurial mindset of a merchant.[1] Aseffa, in contrast, sees in running freedom from the disposition of the merchant, which in his view is scheming and deceptive. When he says that with running "you get what you deserve," he portrays running as a career choice that affords a straightforward relationship between work and success that does not require the demeaning behaviour of scheming and cheating.

FIGURE 3.1 The runners prepare to begin a run in Akaki, 20 January 2016. (Source: Michael Crawley)

During the 15 months of ethnographic fieldwork I conducted in Addis Ababa, Ethiopia, and at rural training camps in the northern highlands of Ethiopia, I lived and trained with runners at a range of levels, from those who had just started their training and who did not yet have a passport to those who regularly travelled overseas to compete for tens of thousands of dollars (Figure 3.1). I also travelled with the runners to races in Europe, Turkey, and China. Much of my fieldwork took place with the training group of Moyo Sports Management, an athlete management agency based in the United Kingdom, whose athletes were primarily Amhara (with a minority from Oromia) and Orthodox Christian (with the exception of two Protestants). Choosing to become a runner involves speculating and taking risks, as well as actively rejecting other forms of precarious work, which runners perceive as failing to offer a "chance" of "changing one's life" for the better. Running, eating and resting alongside runners, I gained an understanding of how people attempt to navigate what I call an "economy of limited energy" (Crawley 2018), whereby their everyday actions, attitude to the environment, and relational ethics all focus on how to deploy their energy, how to share it with others, and how to pursue a future in the sport.

While the epigraphs illustrate a dichotomy between two dispositions, in reality runners seek to find a balance between dispositions of patience and submission on the one hand and self-promotion on the other as they navigate the ultra-competitive world of professional athletics. In some cases, they switch from one to the other or use one to attain the other. The analytical distinction between two notions of "chance" that Ethiopian runners draw upon rests on two theories of agency: both are individual, but they diverge in how they enlist other people's help, how runners deploy them over time, and how they produce results. While the first disposition, silent submission to the authority of coach and sub-agent, was open to both male and female runners, only my male interlocutors pursued the second. Living as a male runner was to teeter between two ideologies, to have faith in your-self but also to place yourself in the pull of social and environmental forces in such a way as to increase the likelihood of "changing your life." What we often think of as "neoliberal" transformations represent, in the Ethiopian context at least, a partial reproduction of pre-existing cultural values.

A simple version of the way in which "neoliberal" practices transform sporting subjectivities assumes a shift from an understanding of the self as collectively produced towards what Michel Foucault characterized as the "entrepreneur of the self, being for himself his own capital, being for himself his own producer, being for himself the source of [his] earnings" (Foucault 2008, 224). This kind of trans-formation is, of course, not confined to the sporting world, and a process in which the Ethiopian state is actively engaged. It is a mistake to assume that neoliberalism is necessarily opposed to the intervention of the state; in fact, as many have pointed out, the state is an active agent in neoliberal transformations.

Former Prime Minister Meles Zenawi, the architect of Ethiopia's develop-mental state, stated clearly that his aim was to create an atomized peasantry who would abandon their allegiances to intermediate social entities such as the church and extended family (De Waal 2018). For example, in state-run entrepreneur-ship schemes in Addis Ababa, the state casts unemployed youth as personally responsible for their poverty and exclusion. The statute adopted by the Ethiopian People's Revolutionary Democratic Front's (EPRDF) 4th General Assembly states that the government's system of entrepreneurship schemes was intended to work in such a way that "those who show productive results obtain progress, and those who do not, will receive nothing" (EPRDF 2006, 39, quoted in Di Nunzio 2015, 1194).

The Ethiopian state then is involved in a project of attempting to create the kind of individualized and responsibilized citizen, who, as James Ferguson puts it, "comes to operate as a miniature firm, responding to incentives, rationally assessing risks, and prudently choosing from among different courses of action" (2010, 172). This was the disposition that our coach, Messeret, encouraged by repeatedly telling athletes that they needed to take "responsibility" for their own performances and think of themselves as merchants of their own one-person business. This is a discourse of individualization and internalization that Ferguson claims is absent in the African context. In Africa, he writes, neoliberalism has meant the "policy measures that were forced on African states in the 1980s – policies that have more in common with older, liberal, laissez faire economic policies" (2010, 172). In short, for Ferguson, neoliberalism is something that is done *to* African countries, the "crude battering open of third world markets" (172). However, how Messeret wanted runners to plan their careers and "take responsibility" actually resembles closely the "Anglo-Foucauldian" rationality Ferguson claims is absent in Africa. But it was not the only way in which runners thought about their running.

The idea of a straightforward transition from thinking of the self as collectively produced to an entrepreneurial habitus recalls Pierre Bourdieu's assertion that there is such a "mismatch" between "the economic dispositions fashioned in a pre-capitalist economy" and the "rationalised economic cosmos" of (colonized) modernity that we must speak not of "adaptation" but rather of "conversion" of the "whole mindset" to the "spirit of calculation" (2000, 23). This simple dichotomy has been often been taken up by scholars of global sport such as James Esson (2013; 2015), who has argued that Ghanaian footballers seek to become Foucauldian "entrepreneurs of self" by investing in their human capital in order to become a professional footballer.

To speak of "conversion" to a completely new, individualistic mindset, however, is oversimplifying in the Ethiopian context. While Bourdieu rejects the term "adaptation," I think it is useful, not least because the word that Ethiopian runners most often used to describe training in Amharic, the dominant language of Ethiopia, was *lememid*, "adaptation." How neoliberalism asserts itself as the partial reproduction of pre-existing cultural values is far better described as one of "adaptation" – and selective "adaptation" at that – than one of "transformation."

Crucially, this adaptation is different from a neoliberalism-inflected ideology of entrepreneurship, which attempts to create a "chance." The idea of individualism is already there at the heart of Amhara culture, which understands people to be driven by personal and even selfish desires, urges that must be tempered through discourses of togetherness and practices of commensality (Levine 1965; Kebede 1999; Malara and Boylston 2016; Boylston 2018). The question is how this pre-existing individualism is transformed when it comes into contact with neoliberal impulses. It is this new object that I seek to uncover by delineating the two ideologies of "chance" separately before explaining how they interact with one another. I call these ideologies the "ideology of silence and deserving" and the "ideology of chance creation." What kinds of skills does a runner need to succeed, beyond the skill of running? How does he or she cultivate a running self in relation to others? What kinds of capital does he or she need to learn and how? And above all, how do runners experience and mediate "chance"?

Two ideologies of "chance"

In Addis Ababa, cheaply printed self-help books in either Amharic or English are ubiquitous at roadside stalls. Members of the public see these books as a problem and some, like exorcists, even see them as a demonic threat (Di Nunzio 2015; Malara 2017). Our coach Messeret almost always had one of these books with him on our bus journeys to training. At one of our post-training meetings, he spoke to the athletes about the difference between the psychology developed in such books and that of the runners themselves as follows:

> Do you know the difference between Americans and people from other countries? There is a huge difference in terms of psychology. Most Americans think: I am the only person who can do this (he points to himself). I, I, I. I know, I have read many of their books. Psychologically they convince themselves: I, I, I am the person who can do this. I am first, I am first, I am first. They grow up like this. Go away Selamyhun, you can't do this, Mekasha you can't, Berhanu is ill, you can't. you can't you can't. We have to try to come to this kind of thinking.

The self-help books were popular not only because they contained the allure of the outside world and Western success but also because they resonate with a pre-existing ideology of ambition and the self-aggrandizing view of one's life possibilities (Levine 1965; Kebede 1999). What is new and different is not so much the beliefs themselves but how these books allow these beliefs to be openly articulated. Messeret would lean on them as he was writing down the athletes' times in training and often snatched some reading time on our jolting bus journeys back from training. The mindset of books like *The Seven Habits of Highly Effective People* was one he sought to instil upon the athletes in our post-training meetings. These books rely upon an idea of discipline in line with Foucault's notion of work of the self upon the self. In the Ethiopian context, however, this discipline is not merely self-focused, but rather entails dyadic hierarchical relations (between the runner and the coach) as well as a relational work environment, which in the runners' case consisted of the training group in which people "share" the responsibility to set the pace and emphasize "improving together."

A tension sometimes arose between the ideas of entrepreneurial spirit and individual responsibilization associated with modernity on the one hand and a faith in chance, associated with passivity, on the other. Marco Di Nunzio quotes an inscription on the gate of one of the colleges in Addis Ababa which read, "Development is not by chance (*idil*), it is a matter of choice (*mirca*)" (2015, 1193), using this to emphasize the extent to which, for his interlocutors, "chance" in the sense of a stroke of luck *could* bring about development. My interlocutors, however, were opposed to this view of *idil* as operating at random and independently of an individual's actions. They saw chance as something that happened to someone but also something for which you had to work hard in order to be ready to seize the opportunity when it was presented. While my interlocutors saw gaining a "chance" to run abroad as vitally important to their success, they often saw that the best way to approach this was a disposition of patient hard work, submission to the authority of the coach, and a discourse of intersubjective dependence.

Idil was central to how my interlocutors thought about running. But they did not associate *idil* with passivity or frame it as the opposite of choice. For them, *idil* both helped to rationalize failure and essentially remained speculative and hopeful. They spoke of *idil* in Amharic and "chance" in English to describe a specific opportunity that was usually offered by a foreign manager. The two concepts are not the same, however: *idil* referred to a disposition of deserving, while "chance" referred to particular opportunities which can be attained by adopting an entrepreneurial disposition. It is important to distinguish cultivating a moral economy of "deservingness" likely to improve one's *idil* (Malara and Boylston 2016) and capitalizing on a fleeting "chance," which may in fact be detrimental to *idil*.

Idil depends on the belief that everything that happens reflects the active will of God and that this will is, above all, mysterious. This means that "the grace which distributes different and unequal destinies to individuals is extremely unstable and shifting," a belief that is "imbued less with the idea of fatalism than with the idea of changing destinies" (Kebede 1999, 204). Endurance and patience (*tigist*) rank among the highest virtues, while arrogance (*tigab*) or not knowing one's place is a serious vice. *Idil* is thus strongly inflected with moral values, comparable with "destiny" (Guinness 2018), which includes the future orientation of hope as well as a moral imperative for action and endurance. This orientation is less about continuity and progression and more about "sensitivity to reversals ... of ups and downs in a cyclical fashion" (Kebede 1999, 216). Because runners think about talent or capacity primarily in terms of grace (*tsega*) or *idil*, the social system must be open and people must be open to the possibility of both the sudden improvement and equally sudden deterioration of their situation.

Idil relies on the knowledge of one's place within a hierarchy. Ethiopian runners understand themselves to be part of a hierarchy that is constantly in flux, where nothing is final, all is reversible according to the will of God, and arrogance can lead to the reversal of one's fortunes. This is at odds with Max Weber's (2002) analysis of the Protestant work ethic, the believers of which seek signs of election in work and the accumulation of wealth. It is also different from the way in which athletes relate to Christianity elsewhere (e.g., Rial 2012; Kovač 2016; Guinness 2018). For an Amhara runner, one is never elected once and for all. The physical "condition" on which success depends can "disappear" abruptly and may never return. In contrast, it can "suddenly come" to an athlete who has been struggling for months. In traditional Amhara society, the belief in *idil* means that a person's potential or real worth is often obscured, or at least not necessarily reflected in their outward bearing or level of wealth. This explains why the self-made person who has improved him- or herself through work or the accumulation of money is often not looked upon positively (Kebede 1999), as the opening epigraph from Aseffa illustrates.

For runners, *idil* is cultivated through a moral economy of patient hard work and submission. It is inextricably tied up with the notion of "condition," a fickle state of health and fitness that enables athletic performance, defined by patience, acceptance, and a particular way of relating to fellow runners. Within the group, morally appropriate training behaviour demanded that training be visible and synchronous, and that pace-making responsibilities be equally shared to ensure that no one gained an unfair advantage. "Condition" was reliant upon training hard and a lifestyle characterized by seclusion and the avoidance of many aspects of normal social life in Ethiopia. Runners warned me and each other against "warming up café seats," as one of my informants put it, emphasizing the importance of properly resting at home between training sessions and the careful monitoring of energy levels. In contrast to the beliefs in innate talent held by many people involved in elite sports, runners believed that patient and consistent work and adequate rest could help anyone to become "changed" and succeed. In parallel was a more active disposition that does share characteristics with the entrepreneurship of the self, in which runners actively sought opportunities or "chance" by nurturing networks with managers, race organizers, and other foreigners who may have access to races "outside."

"Not a single word": The ideology of silent submission and deserving

The disposition most commonly adopted by the runners I knew was one of patience and silent hard work. Aseffa was one of the more experienced runners in the group of athletes with whom I trained in Addis Ababa. He had travelled to races in the United Kingdom, Europe, and China, and had won a few thousand dollars on several occasions. In spite of this relative success, most of his earnings had thus far been reinvested in his running career.[2] He had moved to a more comfortable house with his girlfriend, and was spending money on the kinds of foods associated with maintaining energy levels such as meat, fresh juice, and avocados. He was also spending around 600 birr (US$24) a month on "milk rent," a litre of milk per day from a local farmer. His relationship to our sub-agent Hailye was one of friendly deference, and he was philosophical about his access to races outside of Ethiopia.

As the epigraph with which I started this chapter suggests, he saw running as a transparent process that enabled someone to make their *idil* visible. In contrast to the scheming and dissembling that he sees as characteristic of other professions (merchants being the archetype), running allowed an individual to "prove what [he] has … in front of people." This has parallels in warfare, which, as an encounter with clear winners and losers, best reveals warriors' *idil* (Kebede 1999). By emphasizing the importance of competing "in front of people," Aseffa evokes the race – as the culmination of all the patient training that has led up to it – as a means to render one's *idil* visible. "Proving" oneself happens at the race itself, when the competing runners are sorted into winners and losers, but it also happens more frequently at the training sessions around Addis Ababa attended by the sub-agent, who then reports to the manager on athletes' "performance." The visibility of "proving" yourself was an important part of gaining a chance.

Because visibility and synchronicity are important in training, Coach Messeret spoke constantly about the problem of missing group training sessions. This is how he spoke about it after training one day:

> If someone is poor and sleeps on a bed of mud in a blanket of flies, sewn by needle and thread, then he covers himself in a white cloth, he will consider

himself a rich man in front of his friends and neighbours, won't he? You see, the white cloth is clean because he washes it, but not the blanket on the inside. The question is, does he sleep in it or not? The one who is accustomed to it will sleep in it, the other will not. If you get used to knowing how to keep condition you will keep it, if not you won't.

This quote lends itself to different interpretations and conveys more than one message. The first point is about authenticity and appearances. What Messeret seeks to make clear is that there is no point trying to hide one's true "condition," which will in any case be revealed in a race. In this sense, "condition" is somewhat like *idil*, an interior state that only God knows. The second point is about being accustomed to hardship and virtuous suffering. One needs to be able to "sleep in" one's "condition," to accept the discomfort and fatigue that come with heavy training and to patiently wait to improve (compare Kovač, this volume).

An athlete does not generally contact a manager directly, as this would be seen as inappropriate and clumsy. As mediators, the sub-agents who work on behalf of managers therefore have significant power over which athletes would race abroad. Runners in the group I trained in needed to learn to cultivate a moral economy of "deserving" characterized by consistent attendance of training sessions, hard work, and above all silence. This was the behaviour most likely to influence the sub-agent positively. When they receive commands from a superior, subordinates need to keep silent to index obedience and deference. Aseffa seemed to understand this well, and his relationship with Hailye was good. He would regularly stop by our compound on the way back from training to exchange greetings and chat about running. These conversations would be about training, and about other athletes' races, but Aseffa was careful not to ask for races for himself or to talk about money. Often prize money from races abroad could take months to arrive (via the manager) in the athlete's bank account, but this was another thing Aseffa was careful not to mention in his conversations with Hailye. In conversations about his own running, future plans and finances, he displayed silent acceptance. As Hailye himself put it, "Aseffa understands, he's a good guy."

For Aseffa, the important thing was for Hailye to see him as working hard. He had heard Hailye complain that the other athletes "nagged" him, constantly asking him when they would get to race abroad, so he avoided doing so himself. His respect for quiet, unassuming hard work was revealed on one particular occasion when he called a meeting of the athletes to discuss our training bus conductor Tadesse. The manager of the group hired a bus three mornings a week to take us to various training locations. Sitting alongside the driver, Tadesse opened the door for the athletes and prevented members of the public from boarding the bus, which looked like a regular city bus. Tadesse had been a runner himself for a few years before finding himself under too much pressure to earn money and without the time to train, and as the bus followed the runners on a training run he would jump out every five kilometres clutching an armful of water bottles, sprinting alongside

FIGURE 3.2 Tadesse hands out water bottles during a training session in Sendafa, 21 March 2016.
(Source: Michael Crawley)

the athletes to hand them out and then collecting them up again after they had been discarded (Figure 3.2).

He did all this without the athletes explicitly asking for it, and seemingly without any expectation of reward, and he seemed to enjoy the challenge of trying to hand out water bottles while sprinting in jeans and flip-flops. Aseffa wanted to reward this behaviour by collecting money for Tadesse to pay for driving lessons. This is how he and Hailye pitched the idea to the group:

> *Aseffa:* I have been thinking about Tadesse for a while. In God's name, I think we should facilitate something for him …
>
> *Hailye:* I will contribute, and coach will contribute 100 birr, others can contribute 50 birr each. … He deserves a lot, giving water even though he is very busy. He is working very hard …
>
> *Aseffa:* He's working so hard!

Aseffa and Hailye are rewarding behaviour they see as exemplary – hard work with no complaints and no expectation of reward. This is also the ideal behaviour of the runner, who is expected to trust Hailye completely and not question anything, especially concerning money. On several occasions, I witnessed Hailye attempting to show athletes the printed "breakdown" from the races in which they had competed abroad. These were calculations made by the manager showing the prize money won, the amount deducted as a percentage by the manager, and the various other deductions for flights, meals, and transfers. The most common reaction I witnessed to this was for athletes to push the paper away in mock offence. I was present on one occasion when Hailye attempted to show an athlete a "breakdown" showing that they had won a net amount of $15,000 and would be receiving just over $8,000 to their bank account after the deduction of 20% tax, the 15% Athlete Representative fee and the cost of flights to China. Hailye was concerned because while the calculations were correct, some athletes would question why so much money had seemingly been deducted from their winnings. Asmara, the athlete in question, refused to look at the paper. Instead he insisted, "No, coach, I trust you in everything." As we walked away, I expressed surprise that he wouldn't want to see the details. Hailye just said, "Asmara is good, he is very happy after that race." When I mentioned this to the manager of our team he had this to say:

> You know what, I said to Hailye, if there's an athlete who's not under sponsorship then there's prioritisation of who gets kit and Asmara 100% gets some of the best stuff because he does the hard work in training, he accepts the races that we think are best and then he agrees with the breakdowns and doesn't cause any problems.

Adopting a disposition of silent acceptance of the decisions of those in positions of authority can bring material rewards. In refusing to scrutinize the "breakdown" and showing trust in his manager and sub-agent, Asmara was given new Nike shoes and training kit from the supply Hailye had in his compound.

For Amhara Orthodox Christians, the marker of hierarchy is not only obeying one's superiors, but also not questioning them (Malara and Boylston 2016). The driver of the team bus articulated this idea during a team meeting, when he said "the government uses the word 'integration.' This work needs integration. The words of God and the words of bosses must be respected." Various ideas about submission to authority, whether divine or government-orchestrated, are reproduced in fostering a sense of team "integration." For Berhanu, who was at least 20 years older than the runners, "integration" essentially meant for the runners to obey the wishes of their superiors, namely the sub-agent Hailye and the coach Messeret.

It was important for runners to know their place (*lil mawek*) and demonstrate it visibly. Performing submission, in fact, can be as important a strategy for creating a "chance" as more assertive attempts to do so. For Hailye, the worst behaviour an athlete could exhibit was to question his decision and ask him to be chosen for a race. He would deliberately reward athletes for their submission and silent hard work. For example, Melaku was a young athlete who had recently moved to Addis Ababa from a rural training camp and barely had enough to rent a one-room house in Sendafa, 30 km outside the city. He would get up before 4 A.M. to take a bus to Maganegna, the main transit hub in the east of the city, where our team bus could pick him up. In his first few weeks with us, he barely spoke. Hailye selected him to travel to a race in Turkey after just six weeks with the group, and justified his decision thus:

> Melaku is a really good person. I'm really pleased that he got this chance. But some of them, like, you know, they don't tell me straight, they tell Tsedat, or someone who is very close to me, they say "if he doesn't arrange [a race] for us we're going to go with another manager." So if they are dishonest, we should give a chance to the honest ones, especially if they are strong. There is no one like Melaku. He is the one person who never said anything about a race. Not a single word. He just keeps working.

To deserve a race was to work hard and in silence and to accept the decision about where you were sent to run and the result. A strong belief in one's *idil* was demonstrated by acceptance of poor performances as well as good ones. This is how Aseffa described his response to a poor race:

> If I run and don't get any prize money, I don't complain. I'm not sad because I know that if that money came I might use it to do sin, or to do bad things with it. God has a purpose, he knows what is useful for you. Like, if you get money, and you buy a car, then you get hit by another car and you die, that is not useful for you.

This acceptance of a poor competitive performance was frustrating for the manager of our group, who took it as a sign that the athlete didn't care sufficiently about their career. However, there was a very clear sense that runners had to accept God's role in the unfolding of their *idil*. For someone like Aseffa or Melaku, to question Hailye's judgement and to "nag" him for a race without deserving it could have serious and potentially fatal consequences. The runners in the group associated rewards not with striving and seeking to create a "chance" by negotiating but rather by being loyal and submissive over the long term. This moral economy of deserving and acceptance of the very real likelihood that all the work done in training may amount to nothing in material terms extended to the fact that runners insisted that money should not be considered the main indicator of success. Mekasha explained the failure and disintegration of his previous training group as follows:

> We had a group, we discussed things and learned things together, but we were from different religions and money came and it disrupted everything. What I learnt from that is that if money destroys our unity, if it detaches us, if it turns us into show-offs, tomorrow we may not have our legs – there are athletes who are committing suicide with their own cars!

Here we have Mekasha making a causal connection between short-term economic interest and religious diversity. Elite Ethiopian runners are primarily from two ethnic groups, the Amhara and the Oromo, and while most are Orthodox Christians, there are also fairly large proportions of Protestant, Pentecostal, and Muslim athletes. In spite of this, the Moyo Sports group was religiously homogenous, with all but a couple of runners being Amhara Orthodox Christians. On the social occasion on which Mekasha made these comments, the two non-Orthodox runners were not present, and he associates the moral economy of deserving with Amhara Orthodox morality. These two warnings against short-term economic self-interest leading to fatal car accidents demonstrate the analytical distinction between the categories of *idil* and "chance": getting a short-term opportunity can be detrimental to *idil*.

Hailye and other runners often interpreted the values of silence and submission to authority as *rural* values that life in the city potentially threatens. For two young athletes from Gondar, in northern Ethiopia, who were selected to compete with the national team in the World Junior Championships in Poland, what struck them most during their "pre-competition" training time in Addis Ababa was the non-authoritarian nature of the coaching. This is how Kidane, who competed in the 3,000 metre steeplechase, described it:

> In Gondar, the coaches look after you very well. They say, "where have you been, what have you been doing?" There is seriousness there … The coaches even hit and punch you to encourage you to run well, but here you have to do things and deserve for yourself.

Coercive power can co-exist with love and care, and athletes would often ask our coach to be more authoritarian because they knew that authoritarianism was also caring. Messeret would often end our post-training discussions by asking athletes for comments, a democratic gesture he had learned from a coaching course he had attended in the United States and from the self-help books he read. Much to his frustration, it was almost always met with silence. Privately, the athletes told me that they felt that Messeret undermined his authority by asking them for their opinions, and that it was his job to tell them what to do and ensure that they did it.

Ethiopians traditionally have "difficulty in seeing the merchant as a person of value" given that their efforts "betrayed an attempt to become what they were not, to occupy places to which they were not entitled" (Kebede 1999, 221; Mains 2011). Yet Coach Messeret often encouraged runners to think of themselves as "merchants" responsible for their own "bankruptcy and profit." This encouragement to adopt a disposition of striving and self-promotion came into tension with the disposition of deserving, silence, and submission. Nevertheless, runners slipped in and out of these dispositions according to their circumstances. To adopt an entrepreneurial disposition was often associated with the acceptance of a lesser athletic future.

Chasing chance

> There are someone who is sending invitation from Panama. On a website, "Panama is one of the most attractive cities in the world," it says. So the economy is strong, one dollar is equal to 0.98 Panama money …
>
> *(Mesgebe, October 2015)*

> Panama is gone, but still I try with Peru. And today I will meet with a man from Finland and I am also contact a man from New Zealand.
>
> *(Mesgebe, March 2016)*

> In Brazil, they will pay you 60,000, 80,000 Brazilian money. Which is you divide by 3.9 something because one dollar is equal to 3 point something. … The money is like this. They have so many races but they could not speak English. Even though there are different websites, Facebook, Twitter, everything but they are not able to speak English. I don't know why.
>
> *(Mesgebe, July 2016)*

Like other runners in Addis Ababa, I would often pass time in the various juice houses (*chemaki bets*) around Kotebe after training. On one particular morning, it took me a while to recognize the men who sat opposite me, despite the fact that I had met them on many occasions. So used to seeing them in tracksuits in the forest, their jeans and shirtsleeves looked strange on them as they pored over three phones like businessmen. After chatting for a while, I asked why Mesgebe had two phones. "One is for international running contacts," he told me before showing me the web page of AIMS World Running, a site which features the organization and contact details of many of the world's most important road races. Mesgebe and Danny occasionally trained in what they called the "management system" (a group similar to Moyo Sports, described above), but they organized their own trips to races as well. As the quotations above suggest, Mesgebe actively sought opportunities abroad by sending speculative e-mails attempting to create networks with race directors. He often experienced these interactions as opaque and frustrating, and they demanded a lot of time and effort to pursue.

In fact, in the time I was in Ethiopia, instead of the vast global reach they were hoping to master, Mesgebe and Danny only managed to travel to India to race, which represented a compromise in a number of ways. They had to raise the money from friends and relatives, many of whom had already been abroad themselves, but India was a cheap place to fly to and didn't require complicated visa arrangements. Mesgebe was keenly aware of the problems associated with trying to travel to races independently, and several consulates had refused him visas in the course of my fieldwork. In spite of this, he still thought he could "make business" by being strategic about his applications. India was intended as a first step that would prove to other consulates that he was not merely trying to "disappear," as he put it. After going to India, he spoke of plans to travel to Romania, the Czech Republic, and

Italy, which he thought had less stringent visa requirements, before then being able to travel to the United Kingdom or France. In a sense, a trip to India would enable him to create a chance, though on a different scale, by demonstrating to state authorities that he was an obedient servant. Mesgebe had developed a clear awareness of the strategies necessary to access races, but his experiences in India had been exhausting and fraught with problems. On his return, this is how he described the trip:

> Oh, India, India was tough. It was just too hot, the lifestyle was not adequate for me. We had a lot of suffering because if you have a competition in Mumbai, then the next day you will travel for 1,300 km, 1,500 km, something like that. And no training at all. If today is Sunday, today you compete, for the next Sunday you will compete 1,500 km away or something like that. It takes two nights, two days of travel. You may win 20,000 rupees, but for food, for bedroom, for transportation, for everything it will go. Because normally I train hard in the morning and the afternoon, my body became locked and I couldn't sprint at all.

Ethiopian runners pay considerable attention to the environmental resources of different areas surrounding Addis Ababa, and on the benefits of the climate of highland Ethiopia. To remain away from Ethiopia for more than a few days means a big drop in an athlete's "condition," and therefore to stay in India for so long required sacrificing long-sought "condition" in order to make a few thousand rupees. The second time he went to India, Mesgebe decided not to run at all, but rather charged other runners for getting them invited to races and facilitating their travel. "Because the runners don't know English," he told me, "I facilitate for them. Two even went for hospital treatment, because I know a big hospital in India that is better than in Ethiopia." Here it was his English-language skills and ability to network that enabled him to make money. He became an agent, at least temporarily. Mesgebe still had dreams of making it as a runner, but mobility in itself was not enough to do this. Successful running required a specific kind of mobility involving travelling to a race for a couple of days and then immediately returning to Ethiopia, rather than the drawn-out process of competing in several races in order to make ends meet.

Small races, small money

In Mesgebe's eyes, success was tied to the environment in Ethiopia, which was why spending so long in India was so problematic. "To be successful, you have to use all the good working places around Addis," he told me at one point, assuring me that if I stayed in Ethiopia I would have an advantage over runners in Europe. When I explained to him that there were actually a number of Ethiopian and Kenyan runners residing in Britain, he shrugged and replied, "you work here though, you can beat them if they stay there." The ideology of silence and deserving described in the previous section relied upon patience and delayed gratification. Seeking a "chance" of one's own accord, however, often meant that while a "chance" may be more immediate, it involved accepting diminished returns from running. Mesgebe told me about a friend of his who travelled to Belgium in the following terms:

> One guy I know went to Belgium. He went for a race in Italy and then dir-
> ectly he went to Belgium and he is doing his best now. He is winning small
> races. In Ethiopia he couldn't even follow us in training but he got a chance
> because he got an Italian visa because he knew someone there who could
> send him an invitation. He paid 5,000 birr for the invitation and then when
> he got to Italy he disappeared to Belgium.

Michael: Why did he decide to go to Belgium?
Mesgebe: Because here he decided he could not be a good athlete anymore.
Because he turned 35 years, he became old.
Michael: So is he doing a different job now?
Mesgebe: No, just he is running. Small races, small money. What is good is that
in developed countries there are many small races, he can collect a little bit
every week.

A conventional narrative of neoliberal sporting aspiration might assume that to gain permanent residence in a country in the Global North in which to compete would be the ultimate aim of an athlete in the Global South. As the conversation above demonstrates, however, Ethiopian runners see migrating to the Global North as a last resort or at least a categorically different form of mobility to that which they sought in hope of "changing their lives" (compare Hopkinson, this volume, on a similar pattern among Ghanaian boxers). The following is an extract from a conversation between two runners, Berhanu, who had just returned from a couple of races in the United States, and Teklemariam, who sought his advice about going there himself:

Teklemariam: Can you run for a club there?
Berhanu: Yes, but you run voluntarily.
Teklemariam: Just for the sake of running?
Berhanu: Yes. For instance, if you run a race and you finish in the top five you will
make $200. No other benefits.
Teklemariam: No other benefits?
Berhanu: No, you just go there instead of sitting around here.
Teklemariam: If I get a chance to go, what would your advice be?
Berhanu: Go, but if you want to run make sure you are strong first. Otherwise, if
you are just average even if you get something you will just spend it – there is
no profit. You'd better work, you understand? If you stay here and train you'll
have a better chance. Here it is better, massage is cheap and the food is good.
I will prepare for my next race here, if you stay there you can't be successful,
and when you get back here it is difficult to re-adapt to the altitude.

This passage demonstrates how "getting a chance," as Teklemariam puts it, may be detrimental to his progress as a runner, just as it was for Mesgebe in India. In the time I knew him, Teklemariam often wavered between wanting to focus on his own running ("I need to just train and nothing else for six months") and seeking other strategies to make money. One of these, which he reverted to on a couple of occasions, was to work as a pacemaker for the female athletes in our group. As prize money in athletics is equal for men and women, and because fewer female athletes compete, it was a widely held perception amongst male Ethiopian runners and coaches that it was "easier" for female runners to make money. It was rare to see female runners training in the forest on their own, however, and a male pacemaker usually preceded them.

"All Ethiopian females need a male pacemaker"

Teklemariam, who lived a few kilometres to the east of Kotebe, would sometimes come to stay with Hailye so that he could run as a pacemaker for a female runner he knew. This involved getting up at 3.30 A.M. in order to avoid the traffic on the asphalt roads in the city centre. Hailye explained this to me by saying, "You know, if you are not able to run well on your own, you will find a girlfriend to pace and she will run well." Male runners were usually paid a small salary for this, but Hailye said that "often after two or three runs the man will say, 'Don't worry about the money, you can be my girlfriend instead.'" For Teklemariam, pacing was a strategy employed in tandem with his own running career. He would pace for a couple of months in order to make enough money to continue his own training, and hoped that if he did a good enough job he might be sent abroad to pace a marathon. This was a path that had been followed by one of the more successful athletes in our group when he first arrived in Addis Ababa. As Hailye put it, "I told him to pace females, and that is how he changed his life." He was able to "eat well and set goals for himself" while he was pacing, and save enough money to completely focus on his running.

Management groups paid a reasonable fee for pacing, and it could create a "chance" to race abroad. Fasil, a young runner in our group, saw pacing as an opportunity to save enough money to pay his own way to a race. He calculated the number of months he would have to save up for, allowing for a final month of training alone and some money to frequent a gym. However, much like running "small races for small money," runners like Teklemariam and Fasil saw pace-making as something that interrupted an athlete's attempt to improve their "condition" to a point where they could compete for significant prize money, even though it constituted a "chance" that was preferable to other forms of work in the city. Like competing in India, working as a pacemaker (which meant training at a slower pace) was associated with gradually diminishing "condition," which therefore lessened the likelihood of winning prize money that would "change your life." They were, however, strategies that could be employed in order to facilitate the kind of training that might allow you to run in a big race eventually.

From conversion to adaptation

The dispositions that characterize the two ideologies of running I have described here, silent submission and actively creating a "chance," are different. The first is associated with developing an athlete's "condition" and, concomitantly, their *idil*. The second operates alongside the first, and the two are sometimes compatible, sometimes antagonistic. To seek a "chance" can be detrimental to a runner's "condition," to their development as an athlete and to their *idil*, but it can also allow them to keep the dream of one day winning a big race alive by allowing them to save enough money for a period of devoted training.

Ethiopian runners train for years to improve their "condition" – the fickle state of health and fitness necessary to sustain a career in the sport. Training as a long-distance runner requires acceptance of a simple, repetitive lifestyle characterized by a cycle of work, food, and rest, and by the virtues of patience and consistency. I have demonstrated that conventional narratives of "conversion" (Bourdieu 2000) to an individualistic and entrepreneurial mindset fail to account for pre-existing notions of individualism, contributing to the understanding of how these concepts meet neoliberal impulses and give rise to new and interesting objects. Rather than seeing running in terms of entrepreneurship of self, I have shown how to survive as a runner in Ethiopia means to teeter between two ideological systems, to cultivate one's *idil* but also to place oneself within the pull of social and environmental forces in such a way as to create a "chance" to change one's life. The disposition required to create a "chance" to run abroad may not look like the strategies of self-assertion one associates with the figure of the entrepreneur, but may instead be characterized by silence and submission to authority, an orientation that may not become clear at first sight.

Acknowledgements

I wrote this chapter with the support of a studentship and postdoctoral fellowship from the U.K. Economic and Social Research Council. The material on which it is based is from my doctoral thesis (Crawley 2018). I want to thank Niko Besnier and Daniel Guinness for the exceptional editorial support, and I am grateful for comments on earlier versions from Diego Malara, Neil Thin, Jamie Cross, Roslyn Malcolm, Nick Long, and Tom Boylston. I also want to thank Malcolm Anderson, Hailye Teshome and the athletes of Moyo Sports Management for letting me in and for all the hours of running and conversation we shared.

Notes

1 I use real names in this text because this was my interlocutors' preference.
2 In contrast to many popular accounts of runners supporting large numbers of people through their race winnings, many of those I talked to provided limited support to their families, who they often criticized for failing to understand why they wanted to pursue athletics at the expense of education.

References

Bourdieu, Pierre. 2000. "Making the Economic Habitus: Algerian Workers Revisited." *Ethnography* 1, no. 1: 17–41.

Boylston, Tom. 2018. *The Stranger at the Feast: Prohibition and Mediation in an Ethiopian Orthodox Christian Community*. Oakland: University of California Press.

Crawley, Michael. 2018. *"Condition" Energy, Time and Success Amongst Ethiopian Runners*. Ph.D. dissertation, Department of Social Anthropology, University of Edinburgh.

De Waal, Alex. 2018. "The Future of Ethiopia: Developmental State or Political Marketplace?" *World Peace Foundation Occasional Paper*, 20 August 2018.

Di Nunzio, Marco. 2015. "What Is the Alternative?: Youth, Entrepreneurship and the Developmental State in Urban Ethiopia." *Development & Change* 46, no. 5: 1179–1200.

Esson, James. 2013. "A Body and a Dream at a Vital Conjuncture: Ghanaian Youth, Uncertainty and the Allure of Football." *Geoforum* 47 (June): 84–89.

Esson, James. 2015. "Escape to Victory: Development, Youth Entrepreneurship and the Migration of Ghanaian Footballers." *Geoforum* 64 (August): 47–55.

Ferguson, James. 2010. "The Uses of Neoliberalism." *Antipode* 41, no.1: 166–184.

Foucault, Michel. 2008. *The Birth of Biopolitics: Lectures at the Collège de France, 1978–1979*. London: Palgrave Macmillan.

Guinness, Daniel. 2018. "Corporal Destinies: Faith, Ethno-Nationalism and Raw Talent in Fijian Professional Rugby Aspirations." *HAU* 8, no. 1–2: 314–328.

Kebede, Messay. 1999. *Survival and Modernisation, Ethiopia's Enigmatic Present: A Philosophical Discourse*. Lawrenceville, NJ: Red Sea Press.

Kovač, Uroš. 2016. "Football Dreams, Pentecostalism and Migration in Southwest Cameroon." GLOBALSPORT (blog), 7 September 2016. http://global-sport.eu/football-dreams-pentecostalism-and-migration-in-southwest-cameroon.

Levine, Donald. 1965. *Wax and Gold: Tradition and Innovation in Ethiopian Culture*. Chicago: University of Chicago Press.

Mains, Daniel. 2011. *Hope Is Cut: Youth, Unemployment and the Future in Urban Ethiopia*. Philadelphia: Temple University Press.

Malara, Diego. 2017. "A Geometry of Blessing: Embodiment, Relatedness and Exorcism amongst Ethiopian Orthodox Christians in Addis Ababa, Ethiopia." Ph.D. dissertation, Department of Social Anthropology, University of Edinburgh.

Malara, Diego, and Tom Boylston. 2016. "Vertical Love: Forms of Submission and Top-Down Power in Orthodox Ethiopia." *Social Analysis* 60, no. 4: 40–57.

Rial, Carmen. 2012. "Banal Religiosity: Brazilian Athletes as New Missionaries of the Neo-Pentecostal Diaspora." *Vibrant* 9, no. 2: 128–159.

Weber, Max. 2002. *The Protestant Ethic and the "Spirit" of Capitalism, and Other Writings*, translated and edited by Peter Baehr and Gordeon C. Wells. London: Penguin. (First published 1905.)

4

LABOURING ATHLETES, LABOURING MOTHERS

Ethiopian women athletes' bodies at work

Hannah Borenstein

"I've become fat now, haven't I?" Tigist asks, laughing.[1] It's a question that's difficult to answer correctly. In Ethiopia, a person becoming fat is generally seen as a good thing. It is a sign that they may have come into money, that they have been on a relaxing vacation, or at the very least, that they are doing comfortably well. I have come back from a long weekend and been told, "you look good, you've gotten a little fat."

For Ethiopian athletes, however, becoming fat is a concern. It is a way of talking about one's current "condition." As Michael Crawley (2018; this volume) argues, Ethiopian runners talk about "condition" as a way of inhabiting the world in which concerns about energy are front and centre in an athlete's mind. A concern with "condition" dominates all aspects of their lives. While true for all athletes, for women athletes condition is doubly complicated. When someone gets injured, they fear becoming fat, which may mean gaining just a few kilos – going from a wiry 48 kg to a lithe 51 kg. Becoming fat is a concern not because beauty is at stake – it may in fact be the opposite – but because it weakens one's capacity to run fast. If athletes are "fat," their "condition" is probably not good. They are not ready to work in athletics. Being fat means one cannot race, win, or make money.

"Yes, she's more fat, I'm a little fat. You. You're always the same," our friend Kalkidan chimes in, as we sit in silence in Kalkidan's house in 2019. It is one of the first moments of silence in this reunion. They are both breast-feeding their daughters. Tigist's daughter is 10 months old, quiet, and tiny. Kalkidan's daughter is just shy of two years, can do a drunken sailor walk, and enjoys the pastime of knocking things off tables. Kalkidan's older son, who manages to wreak havoc no matter how child-proofed the house is, has gone outside to greet family members in the compound.

There is something a bit sombre about my two friends "becoming fat," even though their husbands, family members, and most friends see them as healthier, more beautiful, and more capable of raising healthy families. Normally a moment to rejoice, now that our days of training together and their days of training all together are long over, my friends' keen attention to caloric intake and bodily musculature have significantly changed. But how my two friends relate to their bodies is indelibly marked by having worked as athletes.

Like Tongan rugby players who migrate to Japan (Besnier 2012), Ethiopian female athletes shed light on how notions of "habitus" – how structures can inscribe social class and status onto bodies (Bourdieu 1990) – fall short of adequately assessing subjects' relationship to their bodies and their social and class position. Indeed, the global circulation of professional athletes is an interesting place to examine the body as athletes become "object[s] of multiple expectations, demands, and hopes, many of which have little to do with sport and everything to do with kinship, communities, congregations, villages, and the state" (Besnier 2012, 494). Similarly, in Ethiopia, women athletes become objects of multiple ideals of a working body. They deal with tensions between duelling body types as they pertain to different ideas of work. These tensions are brought about and sharpened by political economic structures in which athletics is embedded and which international sporting industries help to produce (Besnier, Calabrò, and Guinness, this volume).

An anthropology of sport offers insights into how migration in the neoliberal age affects how bodies are valued and the embodied experiences of this valuation (Besnier, Brownell, and Carter 2018, 239–248). While in certain realms many actors in Ethiopia attempt to confine women's child rearing work, both reproductive and productive, of giving birth and raising families to a separate sphere, women athletes demand something different as they try to migrate or work outside the country. The body is a privileged site to examine how agents demarcate production and reproduction, as women athletes in Ethiopia attempt to satisfy the demands of international athletics and Ethiopian motherhood, demands that are simultaneously necessary and incommensurable.

As social reproduction theorists has shown (Vogel 1983; Bezanson and Luxton 2006; Bhattacharya 2017), the division between the public and the private has always been flawed, especially in reference to gender, and recent shifts under capitalism have exacerbated the ramifications for women who are implored to embody this impossible tension. Ethiopian female athletes desire to be successful runners and healthy mothers simultaneously, but as social reproduction theory makes clear, the separation between production and reproduction under capitalism is a fabrication that needs to be undone.

Mothering is reproduction *and* production but appears incommensurable with the transnational athletics market. Working as a professional athlete is production *and* reproduction, but sometimes it appears incommensurable to many extensive social and familial networks in Ethiopia. Women's struggles to work in these seemingly incommensurable roles demonstrate that the incommensurability is inorganic. It is not so much that the contrasting bodily ideals mirror the contrasting realms of production and reproduction – although at times they seem isomorphic – but that the impossibility of being both are evidence of deeply rooted problems systemic in capitalism, that are exacerbated in a neoliberal migratory landscape that tries to obfuscate the constructions of production and reproduction as domains at all.

The international athletics market in which Ethiopian athletes must work is predicated on migrating, and global political economic shifts in neoliberal capitalism have both augmented and been augmented by political economic changes in the business of athletics. Ethiopian women athletes and the relationships to their bodies within and through these processes elucidate how the capital and power differentials in this system play a role in how women experience their bodies. And the lived experiences of Ethiopian women athlete workers and mothers, in turn, shed light on the aftermath on neoliberal capitalism's effects on women's transnational and migratory work.

Production and reproduction, public and private

In his analysis of capitalist production and accumulation, Karl Marx defines free labour as being "free in the double sense that as a free individual he can dispose of his labour-power as his own commodity, and that, on the other hand, he has no other commodity for sale" (Marx 1976, 276). Labour power – not the hours worked but the capacity to work – then appears on the "free market" if "the individual whose labour-power it is, offers it for sale or sells it as a commodity... be[ing] the free proprietor of his own labour-capacity, hence of his person" (1976, 271).

In a preceding footnote, Marx mocks texts of classical antiquity that have been used to explain and justify the free market and free labour: "in encyclopedias of classical antiquity one can read such nonsense as this: in the ancient world capital was fully developed, 'except for the absence of the free worker and of a system of credit'" (1976, 271). In short, the notion of freedom, the "free market," "free labour," and "freedom" more generally are deeply flawed.

As the capitalist profits off of the worker, who sells labour power on the market for a wage, it is the reproduction of this labour power that becomes a principal site of capital exploitation: "Capital therefore announces from the outset a new epoch in the process of social reproduction" (1976, 274). While the labour that the worker sells on the "free market" may be underpaid, the maintenance of the labour power, such as ensuring that the basic needs of the worker are met, is generally not paid nor acknowledged to be part of the production process.

The labour power that people sell in the market needs to be reproduced, most straightforwardly by producing children, who become workers in turn. The worker must also be fed, clothed, sheltered, cared for, loved, and entertained in order to keep working. It is this type of unacknowledged and unpaid work that in the 1970s drew the interest of feminists, who wanted to showcase reproductive and other forms of gendered labour as fundamental to capital production (Dalla Costa and James 1972; Federici 1975). The accumulation of capital exploits not only the workers, but also those who do not receive wages and whose work is not recognized as work; a work force that is predominantly comprised of women.

Debates about invisible feminized forms of labour were tense, as many felt that social reproduction theory in its original form did not adequately address racialized domestic workers who were paid, although most often underpaid (hooks 1981; Collins 2009; Davis 1983) or work performed by migrants (Arat-Koç 2001; Blackett 2019; Hopkins 2017). Yet both performed the work of social reproduction. The role of domestic and migrant workers was instrumental in bringing to light the fallible separation of private and public spheres, in that these workers are not "private" or "unwaged" in the strict sense of the term. Social reproduction that takes place outside the private (Vogel 1983) and, more recently, in the context of globalized financial capitalism and labour outsourcing (Fraser 2017) demonstrates that social reproduction is part-and-parcel of the production process.

In the 1970s, while scholarly attention to social reproduction was growing, neoliberalization was transforming the world (Harvey 2005). Private enterprise was fundamentally altering work, labour, and migration, blurring even further the (already flawed) distinction between private and public life. The liberalization of economies, roll back of social services, and state withdrawal from welfare services oriented to fix the economic crisis impacting the Global North in the 1970s led to the collapse of many economies in the Global South, and strengthened certain financial centres of the world and multinational private conglomerates (Besnier, Calabrò, and Guinness, this volume).

As a result, especially in the Global South, most people's lives, which had already been precarious under capitalism, have become even more hazardous, and working conditions in many places have become even more exploitative. In response, some theorists have called for a theoretical return to social reproduction to

> revise the commonsense perception that capital relinquishes all control over the worker when she leaves the workplace ... because it is the attack by capital on global labour to try and restructure *production* in the workplaces and the social processes of *reproduction* of labour power in homes, communities, and the niches of everyday life.
>
> *(Bhattacharya 2017, 183)*

In other words, although many of the fundamental processes of production have not changed under neoliberalism, we must turn to workers themselves to understand how life has changed for working people with capital explicitly attempting to seize control of their public and private lives.

The experiences of athletes are particularly fruitful ground to understand how some of these changes are being played out because the athletes' stories that one generally hears are ones of steep upward mobility, whereas many who attempt to pursue sport at the highest level often do not reach these heights. Sport is often depicted as the opposite of work because of its association with leisure. Sport fans' remote and emotional attachment to teams that provides them an escape from the mundanity of everyday working life contributes the perception that sport is not labour (Eckert 2016, 6). Oft-cited athletes' rags-to-riches stories contribute to the perception that their labour is free. Even when athletes speak of their work as work, their narratives do not lend themselves to a critique of labour.

Yet global athletics are actually some of the most significant sites of capital accumulation, in a dependent and dialectical relationship with the accumulation of labour (Denning 2016, 274). Apparel companies and other sponsors (insurance companies, telecommunications corporations, airlines, and petrochemical corporations, to name a few) promote their brands through the wide spectatorship opportunities that global sport affords. The governing bodies of international sports, such as the International Olympic Committee (IOC) and the International Association of Athletics Federation (IAAF, renamed World Athletics, or WA, in 2019), elect members closely affiliated or in support of certain interested parties, and thereby influence the direction sponsorships and corporate investment to suit the interests of certain people and entities.

Thus global athletics are not merely a microcosm of global economic and social transformations, but are also part-and-parcel of them. The financial centres that yield disproportionate economic influence have also become some of the most important sites of major global sporting events. For example, cities such as Tokyo, Boston, London, Berlin, New York, and Chicago participate in the Abbott World Marathon Majors, the most elite marathon racing series in the world. Athletes who run in marathons hosted by these cities score cumulative points based on their finishing places; at the end of each year, these points are added together and the top scorers receive prizes, resulting in a system that binds these metropoles even more tightly.

Even though athletes from Ethiopia and other countries of the Global South are the primary value producers in this transnational operation, most of the capital remains in the Global North. As a result, while Ethiopian long-distance athletes spend years undergoing gruelling training and pre-professionalization, being an athlete in Ethiopia means being an athlete outside Ethiopia, as they must travel internationally to make money. This has created an array of paths of migration to run for prizes, to switch nationalities, or to use athletics to leave Ethiopia for alternative futures. Underlying the diverse experiences of athletes – from those who develop through clubs and race abroad, to those who change their nationality to compete for another country, to those who never make it at all, and to those like Tigist who use sport to migrate for ulterior means – is a broader connection the interconnected processes of production and reproduction of capital and labour.

Running between the lines

While athletes who succeed at the highest level are the most visible, athletes who attempt to work in this neoliberal sporting realm for alternative migratory ends illuminate the relations of production and reproduction work within a transnational sporting business, and how working in this business affects embodied gendered experiences of working elsewhere.

In 2013, when I came to Ethiopia for the first time, Tigist and Kalkidan were coming into peak form. Tigist in particular seemed for the first time to be able to train consistently, without interruption, and with reliable financial and emotional support. Born in a town called Chereka not far from Bahir Dar, she developed health problems in early childhood and she was sent to live with her aunt and uncle in Addis Ababa. People in the town thought she might have been marked by the *buda* "evil eye" and her family feared her reputation was ruined. At her aunt and uncle's home, she was responsible for doing a great deal of the housework. When she saw children playing soccer in the neighbourhood, she would join them. But when her uncle learned about it, he called her a *dooriye* "delinquent, hooligan" and beat her up. This was no proper behaviour for a young woman.

As soon as Tigist could move out, she did. She took a job at a café in Akaki, south of Addis Ababa, where top-tier athletes often go to do hard training on soft surfaces. After training, runners would often come to the café in their track suits, which kindled Tigist's dreams of being an athlete (Figure 4.1). They would talk about their experiences racing in France, Turkey, Japan, and the United States, and don sports wares that can only be purchased outside Ethiopia. She asked to change her work shifts at the café so that she could train in the morning and work in the evening.

In the following years, she trained, got injured, took up a new job, and did it all over again. She worked at an ale house, then worked as a domestic help in a Canadian family's home, then worked in a supermarket, all the time continuing training. As was common among young athletes who were not members of funded

FIGURE 4.1 A training session of elite women athletes in Sebeta, Ethiopia, 2019. (Source: Hannah Borenstein)

clubs, Tigist would join a group of athletes who would each contribute a small sum every month to pay a coach for instruction. She reflected:

> At the beginning I didn't have a lot of demands for running. I didn't ask for many things. But later on, the more I ran, the more my expenses were for shoes. So I had to work in the afternoon to cover those expenses. I sold Sambusa and made 400 birr [US$6] a month to use for expenses and I had to quit education to continue running so I could make enough money.[2] If all of your needs are fulfilled – like shoes, and sports clothes – like you use for asphalt or *korokonj* and so on, then it's just your strength that is required to win and I think that's easy.[3] But if those things aren't fulfilled it won't be easy.

Tigist refers to the "needs" she has to meet in order to keep working as an athlete, but in her case, she had to work other jobs rather than relying on a partner, family, club, or coach for support.

Despite lacking basic resources, athletes like Tigist use every ounce of their ability to appear as if they had at least basic support and often more (compare Hopkinson, this volume, on Ghanaian boxers). This means diligently scrubbing their clothes and shoes so that they look new at every training session, only to get muddied again. In addition, they often identify themselves as athletes even before they secure a spot in a club or with management. When they are offered a contract or when they enter a race, they are already athletes. These dynamics are a form of pre-professionalizing characteristic of neoliberal work (Weeks 2011; Gershon 2017). Without basic needs being met, most workers in the neoliberal economy are encouraged to form attachments to their working subjectivities and for work to pervade all sectors of their lives.

However, this does not mean women, including athletes, are free from the responsibility of producing and reproducing domestic spaces. For example, Tigist noted:

> My brother always told me to stop [running] and so did my mother. My father was a little bit more encouraging but overall my family didn't like the idea of me running. Whenever, I would talk to my brother he would say "Are you still running? Why? There's no point. You should stop now." My family thought that I was wasting my time here with the running. I always felt anxious when I would go home to visit because they wouldn't see any big changes in my lifestyle, they had hoped that I would make something of myself once I got to the city but I hadn't really had much success. They thought I was struggling for no reason. For them, they would hope to see me married with a good life. Maybe I would have a child. They would want me to be able to support myself and this lifestyle here. They would also want me to bring some of that home and be able to support them to some extent. Those were the kinds of significant changes they had in mind. More important than money and success was marriage. I would come home unmarried, without kids and they would be disappointed.

Pursuing athletics did not mean that Tigist would be free from the expectation of raising a family. While a relative lack of athletic success amplified this expectation, this is sometimes even true with those who finish atop podiums. For example, a nurse in Addis Ababa told me she was treating an athlete for complications after childbirth who had won one of the world's major marathons. While she too may have wanted a family, it was her husband who was urging her, against medical advice, to resume intensive training. She had "gotten fat, which was necessary for the baby, but needed to become skinny again to work as an athlete."

In Tigist's case, the pressures were somewhat reversed. Her family wanted her to become *more* fat, get married, and start a family. But the underlying circumstances that emphasize that women athletes are somehow expected to be able to do both forms of work complicate the pursuit of sport. Broad structural changes in the neoliberal turns beginning the 1970s have encouraged women in Ethiopia to pursue sport and make it pay off by being thin and fit throughout the year. But often, at the same time, family members want them to devote their body to the work of childbirth that leads to an incommensurable embodied state.

Ethiopia's place in neoliberal sport

Although the media lionizes Ethiopian athletes who often come from poor backgrounds and appear to be exceptions to the economic and social stratification that comprises capital's production and reproduction, there are tensions at every turn. While a select few do indeed seem to chart dramatically different pathways than those they were expected to follow – becoming a world-class performer instead of a subsistence farmer, for example – this is hardly the case of most who attempt to pursue a career in athletics. And even for those who successfully land atop podiums in major world cities, a select few financial centres around the world benefit from the transnational movements and frictions of several athletes. It is even the case that some of the most successful athletes do not end up netting the substantial amounts of money and fame that the media indicates they earn.

Rather than sport as being an avenue for representation or something outside the throws of neoliberal rationality, the work of Ethiopian women athletes is part-and-parcel of the various phases of capitalism's development. As modern sport grew in popularity and influence, the urban bourgeoise was intent on organizing and regulating sport to reify the idea that "fair play" – comparable to the notion of "free labour" that Marx mocked – was a ruling ideology (Collins 2011, 29). Institutions like the IOC and the IAAF were established long before Ethiopia entered the global sports market.

The revival of the Olympic Games in 1896 – two years after the Berlin Conference in 1884 where Europeans sought to divide up and colonize Africa – coincided with the Ethiopian victory over an Italian invading army at the Battle of Adwa, which heralded the country's campaign to be recognized as a strong African independent nation, and sports would come to play an informative role in that formation.

As early as 1868, some members of the Ethiopian nobility were going abroad to receive a Western education that included sport and physical education. But modern athletics only emerged in the 1920s, as part of Emperor Haile Selassie's project to modernize the country (Gaudin and Gebremariam 2019, 196). In addition to introducing spaces to practice and regulate sport, such as the public playgrounds in Jan Meda and Haile Selassie I Stadium in Addis Ababa (Bromber 2013, 61), Selassie also used diplomacy to help Ethiopia join the ranks of European and American nation states competing in the Olympic Games. In 1924, he went to the Paris Olympic Games as a guest.

In 1935–40, Italy occupied Ethiopia and Haile Selassie was exiled. When he returned at the end of the occupation, during which sport had been sidelined, he turned to Sweden for aid, as it was a country with a strong economy but that did not yield as much political clout as others at the time. Among the 700 Swedes sent to work with Ethiopian government officials, teachers, and soldiers was a coach, Onni Niskanen. He set up sporting competitions and became close to the imperial family, and eventually was employed in the Department of Education to build the sports programme in schools (Bergman, n.d.; Rambali 2006; Judah 2008).

In 1948, the Ethiopian Olympic Committee was formed and Onni Niskanen was selected to act as an observer for Ethiopia at the 1952 Helsinki Olympics. By this time, he had started to coach a cadre of athletes for future Olympic Games, including a member of the Ethiopian Imperial Guard to Haile Selassie, Abebe Bikila, who competed in the marathon at the 1960 Olympic Games in Rome, where no one paid attention to him prior to the competition. The race was run in the evening and, televised for the first time, showcased Rome's iconic structures. As the whole world watched, Bikila became the first black African gold medallist, running past the Coliseum, the Circus Maximus, and the Obelisk that the Italian fascist state had stolen in Ethiopia, radically shifting sporting politics for decades to come (Goldblatt 2016).

Bikila's victory also came at the beginning of African decolonization and radical politics, and the increasing visibility of African athletes in international sport. Between 1950 and 1970, 48 new National Olympic Committees were formed and newly independent nations were eager to demonstrate their athletic prowess to the world (Krieger 2016, 1342). However, as the IOC and the IAAF allowed more countries to enter international competition, they also sought to control the movements of athletes, resources, and capital. Thus, in the 1970s, the IAAF introduced a Technical Aid Program that established a top-down approach wherein the IAAF was the expert organization responsible for athletics in developing emerging nations and increased its funding for coaching activities in Africa from a negligible £1,711 in 1974 to a meagre £15,000 the following two years. The rhetoric of development helped to justify the IAAF's efforts to maintain control over new national federations primarily from the Global South, keep the money centred on a select few federations in the Global North and bring a commercial direction to the association (Krieger 2016, 1345).

In 1978, the IAAF took a new commercial turn when it contracted Dubai International – an arm of the global investment company Dubai Holding – to sponsor a Golden Mile race, which paid US$400,000 to the IAAF for its development initiatives in Africa. Most of these initiatives were coaching courses but were set up with little consultation from African countries. The African Athletics Federation then approached the multinational sport clothing corporation Nike about the possibility of opening up aid programmes, and the president of the IAAF Primo Nebiolo issued a statement imploring African countries to do more to help themselves (Krieger 2016). In the meantime, the USSR was providing hundreds of Soviet coaches to new member federations, but the commercialization of sport by capitalist countries would eventually win out.

Shortly after being elected in 1981, Nebiolo and his new administration accelerated the commercialization of the IAAF through sponsorship and television rights, making the IAAF less dependent on the sales of broadcasting rights from the IOC. East African dominance in the 1968 Mexico City Olympics in particular meant that Ethiopian athletes became increasingly visible in the 1960s and 1970s. After continued Olympic success, they also began winning major IAAF competitions, yet did not seem to be reaping the profits of major revenue increases driven by a coterminous increase the television exposure (Besnier, Calabrò, and Guinness, this volume).

Moreover, athletes, coaches, journalists, and officials were frustrated that national federations were not granted a vote in IAAF elections and decisions. In 1987, Ethiopian journalist, Fekrou Kidane, addressed the IAAF president directly, calling the IAAF "the sole anti-democratic federation in the entire Olympic movement" for not having a one-country-one vote rule (Krieger 2016, 1353). Neoliberal policies in other sectors as well as sport saw privatization and centralization of finance in the hands of a select few wealthy conglomerates, diminishing truly democratic practice. Ultimately, this allowed the West to extend its control over economic, technological, political and knowledge resources in global sport, which top Ethiopian athletes would have to then navigate.

Although most decisions were being made in a select few offices and cities, around the world, the broadcasting of commercial sport was making its way into bars, cafés, and homes, instituting new hopes of migration, chance, and joy to new onlookers. People all over the world, especially in the Global South, were exposed visually to the idealistic lives and competitions of elite athletes around the world. The effect of the neoliberal corporatization of sport has been not only the profit making of television, but also dreams of "migrating, playing in front of global audiences, and earning enough money to support large numbers of people" (Besnier, Calabrò, and Guinness, this volume).

Many Ethiopian athletes I know told me that they started running after seeing early icons succeed on television and learning about their stories inspired them to pursue athletics. Kalkidan noted that one of her greatest role models in her life was Meseret Defar:

I remember I saw her win on TV and I wanted to start training. She's been a big influence. She's had a lot of obstacles in life. Meseret grew up in Addis Ababa but she had to really work, she had a lot of jobs. She worked hard and got to a really good place in her running career. Now she runs all over the world.

When I interviewed young athletes, they often cite Meseret Defar or Tirunesh Dibaba as their role models. Defar and Dibaba have been some of the most successful Ethiopian women runners who competed during the same period and have dozens of Olympic medals, World Championship titles, and World Records Between them.

Although Derartu Tulu, Ethiopia and Africa's first black woman Olympic Gold Medallist in 1992, has not been forgotten, it was the more recent and highly televised performances of the previous two women that most athletes often cited as inspirational. Tigist noted:

It used to be Derartu [Tulu], but for me when I heard about Tirunesh's victory I was inspired to be a renowned athlete like her. I used to think that I would be able to do that through my education but that didn't work out, so at least I could win and change myself and my circumstances. It was still possible through running. It became a dream of mine. I hoped it would happen instantly, but it became very difficult.

In addition, these athletes offered, and newer athletes continue to offer, entertainment for the millions who tune into the Olympic Games, World Championships, and other major events. As Nathan Kalman-Lamb (2019) has argued, sport fandom has become a way in which masses of workers experience social connection and relief from the pressures of work. Watching sport is what people do to recharge and to be able to return to work the following day. Although often paid and sometimes very well paid, athletic work is central to social reproduction.

While corporations and international federations have sought to maintain control over the movements of athletes and capital in sport, the work of the athletes is central to reproducing their own families, new generations of athletes, and the institution of sport itself. All actors are important in understanding this multi-faceted process of production, but the experiences of some of the lesser-known athletes who often end up in systems of neoliberal transnational capital are often brushed over. Thus, Tigist's experiences attempting to work in athletics, and the alternative paths she ended up taking, show some of the far-reaching effects of women's work in the global sporting enterprise.

Going "outside"

Ethiopian women runners work to serve numerous ends simultaneously. But being a thin and productive athlete has a geographical teleology. The density of spatial and financial organization in economic metropoles means that Ethiopian athletes train to run outside Ethiopia because this is where the money to be made in athletics is located – *Ethiopia wuch*, or "outside Ethiopia." But the gruelling training schedules athletes endure to get a coveted chance to run overseas has a profound effect on social and familial dynamics.

For women athletes, the need to go "outside" can be significantly more complicated because women's bodies are valued differently in different circumstances. Working as a woman athlete in different contexts puts the athlete's body not just in tension with ideas of tradition or modernity, but also blurs values associated with the different but intersecting domains of work (Besnier 2011). Even as Ethiopian women athletes have developed a relatively well-known working stream to race abroad and alter their lives, simultaneous demands to both rear children and be athletic demands drastically different ideal bodies.

The opportunity for Tigist to go "outside" came in 2014, after a series of health complications, which meant that she would not become one of the next Ethiopian greats. The previous year, she suffered from tendonitis in the knee but at the time she managed to control it with a rigorous stretching programme and by over-using anti-inflammatories, and she did not miss more than two consecutive days of training.

It was also in that year, when she was fit and showed promise, that she met Roberto, a running enthusiast from Spain who came to Ethiopia to train in the highlands. Tigist ran with him frequently during his stay, showing him the best routes to take through the forest and the flat meadows ideal for interval training. Before leaving Ethiopia in 2013, he gave Tigist a training t-shirt from his running club in Spain and told her he would invite her to race with the club.

Roberto was not an IAAF-registered agent and did not intend to help Tigist find a sponsor or contract. While most athletes in Ethiopia seek a foreign manager to find them races abroad, some like Tigist have found less conventional means of going "outside." She acknowledged that she might be risking her chance to sign in the future with a registered agent, but that "it was a good chance."

If running did not work out, Tigist often said that she would likely move to the Middle East (Lebanon or Kuwait) like many women she knew had done to find domestic work, which was often underpaid and risked exposing them to sexual, physical, and verbal abuse, but could still enable them to send remittances to their families. Tigist having hoped for years for a chance like this one, against the desires of many of her family members, an opportunity to race with Roberto's sub-elite club in Spain was a welcome opportunity.

Roberto and Tigist connected on Facebook before he returned to Spain and he assured her that he would be in touch. However, he did not reach out for several months, and thus did not know about Tigist's pregnancy, miscarriage, and knee problems. He assumed that she was still training full time and she reassured him that this was the case. Roberto's club had three races coming up in a few months and he wrote her that as long as she got a visa (an enormous hurdle for early-career athletes), his club would sponsor the visit.

Tigist and her husband Chalu asked me to write to Roberto a long message on Facebook to ask him for a formal invitation letter to take to the embassy, which even the most elite athletes are required to have to apply for visas. Tigist's passport showed no evidence of international travel, so it was far from guaranteed that should would be issued the visa. But Roberto phoned a friend who could write her an invitation letter for the race and she returned from the Spanish embassy one week later, visa in hand.

Tigist was relieved but also nervous, not only because she had not been training – and Roberto expected her to arrive in strong running shape – but also because she had not decided whether she would return to Ethiopia. She would eventually come back, a little more than two years past her three-month visa expiration date, and from Belgium rather than Spain.

Tigist left for Spain and when she arrived Roberto was surprised by the weight she had gained and her poor condition. In the first scheduled race she came in third; one year before, she would easily have won the race. After the race, she walked with a limp. Roberto told her he was going to send her back home early because she could not perform. Two weeks later, he dropped her off at the airport and her bags arrived in Addis Ababa, but she did not. She had gathered up as much money as she could and boarded a bus to Belgium, where she spent the next two years living in refugee centres, attempting to navigate an exceedingly complicated labyrinth of immigration policies, strategies, and necessary deceit:

> Everyone told me to lie. They told me to tell the authorities I was Eritrean, or Oromo. They also told me to tell them I had no family, they had all died, my husband, my father. I was so stressed, I got sick. I thought that if I lied and said those things they would be true. I don't like to talk like this, to zig zag. I was so stressed I lost so many kilos at that time.

When she was initially leaving for Spain, she had fretted about her weight gain, but now Tigist was concerned about losing weight. She was more concerned by daily survival than pursuing an athletic career, and losing weight turned from a goal to a worry.

She reached out to a Somali-born runner who represented Belgium and frequently travelled to Ethiopia to train. When he found out she was in Belgium, he visited her at the centre and invited her to a training session. The coach was impressed by her trial run and she began coming regularly to training. She began to think that her purposes for going abroad were morphing into something new, having hoped for so many years to emigrate for athletics, meant that she still held on to the coveted aspiration of becoming an elite runner.

But the body does not forget, and Tigist's knee certainly did not. Because she was able to see a doctor at no cost, she got her first MRI and was told that without surgery, she would probably never be able to run competitively, although undergoing surgery was out of the question. Not only could she not afford it, but she also lacked a strong network of people or resources to support her after the surgery.

She called Chalu and

> told him how depressed I was. I wanted to come home. But he kept telling
> me to stay and try to get work. That he would join me later on. But people,
> they don't believe you. They don't want to believe you.

Tigist often reflects about how her husband and family members did not believe
how difficult life was in Europe. They were confused as to why she had not yet
found a job even though she had explained that she was not legally allowed to
work. She spent two years without documents and began to meet other asylum-
seekers who had been waiting more than a decade to get proper documentation.
She often remarked that people in Ethiopia whom she loved dearly did not *want*
to believe her.

The lawyer whom she had consulted urged her to stay and wait to be granted
asylum, thinking that her case would eventually go through. She had a former
coach and employer write her a letter of support, noting that she was smart and
hard-working and would be an asset to Belgian society. However, when both her
coach and her lawyer learned that she wanted to return to Ethiopia, they did not
want to believe her either.

In 2016, when I was in Ethiopia for my first pre-dissertation fieldwork, I went
to visit Chalu. When I arrived, he told me Tigist had come back to Ethiopia three
weeks before. Excited and shocked, I ran over to their house and we spent the next
several hours catching up. She brought out a jar of Nutella and asked me, "Hannah,
have you seen this one before?" I laughed and when I declined eating it by the
spoonful, she said, "I love this one. But in Belgium, I did not eat it. Now already
I'm becoming fat. But I need to start working again." By working, she was referring
to training.

Later in the evening, Chalu came home from work and we all had dinner. He
noted that when she came back from Belgium, "her kilos had gone down too
much. She wouldn't eat there." When they spoke over the phone shortly before
she returned, she told him that she could not eat. Chalu kept hearing that she
was too sad and her health was declining and finally agreed that she should give
up on her asylum procedure and return to Ethiopia. That was the end of his own
dreams of a future life for the two of them in Belgium. More relaxed, he said,
"Now she's starting to get fat. I think it's enough training." Even though her
athletic pursuits had given them the desired chance at migrating, he wanted her
to stop running.

In the following few months, Tigist slowly realized that her plans of working as
a competitive athlete were behind her. Yet, with persistent and intense knee pain,
she kept training. "I know I want to do something, but I don't know anything but
training," she told me. "It would be nice to start a business, but that would be difficult." When I stayed at her house and attempted to reduce the portion size of wots
(Ethiopian stews) that she was serving me, she would urge me, "but this is good for

sport." And on the few mornings on which we went running together, neither of us in the shape that we had once been in, we still carried the mindset. "Running is more difficult when we're fat," she joked.

In Ethiopia, training is something aspiring athletes do. It is work – and it is deeply pre-professionalized. When I introduce myself as a student to the sub-elite athletes I have spent time with since 2013, they introduce themselves to me as athletes. They treat their bodies as if they had already secured contracts. They talk about training in the language of serious work. Exercise or jogging is an activity that a few wealthy people engage in. A friend once noted that, in a neighbourhood of Addis Ababa where wealthy Ethiopian migrants living overseas have built second homes in their native country and spend part of the year, "you see many people jogging here in the mornings because they are rich, so they want to live longer." In contrast, running for the purpose of bettering one's health is not what drives pre-professional athletes in Ethiopia. Rather, the principal goal of exercise is to make a living.

One aspect of this pre-professionalizing is being wire-thin. When an athlete is bigger than the others in the group, his or her training mates commonly comment on him or her being "fat." It is not a dig at their looks but a negative comment on their work ethic. Being fat means not taking running seriously. This self-reflexive concern about body image, which is more anxiety-provoking for women than for men, sheds light on how the working conditions of even "trying" to be an athlete permeate every aspect of everyday life.

After returning from Belgium, Tigist became pregnant again. She had terrible morning sickness, which ushered in anxieties about being fat enough for the baby. And though she did deliver a healthy baby, she spent the following month sick in the hospital, which made her fearful about being able to nurse and care for her child. Chalu was also worried. He often told me, "I was scared when her kilo would go down. Now she's fat" – they both laughed – "it's good for the baby."

When I visited Tigist shortly after her baby's first birthday, we nostalgically looked through old photographs together. With nearly every picture, she remarked about how skinny she used to be. She missed being thin and fit and identifying as an athlete. "I want to start training again, but you know, when I say this, Chalu gets very stressed. He worries when I do not eat enough that I won't have enough milk for the baby. Maybe when I stop breastfeeding."

Tigist also realized that to be training only for her health in the Ethiopian countryside would raise eyebrows about her work ethic as a mother. Like training for athletes, caring for children is serious work that requires enormous physical and emotional commitment. If she was not training to be a professional athlete, engaging in intense exercise might come across as worse than a waste of time: she might be seen as irresponsible and selfish, damaging her body and not looking after her family. Despite this, having spent so many years seeking a body that is valued as an athlete, the occasional euphoria of endurance training has not escaped her embodied memory. Tigist sometimes just misses running.

Labours of love

"*Tinnish wofri*," Tigist urges me. "Become a little more fat." "*Tinnish chemeri*," "add a little bit," she pleads, holding a spoonful of *shiro*, a chickpea stew, over my plate. "*Baka, baka*," I insist. "I have had enough." This is a typical daily exchange in Ethiopia; encouraging others to eat more food is as much a part of daily life as drinking coffee. But here, the context is more loaded. Before, Tigist would urge me to eat more because I would burn off the calories in training. Now, as she holds her baby girl and remarks that I will soon be ready to have children too, she insists that I need to become fatter.

As evidenced by expectations about one's body, the transnational athletics market and familial and social expectations in Ethiopia seem to conspire to keep spaces of biological reproduction and waged production separate. But the experience of athletes like Tigist, especially as they have played out in neoliberal landscapes, shows how the demands of working as a mother and working as an athlete are actively made incommensurable. When the possibility to be productive and reproductive as an athlete presented itself to Tigist's husband and some family members at home, they might desire a thin, wiry, and strong athletic body. This body type was predicated on going elsewhere, and making a lot of money to support the needs of many people in her social sphere. However, in tension with migratory opportunities were the constant expectations that doing the work of motherhood – reproductive and productive – demanded a different working body – a bigger body that conserves more energy and substance to pass along.

International sport and Ethiopia's place within it bring together gendered work experiences, only a few of which inform the global public image of Ethiopian distance runners, which focus solely on athletes who finish atop podiums in major cities of the world. Missing from these images are the masses of other athletes, especially women, who contribute to international sport in both their sporting and non-sporting endeavours. In theory, Tigist could have worked as an athlete and a mother at the same time, but spatially specific knowledge asserted that a skinny athletic body was for one purpose, whereas a bigger body was more proper for motherhood. As a result, she was urged to respond in kind.

Acknowledgements

First and foremost, I would like to thank Tigist, Kalkidan, Chalu, and several other friends in Ethiopia who opened their lives to me and shared with me their stories, making me a better scholar and person. This research would also not be possible without the funding support of the Wenner-Gren Foundation, the Center for French and Ethiopian Studies, the Olympic Studies Center, and Duke University. Finally, I appreciate the generous feedback and support of my adviser Orin Starn, graduate students who always read my work and provide generous feedback (Can

Evren, Chris Daley, Jake Silver, Jieun Cho, Koffi Nomedji, and Claire Ravenscroft), and especially Niko Besnier, who worked closely with me on a tight schedule to be included in the volume.

Notes

1 All names are pseudonyms.
2 *Sambusa* is a popular street food made up of lentils and fried dough.
3 *Korokonj* is a surface that is either very rocky or cobble-stoned.

References

Arat-Koç, Sedef. 2001. *Caregivers Break the Silence: A Participatory Actions Research on the Abuse and Violence, Including the Impact of Family Separation Experienced by Women in the Live-In Caregiver Program.* Toronto: INTERCEDE.

Bergman, Pia. n.d. "The Swede Who Became an Ethiopian." Accessed 11 July 2020. http://onniniskanen.se/eng/swede_who.php. (First published 1984.)

Besnier, Niko. 2011. *On the Edge of the Global: Modern Anxieties in a Pacific Island Nation.* Stanford, CA: Stanford University Press.

Besnier, Niko. 2012. "The Athlete's Body and the Global Condition: Tongan Rugby Players in Japan." *American Ethnologist* 39, no. 3: 491–510.

Besnier, Niko, Susan Brownell, and Thomas F. Carter. 2018. *The Anthropology of Sport: Bodies, Borders, Biopolitics.* Oakland: University of California Press.

Bezanson, Kate, and Meg Luxton. 2006. *Social Reproduction: Feminist Political Economy Challenges in Neo-Liberalism.* Montreal: McGill-Queen's University Press.

Bhattacharya, Tithi. 2017. "How Not to Skip Class: Social Reproduction of Labor and the Global Working Class." In *Social Reproduction Theory,* edited by Tithi Bhattacharya, 68–93. London: Pluto.

Blackett, Adelle. 2019. *Everyday Transgressions: Domestic Workers' Transnational Challenge to International Labor Law.* Ithaca, NY: Cornell University Press.

Bourdieu, Pierre. 1990. *The Logic of Practice.* Stanford, CA: Stanford University Press.

Bromber, Katrin. 2013. "The Stadium and the City: Sports Infrastructure in late Imperial Ethiopia and Beyond." *Cadernos de Estudos Africanos* 32: 53–72.

Collins, Patricia. 2009. *Black Feminist Though: Knowledge, Consciousness, and the Politics of Empowerment.* New York: Routledge.

Collins, Tony. 2011. *Sport in Capitalist Society: A Short History.* New York: Routledge.

Crawley, Michael. 2018. "'Condition': Energy, Time and Success Amongst Ethiopian Runners." Ph.D. dissertation, Department of Social Anthropology, University of Edinburgh.

Dalla Costa, Mariarosa, and Selma James. 1972. *The Power of Women and the Subversion of the Community.* New York: Falling Wall Press.

Davis, Angela. 1983. *Women, Race & Class.* New York: Penguin.

Denning, Michael. 2016. "Wageless Life." In *Global Histories of Work,* edited by Andreas Eckert, 273–290. Berlin: Walter de Gruyter.

Eckert, Andreas. 2016. "Why All the Fuss about Global Labour History?" In *Global Histories of Work,* edited by Andreas Eckert, 3–23. Berlin: Walter de Gruyter.

Federici, Sylvia. 1975. *Wages Against Housework.* New York: Falling Wall Press.

Fraser, Nancy. 2017. "Crisis of Care? On the Social-Reproduction Contradictions of Contemporary Capitalism." In *Social Reproduction Theory*, edited by Tithi Bhattacharya, 21–36. London: Pluto.

Gaudin, Benoit, and Tamirat Gebremariam. 2019. "Sports and Physical Education in Ethiopia during the Italian Occupation, 1936–1941." In *Sports in African History, Politics, and Identity Formation*, edited by Michael J. Gennaro and Saheed Aderinto, 196–205. London: Routledge.

Gershon, Ilana. 2017. *Down and Out in the New Economy: How People Find (or Don't Find) Work Today*. Chicago: University of Chicago Press.

Goldblatt, David. 2016. *The Games: A Global History of the Olympics*. London: W. W. Norton.

Harvey, David. 2005. *A Brief History of Neoliberalism*. Oxford: Oxford University Press.

hooks, bell. 1981. *Ain't I a Woman: Black Women and Feminism*. New York: Routledge.

Hopkins, Carmen Teeple. 2017. "Work Intensifications, Injuries, and Legal Exclusions for Paid Domestic Workers in Montréal, Québec." *Gender, Place & Culture* 24, no. 2: 1–12.

Judah, Tim. 2008. *Bikila: Ethiopia's Barefoot Olympian*. London: Reportage Press.

Kalman-Lamb, Nathan. 2019. "Athletic Labor and Social Reproduction." *Journal of Sport and Social Issues* 43, no. 6: 515–530.

Krieger, Jörg. 2016. "'The Sole Anti-Democratic Federation in the Entire Olympic Movement': Early International Association of Athletics Federations Development Initiatives Between Commercialization and Democratization, 1974–1987." *International Journal of the History of Sport* 33, no. 4: 1341–1360.

Marx, Karl. 1976. *Capital: A Critique of Political Economy, Vol. 1*, translated by Ben Fowkes. New York: Penguin. (First published 1867.)

Rambali, Paul. 2006. *Barefoot Runner: The Life of Marathon Champion Abebe Bikila*. London: Serpent's Tail.

Vogel, Lise. 1983. *Marxism and the Oppression of Women: Towards a Unitary Theory*. Chicago: Haymarket.

Weeks, Kathi. 2011. *The Problem with Work: Marxism, Antiwork Politics, and Postwork Imaginaries*. Durham, NC: Duke University Press.

5

FROM LIBERATION TO NEOLIBERALISM

Race, mobility, and masculinity in Caribbean cricket

Adnan Hossain

Every year, male cricketers from many countries in the Caribbean migrate temporarily to the Republic of Trinidad and Tobago, one of the richest countries in the region, to play for Trinidadian cricket clubs. Many had originally aspired to play for the West Indies Cricket Team (or "West Indies"), a multinational team composed of players from 15 countries, British dependencies, and other territories in the Caribbean, but mostly selected by the West Indies Cricket Board from the regional competitions that showcase the most talented players from six constituent cricket associations.[1] Many young men across the Anglophone Caribbean continue to dream of being part of the West Indies as these cricketers were and continue to be some of the most celebrated public figures in the region. Since 2008, many young men have also been dreaming of competing in the Indian Premier League (IPL), the most expensive cricket tournament in the world, currently featuring eight teams representing Indian states and cities.

While regular media glamourization of West Indies cricket superstars like Chris Gayle and Sunil Narine showcases the stories of a tiny number of Caribbean cricketers who are globally mobile, it is their success, glamorous lifestyle, and global mobility that fuel the dream and aspiration of young Caribbean hopefuls. In reality, only a select few Caribbean cricketers regularly play for clubs in the IPL or the West Indies. Realizing at an early stage that their dream of playing for either the West Indies or the IPL will not translate into reality, many young men seasonally migrate to Trinidad to play in a semi-professional cricket league, Trinidad being the only Caribbean country with a domestic cricket league that offers financial opportunities. Thus the Trinidadian cricket league attracts many who have given up completely on playing for either the West Indies or the various tiers of the national team in their respective countries, and former West Indies players who have been dropped from the squad.

In contrast to the migration of athletes from the Global South to the Global North in a bid to translate their sporting talents into economic success (Carter 2011a, 2011b; Darby, Akindes, and Kirwin 2007; Klein 2014), intra-regional migratory dynamics in cricket within the Caribbean brings into view the shifting and multiple relations that these athletes develop with the sport (Gupta 2004; Castles 2008; Byron 2014; Muhr 2016; compare Crawley, this volume; Hopkinson, this volume). The athletic ambitions of young Caribbean men are formed today within the context of a global cricket industry dominated by the IPL and the imageries of glamour, entertainment, sex, conspicuous consumption, and international mobility associated the domestic franchise-based cricket leagues around the world. More significantly, the Caribbean players today are not only the most coveted overseas players in the IPL and other franchise-based cricket leagues, but also some of the highest paid for their distinctive style of play and performance, which showcase speed, strength, height, and a fun-loving disposition (Wigmore 2017).

Guyanese players are the largest group of overseas athletes in the Trinidadian domestic cricket league. Although geographically located in South America, Guyana is historically and culturally part of the Caribbean and one of the poorest economies in the region. Cricket is the national sport of Guyana and, as my Guyanese interlocutors contend, it is inextricably entwined with Guyanese identity (Seecharan 2009). For most Guyanese athletes, Trinidad is the first gateway from home and provides their first exposure to consumer capitalism, in that Trinidad's position in the Caribbean is defined by the global political economy of oil and gas, which has shaped regional structures of inequality and power. Being in Trinidad enables the young men to send remittances home and thus regain a productive masculinity that successive economic downturns have severely eroded. Trinidad also operates as a migratory node for Guyanese athletes that opens up various other cricket and at times post-cricket career possibilities both within and beyond Trinidad, particularly in the Caribbean diaspora in the United States and Canada. Guyanese athletes in Trinidad therefore provide a perspective on how the regional mobility of athletes is directly linked to, but not determined by, an encompassing global economy. Furthermore, they bring into view the unequal relations of production within the global cricket industry.

Intra-regional migratory dynamics in cricket in the Caribbean are entangled with the formation of ethno-national and regional identities in Trinidad. During nine months of fieldwork with Guyanese athletes in Trinidad in 2015, I came to understand it is not only these migrants' aspirations, cultural dislocations, and adjustments but also the discourses of mobility, money, masculinity and ethno-racial ideologies that continue to shape contemporary Caribbean cricket. The entanglement of the Guyanese cricketers' lives in various dynamics of mobility not only conjures the complex interplay of connections (human, economic, socio-political) between disparate locations (Besnier 2012), but also demands a rethinking of the readymade adoption of a place-based "ethnic lens" (Glick Schiller, Çağlar, and Guldbrandsen 2006; Çağlar 2013) in works on athlete migration (Carter 2011a, 2011b), namely a lens that takes migrants' country or region of origin as an overarching framework that privileges one subjectivity and forecloses others. This is particularly significant in the Caribbean, where ethno-racial identity and nationality have been privileged as a framework for understanding regional dynamics of race and ethnic relations (Thompson 1995; Devonish 1995; Yelvington 1995). This has obscured other critical factors, including social class (Allahar 2002; Guadeloupe and de Rooij 2014) and a changing political economy in which symbolic capital, money, and dreams flow along migratory pathways within the Global South and beyond.[2]

Mobility and the changing meaning of Caribbean cricket

Ever since the British colonial military introduced the game of cricket to the Caribbean in 1806, it has represented a symbolic and real possibility of mobility for the colonized. Although the British used cricket as a tool to assert their moral and physical superiority, before long it became a cultural space through which the enslaved and indentured populations and later their descendants challenged the ruling class. Cricket in the Caribbean thus became not just a sport but also a means of self-expression for the enslaved Africans and the indentured Indians.

As a tool of anti-colonial resistance, cricket exemplified the possibility of freedom from the yoke of colonial power, a phase of cricket in Caribbean history that is often described as "liberation cricket" (Beckles and Stoddart 1995). This quest for liberation that historically defined young people's desire to excel in cricket just as West Indies's cricketing success on the world stage has actively stimulated and fuelled the rise of nationalist self-consciousness and the quest for independence (Burton 1985). It is a quest that led the West Indies to be one of the strongest sides in world cricket, particularly from 1975 to 1995, during which they not only won two world cups but also were undefeated in 29 test series (Wigmore 2017).[3]

At least since 1900, for both Afro- and Indo-Caribbeans, the two ethnic groups that constitute Trinidad's population, involvement in the West Indies became an index of social position for individuals and by extension an indication of the standing of various racial and ethnic groups and their relative access to social position and prestige (Beckles 1998a). For example, the selection of Afro-Caribbean athletes into the West Indies since 1900 was a sign of their advancement in political terms, but their real ascendency took place in 1960 when the first Afro-Caribbean man was appointed captain after the mediocre performance by White captains in the previous years. It was not until 1950 that an Indo-Caribbean man was selected for the team (Rampersad, Anand 2014). Although the memory of colonial cricket has become rather faint in the contemporary Caribbean, cricket is still seen as a ground in which ethnic groups can establish themselves and contest for social position. In Trinidad and Guyana, the two Caribbean countries with sizeable people of Indian and African origins living side-by-side, Indo-Caribbean people often point to a long running race-based policy of their exclusion from West Indies cricket (Rampersad, Anand 2014; Hossain 2016).

Caribbean cricketers have long been migrating to play in foreign nations, particularly England. In *Beyond a Boundary*, the Trinidadian postcolonial Marxist intellectual C. L. R. James (2005) offers the example of Learie Constantine, the first Afro-Caribbean cricketer to move to the United Kingdom in 1928 to play professional cricket as an example of cricketers' quest for material wellbeing. The trend of migrating to England to play in the ECB Premier Leagues tournaments reached its peak during the 1980s and 1990s. With the gradual demise of county cricket, England today is no longer the desired destination for young cricket hopefuls across the world, including Caribbean youths. Rather, they aim to be part of franchise-based commercial cricket tournaments around the world that allow them to earn more than they do playing county cricket or representing the West Indies.

This development coincided with a gradual decline of West Indies cricket performance on the global stage, which has been a source of much angst and debate among cricket lovers and scholars. According to Hilary Beckles, a Caribbean cricket scholar and historian:

> the collapse of West Indies cricket performance standards in the mid-1990s, from the pinnacle of 1980s, remains one of the most dramatic examples of nationalist dislocation and demobilization in the face of a refashioned global circumstance.
>
> *(Beckles 1998b, XVII)*

He further contends that:

> today's cricket heroes, therefore, now see themselves as individuals who wish to be identified as professional craftsmen with no primary responsibility for the wider socio-political agenda carried by their predecessors. ... They do not wish to be role models for the youth, nor carry the burden of responsibility for nationalist pride, regional integration and the visibility of the nation state. They see themselves as apolitical, transnational global professionals, who desire to maximize professional earnings within an attractive market, and are motivated and guided by no other consideration.
>
> *(Beckles 1998b, 19)*

In other words, motivations of anti-colonialism and establishing one's ethnic community have been supplanted in current times by an orientation to entrepreneurship and consumption, and expectations of eventual self-realization. Thus the declining cricketing performance in the conventional international formats of the game is also often the result of a declining sense of West Indianness.

Since then, a new and shorter format of the game has emerged, referred to as "T20 cricket" (T20), which has enabled West Indies Cricket to regain their lost glory. The T20 format has significantly increased the prominence of cricket as a television sport and marks the onset of a neoliberal commercialization of cricket on a global scale (Rumford and Wagg 2010). In particular, the IPL, fuelled by a massive injection of corporate capital and sponsorship, television viewership, and the involvement of Bollywood superstars, has drastically changed how the game of cricket is played in India and has been able to tap into the huge commercial potential of the sport. In contrast to the conventional Test format of the game, T20 is a high-paced electrifying spectacle.

Other T20 franchise-based tournaments have been established since 2008 that emulate the IPL business model, including the Caribbean Premier League, introduced in 2013. It is also organized to allow abundant foreign and local sponsorship on a scale never seen before in the region, greater opportunities for local players to be part of the cricketing world, higher prize money and salaries, the inclusion of foreign players in local teams, and high entertainment value (Rampersad, Anngell Amber 2014).

Caribbean cricketers are internationally regarded as the specialists in the T20 format of the game, particularly for their aggressive risk-taking play, long a feature of the regional style. However, very few young men are actually able to play in lucrative T20 tournaments, while the majority only dream of doing so. Caribbean cricket is thus made up of groups of men located at different poles of economic freedom: those who have made themselves visible in the new socio-economic environment through their success, and those whose expectations of liberalization are constrained by their socio-economic circumstances. It is the men who have failed to qualify for franchise-based cricket or the West Indies to whom I now turn.

Trinidad, cricket leagues, and overseas athletes

Trinidad is a multi-ethnic immigrant society that emerged out of a history of African slavery and Indian indentureship. It is also a country with a long history of free movement of people from both within and outside the Caribbean region. The major ethnic groups are descendants of Africans and Indians, accounting for 37 and 40 percent of the population, respectively. Other ethnic groups include Chinese, Portuguese, Syrians, and Lebanese. There is also the category of Dougla, a distinct Caribbean mixed-race identity comprised mainly of people of Afro-Trinidadian and Indo-Trinidadian descent (Barratt and Ranjitsingh 2018). The social organization of cricket in Trinidad reflected the widespread race and class-based societal inequalities and mobility (James 2005). While many of the cricket clubs that James described have now disappeared, cricket clubs in Trinidad continue to remain important sites for the staging of various ethno-racial, class and gender-based ideologies, solidarities, and hierarchies (Joseph 2015; Rampersad, Anand 2014).

A significant trait of Trinidadian cricket today is the growing influence of Indo-Caribbeans, who act not only as chief patrons, owners, and managers of cricket clubs, but also as spectators and players (Rampersad, Anand 2014). For example, the majority of those holding various management positions on the Trinidad and Tobago Cricket Board (TTCB) are Indo-Caribbeans. The relocation in 2000 of the TTCB from the country's capital Port of Spain to Indian-dominated southern Trinidad also worked to reinforce the popular perception that cricket in Trinidad today is an Indian sport. However, this has not necessarily resulted in a greater number of Indo-Trinidadians being selected for the national team. In other words, just because there is greater display of enthusiastic support for cricket among the Indo-Trinidadians today does not mean that they are necessarily good at it.[4]

Trinidad's domestic cricket league, currently known as the Premier League, was established in the early 1980s to nurture local talent, under the auspices of a group of Indian businessmen and sponsors. In its initial years, the players were only paid stipends and awarded prizes for their performances. In the late 1980s, one local club brought two Guyanese players from Berbice, a county in Guyana, to play in the domestic cricket league. The man behind this initiative told me that, after he brought these athletes over, his club's performance improved dramatically. In his view, his efforts set the trend for other clubs to bring more Guyanese athletes over to Trinidad.

The introduction of foreign players also led to a shift in the meaning of cricket from an amateur sport fuelled by passion to a sport played by paid labour. At the time of my fieldwork, almost all the roughly 15 Premier League clubs had contracted overseas players. To prevent some clubs from having an unfair advantage, the TTCB set guidelines that regulate the number of foreign players each club is allowed to play in tournaments. Today, the clubs are also required to register foreign players with the TTCB and have them sign formal contracts.

The relationship between the clubs and the athletes they hire is often complicated. In practice, TTCB is minimally involved in the way clubs deal with the cricketers or negotiate their salaries. Athletes and managers often refer to "contracts," but these are actually verbal agreements based on trust. Players are often recruited on the recommendations of former players or through "friends-of-friends networks" (Bale 1991). In fact, many of my Guyanese interlocutors arrived in Trinidad after only a telephone conversation with a manager or a former player.

Club managers I met argued that the lack of written contracts helps the players to remain vague about their salaries, a strategy that allows them to avoid paying taxes to the Trinidadian government. Although this may lead to the possibility of exploitation, both the clubs and the players find this arrangement acceptable. Generally, foreign players are paid US$2,000–5,000 per cricket season (from the end of January to the beginning of June), although those with West Indies or national level experience can earn more. Clubs also provide the players with accommodation, meals, and transportation during their stay in Trinidad. Disputes sometimes break out between club management and players over matters of housing and food quality, or the players' poor performance. When a cricketer wants to leave a club because of a disagreement, he has to obtain a release from the club before joining another one, which places him at the mercy of the club. However, not a single player I interacted with ever mentioned the lack of proper contracts as contributing to these disputes.

While Trinidadian cricket club managers pride themselves on having the only domestic league in the Caribbean, they also recognize that players cannot support themselves solely as cricketers. Thus, in addition to playing cricket, most players also do menial work arranged by the clubs, even though the visa category they come under strictly prohibits them from taking up other work. The Caribbean Single

Market and Economy, an integrated development strategy envisioned in 1990 to enhance regional integration, recognizes the category of sportsperson and their right to free movement within the jurisdiction of the member states of CARICOM, an organization of 15 Caribbean nations and dependencies whose primary objectives is to promote economic integration and cooperation, to which both Trinidad and Guyana belong. Yet most Guyanese athletes who compete in Trinidad do not fall in this category. Obtaining certificates to be recognized as a sportsperson involves complicated bureaucracy and most Guyanese athletes in Trinidad are simply not aware of this scheme. Moreover, even though they may show invitation letters from the cricket clubs to immigration authorities upon arrival, the latter only grant them temporary visitors' permits of six months or less. In other words, an unwritten and informal arrangement between the clubs and immigration authority allow the Guyanese athletes to play cricket in the domestic Trinidadian cricket league, even though they are only admitted into the country as general visitors.

Most of the overseas athletes I befriended initially concealed from me the fact that they were also engaged in odd jobs. Coura Cricket Club arranged part-time work in a car-parts factory for all five overseas athletes on its squad.[5] Club managers told me that such activities can help Guyanese players earn extra cash before they return home. What emerges is an informal economy around cricket and the transnational and intra-regional migrations it involves, wherein players are engaged in non-sporting activity to support their efforts to be recognized as professional cricketers.

Guyanese athletes in Trinidad: Material and symbolic possibilities beyond cricket

As one of the richest countries in the Caribbean, Trinidad has been a destination for economic migrants from other Caribbean countries for decades. However, sport migration to the Trinidadian domestic cricket league is a much more recent phenomenon. The numerical preponderance of Guyanese players in Trinidad club cricket is not a coincidence. Trinidadian club managers, club sponsors, and cricket enthusiasts contend that this presence is at least partially due to the fact that Guyanese players are "cheaper" than cricketers from other Caribbean countries. As one of my Trinidadian interlocutors explained, bringing players from Guyana is logistically easy as the airfare between Trinidad and Guyana is cheaper than airfares between Trinidad and Jamaica or other islands, which are prohibitively expensive.

My Trinidadian interlocutors also suggested that the Guyanese tend to fit more easily into Trinidadian society than athletes from other Caribbean countries because of felt cultural similarities between Trinidad and Guyana, which share a history of African slavery and Indian indentureship. According to my Trinidadian and Guyanese interlocutors, these are the two countries in the Caribbean where people of African and Indian origins live side-by-side, a feature that is foreign to cricketers of most other Caribbean countries. Many Trinidadians also explained to me that the Guyanese tend to do well in Trinidad because of similar playing conditions and styles of play.

In contrast, my Guyanese interlocutors interpret Trinidadian interest in Guyanese athletes as a recognition of Guyanese talent and cricketing abilities. While they agree that cultural familiarity and similar race composition make it easy for Guyanese to navigate the Trinidadian social world, they also insist that they are different from Trinidadians. In the words of Nishal, a Guyanese cricketer, "we are more appealing to the Trinidadians because we are more hard working, will do things that Trinidadians will not do, and we perform better on the cricket field." Roopram, another Guyanese athlete, commented, "there is a distinct flair that the Guyanese bring to cricket, not only in Trinidad, but also in the West Indies Cricket Team."

According to some Guyanese and Trinidadians, the difference stems from the fact that the Guyanese athletes who manage to become part of the West Indies or the domestic Trinidadian cricket league have frequently done so without the privilege of formal training or sponsorship. Frequently, these athletes have not even had the financial capacity to purchase basic cricket equipment like helmets, gloves, bats, or balls. Many have learned cricket by playing on the street. According to a cricket coach in Trinidad, the Guyanese context of today can be compared to Trinidad's situation some 20 to 30 years back, when the country started experiencing dramatic shifts in its socio-economic development thanks to the oil boom, which led to a sudden rise in the standard of living, cost of labour, and infrastructure development, and colossal investments in health, education, and social welfare.[6] This phenomenon also intensified rural to urban migration and a radical shift in consumption patterns. Importantly, Indo-Trinidadians, who historically occupied the rural hinterlands, abandoned the agricultural sector as they increasingly took up jobs in the oil-related sector or set up small and medium-size businesses. However, the overdependence on oil eventually backfired as the oil price fell in the 1980s. The changing global economic scenario led to unemployment and pockets of poverty, which fuelled migration out of Trinidad, mainly to the United States and Canada (Green and Scher 2007).

Today, it is the Indo-Trinidadian business class that dominates the management, governance, and sponsorship of Trinidad cricket. Most Premier League clubs are also owned by Indo-Trinidadian businessmen, many of whom have both Trinidadian and American or Canadian nationalities. Davindra, the sponsor and owner of the Coura Cricket Club, ran real estate businesses in Florida alongside many other business activities in Trinidad, such as car imports. While he would divide his time between Trinidad and Florida, his wife and two daughters were settled in the United States and visited Trinidad only for holidays. As an avid cricket lover and organizer, Davindra was also actively involved in organizing cricket matches and tournaments in various areas in the United States, especially in New York and Florida. He would recruit Guyanese players from Trinidad and arrange for their trips to the United States. More recently, there has also been a steady increase in the demand for and popularity of Guyanese athletes in cricket clubs in Canada, where cricket is played by migrants from the Caribbean and South Asia.

For many Guyanese cricketers, coming to play in Trinidad's domestic league can thus open up other prospects beyond the Caribbean. While it is generally difficult for Guyanese people to obtain a visa to the United States, it is much easier to secure one to Canada for an athlete sponsored by a Canadian cricket club. However, many who make it to Canada or the United States have first displayed their performance in Trinidad's domestic league and built relations with Trinidadian cricket organizers and sponsors. On many occasions, Davindra brought to my attention that he had helped one Guyanese athlete to obtain a visa to stay in Canada for a whole year through his connection with a cricket club in that country.

The case of Canada is particularly interesting, as the cricket season there starts in June or July, just when the season in Trinidad ends. Many Guyanese cricketers who manage to secure a contract to play in Canada through Trinidadian sponsors return to Guyana in June after a season in Trinidad, leave for Canada after two weeks to play the season there, return to Guyana in November or December, and move to Trinidad once again in January or February. In this cycle of cricket migration, Trinidad serves as a critical node that connects the Guyanese to other material possibilities. In the last five years that Davindra had owned a cricket club, he has arranged several cricket competitions in New York and Florida, for which he helped several Guyanese athletes fly to the United States. In addition to earning a one-time salary for playing, the Guyanese athletes also took on blue-collar jobs in the United States to earn extra cash.

Davindra also plays a crucial role in importing cricket gear like balls, pads, and jerseys from South Asian countries like Pakistan to the United States, Canada, and even Trinidad. At the time of my fieldwork, he was helping a Guyanese cricketer affiliated with his club set up, as an alternative career, a small-scale business in Guyana to take order for cricket gears. A well-established Guyanese athlete who had taken part in cricket migrations from Guyana to Trinidad and beyond for a few years recently set up a sports agency to recruit athletes, especially from Guyana, to play in the United States, Canada, and Trinidad. The sports agency produced flyers for recruitment that were in transnational circulation through various online platforms.

Foreignness and the valuation of Guyanese in Trinidad

Mango Tree, the club where I was based during my fieldwork, had four Guyanese players. They all stayed in a two-bedroom apartment that the club had arranged. Located in an Indo-Trinidadian neighbourhood, the apartment was a 20-minute drive from the club. The Guyanese cricketers lived on the first floor while the ground floor apartment was occupied by a group of women from the Dominican Republic working in local massage parlours. The club supplied food but the athletes had to cook for themselves. During the five-month Premier League season, the athletes spent most of their time at the apartment or on the cricket grounds. Whatever spare time they had was devoted to various kinds of income-generating activities organized by the club.

One club manager I grew close to often complained about what he considered to be the "monster-like" eating habits of the Guyanese athletes, as food supplies ran out faster than he would have liked. The athletes, in contrast, frequently complained, as I grew closer to some of them, about being mistreated by the club, giving as an example the fact that food was not delivered in a timely manner, but they pleaded that I not divulge their feelings to the manager. Typically, foreign athletes refrain from saying anything negative about either Trinidad or club managers. One Guyanese athlete, tangled up in a row over payment with a club, once asked me to intervene and secure his release from the club with the help of another influential club manager and sponsor who was also my friend, Jhatu Lal. One evening, during a "lime" (as the art of doing nothing is called in Trinidad), I raised the issue of the Guyanese athlete seeking release from the club with Jhatu Lal. He did not seem very keen on helping that particular athlete, stating that his wish to leave was tantamount to betrayal, as a club had invested massively in him, attending to logistics like airline tickets, food, and accommodation, and offering him an allowance plus additional loans. In particular, Jhatu pointed to the fact that Trinidad offers opportunities to the "hungry" Guyanese and that "these foreign athletes should not be complaining" (Besnier 2012, 503).

The Guyanese's guarded and self-conscious behaviour would often strike me, as if their every move was being judged in both cricketing contexts and wider society. Compared to Trinidadian players, who were often spontaneous, the Guyanese were tense and tongue-tied. In my first month of fieldwork, I thought they were perhaps polite and unassertive. I also felt that I was perhaps reading too much in their apparent lack of frankness. But I soon realized that Trinidadians routinely mocked the Guyanese, denigrating them as "small islanders." The roots of these "small island" jokes can be traced to a cricket match between Trinidad and other Caribbean countries in 1975. Migrants from other Caribbean countries based in Trinidad turned out in droves to support the visiting team. When Trinidadians lost that match, newspapers the following day were flooded with commentaries questioning the allegiance of migrants from other islands and their right to work and stay in Trinidad. Apparently, during another match in the 1980s, Trinidadian immigration officers were called in to check the legal status of the supporters of the Guyanese team playing against Trinidad (Devonish 1995). Such incidents, I contend, provide the backdrop for the current Trinidadian attitude towards the Guyanese.

But Guyana is not an island, let alone a small one. In fact, with 215,000 km^2 compared to Trinidad and Tobago's 5,100 km^2, it is the largest country in the Caribbean. So the label "small islander" refers not to the size of the country but to the pervasive poverty in Guyana and the stereotype about Guyanese being generally "backward." Club managers and Trinidadian players often jokingly called Guyana a "bush." The Guyanese dialect of English was a constant source of their amusement. Although my Guyanese interlocutors were aware of these taunts, they barely reacted to them and even sometimes laughed along. Their tendency to refrain from reacting to or to disregard such taunt needs to be understood in the context of their dependence on Trinidadian club members, cricketers, and friends. For example, most athletes during their stay have limited physical mobility because the clubs are often located in semi-urban or rural areas with no public transport, and hiring private cars in Trinidad is prohibitively expensive. The athletes thus often have to depend on the clubs or Trinidadian athletes and friends to travel or even visit the nearest township. Against this backdrop, the choice of these athletes not to react to taunts may be read as a way to navigate the challenges of living in a foreign environment.

In addition, Guyanese identity is constructed in Trinidad in a way that is entangled with the production of athletes' mobility, immobility, and precarity. Being Guyanese in Trinidad engenders both negative and positive value. Here is it important to examine the conditions under which the registers of race and foreign-ness are constructed. For example, while being from Guyana creates the conditions of the athletes' mobility, namely the opportunity to play cricket, it may also become an obstacle in everyday life, as when they are perceived as foreigners because of their accent. Emplacement processes are significant as the athletes are located within the social and economic life of these places (Glick Schiller and Çağlar 2016). In one cricket club in a remote village in southern Trinidad, the only site of entertainment for the locals and athletes was a local rum shop in which players would gather to drink, dance, and lime after a hard day of practice. Jason Persaud, a cricketer who was in Trinidad for a third stint, had by then developed a close friendship not only with the owner of the rum shop but also the local inhabitants. While the Trinidadian cricketers would visit the club premises and the cricket ground only during matches, Jason would hang out in the club premises and the adjacent rum shop day in and day out. In other words, because many foreign athletes such as Jason were located in the neighbourhoods, various forms of sociabilities emerged between the emigrant athletes and the local inhabitants based on "domains of com-monality" that transcended difference (Glick Schiller and Çağlar 2016).

Masculine anxiety and the "stealing" of Trinidadian women

One theme that often emerged in conversations among the Trinidadian cricket club managers and athletes was Guyanese men flirting with Trinidadian women and getting seriously involved with them. While men located in remote rural clubs had fewer opportunities to meet Trinidadian women, at least two cricketers from a village-based club whom I befriended were dating women whom they had met through Trinidadian cricketers of the same club. A few times a week, after a day's play, athletes of the Coura Cricket Club would gather in the forecourt of the club manager's house for a lime, followed by drinking and a dinner of goat curry and rice. After a while Trinidadian athletes would leave, but the Guyanese group would stay and continue liming. Men and women in the club manager's network, including his friends and business colleagues, would also often drop by. Taking part in such limes was also an opportunity for the Guyanese to meet Trinidadians outside the club, including women. A few former Guyanese cricketers and their Trinidadian wives would regularly join the limes, through whom newly arrived Guyanese could connect with wider networks.

Many Trinidadians think that "small island" Guyanese men of both Indo-Guyanese and Afro-Guyanese origin "steal" Trinidadian women: they come over to Trinidad, earn Trinidadian money, marry Trinidadian women, and settle down. Particularly at the Mango Tree Club, the popularity of two former West Indies players among Trinidadian female fans was a frequent topic of comments by club managers and Indo- and Afro-Trinidadian athletes. But Indo-Trinidadian men also complain that Afro-Trinidadian men "steal" Indo-Trinidadian women, which places race at the centre of masculine anxiety. In contrast, in the Trinidadian club managers' displeasure with Afro- and Indo-Guyanese athletes' erotic exploits, it is national identity rather than race that contributes to their emasculation.

Trinidadian men's masculine anxieties do not result from their inability to form sexual relations with Trinidadian women; in fact, the club managers and Trinidadian athletes at Mango Tree Club had multiple sexual partners. Some women would frequent the cricket grounds to cheer for the team and the club managers' "mistresses" would often visit the club and spend hours hanging out with the managers and athletes. Thus, rather than a case of individual inability to "access" women, Trinidadian club managers' displeasure with Guyanese athletes' involvement with Trinidadian women stems from a concern to maintain boundaries between poor Guyana and wealthy Trinidad.

Many Trinidadians also argued that the Guyanese became involved with Trinidadian women not because of love but because Trinidadian women were often wealthier. One club manager categorically pointed out that many athletes get involved with divorced Trinidadian women with children and eventually married them because marriage, whether legally sanctioned or common-law, guaranteed financial security. However, my Trinidadian interlocutors' vexations did little to discourage Guyanese men from trying their luck with Trinidadian women. In fact, many Guyanese I met during my fieldwork were married to Trinidadian women and lived in Trinidad permanently. My Guyanese interlocutors saw the many Guyanese men married to Trinidadian women as proof that they were more reliable than Trinidadian men.

Guyanese cricketers return home: Aspirations and dreams reassessed

Curious to learn more about my Guyanese interlocutors and the meaning of cricket in Guyana, in June 2015 I travelled to Berbice, a county located a four-hour drive from the country's capital Georgetown, which was home to at least ten cricketers whom I had befriended in Trinidad. Within moments of my arrival, I noticed billboards depicting local cricket talent who have played for the West Indies. When I arrived, most of my Guyanese interlocutors had been back home for two weeks. Some had taken up part-time work such as taxi driving while others were simply passing time, waiting for the next cricket season in Trinidad to begin.

The first thing that struck me after I reached New Amsterdam, the capital of the county, was the cricketers' frankness and spontaneity. I felt as if I was talking to completely different people from the ones I had known in Trinidad: convivial, eloquent, and self-assured. I visited their families and parents, who invited me for lunch or dinner. In the neighbourhoods and the cricket circles I hung out in, it was evident that those who had returned from Trinidad exuded greater confidence in their interaction with others than those who had stayed home. The parents of the young men, all connected to a local sugar estate, were happy to have their sons back home. At one of the matches of bumper ball, a popular local variant of cricket, organized by a Presbyterian church, I met several young people interested in pursuing a cricket career. Many wanted to travel to Trinidad to play. Knowing my connection with cricket clubs in Trinidad, some asked if I could link them up with my networks. The Guyanese cricketers who returned to Trinidad were also acting as advisers to the many young men aspiring to make it in the profession. Those who returned from Trinidad stood out not only for the wealth of stories they told but also because of their new sartorial styles, including flashy clothes and sunglasses easily identifiable as being from Trinidad or abroad. For many Guyanese cricketers, Trinidad was their first experience of a consumer capitalist society and it is only by playing cricket that they had experienced it. As many Guyanese told me, "those who have come back from Trinidad are changed for good." Some viewed this change positively, as the Guyanese boys were more confident. Others suggested that they had returned with attitudes not compatible with Guyanese values and that many locals found them disrespectful.

One evening, I joined a few cricketers at a nearby rum shop to enjoy chilled beer and wild meat, chatting about cricket, Guyana, and their sexual experiences in Trinidad. While the cricketers had enjoyed their time in Trinidad, some were upset about the fact that they had not established connections that would have led to their recruitment in Canadian clubs and that they would have to try harder next season. A few were unsure about whether they would even be invited back to Trinidad next season because of their poor performance. The athletes did not talk candidly about these anxieties with other people nor did they discourage other young men from pursuing their cricket dreams. Because no systematic recruitment structure was in place, the cricketers returning from Trinidad are the ones who not only operate as talent scouts for the Trinidadian clubs but also represent beacons of hope for their younger compatriots.

Conclusion: Caribbean cricket at multiple spatial and temporal scales

Introduced to the Caribbean as an elite sport by the British, cricket soon became a site of anti-colonial resistance. The literature on Caribbean cricket focuses primarily on the complex relation between the sport and colonial power and the sport's contribution to the emergence of a common Caribbean or West Indian identity. However, in the rapidly changing context of the postcolonial Caribbean, cricket has taken on new meanings. Rather than being a symbolic battlefield for the assertion of Caribbean power against colonial oppression, cricket today is often associated with the emergence of wealth and individual glory, and the glamour and ostentation of a capitalist consumerist lifestyle (Beckles 1998b). While many Caribbean cricket analysts mourn the declining performance of the West Indies in the traditional formats of the game, West Indies cricketers and Caribbean cricketers more generally have gained the reputation of being specialists in the T20 format of the game.

In reality, however, only a tiny minority manage to make it to play for franchise-based T20 cricket and to enjoy the lifestyle it affords, even though the few examples of success continue to drive the dreams and aspirations of thousands of young men who bank on cricket to move out of poverty and obscurity. The lives of some Caribbean athletes, such as Guyanese cricketers, are constructed through multiple trajectories of mobility, uncertainty, and precarity. These lives reveal the continued importance of the legacies of colonialism, which shape the opportunities for and constraints on the athletes' social and physical mobilities within current global and regional dynamics of inequalities.

Many scholars have characterized the relationship between the sending and receiving countries of sport migration from the Global South to the Global North as a neo-colonial relationship (e.g., Darby, Akindes, and Kirwin 2007). In contrast, relationships and movements within the Global South (though not in the context of sport) have often been viewed as promoting alternative development, cooperation, and "third world" liberation and emancipation (e.g., Muhr 2016). It is often out of such an understanding of alternative possibilities that regional blocs have been brought into being in a bid to counter the Northern domination of the world.

Guyanese cricketers' experiences demonstrate the problems with frameworks anchored in binaries, be they framed in terms of Global South versus Global North or centre versus periphery (Besnier, Guinness, and Calabrò, this volume). Instead, they bring to the fore multiple and intersecting networks in which actors, including individuals, institutions, and corporate entities, are connected to various places and hold uneven power. The seasonal migration of Guyanese athletes to Trinidad and their entanglement with Trinidadian cricket clubs and society require us to braid together economic, ideological, and human connections, not only between Guyana and Trinidad but also other locations in the United States and Canada, both real and imagined. Focusing on the point of origin and the point of destination of migration trajectories is limiting, for the latter is also a point of departure towards new possibilities, including post-career ones. Trinidad thus becomes a means to other cricket and post-cricket possibilities, as well as an end in itself. The experience of the Guyanese athletes' migration to a semi-peripheral cricket economy (Akindes 2013) and the changing meaning of cricket in the postcolonial Caribbean countries necessitates taking into account not only the old colonial relations between the colonizer and the colonized or the centre and the periphery but also new relationships of inequality and dependency between and among countries in the Global South and within regional context like the Caribbean.

In this complex engagement, while the sense of these athletes being Guyanese is often forged and reinforced in their various encounters in Trinidad, the simultaneous presence of diverse locations and possibilities, the various real and imagined worlds with which Trinidad is associated and within which they are set bring into view the limits of an "ethnic lens" (Çağlar 2013; Glick Schiller, Çağlar, and Guldbrandsen 2016) in understanding the cricketers' subjectivity.

Although part of my aim in this chapter has been to jettison the overarching use of the lens of an ethnic and racial difference, I also recognize that there is an uneasy fit between a theoretical approach that points away from race and ethnicity and a system of international cricket migration that is structured by these categories, at least as they are reinforced by nationalisms and subnationalisms within the global cricket industry. Furthermore, Trinidadians often employ racial and ethnic differences as the dominant lens when they speak about the Guyanese (and others) in everyday settings, as much as the Guyanese mobilize racial, ethnic, and national perspectives in trying to create positive value for themselves. One cannot overlook the everyday production of race and race-based differences. Race and ethnic differences are not static even when they are made to appear so, such as in the way many people in Trinidad and Guyana spoke about these differences.

Approaching my interlocutors through the lens of ethno-racial and national categories is to turn a blind eye to the complexities of everyday interactions and transnational dynamics that actively constitute the experiences of Guyanese in Trinidad. In order to understand the dynamics of valuation, the social production of various registers of difference needs to be situated within the broader fields of power. The various negative stereotyping of the Guyanese in Trinidad as well as the positive valuation of these athletes need to be understood in conjunction with the political economy of contemporary racialized circulation of athletes both within the Caribbean region and the global cricket industry. More generally, the production of Guyanese identity in Trinidad needs to be contextualized in its relationship to the larger macroscopic structure of transnational Trinidadian society, such as the constraints of occupation, residence, social network, club affiliation, and sociocultural and economic dynamics in Trinidad, the Caribbean, and beyond.

Acknowledgements

I would like to thank the Institute for Gender and Development Studies, University of the West Indies, St. Augustine, for hosting me as a visiting scholar during my fieldwork in Trinidad and Tobago in 2015. I also want to thank Gabrielle Hossein, Anand Rampersad, Leanna Ganga, Allen Sammy, Corey Gilkes, David Ramsing, and Davindra Singh for their time, conversation, and friendship. Thanks are also due to all the athletes I interacted with during my time in the Caribbean. Special thanks are also due to Daniel Guinness, Domenica Gisella Calabrò, and Niko Besnier for their comments and editorship. This research received funding from the

European Research Council (grant agreement no. 295769) for the project titled "Globalization, Sport and the Precarity of Masculinity" (GLOBALSPORT) based at the University of Amsterdam.

Notes

1 The West Indies Cricket Board, the governing body of the team, consists of the cricket associations of Barbados, Guyana, Jamaica, Trinidad and Tobago, Leeward Islands, and Windward Islands.
2 While the general consensus is that ethnicity refers to cultural differences whereas race refers to phenotypical differences, neither term has a fixed referent. Rather, they are embedded in academic, popular, and political discourses that are themselves constitutive of relationships and practices (Wade 2010). For example, in our conversations, my interlocutors in the Caribbean never used the term "ethnicity" although they frequently invoked "race" to refer to both cultural and physical differences.
3 International cricket is played in two different forms: test matches and limited-overs games. The most important difference is their lengths. Test cricket is played over five days, with each day's play lasting six hours and at least 90 overs bowled per day. Limited-overs cricket, as its name suggests, is restricted to a maximum number of overs. In the modern era, international limited-overs cricket is divided between one-day internationals (ODIs, 50 overs in length) and Twenty20 internationals (20 overs in length).
4 That Indo-Trinidadians express enthusiasm for cricket in public also has to do with their relatively higher economic status. In other words, because they have money, they are able to buy tickets and watch games.
5 All names of clubs and people are pseudonyms.
6 The oil boom was caused by the tremendous increase in the price of crude oil starting in 1973.

References

Akindes, Gerard A. 2013. "South Asia and South-East Asia: New Paths of African Footballer Migration." *Soccer and Society* 14, no. 4: 684–701.
Allahar, Anton. 2002. "'Race' and Class in the Making of Caribbean Political Culture." *Transforming Anthropology* 10, no. 2: 13–29.
Bale, John. 1991. *The Brawn Drain: Foreign Student-Athletes in American Universities.* Urbana: University of Illinois Press.
Barratt, Sue Ann, and Aleah Ranjitsingh. 2018. "Recognising Selves in Others: Situating *Dougla* Manoeuvrability as Shared Mixed-Race Ontology." *Journal of Intercultural Studies* 39, no. 4: 481–493.
Beckles, Hilary. 1998a. *The Development of West Indies Cricket, Vol. 1: The Age of Nationalism.* London: Pluto.
Beckles, Hilary. 1998b. *The Development of West Indies Cricket. Vol. 2: The Age of Globalization.* London: Pluto.
Beckles, Hilary, and Brian Stoddart. 1995. *Liberation Cricket: West Indies Cricket Culture.* Manchester: Manchester University Press.
Besnier, Niko. 2012. "The Athlete's Body and the Global Condition: Tongan Rugby Players in Japan." *American Ethnologist* 39, no. 3: 491–510.
Burton, Richard D.E. 1985. "Cricket, Carnival and Street Culture in the Caribbean." *International Journal of the History of Sport* 2, no. 2: 179–197.

Byron, Jessica. 2014. "Developmental Regionalism in Crisis? Rethinking CARICOM, Deepening Relations with Latin America." *Caribbean Journal of International Relations and Diplomacy* 2, no. 4: 23–50.

Çağlar, Ayşe. 2013. "Locating Migrant Hometown Ties in Time and Space: Locality as a Blind Spot of Migration Scholarship." *Historische Anthropologie* 21, no. 1: 26–42.

Carter, Thomas. 2011a. *In Foreign Fields: The Politics and Experience of Transnational Sport Migration.* London: Pluto.

Carter, Thomas. 2011b. "Re-placing Sport Migrants: Moving Beyond the Institutional Structures Informing International Sport Migration." *International Review for the Sociology of Sport* 48, no. 1: 1–17.

Castles, Stephen. 2008. "The Factors that Make and Unmake Migration Policies." In *Rethinking Migration: New Theoretical and Empirical Perspectives,* edited by Alejandro Portes and Josh DeWind, 29–61. New York: Berghahn.

Darby, Paul, Gerard Akindes, and Matthew Kirwin. 2007. "Football Academies and the Migration of African Football Labor to Europe." *Journal of Sport & Social Issues* 3, no. 2: 143–161.

Devonish, Hubert. 1995. "African and Indian Consciousness at Play: A Study in West Indies Cricket and Nationalism." In *Liberation Cricket: West Indies Cricket Culture,* edited by Hilary Beckles and Brian Stoddart, 179–191. Manchester: Manchester University Press.

Glick Schiller, Nina, and Ayşe Çağlar. 2016. "Displacement, Emplacement and Migrant Newcomers: Rethinking Urban Sociabilities within Multiscalar Power." *Identities* 23, no. 1: 17–34.

Glick Schiller, Nina, Ayşe Çağlar, and Thaddeus C. Guldbrandsen. 2006. "Beyond the Ethnic Lens: Locality, Globality, and Born-Again Incorporation." *American Ethnologist* 33, no. 4: 612–633.

Green, Garth L., and Philip W. Scher. 2007. *Trinidad Carnival: The Cultural Politics of a Transnational Festival.* Bloomington: Indiana University Press.

Guadeloupe, Francio, and Vincent A. de Rooij. 2014. "Pimping and the Deconstruction of the Natural: A Perspective from Saint Martin and Sint Maarten (SXM)." *Women's Studies International Forum* 43 (March–April): 5–12.

Gupta, Amit. 2004. "The Globalization of Cricket: The Rise of the Non-West." *International Journal of the History of Sport* 21, no. 2: 257–276.

Hossain, Adnan. 2016. "Race and Cricket Narratives in the West Indies." *Anthropology News* 57: e1–e4. doi:10.1111/AN.77. Accessed 11 May 2019.

James, C. L. R. 2005. *Beyond a Boundary.* Durham, NC: Duke University Press. (First published 1963.)

Joseph, Janelle. 2015. "A Narrative Exploration of Gender Performances and Gender Relations in the Caribbean Diaspora." *Identities* 22, no. 2: 168–182.

Klein, Alan. 2014. *Dominican Baseball: New Pride, Old Prejudice.* Philadelphia: Temple University Press.

Muhr, Thomas. 2016. "Beyond 'BRICS': 10 Theses on South-South Cooperation in the 21st Century." *Third World Quarterly* 37, no. 4: 630–648.

Rampersad, Anand. 2014. "Ethnicity, National Identity, and Cricket in Contemporary Trinidad and Tobago." In *Beyond C. L. R. James: Shifting Boundaries of Race and Ethnicity in Sport,* edited by John Nauright, Alan G. Cobley, and David K. Eiggins, 239–252. Fayetteville: University of Arkansas Press.

Rampersad, Anngell Amber. 2014. "CPL: The New Star of Cricket? The Commercialization of the Caribbean Premier League and Its Influence on the Culture of Cricket." Master's Thesis in Sociology, University of the West Indies, St. Augustine Campus.

Rumford, Chris, and Stephen Wagg. 2010. "Cricket and Globalization." In *Cricket and Globalization*, edited by Chris Rumford and Stephen Wagg, 1–17. Cambridge: Cambridge Scholars.

Seecharan, Clem. 2009. *From Ranji to Rohan: Cricket and Indian Identity in Colonial Guyana, 1890s–1960s*. Hertford, UK: Hansib Publications.

Thompson, L. O'Brien. 1995. "How Cricket Is West Indian Cricket? Class, Racial, and Color Conflict." In *Liberation Cricket: West Indies Cricket Culture*, edited by Hilary Beckles and Brian Stoddart, 165–179. Manchester: Manchester University Press.

Wade, Peter. 2010. *Race and Ethnicity in Latin America*. London: Pluto.

Wigmore, Tim. 2017. "Kings Again: How West Indies Got Their Groove Back and Changed the Face of T20 cricket." *The Cricket Monthly*, 15 September 2017, www.thecricketmonthly.com/story/1119424/kings-again.

Yelvington, Kevin A. 1995. "Ethnicity 'Not Out': The Indian Cricket Tour of the West Indies and the 1976 Elections in Trinidad and Tobago." In *Liberation Cricket: West Indies Cricket Culture*, edited by Hilary Beckles and Brian Stoddart, 205–221. Manchester: Manchester University Press.

6

FRIENDSHIP, RESPECT, AND SUCCESS

Kenyan runners in Japan

Michael Kentaro Peters

The reggae music of South African musician Lucky Dube was blasting on the speakers. Julius, a senior three weeks away from his university graduation in March 2018, prepared afternoon tea while I glanced at the photos and medals that decorated his apartment.[1] He lived in a dormitory for student athletes on a suburban campus of a private university on the outskirts of Tokyo. A framed picture depicted him among the top finishers at a national championship race during his freshman year. That reminded me of the day we first met in the stadium of that event. That performance reflected the reason that his university originally gave him a full scholarship for: to enhance its brand name. For Julius, it fuelled fantasies of a life-changing future. Running and becoming a top high school runner in Kenya had earned him a ticket to Japan, enabling him to provide for his family and many others. As Lucky Dube's (2006) lyrics from the single "Shut Up" played, Julius sang along: "Your best friends today could be your worst enemies tomorrow. Your worst enemies today could be your best friends tomorrow. Don't burn that bridge. Don't close the door." These lyrics had been in the background of conversations during my multiple visits with Julius, and more than once our conversation had taken a momentary backseat while Julius performed an imaginary duet with the artist he reveres. The metaphorical resonance is vividly present in the verse and ironically reverberated as a theme for our meetings. The cautionary language provided maxims that were directly relevant to how Julius makes sense of his friendships. Julius cannot afford to burn bridges as it is thanks to friendships that he has been able to remain in Japan.

There are no major international running competitions in Kenya, so Kenyan athletes must be internationally mobile to increase their visibility and value (Njororai 2010). A few of the most fortunate athletes have ended up in Japan, a country with a strong demand for fast runners to augment high school, university, and corporate level teams; the willingness to recruit overseas to fill their ranks; and the financial resources to do so. Japanese educational institutions and companies sponsor Kenyan runners solely in the hope that the athletically talented Kenyans will lead their teams in road relay races known as the *ekiden*. Many top Kenyan runners are based in Japan, such as Paul Tanui, who recently ran for the Kyudenko Corporation and who earned a silver medal in the 10,000-metre race at the 2016 Olympic Games in Rio de Janeiro. While about half the Kenyan runners in Japan in any given year are on corporate teams, the others are students like Julius, who arrive on scholarships hoping to one day earn a salary through running. These rely on agents, coaches, and employers to remain in Japan. However, the prospect of losing a scholarship because of poor performance or one's place on a corporate team because of injury is an ever-present shadow.

Julius's collegiate racing career could have helped him secure a position in a Japanese corporate running club and the lucrative salary that comes with it. Unfortunately, a flurry of debilitating injuries ensued within months of the event where I first met him. As his student visa was expiring weeks after his graduation, and with no visa extension or job offer in sight, his days in Japan were numbered. Caught up in the neoliberal promises of success through sport (Besnier, Guinness, Hann, and Kovač 2018; Besnier, Calabrò, and Guinness, this volume), he displayed no particular anxiety or panic despite the slim odds of making it as an athlete or remaining in Japan. When I hesitatingly pointed out that he seemed to have gained weight, he downplayed it and said that he had only put on under ten kilograms, defiantly boasting that he only needed two months to make a full comeback. Our conversation paused and we sipped the piping hot chai that was now ready.

A year and a half later, in the summer of 2019, Julius was still in Japan. When I visited him in his new dwelling, Lucky Dube's "Shut Up" was once again playing in the background, his physique had not improved, and running for a living seemed even more unlikely. Julius now works for a local company (with five employees including the owner) that rents out motorboats and yachts to tourists on a scenic lake surrounded by mountains, hundreds of kilometres from Tokyo. He lives in a prefabricated home that he and his boss had converted from a shipping container, located in a parking lot alongside another shipping container that serves as the company office (Figure 6.1). Julius and his boss had also built a separate unit behind the containers that included a shower, a sink for washing dishes, a washing machine, and a bathroom. Julius's rent is deducted from his monthly salary, which is much more than he received from his university stipend, but clearly far less than what his friends earn running for Japanese corporations. The parking lot where Julius's life now unfolds lies directly across the street from a row of newly built two-story homes in an upper-middle-class neighbourhood. The only bridge linking the two worlds are the greetings of "Good morning" that Julius occasionally exchanges with the families who live there.

Julius was reluctant at first to explain how he got the job that enabled him to legally remain in Japan. Eventually, he admitted that his job resulted from a favour by a "friend of a friend" of his former coach, who also happens to have deep ties to and

FIGURE 6.1 The shipping crates on the right is where Julius currently lives, the shipping crate on the left is his company's office, Japan, 4 May 2019.
(Source: Michael Kentaro Peters)

clout in the distance-running world in Kenya. In the five years that I have known Julius, he periodically mentioned his former coach and other Kenyan runners he met during his time in Japan. At times, he called them friends and lauded them; in other instances, he denigrated them. These fluctuations in Julius's assessments of fellow runners offers an opening into an exploration of how friendship operates in the Kenyan athletes' strategies to navigate their migratory experience in Japan. Their friendships are crucial for realizing the distinct but interconnected goals that illustrate their success: surviving the neoliberal sport industry and surviving the expectations grounded in Kenya. Such friendships build upon values they are socialized into in Kenya: notions of respect and understandings that individual achievements will translate into immediate and drastic improvements for one's family and friends. Disappointment seems to arise when friends, comprised of current or former Kenyan runners, seem to disrupt those local values, circumscribing their friendships within neoliberal parameters.

In the context of Kenyan runners aspiring to go overseas, hopes of satisfying individual desires are secondary to hopes of generating collective wellbeing. Validating one's journey does not necessarily mean winning bronze, silver, or gold hardware at the Olympics, nor the fame or prestige that may come with it (Figure 6.2). The

FIGURE 6.2 Kenyan runners dominating at a track meet in Japan, 5 November 2014.
Note: Part of this image is blurred to protect the person's identity.
(Source: Michael Kentaro Peters)

athletes' legacy is indeed contingent on securing the rapid improvement of the lives of many others who attach their hopes to the runner (who in many cases may no longer be a competitive runner). Runners like Julius are caught in what they perceive and experience as two divergent value systems within Kenya: one that showcases the individual, and another that showcases communalism. Kenyan responses to global and local economic circumstances steer individuals to create their own route to a better life, and yet discourage moral individualism, for individual entrepreneurship needs to be at the service of many others. However, the communal values in turn generate the friendships which help the Kenyan runners in Japan express their individual entrepreneurship and remain accountable to many others back in Kenya. The athletes manage a balancing act between desires of individual wellbeing and responsibility towards fulfilling the expectations placed on them, affecting the expression or perceptions of friendships. The interpersonal relationships between runners requires as a prerequisite a degree of respect but also offers the potential to earn more respect for oneself.

How does running in Japan earn Kenyan women and men respect? What roles do their friendships with other Kenyans in both Japan and Kenya play in this objective? The athletes' experiences and interactions with each other provide further insight into how respect is culturally generated and maintained. Moreover, refined meanings and images of what it means to be successful in different contexts emerge by following their journeys.

Maendeleo: **Neoliberal logics and communal worldview**

> Because of our poor political country, getting a job is a problem. The creativity of any income must be done individually to get something to sustain their needs. I better help them with capital and let them run something that will get income and later back my money. I wonder how this country will develop. No *maendeleo* in the country. (Alice, former runner in Japan)

The Swahili word *maendeleo* literally translates as "development" or "improvement" (Ahearne 2016; Karp 2002; Mercer 2002; Smith 2008) and people and organizations use this ideologically laden concept widely across East Africa. For example, the term appears in the names of many NGOs, funds, and charities throughout Kenya and neighbouring Tanzania, such as the Maendeleo Ya Wanawake Organization (improving the lives of rural communities with a focus on women and youth), the Maendeleo Agricultural Enterprise Fund (providing grants for small-scale farmers), and the Rafiki wa Maendeleo Trust (empowering the poorest communities).

While the definition of the term is open to local interpretations, a common theme relates specifically to development or betterment (Hunter 2014). Kenyans perceive development to be a state that they are constantly lacking but perpetually desiring, particularly in the context of the deregulation of the economy in 1993 (Smith 2012). Public spending was slashed, dramatic downsizing in the public sector reduced employment opportunities for civil servants, and higher education no longer guaranteed a job (compare Hann, this volume, on Senegal; Kovač, this volume, on Cameroon; Besnier, Guinness, Hann, and Kovač 2018). Power structures, mainly educational institutions and the state, were no longer reliable means to foster development (Green 2000). Kenyans can no longer depend on a paternalistic state to provide aid for development and improvement (Prince 2013), but can only count on their individual resourcefulness. Someone like Alice, whom I quote in the epigraph of this section, tries to contribute to *maendeleo* with the money she earned in Japan thanks to her resourcefulness to provide fellow Kenyans with the capital to express their own entrepreneurship in securing a better life.

Alice's remarks highlight how *maendeleo* has incorporated neoliberal logics. In the neoliberal context, it is up to the individual to become an "entrepreneurial" actor, in the sense that one must create strategies to make ends meet and is personally responsible to manoeuvre obstacles and overcoming failure in the quest for an improved life (Brown 2005; Cornwall 2016; Gershon 2011; Gershon and Alexy 2011; McGuigan 2014). However, *maendeleo* also requires individual achievements to deliver on the hopes of many others. Alice's story is exemplary: aged 15, she managed to be among the best in the world at the 3,000 metres in the world junior rankings, which made her well-known among recruiters. In her final year of high school, she was offered two opportunities to go overseas: a full athletic scholarship at a university in the United States or a contract with a Japanese corporation. After consulting with her family, she opted for the latter. She realized that with the salary she was offered, she could support her mother, her nine siblings, and her extended family, and open up a path for her younger sister to go to the United States in the future. Years later, her younger sister earned a scholarship to run cross-country and track at a U.S. university. Alice felt, that since she had brought financial stability to her family and relatives in Kenya, it was easier for her sister to accept the opportunity to study abroad.

Discourses around *maendeleo* tend to pit the personal goals of being responsible for one's own wellbeing under neoliberalism against the goals of fulfilling obligations and hopes for many others. The latter goal speaks to the collective heritage of reciprocity encompassed in Kenya's "economy of affection" (Hyden 1987, 119). From an early age, people learn to participate in obligatory acts of giving, receiving, and reciprocating to maintain a favourable social standing among their families and locally, in other words gain and maintain respect (Taylor, Wangaruro, and Papadopoulos 2012). Patrick Kamau, a longtime running coach based in Nyahururu, Kenya, who has worked with athletes who ended up in Japan, stressed to me the importance of giving: "If one has to go back to the original place, one must assist. We believe it's a curse if you don't assist. If one doesn't assist, it's not like he's kicked out, but he kicked himself out." Kenyan runners thus comply with "rule one of social life in western Kenya: never look selfish" (Shipton 2010, 174).[2] Individuals like migrant runners are thus deeply aware of social expectations that whatever they may achieve will contribute to also changing the future of many in Kenya, producing the desired *maendeleo*.

Sending remittances is the most common and immediate method of meeting the expectations placed on Kenyan nationals overseas (Rutten and Muli 2007). Remittances not only meet the recipients' temporary needs (e.g., building new homes, paying school fees, meeting ceremonial expenses), but also accelerate the elevation of the status and reputation of the migrant. Among Kenyan migrants, the runners are under particular pressure as their families, friends, and others expect them to deliver miraculous economic contributions.

As a result, migrant runners develop strategies to enable them to weigh to whom they can give, how much they give, and when they give. It is crucial for athletes to have the ability to say "no" to certain requests from other athletes or to people requesting remittances back in Kenya. Some classic avoidance strategies are for athletes to change their phone number or give an incorrect number to potential money seekers. Many of my interlocutors found it difficult to say "no" directly to someone in Kenya, and even more so to other Kenyans living much closer in Japan. Some phrases athletes use to decline a request are, "Let me think about it" or "Give me time." Both phrases do not necessarily imply that they actually intend to give money at a later date, but can be used to soften a rejection. This can eventually be followed with, "I'm sorry, I don't have money right now" or "I am bankrupt, so maybe next time."

One perceived advantage athletes claim to have of being in Japan is that it is far from Kenya. Family or friends in Kenya have to make an international call to reach an athlete, which is costly. Another factor working in favour of the athlete is the six-hour time difference between Japan and Kenya. An athlete can pretend they were asleep or unavailable when the phone rang. These avoidance strategies are not unique to migrants in other contexts as highlighted earlier by what Ilana Gershon (2000) describes as "strategic ignorance." Since families also employ their own strategies of "not knowing," the great distance between Kenya and Japan may be disadvantageous for athletes in Japan. Families in Kenya can pretend that they are unaware what their relatives are facing in Japan defending their actions of making incessant requests. They also know that athletes put their social standing back in Kenya at risk if they are uncooperative by refusing to lend. Therefore, athletes continuously look for ways to protect themselves when the demands from family or friends are overwhelming. Athletes can also pacify family and friends making requests by conceding a smaller sum of money than requested. Finally, for some athletes, being straightforward may be the last resort. One athlete bluntly told his parents that he had only been in Japan for a month and a half, and needed time to adjust to life before sending money.

Athletic careers are brief and often end abruptly – the onset of which Julius is grappling with and hopes to curb. Several other talented Kenyan runners who were unable to secure a contract with a corporate club are forced to adopt a flexible approach, remaining in Japan by capitalizing on other skills, for instance as English language instructors. The money they do earn from running is often insufficient to finance all of the growing expectations pinned on them, and they thus need to strategize to generate income.

Both current and former athletes commonly use a portion of their savings to diversify their sources of income by starting their own businesses in Kenya. These are a prevalent neoliberal type of investment or risk management in rural Kenya, which Parker Shipton calls "an eclectic agrarian living" (2009, 66; see also Haugerud 1995). While they remain in Japan, runners commonly employ friends and relatives to operate these businesses, creating jobs for many who would otherwise remain unemployed. The most common enterprises are importing used vehicles that fail the rigorous Japanese inspection standards (a common strategy in left-hand-driving countries of the Global South), general stores, minibus used as a taxi service (*matatu*), farms, private schools, real estate ventures, and restaurants. These businesses demonstrate in a public way that runners are capable of achieving not only *maendeleo* for themselves but also for their friends, families, and other dependents in their networks.

Foundations of respect, friendship, and success

In Japan, athletes assist one another by borrowing money. Julius had mentioned to me that a fellow Kenyan runner named Ezekiel, who at the time ran for a Japanese corporate team, "is a very kind man and a very good friend because he lends me money and is always able to help me out when I need it for my family in Kenya." Julius, who had at that time been in Japan for six months, often borrowed, received, and accepted money from Ezekiel, on top of the stipend that his coach was yet to start siphoning off. The money he wired to Kenya contributed to fulfilling hopes that his friends and family placed in his going to Japan and what that could generate for them. This helped Julius earn the respect of his family and friends. In turn, by helping a friend gain respect, Ezekiel also earned respect or maintained his respected status, for many in Kenya read a reluctance to share as antithetical to friendship (Haugerud 1995; Shipton 2007).

At a training camp in Kenya where Japan-based runners get together and workout intensively when they are back in the country during the off-season, Elijah, an Olympic medallist in the marathon, and Vincent, one of the fastest marathoners in history, distinguished between lending money and helping a friend out of respect. Vincent emphasized the importance of trustworthiness, because "if you don't have the trust with the person, even the respect cannot be made," while Elijah identified that trust is a form of respect on its own, for "if you don't have that respect, then you would not give me." Respect between individuals is thus the prerequisite for monetary transactions as well as their goal. It is not imperative that a friend always returns money:

> So you find that when it comes to the time of respect, there is no measure of value. (laughs) You can't measure. But what you need to do is to respect your friend, help him when he is need and he will also help you when you need it. … You don't need that person to pay back. You have helped him. So it brings friendship for you have helped and then forget. Yeah help and forget. … What is important there is to help one another to succeed.
>
> *(Vincent)*

Helping another to succeed in turn leads to success for both because success is contingent on earning respect. As they assist each other, athletes thus uphold an image of success that is embedded in the expectations of friendship.[3]

Helping a fellow runner does not necessarily involve wiring money. When Julius began to have lingering injuries that prevented him from competing, his coach recruited a freshman runner from Kenya to replace him. It was painful for Julius to watch the new addition to the team not only take over his spot on the roster in races, but also the attention and adulation he had once received. Out of respect for his new teammate, Julius swallowed his pride and tried to give advice to his younger compatriot so that he not meet the same fate. Friendship also manifested itself in the job that enabled Julius to remain in Japan. In their attempts to serve collective aspirations of betterment through their individual endeavours, the Kenyan runners in Japan rely on a transnational network of friendships: "friends" back home support the investment of savings and help the runners migrate, and "friends" in Japan help runners send remittances and navigate the sporting industry and life in Japan.

People in Alice's hometown in Kenya often refer to her as "the chosen one" because she was the first member of her family to complete secondary school and in reference to her strong leadership and the businesses she has started with the money she earned in Japan. This was particularly significant because of her gender, as women are less likely to be able to choose running as a career than men (Sikes and Jarvie 2014). Fewer girls than boys have the opportunity to attend school, which translates into fewer chances to participate in organized sports and be noticed by agents and recruiters. Kenyan society also expects women to be subservient to their husbands, who are typically considered the breadwinners (Silberschmidt 1999), and women are expected to be the primary caregivers at home, which is antithetical to pursuing a career in sport (compare Borenstein, this volume, on Ethiopian women runners). However, a few women have paved the way through their Olympic achievements, becoming role models for today's young female Kenyans.

Women and men support each other in trying to meet the expectations placed on Kenyan runners. Their friendships at first suggest forms of non-gendered socialization, but the dynamics of these friendships prove nonetheless to be gendered because of the different expectations placed on women and men. For example, when Vincent explained why one should help a friend with money, he eventually framed his explanations in masculine terms: "Yeah, when you are doing that you want someone also to succeed so you help one another to succeed. If you are two guys, that remains like a secret. It's your secret." The circulation of money between "two guys" is an unspoken pact between two male athletes who understand the importance for overseas male athletes to appear successful back home in Kenya.

Knowing when to step back

In the summer of 2016, during his junior year of university, Julius made his first visit back to his old high school in Kenya since migrating to Japan. His friend Justus, an older runner who has served as his mentor and coach, especially on his return visits to Kenya, and Claudia, a former runner visiting from Japan, joined him for the afternoon. Students quickly flocked over to see Julius, who pulled out his smartphone to show photos of his life in Japan. Glowing with pride, he held both arms up above everyone else and told them to look up for a group selfie (Figure 6.3). The latest smartphone model, the expensive Lacoste shirt, the brand-new black leather boots, the silver chain, and the running watch were material markers of success Julius had on full display. The school vice-principal, who was also Julius's running coach in high school, then asked him whether he had anything for the school, such as a few new computers. He also pulled his cell phone out of his back pocket, an old flip-phone with a cracked screen and a battery that he said lasted only two hours at best and asked, "why can't you buy me a nice phone?" Looking down at the ground, Julius replied that he was a student with no income, but that in a few years' time he would take care of the school.

As sunset was approaching, everyone gathered for some last-minute photo opportunities. While Julius was shaking hands with the students, Justus asked Claudia for KSh200 (approximately €1.80). He did not specify to her why he needed it, but Claudia promptly handed him the money. Without telling Julius that the money was from Claudia, Justus passed the money on to Julius, who then walked over to four young girls. While shaking their hands, Julius discreetly slipped a KSh100 bill

FIGURE 6.3 Taking a selfie with friends, Kenya, 9 August 2016. Note: Part of this image is blurred to protect the person's identity.
(Source: Michael Kentaro Peters)

to two of them and looked around to see whether other students had noticed it, anxious that they might hope to receive whatever he could offer.

Claudia was not able to secure employment running for a Japanese corporation but continues to work in Japan in foreign language instruction on renewable one-year contracts. At the end of every year, she is anxious about not having her contract renewed and having to return to Kenya earlier than she may have hoped, since her residence permit is contingent on her being employed. Despite no longer being able to make it as an athlete, she has managed to forge ahead with financial prospects and living conditions that are markedly more favourable than those of Julius. A few days after the visit to Julius's high school, when nobody else was around, she admitted to me that Justus's action had left her slightly agitated. She chose not to say anything to or about Justus, presumably calculating that it was not worth embarrassing someone whom Julius looks up to over what to her was an insignificant sum of money. She also pointed out that nobody at Julius's school would accept that Julius had lived in Japan for over three years but had nothing to offer to his alma mater. Claudia played her part as a good friend by first letting Justus's act slide and then allowing him to assist Julius and make it look like an act of friendship.

Paradoxically, her gesture confirmed gendered definitions of respect. As Justus maintained the image of a successful man and good friend before Julius and elevated Julius's masculinity before the two school girls, he also prevented Claudia from taking on the role of patron, which she regularly plays from afar by providing material support. On this day, Claudia internalized her frustration and let Justus and Julius display what was expected of them as migrant male athletes. This actually speaks to the much higher degree of pressure placed on male athletes to be successful neoliberal workers and good friends. At the same time, as Justus turned the transaction into a secret between Claudia and him, he "admitted" her into what would have normally been a masculine practice, as Vincent and Elijah explained.

On the following day, Claudia and I took the several-hour drive to visit Alice in the city of Eldoret in Uasin Gishu County. Even though she was in the peak years of her running career and her employer had guaranteed her a contract for another year, Alice had returned to Kenya after living in Japan for nearly a decade and her new home was in the final stages of construction. But most of her income was now from the investments she had made with the money she had earned in Japan and from appearance fees and cash prizes she earned competing on the track and road-racing circuit in Europe. Alice wanted to be in Kenya to be with her child, whose care she had entrusted to her mother, together with some orphans she had adopted. Alice's marriage had collapsed while she was in Japan, and her husband had cheated her of all her properties because the land she had purchased was registered in his name, as Kenyan laws at the time did not allow women to own land. Alice's experience is not uncommon among Kenyan female athletes who have lived and competed overseas and are the primary breadwinner of their families. In the same vein, it is not unusual for a Kenyan female athlete in Japan to return home in her athletic prime because of the gendered expectations that women conform to in order to start a family, raise children, and yield to the demands of their male partners (compare Borenstein, this volume).

Alice and Claudia's stories reveal that female runners' respect may be secondary to male runners'. Alice moved on, built a new house, which is now registered in her own name, and purchased new properties to rent out. She sacrificed the other properties that she had originally purchased when she separated from her husband without publicly challenging him, as doing so would likely have tarnished her reputation and accomplished little in undermining the patriarchal order. She provides for her child on her own and delegates the care of her biological and adopted children to her own mother. Her child and mother now live with her, and some of the orphans she raised are now studying at university at her expense. She continues to be revered as "the chosen one." As for Claudia, on the day she visited Julius's school, she had markers of success such as a tablet, black leather jacket, designer jeans, and elaborate hairstyle with red highlights that were prominently visible. Claudia's job teaching in Japan is one that Julius's former coach dreams of having, and she was living proof to the boys and girls at the school that success is indeed possible outside of Kenya. While the respect one can earn as a runner overseas is palpable, it is always subject to being overshadowed by prevailing gender inequalities.

Dreams of success

Julius took me to visit Justus, whom he often refers to as a very good friend, at his home (Figure 6.4). As Julius and I were drawing water from the well in the yard, he surveyed the perimeter of the property and then turned to me:

FIGURE 6.4 The home of Justus and his wife in Kenya, 10 August 2016.
(Source: Michael Kentaro Peters)

> Justus does not have to pay rent to anyone. He built this home by himself. In three years, I'm going to build a house like this one. I will build a hotel and restaurant where you can stay for free and eat traditional Kisii dishes, which I will prepare for you. You can use my car to get around whenever you like. You have my word.

Although Justus has never run in Japan, he has competed in long-distance races overseas and his wife currently competes sporadically in international competitions, and the income they have generated has enabled them to live the way they do. Yet Justus never mentioned his wife's financial contributions to their wellbeing nor acknowledged her efforts. Justus is well-respected locally as he coaches up-and-coming athletes who, like Julius, hope to make it by going abroad. The hearty meal that Justus was preparing for Julius and what was about to occur later that afternoon reinforced Justus's sentiment of Julius being a good friend.

On a training run with Julius earlier in the morning, Ezekiel's name surfaced in conversation. Ezekiel happens to be from the same region as Julius and had graduated from the same high school a few years before him. By this time, Ezekiel had returned to Kenya because the company he ran for did not renew his contract and he was unable to secure employment running for another corporate team in Japan. According to multiple sources, including coaches and agents in Japan, Ezekiel's performances in races lagged behind that of other Kenyan runners in Japan. With thousands of runners in Kenya just hoping to make it out of the country, and among them several hundred whose recent performances eclipsed those of Ezekiel, his days running in Japan came to an abrupt end. Like other Kenyan athletes, Julius was seemingly unaware of the actual reason why Ezekiel was back in Kenya mainly because Ezekiel let it be known that he had left Japan on his own terms. Proud as he was of his running prowess, Ezekiel would have been ashamed to admit to others that he was no longer fast enough to warrant a spot on corporate team rosters. Julius, who was still a year and a half away from graduating from university and hoping to land a running contract with a Japanese corporation as Ezekiel had, could not understand why Ezekiel would "give it all up after you are lucky enough to have a chance [to run in Japan]" and be "useful" to others.[4] Julius then added disapprovingly that Ezekiel had been "acting big driving around in a nice car":

> Ezekiel should not be buying a car when the money should be spent for more important priorities. A car for what? This is not an investment! If I need to buy something, I need to consult my friends first. If they give me advice, I need to work on that advice. You should buy land. You can buy 10 cars later with the investment made in buying land. You need to invest in something that doesn't take money, but keeps generating money. I hate somebody who buys cars. We were born poor!

For Julius, money should be spent on something durable that would generate additional returns. More importantly, he stressed how important it is to strive to gain the approval of "friends." From Ezekiel's perspective, a car is a status symbol and a masculine marker of respect (compare Archambault 2015; Meiu 2015), a proof of individual neoliberal success (Jeske 2016) that would still enable him to be generous to others by offering them lifts. Julius himself had imagined a future in which he owned a car and would drive me around, but he did not see the contradiction between this dream of consumption and his criticism of Ezekiel for having achieved this dream. The purchase of the car validated Ezekiel from the pressures of proving that he has made it as an athlete. A student at that time, Julius was still nowhere close to being able to buy a car or make similar grand purchases; even later when he was employed, he still was not in a position to do so.

Julius's ambivalence suggests his own internal tension between the desire to gratify himself and the desire to support others. When he moved to Japan in 2014, he had a clear plan that addressed both individual and collective desires:

> Many of the famous athletes we have now in Kenya, they usually train in Japan like [Paul] Tanui and [Bedan] Karoki.[5] Those people are the fastest runners in Kenya right now. So I was aiming to come to Japan because I want to be somebody who is popular. And this is the talent I have. So I have to do it so that I can be able to get what I want from it. That's why I came to Japan after my high school. So I started to come to the university to study Japanese and also I want to work in Japan for my life.

Showcasing a neoliberal belief in talent, Julius harbours dreams of being famous and adulated as Olympic champions are. At the beginning of his stay in Japan, he was performing well and was appreciated by his employers, but he was also struggling because he had to take care of his family and meet the expectations of many others. On this return to Kenya, he contrasted his own situation with that of other Japan-based Kenyan runners or former ones like Ezekiel, realizing he was not quite where he wanted to be in life.

His persistent injuries, the cuts to his scholarship, and his replacement by the coach in competitions with another Kenyan young man made him dread the possibility of having to return to Kenya after four years at university with nothing to show for. "I can't go back empty-handed. My coach has destroyed my life." He saw the coach's action as a breach of friendship as it is understood in Kenya. The coach had acted using the logic of neoliberalism, according to which athletes are commodities and each is responsible for his or her own destiny. The same logic is what led to Ezekiel's skills as a runner no longer being valued in Japan. And it underlies Julius's strategizing for his future: his life living in one shipping container and working in another is not what he envisioned when he arrived in Japan six years ago. He hopes that his friendships with other Kenyan runners in Japan will enable him to better position himself so that he can return to Kenya with something to show for and gain a level of respect that thus far has eluded him.

"Just shut up"

Friendships are crucial in helping migrant athletes negotiate the conflict between neoliberal values and their responsibilities to their kin. Individuals must use their creativity to generate income, which they must then redistribute to others. But in the process, they depend on friendship networks with other Kenyans, as Julius's story illustrates. Using his own experience as a cautionary tale, Julius guides his younger Kenyan teammate so that the latter avoid going down the same path as him. Alice invests her money so that her sister can attend university overseas and others reap the fruit of her efforts. While being a successful runner is always a key factor for the lucky few to secure a ticket out of Kenya, the ticket back to Kenya does not necessarily require one to be a successful runner. Nevertheless, under the parameters of neoliberalism, each current or former athlete is responsible to find her or his own ways to success and earn the respect that comes with it. Friendships play a pivotal role in reaching those objectives.

Alice, "the chosen one," becomes the embodiment of the neoliberal promises of sport: she commands a new form of respect from her individual achievements that articulates with traditional forms of respect based on redistribution, which is usually expected of men. When she was married, she helped her husband be successful, but she sacrificed the peak years of her athletic career and the potential to earn more money to be closer to him and raise their child. When her husband left her, she conceded those assets to avoid a lopsided battle that would have tarnished her reputation while leaving his intact, in a society that structurally safeguards masculinity.

Female athletes participate in the gendered game of strategic friendships and competition for respectability. But gender is complex. On the one hand, Alice's and Claudia's trajectories are success stories of female empowerment, despite an unfair divorce in one case and repressed feelings in the other, while Julius's trajectory is one of male disempowerment. The women have gained the respect of others, while the respect that Julius had managed to command is precarious. Their divergent experiences illustrate the different ways women and men may experience opportunities or face struggles specific to their gender in the global sporting industry in the neoliberal era. Their journeys underscore the importance of friendships, the fragility of respect, and the tiny window for success through sport.

Being no stranger to subscribing to old adages, Julius provided his own rendition of another during one of our meetings: "you can feed a human for three years, he can forget you in three days. You can feed a dog for three days, it can remember you for three years." Julius explained his version of the aphorism:

> even if I am away for one year [from Kenya], they [his three dogs] are happy to see me back home. You can give one-hundred percent for many years, and they [the people in Kenya who depend on Julius financially] forget you.

Julius appeared tired of the constant stream of requests from people in Kenya and felt underappreciated by them despite his perception that he has fulfilled much of what people ask of him.

Despite the slim odds, Julius has remained optimistic that he will be able to run for a Japanese corporate team in the near future. He may not regard his coach very highly at the moment, but he is aware that he is an important bridge not worth burning because he holds the proverbial keys to his future as an athlete in Japan. With no income and only his personal network with other Kenyan athletes in Japan and a few others in Kenya to rely on, Julius cannot afford to burn his bridges with any of them either if he has any hope of preserving local forms of respect in Kenya. It behoves all Kenyan women and men athletes to manage their friendships and how they talk about their friendships cautiously because their worst enemy today could be their best friend tomorrow. To recall some of the lyrics of "Shut Up" I heard Julius sing during the time I spent with him: "And if you can't say something good about somebody, oh shut up. And if you can't say something good about somebody, just shut up" (Dube 2006). For Kenyan women and men to maintain social relations that are instrumental to friendship, respect, and success, it may be best for them to do as Lucky Dube suggests: just shut up.

Acknowledgements

The research reported herein has received funding from the European Research Council under Grant Agreement 295769 for a project entitled "Globalization, Sport and the Precarity of Masculinity" (GLOBALSPORT). I am grateful to all of the current and former athletes for not only their friendships but also for helping me understand what friendship can mean. I would also like to thank their families, coaches, managers, and countless others in the distance-running world in both Kenya and Japan. Finally, thank you to Niko Besnier, Susan Brownell, Domenica Gisella Calabrò, Daniel Guinness, William Kelly, and Glenda Roberts for constructive feedback on this chapter and guiding me through the entire process.

Notes

1 All names including nicknames are pseudonyms, except those of athletes who participated or were medaled at the Olympic Games or World Track and Field Championships.
2 Most Kenyan runners hail from rural western Kenya, either because they were born there or because they moved to run in a training camp hoping to earn a chance to make it out of Kenya. Without a good manager (often used interchangeably with "agent"), it is near impossible for an athlete to increase his or her visibility, which can enhance the likelihood of going abroad. Camps are spaces for living and training where managers gather athletes with the explicit goal of separating them from the distractions of family and friends and preparing them for local competitions and later gaining exposure at national level competitions and entering the global athletic market. Running is a business, and more money earned by athletes at competitions translates into more money for agents. Not all athletes are in camps run by agents, though the most prominent camps may be based in rural western Kenya and funded by transnational shoe corporations, where athletes are recruited and nurtured to represent the brands. Camps often have up to thirty runners living together under the representation of one manager. Many runners from around the Rift Valley who hail from urban areas such as Nyahururu or Nakuru go to camps in these same cities, or opt to train at higher altitude in Kapsabet or Kaptagat. Alternatively, athletes may train in areas like Ngong Hills just outside Central Nairobi or further away in Machakos, southeast of Nairobi, or in Kisii, southwest of many camps in the Rift Valley. Eldoret, at 2,100 metres above sea level, is an urban area that serves as training hub for both aspiring and elite runners; Iten (dubbed the "Home of Champions") is located 40 kilometres north of Eldoret at an altitude of over 2,500 metres, to which thousands of runners move hoping to "make it" in distance running.
3 Appearing successful is also connected to friendship among Salvadorans on Long Island, New York (Mahler 1995) and Malagasy migrants in France (Cole 2014).
4 "Usefulness" and "uselessness" are important tropes in many African societies (Fioratta 2015; Kovač 2018).
5 Paul Tanui would later win the silver medal in the 10,000-metre race at the 2016 Rio Olympic Games and Bedan Karoki would finish seventh in the same race.

References

Ahearne, Robert M. 2016. "Development and Progress as Historical Phenomena in Tanzania: '*Maendeleo*? We Had That in the Past.'" *African Studies Review* 59, no. 1: 77–96.
Archambault, J. S. 2015. "Rhythms of Uncertainty and the Pleasures of Anticipation." In *Ethnographies of Uncertainty in Africa*, edited by David Pratten and Elizabeth Cooper, 129–148. New York: Palgrave Macmillan.
Besnier, Niko, Daniel Guinness, Mark Hann, and Uroš Kovač. 2018. "Rethinking Masculinity in the Neoliberal Age: Cameroonian Footballers, Fijian Rugby Players, Senegalese Wrestlers." *Comparative Studies in Society and History* 60, no. 4: 839–872.

Brown, Wendy. 2005. *Edgework: Critical Essays on Knowledge and Politics*. Princeton, NJ: Princeton University Press.

Cole, Jennifer. 2014. "The *Téléphone Malgache*: Transnational Gossip and Social Transformation among Malagasy Marriage Migrants in France." *American Ethnologist* 41, no. 2: 276–289.

Cornwall, Andrea. 2016. "Masculinities under Neoliberalism." In *Masculinities under Neoliberalism*, edited by Andrea Cornwall, Frank Karioris, and Nancy Lindisfarne, 1–28. London: Routledge.

Dube, Lucky. 2006. "Shut Up." *Respect*. Gallo Record Company. CD.

Fioratta, Susanna. 2015. "Beyond Remittance: Evading Uselessness and Seeking Personhood in Fouta Djallon, Guinea." *American Ethnologist* 42, no. 2: 295–308.

Gershon, Ilana. 2000. "How to Know When Not to Know: Strategic Ignorance When Eliciting Samoan Migrant Exchanges." *Social Analysis* 44, no. 2: 84–105.

Gershon, Ilana. 2011. "Neoliberal Agency." *Current Anthropology* 52, no. 4: 537–555.

Gershon, Ilana, and Allison Alexy. 2011. "The Ethics of Disconnection in a Neoliberal Age." *Anthropological Quarterly* 84, no. 4: 799–808.

Green, Maia. 2000. "Participatory Development and the Appropriation of Agency in Southern Tanzania." *Critique of Anthropology* 20, no. 1: 67–89.

Haugerud, Angelique. 1995. *The Culture of Politics in Modern Kenya*. Cambridge: Cambridge University Press.

Hunter, Emma. 2014. "A History of *Maendeleo*: The Concept of 'Development' in Tanganyika's Late Colonial Public Sphere." In *Developing Africa: Concepts and Practices in Twentieth Century Colonialism*, edited by Joseph Hodge, Martina Kopf, and Gerald Hoedl, 87–107. Manchester: Manchester University Press.

Hyden, Goran. 1987. "Capital Accumulation, Resource Distribution, and Governance in Kenya: the Role of the Economy of Affection." In *The Political Economy of Kenya*, edited by Michael Schatzberg, 117–136. New York: Praeger.

Jeske, Christine. 2016. "Are Cars the New Cows? Changing Wealth Goods and Moral Economies in South Africa." *American Anthropologist* 118, no. 3: 483–494.

Karp, Ivan. 2002. "Development and Personhood: Tracing the Contours of a Moral Discourse." In *Critically Modern: Alternatives, Alterities, and Ethnographies*, edited by Bruce Knauft, 82–104. Bloomington: Indiana University Press.

Kovač, Uroš. 2018. "The Precarity of Masculinity: Football, Pentecostalism, and Transnational Aspirations in Cameroon." Ph.D. dissertation, Amsterdam Institute of Social Science Research, University of Amsterdam.

Mahler, Sarah J. 1995. *American Dreaming: Immigrant Life on the Margins*. Princeton, NJ: Princeton University Press.

McGuigan, Jim. 2014. "The Neoliberal Self." *Culture Unbound* 6, no. 1: 223–240.

Meiu, George Paul. 2015. "'Beach-Boy Elders' and 'Young Big-Men': Subverting the Temporalities of Ageing in Kenya's Ethno-Erotic Economies." *Ethnos* 80, no. 4: 472–496.

Mercer, Claire. 2002. "The Discourse of *Maendeleo* and the Politics of Women's Participation on Mount Kilimanjaro." *Development and Change* 33, no. 1: 101–127.

Njororai, Wycliffe. 2010. "Global Inequality and Athlete Labour Migration From Kenya." *Leisure/Loisir* 34, no. 4: 443–461.

Prince, Ruth. 2013. "'Tarmacking' in the Millennium City: Spatial and Temporal Trajectories of Empowerment and Development in Kisumu, Kenya." *Africa* 83, no. 4: 582–605.

Rutten, Marcel, and Koki Muli. 2007. "The Migration Debate in Kenya." In *International Migration and National Development in Sub-Saharan Africa: Viewpoints and Policy Initiatives in the Countries of Origin*, edited by Aderanti Adepoju, Ton Van Naerssen, and Annelies Zoomers, 182–203. Leiden: Brill.

Shipton, Parker. 2007. *The Nature of Entrustment: Intimacy, Exchange, and the Sacred in Africa*. New Haven, CT: Yale University Press.

Shipton, Parker. 2009. *Mortgaging the Ancestors: Ideologies of Attachment in Africa*. New Haven, CT: Yale University Press.

Shipton, Parker. 2010. *Credit between Cultures: Farmers, Financiers, and Misunderstandings in Africa*. New Haven, CT: Yale University Press.

Sikes, Michelle, and Grant Jarvie 2014. "Women's Running as Freedom: Development and Choice." *Sport in Society* 17, no. 4: 507–522.

Silberschmidt, Margarethe. 1999. *Women Forget that Men Are the Masters: Gender Antagonism and Socio-Economic Change in Kisii district, Kenya*. Uppsala, Sweden: Nordiska Afrikainstitutet.

Smith, James Howard. 2008. *Bewitching Development: Witchcraft and the Reinvention of Development in Neoliberal Kenya*. Chicago: University of Chicago Press.

Smith, James Howard. 2012. "Saving Development: Secular NGOs, the Pentecostal Revolution and the Search for a Purified Political Space in the Taita Hills, Kenya." In *Pentecostalism and Development: Churches, NGOs and Social Change in Africa*, edited by Dena Freeman, 134–158. New York: Palgrave Macmillan.

Taylor, Georgina, Jane Wangaruro, and Irena Papadopoulos. 2012. "'It Is My Turn to Give': Migrants' Perceptions of Gift Exchange and the Maintenance of Transnational Identity." *Journal of Ethnic and Migration Studies* 38, no. 7: 1085–1100.

7

NEOLIBERALISM, MASCULINITY, AND SOCIAL MOBILITY IN CHINESE TENNIS

Matthew Haugen

In October 2018, while wandering the grounds of the China Open, a marquee tennis tournament that plays host to the world's top professional men, women, and juniors, I bumped into Daniel.[1] It had been nearly four years since we had last seen each other. I was surprised to learn he was using the week-long holiday to take a break from studying business at Shanghai Jiao Tong University, a highly respected institution, to provide colour commentary for Beijing TV during the week-long event and promote his newly launched fashion line. Daniel's path is atypical of the route that most of China's aspiring elite athletes take once their career ends. Many fall back on coaching, work as physical education teachers, become personal trainers, or, if lucky, obtain jobs in the sports bureaus. Daniel's career contrasts starkly with these other trajectories, but his story illustrates the dilemmas faced by aspiring tennis athletes in China, who must negotiate between traditional and current modes of masculinity, as well as between the state-supported sports system and the emerging market-based sports sector.

Like other aspects of the Chinese economy, the sport industries have developed by incorporating transnational forces and neoliberal economic principles into "socialism with Chinese characteristics," which refers to the infusion of capitalist market principles to spark economic growth while the state continues to hold the reins of political power. China's sports system reflects how neoliberalism is affecting the society as a whole, as the party dictates how to engage in global markets, which causes frictions since the economy is still 30% state-owned. Some China scholars argue that, because the Chinese state exercises strong oversight over its economic policies, it is less likely to engage in the same type of neoliberalism that has taken over developing countries where the state is weaker (Nonini 2008). Consequently, the state institutions that govern sport are unlikely to give up control of the elite sports training system, but they are trying to incorporate market characteristics into existing structures.

Thus, elite athletes in China who aim to make a living by competing in domestic and international competitions must now alter how they engage with an emerging free-market sports industry that is still controlled by the state. As neoliberal ideologies collide with those of the party state, China's athletes are required to become new subjects and reconfigure their social practices. China's elite athletes must reassess how they commodify their bodies (Besnier, Guinness, Hann, and Kovač 2018; Miller 1998), as they use their physical attributes to decide which sports system, state-supported or free market, provides them with the best opportunity to improve their status in society and to achieve geographic and social mobility.

To further complicate the situation, aspiring male athletes come into conflict with traditional Chinese notions of masculinity. Traditional masculinity was characterized by two poles, *wen*, or cultural attainment, and *wu*, or martial valour (Louie 2002); in its current iteration, *wen* is embodied by the scholar, *wu* by the athlete. As a legacy of Confucianism, throughout Chinese history, *wen* has generally been more valued than *wu*. Social accomplishment is closely associated with academic success and athletes are seen as second-class citizens, unless they achieve considerable international attention. The *wen-wu* distinction can also be understood in terms of social class: *wu* masculinity is that of the working-class manual labourer, while *wen* masculinity is that of the middle-class white-collar man. The attainment of knowledge gives one social standing, and educational success is a driving force of upward social mobility (Lee 1996). Thus, few middle-class families in China allow their children to participate in elite competitive sports, as they see education as the path to a better life, while sports are perceived as an activity that lower-class uneducated people engage in (Brownell 1995).

However, as neoliberal economies, transnational ideals, and the global sports industries encroach on Chinese society, the long-held perception that sport cannot be a path for future success is changing. Upward mobility into China's middle class is generally understood as predicated on four criteria: a high and stable income, a professional occupation, educational achievements, and the ability to consume (Chunling Li 2010; Song, Cavusgil, Li, and Luo 2016). Although educational achievement is the most commonly cited attribute needed for occupational attainment and higher income (Bian 2002; Chen and Qin 2014), in actuality the middle classes consist of citizens who became wealthy through private entrepreneurship, employment in foreign investment enterprises, and the management of state-run enterprises (Lieberthal 2010). China's middle classes are not yet fully formed and avenues for mobility are rapidly multiplying.

The emergent middle class is altering the way it engages with the international community by being active in an interdependent world and informed of transnational cultural currents (Cheng Li 2010). Sport is fast becoming an important industry to the Chinese state. Chinese people no longer associate it with the undereducated working classes and no longer reject the concept of marketization and commercialization of athletics (Chen and Han 2003). They are gradually recognizing that sport achievements can be a marketable commodity. Aspiring athletes themselves push against traditional stereotypes of the working-class sportsperson and see sport as a route to upward mobility. Some athletes choose a conservative route to upward mobility by utilizing traditional state-supported systems designed to bring glory to the nation through sporting success on the international scene, while other athletes choose a more individualistic transnational approach that capitalizes on the free-market economy.

The neoliberal reorganization of sport in China has had a profound effect on its institutions and athletes. As global sport industries integrate with China, athletes dream of success but must alter their pathways and develop innovative strategies to capture the commercial growth of the market. Having worked in China for six years as a tennis coach for both state-run provincial programmes and private academies, I have been privy to and part of the change. Athletes' transitions through a system that is being fundamentally altered by neoliberal economies has inspired my research. As China continues to engage in global sports industries, new social, economic, and geographic mobilities are emerging. Aspiring athletes must navigate the transnational changes to the Chinese sports industries and in doing so reconcile their place in a shifting sporting infrastructure (Figure 7.1).

FIGURE 7.1 An aerial view of the Nanjing Sport Institute and the Tennis Academy of China.
The world-class facility supports both the state-sponsored Jiangsu Provincial Tennis Team, and the independently run Sanchez-Casal Tennis Academy.
(Source: Jiang Hong Wei, Tennis Academy of China at the Nanjing Sport Institute)

State-supported sport and the neoliberal sport sector

Over the past 40 years, the development of the Chinese sports industries has reflected specific political, ideological, and policy objectives. After the Cultural Revolution ended in 1976, Deng Xiaoping announced in 1978 reforms designed to secure the place of China's economy in the world and reopen China to foreign investment and trade. These reforms modernized the country's agriculture, industry, education, science, and defence sectors and led to the establishment of a market economy while the central state continued to maintain strict authoritarian control. Deng also believed that success in international sport competitions would lead to greater international recognition of China's newfound strength and his sports policy emphasized building a positive international image of the country (Luo 1995). Citizens would find in Chinese athletes' international achievements a nationalist rallying cry and a renewed sense of patriotism, which would strengthen their faith in their country's socialist policies (Brownell 1995).

The Chinese state consolidated funding for sport under the State General Administration of Sport (SGAS) and developed a centralized system of provincial sports bureaus and training centres across the nation, known as *juguo tizhi*. Its primary concern was to produce elite athletes for national and Olympic teams. Behind every training centre was the ultimate goal of Olympic gold medals, glory for the nation, and the projection of soft power to the international community (Brownell 2008; Cha 2009; Hong, Wu, and Xiong 2005). The SGAS became a powerful centralized hierarchical organization that recruited and trained professional athletes.

At the Los Angeles 1984 Olympic Games, China had its first moment of international sport glory when the 353-person delegation took home 15 gold, 8 silver, and 9 bronze medals, finishing fourth in the overall medals tally (Luo 1995). From that moment, Olympic success became the mission of sport development in China. However, the 1984 Olympics did more than create a forum for nationalistic pride and patriotism. It was the first Olympic Games to be sponsored by large multinational corporations, which benefited by being able to advertise, and it was the first Games to return a profit. This commercial success encouraged China to infuse its own state sports system with Western capitalistic principles and stimulated the movement to host the Olympics on home soil (Brownell 2015).

Thirty years after the market reforms began, Beijing hosted the 2008 Olympic Games, which showcased its political, economic, and social achievements. Chinese athletes won 51 gold medals, more than any other country. China had finally arrived on the world stage, proved its physical prowess, and entered the era of globalization as a force to be respected. In addition, the Beijing 2008 Olympics did almost precisely for China what the Los Angeles 1984 Olympics had done for the United States, namely to reinforce its sports system as an economically driven enterprise. Investment in the sporting infrastructure and state sports policy leading up to the Beijing Olympics created an environment ripe for an emerging sports market (Brownell 2015).

Since 2008, the role of sport in Chinese society has been in the midst of an ideological shift (Haugen 2016). Like other industries, sport is now incorporating transnational forces and neoliberal rationalities into "socialism with Chinese characteristics" or, as Harvey (2005, 122) calls it, "privatization with Chinese characteristics." As the state-led sports industries integrate with transnational neoliberalism, a particular hybrid type of governance emerges, which in turn produces new subjectivities, forms of citizenship, and social practices (Brown 2005).

Elite athletes who aim to make a living by competing domestically and internationally must now change how they engage with an emerging free-market sports industry. Neoliberalism is creating new institutions, altering management structures, and changing developmental pathways by incorporating Western techniques while relying less on the state. Private sports academies have emerged, luring young talent to train using methods that differ from state-run programmes. Athletes who choose the privatized development system rather than the state-funded development system do so because they want more autonomy over their careers. All this is challenging traditional notions of social mobility, as previously the state system was the permanent fixture in supplying the career trajectory, salaries, and job placement for the nation's top athletes.

The state-run programmes and independent academies systems compete to recruit the best athletes. As a new middle class emerges, an increasing number of families of aspiring athletes have the means to choose between the two systems. The choice between the highly subsidized state-run programme and the more expensive private market is not an easy one for families. Both systems can involve rewards and risks, and athletic achievements can provide economic mobility, but failure can prove to be costly. Thus, the reform of the sports industries is opening new opportunities while simultaneously muddling preexisting state-supported routes to social and geographic mobility.

The transnational tennis system, social mobility, and gender

The state-funded system forms the backbone of development for China's tennis players and is managed by local sport bureaus in conjunction with the China Tennis Association (CTA). The CTA and the sport bureaus manage nearly every aspect of development pathway and athletes' training, including running domestic competitions, allocating coaches, setting schedules, directing the style of play, and providing salaries. In exchange for funding athletes' careers, the CTA and the sports bureaus keep part of the prize money that athletes win and the sponsorship money they earn. Before the 2000s, China's tennis players had little success on the international circuit. Only the most talented players were able to compete outside China, where they would be exposed to international training methods and to how international athletes structured their lives and careers.

In the early 2000s, the governance of the CTA came under criticism from an unlikely source, namely elite women players who, in contrast to their male colleagues, were successful on the international stage. When the doubles team of Li

Ting and Sun Tiantian won the gold medal at the Athens 2004 Olympic Games, China's bureaucratic sports powers began to realize female tennis players' international potential. However, female tennis stars were frustrated by having to fork over their earnings, being chaperoned by state officials while on tour, and having little control over their careers. They realized that, to succeed, they needed more support and independence than the CTA was willing to provide.

Both ranked top 40 in the world, Li Na and Peng Shuai, who had grown up in the state system and were bound to the contractual obligations of their provincial teams, became outspoken advocates of reforms. Their exposure playing on the Women's Tennis Association (WTA) international tour gave them insights into the arrangements that other highly ranked international athletes were operating under. They too wanted to have autonomy over their careers, be decision makers, and profit from the international market value of their athletic accomplishments. In December 2008, the CTA released from state control the nation's top four women's players, Li Na, Peng Shuai, Zheng Jie, and Yan Zi, according to a policy dubbed *danfei*, "fly solo." The players were allowed to choose which tournaments to play, which coaches to train with, and which corporate sponsors to sign up with. They also now kept a major share of their winnings (Yin 2010). After Li's 2011 French Open Singles title, CTA official Sun Jinfang was quoted as saying,

> We took many risks with this reform. When we let them fly, we didn't know if they would succeed. That they have now succeeded means our reform was correct. This reform will serve as a good example for reforms in other sports.
>
> *(Associated Press 2011)*

These events were the impetus for large-scale institutional changes to CTA policies, tournament structures, and coaching philosophies. They also recognized the right of all Chinese athletes to profit from their success, which is grounded in the neoliberal capitalist ideology to which China had now turned. Other reforms included inviting foreign tennis coaches to China in hope of incorporating Western coaching philosophies into the state-run system and developing homegrown talent. International coaching experts were assigned to provincial teams around the country and infused their system with new ideas, philosophies, and playing styles. This is the context in which I became head tennis coach of Hebei Province (Figure 7.2). While progressive, the policy of inviting coaches into China also allowed the state to maintain control over the players by keeping them at home while still giving them a taste of the international game. For Chinese tennis officials, it was a steep learning curve, as they began to understand what was needed to succeed in a global game.

The CTA incorporated other transnational reforms. In the late 1990s, China had hosted only one internationally sanctioned professional tournament, the Shanghai Heineken Open; in 2017 alone, it hosted 82 internationally sanctioned men's, women's, and junior competitions in more than 30 different cities (itftennis.

FIGURE 7.2 The author teaches tennis to children at the Hebei Provincial Sports Centre in Shijiazhuang.
(Source: Ma Tian)

com; Figure 7.3). The CTA saw these competitions as a way to expose Chinese players to international competition. In addition, each tournament provided localities opportunities for urban development, promoting tourism, creating economic investment through sponsorships, and bolstering ticket sales. The most notable of these tournaments are the China Open in Beijing, the Shanghai Masters, and since 2014 the Wuhan Open, which in 2017 attracted more than 18 corporate sponsors (Rossingh 2017b).

For those willing to take the risk of "flying solo," the rewards can be far greater than what the state can provide. Foreign investment in Chinese tennis has allowed domestic coaches to break away from provincial programmes and start independent academies. Independent agents of sports marketing companies such as IMG, Octagon, and Zou Sports now scour the Chinese countryside for the next great talent, securing sponsorships and investments for the players they sign up. For athletes who succeed, such as two-time grand slam champion Li, wealth and riches await. Li's sponsorships at the height of her playing career reached upwards of US$40 million a year from international brands such as Nike, Mercedes, and Rolex (Rossingh 2017a). Money, infrastructure, and human resources now fuel the game's popularity, which is changing how Chinese athletes are engaging with tennis.

The success of China's female tennis players has prompted a series of reforms. It was these women who first explored the idea of reexamining their human capital. The women who pushed for the transnationalization of tennis now drive change

FIGURE 7.3 A match between two junior female players in Nanjing, China. Sponsored in conjunction with the French Open, the winner of the tournament receives a wildcard into the Junior Grand Slam event held in Paris.
(Source: Jiang Hong Wei, Tennis Academy of China at the Nanjing Sport Institute)

in the sports industry, which has resulted in a system in which tennis athletes find it increasingly difficult to rely upon older forms of social support. Tennis players and their families are now confronted with choosing how to best structure their development. The pathway to success runs through multiple avenues, including independent tennis academies, coaches, agents, and sponsors, in addition to the original state-run programmes.

This array of choices also challenges how athletes navigate gender norms. China is still searching for its first male tennis superstar. As of the end of 2019, no Chinese man has ever ranked among the top 100 world players. In contrast, in 2017, six Chinese women were in the top 100, and more than 11 in the top 200 (https://www.wtatennis.com). The CTA hopes that the institutional changes will help China's men capitalize on the riches of its emerging sport market and break into the top 100 in the world rankings.

As China continues to develop its neoliberal economy, policies, commodities, people, and values continue to move in from the West. In particular, Chinese notions of masculinity are being challenged as global images of masculinity are emerging (Louie 2015). To succeed in a transnational global sport economy, Chinese men must compete with and defeat non-Chinese men in international competitions while contending with domestic ideologies of masculinity, in particular the idea that intellectual ability is more valued than physical strength.

Chinese men who pursue tennis as a profession push back against domestic stereotypes by affiliating themselves with sport, in which results are contingent on physical ability. Five elite male tennis players I got to know well illustrate how each navigated the transnational and neoliberal changes to the Chinese tennis industry, which affect traditional notions of masculinity. They must reconcile their place in a shifting infrastructure as they compete daily with other players for social mobility. As the country searches for its first male international tennis star, the five athletes' experiences showcase how male players are following the lead of female players to create social and geographic mobility through an international tennis career.

Five male professional tennis players

I first met Bo in May 2011, when I began working in Shijiazhuang for the Hebei provincial tennis team. The son of farmers from the outskirts of a neighbouring town, Xingtai, Bo was enrolled in a sports boarding school at the age of six because officials identified him as having athletic talent. He eventually joined the Xingtai city team, where he continued to train. However, his results were only subpar. At 14, when most promising athletes have already signed up with provincial programmes, he had not yet secured a spot. Furthermore, because sports boarding schools and provincial or municipal teams place little emphasis on academics, Bo did not score high enough on the national high-school entrance examination to afford him a spot at a good school, a prerequisite to social mobility. With his academic future in question, Bo's parents enrolled him in the state team as a paying player, which means that his family paid for contractual amenities in hope that he would earn a spot on a provincial team and eventually a contract. This method is usually necessary for players who are not particularly talented. Bo registered for the Hebei Province team, but his only guarantee was a place to practice and a chance to climb the ladder within the programme.

At the time, six male players were in training in Hebei and all but Bo had already signed long-term contracts with the team. Contracted (*gongfei* "state-supported") players are provided with a salary, training, coaching, expenses to take part in competitions, equipment, clothing, and room and board. SGAS funds state teams, but not all teams are funded at the same level and every player-support package is different, and becomes a recruitment tool to entice players to state teams.

The strategy that Bo's family adopted is financially risky but potentially rewarding. Bo's rural background disadvantaged him in a country where noticeable social and economic class divisions separate rural from urban citizens. Most notably, these divisions are bureaucratized through the *hukou* system, a household registration system that restricts rural-to-urban migration, ostensibly to regulate the distribution of the population, although it has not prevented the unofficial migration of many unskilled labourers to cities, who then have diminished access to social services such as education, health care, insurance, and welfare, one of the most pressing human rights issues in China.

Bo was always one of the hardest working players while I was coaching the team, in part because his results were a pathway to a paid contract. Finally, after four years with the Hebei team, his determination resulted in a contract and he was able to change his *hukou* from his hometown to the provincial capital, Shijiazhuang, and thus became eligible for city residence and welfare benefits. However, compared to most successful tennis players, his earnings were comparatively meagre. Bo's salary was the lowest on the team and he was given only a few opportunities to compete internationally. He had sacrificed formal education for an athletic career, which has made him unable to attend a university or find a job outside sport. In 2019, still with the Hebei team, Bo hoped that his athletic results would earn him favours with the Hebei Sports Bureau and enable him to aim for a career in the bureau once he retires from tennis. In the meantime, he was on contract with the team for at least another two years through the 2021 quadrennial National Games, China's largest domestic sports competition.

Bo's athletic ability did give him a clearer pathway to stability for his future. The family's investment in tennis has paid off. By acquiring a *hukou* in Hebei's capital, the province's most modern city, he will be able to secure a better job through the provincial team and state connections. The state-sponsored system of sport development worked for Bo. While it may not be a life that capitalizes on participation in a transnational free market, Bo has aligned himself with a state entity and may open up a position in a sport university at the end of his career.

Ricky, who also played for Hebei Province while I coached the team, followed a different pathway. He had grown up in Shijiazhuang, and like most state-supported Chinese athletes, was identified at an early age as having athletic talent, but unlike Bo he did not enrol in a sports boarding school but instead remained in academic schools until the age of 13. Living in Shijiazhuang, he was able to stay on the radar of the provincial sports leaders and was coached for free after school and on the weekends at the province training centre. At 13, Li faced a choice between academics or athletics. He took the national high-school examination but only earned a low score. In an educational testing system that tracks citizens toward jobs and social status according to their early examination results, the low score would have placed him into a lower-level high school and subsequently a low-tier university, and most likely a less specialized career with only moderate earnings potential. Athletes in China are often stereotyped as people who do not do well academically and have no choice but to pursue a sporting career. But Ricky had a solid athletic foundation and an excellent reputation as a tennis player, and his family signed a seven-year contract to play for the provincial team until the end of the 2013 National Games.

Like most players, in following this path, Ricky was relegated to competing within China. His results were not good enough for the provincial team to send him to competitions abroad. In spite of this, Ricky's goal was to medal at the National Games, which would bring him a salary increase, competition bonuses, and future promotion within the provincial sports bureaus. But more important to Ricky was to use his athletic results to enrol in a university. Athletes in China who place in the top three of a major domestic competition are allowed direct entry into a university without having to sit the entrance examination. This is called *mianshi*, or "exemption from examination." Unfortunately, Ricky never placed high enough in any national sanctioned competition. However, as a local who came through the system, and thanks to his amiable personality, work ethic, and leadership skills, he developed good *guanxi* "connections" with the Hebei leaders. The Hebei leaders arranged for him to be admitted at the Hebei Sports University, where he received his degree but was not required to attend classes. It is an open secret that many of China's sports stars graduate from sport universities without attending classes so that they can train for their team.

At the time of writing, Ricky is working as a tennis coach for the provincial team. Although the job is secure and enables him to continue developing *guanxi* and potentially become director, he struggles with his current position, feeling burned out from a lifetime of playing and stuck in a job with no options outside of sport. In 2012, he wanted to leave the team to enrol in Beijing Normal University, where he could have majored in a non-sport-related subject, but he was not able to score high enough on the entrance exam. Ricky's situation confines him to a life centred on sport.

Ricky's story illustrates the struggle that many Chinese athletes face upon retiring from sport. Although he would have liked to work in a non-sport-related field, he is stuck in sport because of his low academic achievements and his subpar athletic result limits him to a regular but stable job as a coach. As often happens with aspiring athletes, he was pushed to drop his academic pursuits and put all efforts into sports. While he struggles with being identified as an athlete and is beholden to that particular label, he has found a way to improve his social status far better than most athletes. Even though it is not the autonomy he would like from China's emerging neoliberal sport market, he has found some stability for the future.

In contrast, players who demonstrate talent can capitalize on the transnational shifts that are taking place in China's sport industries. One such player was Sunny, another player on the Hebei provincial team. He is the first-born son of a low-income family from a small village in Shanxi province, one of the poorest regions in China, best known for its pollution from the coal industry. Once Sunny was identified at a young age as having athletic talent, his family sent him to a small tennis academy in Langfang, Hebei. They understood that the schooling in their poorly resourced rural home province of Shanxi would put their son at a disadvantage, and that tennis was a better option.

In Langfang, Sunny trained under the tutelage of a former Hebei provincial coach, who had started one of China's first independent tennis academies. He also registered for the Hebei state-run team and competed for the province while utilizing Langfang as a training base. When I joined the Hebei team, Sunny was asked by the team director to move to Shijiazhuang to train full-time with the other provincial players under my supervision. This is an example of CTA's initial transnational reforms, which relied on foreign coaches to increase a player's exposure to international training methodologies.

During the three years during which I coached Sunny, his world junior ranking went from 1,000 in the world to top 100, and from the 2013–14 season he was China's second-ranked junior male. Given the dramatic improvement in his ranking, the Hebei team allowed Sunny to travel to international tournaments, a distinction allocated only to China's best athletes. He travelled to Europe, the United States, and other Asian countries, where he was exposed to players from different countries with diverse playing styles, an exposure essential to becoming a top-level tennis player on the international scene.

Sunny has continued to rise in the domestic and international ranks. In 2017, he placed third in the National Games in both singles and doubles. Shortly afterward, he was recruited into the national men's team, which paid for his travels to tournaments in return for a cut of his earnings. With the top three results in the National Games, he was also admitted to Beijing Sports University, the best sports university in China. He represents the school once a year in a university competition, but does not have to attend a full schedule of classes. His enrolment increases his chances of employment in Beijing once his playing career is finished. He has gained favour with local state sports officials who have arranged for him to change his *hukou*, a critical allocation for his family, most of whom have already moved to Beijing. A Beijing *hukou* will allow him to build upon the businesses that his family has started in the city.

Perhaps most important, Sunny's results at the National Games earned him a substantial bonus from the Hebei team in the tens of thousands of dollars and a six-figure endorsement deal with a domestic sports agency. Only 23 years old and with a career-high ranking of 368 in the world in singles and 223 in doubles, he still has time to reach the top 100 and earn the money and fame that comes with such rankings. At the time of writing, according to atptour.com, his career prize earnings were US$131,231. Chinese athletes like Sunny seek to capitalize on their international celebrity and access global sponsorships and marketing deals that far surpass what the state can offer. However, because Sunny is not completely independent of the state-run system, he is required to hand over a percentage of his earnings to the Hebei team in exchange for the athletic development they provided.

Sunny demonstrates how a player can improve his social status far beyond what he could have achieved through schooling. He has utilized the state-run development system to move from Shanxi to Shijiazhuang and then to Beijing, and has emerged in a much better position economically by capitalizing on the hybrid type of marketization that is integrating itself into the state-run athletic programmes.

However, not all athletes have to rely on sport to provide them a stable future. Daniel came from an affluent family, which had introduced him to the game because of its potential social benefits, specifically the well-connected social circles of state sports cadres. He was tall and strong, spoke perfect English, and had the physical attributes and talent to succeed; as a youth, he was widely considered one of the best players in the country. Like his contemporaries, he was recruited into the state-run system and then into the Beijing Men's provincial team, which gave him access to foreign coaches, international travel to competitions, membership in China's national junior team, and a relatively high salary for someone his age.

His family had seen a potentially lucrative future if Daniel could succeed in the international game of tennis. However, the family also understood that men's professional tennis is competitive and careers are short, so they made sure that Daniel was homeschooled during his training. Because the state sports programmes often neglect the education of its athletes, at approximately 12–13 years old, his family employed a private tutor.

When Daniel started having problems with his wrist early in his career, he took a different approach from most athletes in China, who are told to play through the pain and endure hardship for the nation. He ended his contractual agreement with the Beijing team and sat the university entrance examination. As is customary at universities that field sports teams and seek to recruit elite athletes, he was awarded additional points to his score, and his combined academic and sport scores gave him admission to Shanghai Jiao Tong University, and from there he started a fashion and design business. He remains in the public spotlight by providing television commentary on major tennis events for Beijing's sports network.

Daniel's route differs from that of most retired athletes who do not have the educational background or means to find a job outside sports. Daniel has the social means, the educational background, and the strong connections with state officials that he built as an athlete. This is important because state policymakers are now advocating for outgoing professional athletes to capture the transnational nature of China's new commercial sports market though self-employment (State General Administration of Sport 2015). Daniel was successful in balancing athletics and academics and thus was a rare case of someone who was able to combine separate and distinct fields of social achievement. Daniel's pathway is a potential model for other middle-class families as they search for mobility through both sport and education, but of course this is predicated on being born into a privileged family in the first place.

One athlete illustrates another path to social mobility, namely transnational geographical mobility through sport. Aiden was born in an affluent family in Tianjin, northern China, a city of almost 20 million people. Like most children, he was enrolled at a young age in a regular school where he learned basic literacy and numeracy. He was an active boy and to harness his energy his parents kept him occupied by enrolling him in sports programmes. He started playing tennis at age seven, and his parents quickly realized he had talent.

For the next three years, Aiden remained in a traditional school and trained on the side. At 10, because he did not show an interest in education, his parents enrolled him in a spare-time sports school (*tiyu xuexiao*), which the Chinese state has set up for children with athletic talent, many of whom eventually become professional athletes. Having been identified as one of the top prospects in the region, Aiden signed up to train with the Tianjin Provincial Sports Bureau, for which his family had to pay, but this enabled them to control the terms and conditions of his training. He eventually stopped school, training with the tennis team six days a week, but his family paid for a private tutor.

Aiden progressed, but was not the best athlete on the team. Along the way, he met a Taiwanese-American coach, Alex. Concerned that Aiden might fall behind his Chinese counterparts and end up being ignored by the Tianjin team, Alex suggested that he consider training in the United States. At 14, Aiden moved to California to train at a private academy, which his father was able to afford thanks to his lucrative business. In the new training environment, Aiden had to adapt to an entirely new way of thinking. He lived with a host family that helped him learn English and become familiar with life in the United States. He now played sport in his new setting and went to school for half of the day. Aiden's family hoped he would be able to obtain a high-school diploma and obtain an athletic scholarship at a university in the United States.

After three years of training in the United States, Aiden applied to universities. His grades were adequate, his athletic achievements were good, and he did get the athletic scholarship the family had hoped for. However, he was still on contract with the Tianjin government team, which did not want to cut ties with him, so he and his family restructured a second contract with the team that allowed him to continue playing and studying in the United States, but would still require him to compete for the province when needed. His transition to university life was not seamless, as he found his studies strenuous and the new team dynamics challenging. In 2017, he was the only Chinese student athlete on the athletic rosters at his university and only one of two Chinese athletes playing in NCAA Division 1 tennis. In many ways, Aiden is a pioneer.

Aiden's story differs from the four previous stories in that he mobilized international sports migration as a sports career pathway in large part thanks to his family's financial status. In many ways, a merger is taking place as neoliberal ideology is incorporated into Chinese society, especially as it relates to both sport and education. While Chinese students are flocking to U.S. universities, very few are admitted as student athletes: in 2018, of the more than 300,000 Chinese students studying at U.S. universities, only 82 were competing in Division 1 and 2 athletics across all sports (https://www.ncaa.com). Aiden's ability to use sport as a way to enter a university gives him a distinct advantage in finding a job in China or abroad. His story illustrates how young Chinese athletes with means can mobilize both academics and athletics through international geographic mobility.

Duelling sports developmental models and masculinities

As a new generation of athletes takes up sport in China, they are faced with a complex tension between two worlds of sports development and two models of masculinity. Success in tennis can turn an athlete into an international marketing mogul; but athletes must decide what route to success they should take, and this choice is in large part dependent on their class background, as elite athletes depend on their families' resources. They must choose between the private programmes that have emerged since economic liberalization and the traditional provincial programmes supported by the state. The two-track system forces them to question how to reconcile the potential risks of "flying solo" in the new system of tennis development with navigating the state-run system. Further complicating the situation, players must navigate between competing images of masculinity, the traditionally valued image of intellectual masculinity and the image of physical masculinity, traditionally devalued but increasingly seen as a path to upward mobility.

Chinese athletes examine how they engage with an evolving transnational sports industry. They now see themselves as atomized economic subjects whose every action is an "investment" in the future (Figure 7.4). Economic reforms have created wide-scale institutional changes in the tennis industry, which have lasting implications and open up new avenues of upward mobility, in a society where mobility is the object of obsessive attention. The neoliberal political and economic reforms have created new social formations, and individuals have re-examined long-standing cultural assumptions about masculinity.

The stories I have presented illustrate how athletic development intersects with personal circumstances to produce distinctly different outcomes in social and geographic mobility. Each player's journey encompasses many variables embedded in

FIGURE 7.4 Aspiring players participating in an event called the Road to Wimbledon, held at the Tennis Academy of China in Nanjing.
The players have a chance to test their tennis skills on the grass and can dream of playing on the world's biggest stage.
(Source: Jiang Hong Wei, Tennis Academy of China at the Nanjing Sport Institute)

China's historical, cultural, and political context. As transnational forces bring new values to the country, these five athletes and many others like them must analyze their position in the broader context as they try to create a better life through sport. However, there is one crucial similarity in their stories, namely the fact that they all relied, to various extents, on the state-run system as a platform to launch their sports careers. All five athletes began their athletic careers in the late 1990s, before the 2008 Beijing Olympic Games and before sports took off as a commercial market-driven venture.

Chinese athletes who started their sporting careers after the Olympic Games have a much broader array of opportunities. Athletic academies are opening all over the country to meet a growing domestic market. Those with money, power, and influence often bypass the domestic sports system entirely by going directly to foreign countries for athletic training. Although there is growing commercial market for sport, the state-run system still provides meaningful programming and development pathways. Not all aspiring athletes in China have the luxury of choice, and thus entry into the state-run system is an opportunity for many families to improve their social standing through athletic accomplishments. In fact, because of its long-standing history of success in producing international champions, the state-run system remains the pathway that most athletes prefer. This is due to the formative investment from the state in an athletes' career, rather than financial investment by family, which mitigates the potential risk of flying solo. But as China's professional women's tennis players have showcased, the line between government support and open market value is quickly being blurred.

One important element in the transformation of Chinese professional tennis was the important role that women athletes played in bringing about this transformation. Although women are often objectified and sexualized, and told they cannot run, jump, or compete at the same level as men, female Chinese tennis players were some of the first to reap the rewards of the neoliberalized sports industry. The women's tennis players in China have shown great resolve in recognizing, reimagining, and recreating themselves to succeed as modern athletes.

As neoliberal economic reforms in China continue to reshape the sports industry and its institutions, a complicated relationship has formed that affects the development of sport. Athletes who vie to utilize sport as a path to social and geographical mobility navigate the changing configuration of gender, social class, education, and institutional management structures, as well as their own physical and intellectual limits, searching for ways to reimagine their bodies. While China's sporting context is somewhat unique, it is also changing rapidly. Like athletes everywhere, Chinese athletes must deal with the unpredictable nature of sport. Uncertainty lies at every corner, and the athletes who make it to the highest echelons need luck to get to the top. The changes, risks, and uncertainties have not stopped millions of Chinese athletes from trying to become professionals, as they chase dreams of cashing in on China's new commercial sports market and the elusive glory of international superstardom.

Acknowledgements

This chapter is an offshoot of a dissertation project on formal education and sport in China's shifting neoliberal sports industries, funding for which was provided by the Fulbright Commission. I appreciate the comments from Niko Besnier and Susan Brownell on earlier drafts.

Note

1 All names are pseudonyms.

References

Associated Press. 2011. "Li Na Tops Francesca Schiavone for Title." *ESPN Magazine*, 4 June 2011. http://espn.go.com/espn/print?id=6625484andtype=HeadlineNewsandimagesPrint=off.

Besnier, Niko, Daniel Guinness, Mark Hann, and Uroš Kovač. 2018. "Rethinking Masculinity in the Neoliberal Age: Cameroonian Footballers, Fijian Rugby Players, Senegalese Wrestlers." *Comparative Studies in Society and History* 60, no. 4: 839–872.

Bian, Yanjie. 2002. "Chinese Social Stratification and Social Mobility." *Annual Review of Sociology* 28:91–116.

Brown, Wendy. 2005. *Edgework: Critical Essays on Knowledge and Politics*. Princeton, NJ: Princeton University Press.

Brownell, Susan. 1995. *Training the Body for China: Sport in the Moral Order of the People's Republic*. Chicago: University of Chicago Press.

Brownell, Susan. 2008. *Beijing's Games: What the Olympics Mean to China*. Lanham, MD: Rowman & Littlefield.

Brownell, Susan. 2015. "Why 1984 Medalist Li Ning Lit the Flame at the Beijing 2008 Olympics: The Contribution of the Los Angeles Olympics to China's Market Reforms." *International Journal of the History of Sport* 32, no. 1: 128–143.

Cha, Victor. 2009. *Beyond the Final Score: The Politics of Sport in Asia*. New York: Columbia University Press.

Chen, Chen, and Bo Qin. 2014. "The Emergence of China's Middle Class: Social Mobility in a Rapidly Urbanizing Economy." *Habitat International* 44 (October): 528–535.

Chen, Yuqing, and Xiangping Han. 2003. "The Professional Athletes' Economic Value in China: A Thought on the Theory of Human Resource." *Theory and Practice of Finance and Economics* 24, no. 126: 114–116.

Harvey, David. 2005. *A Brief History of Neoliberalism*. Oxford: Oxford University Press.

Haugen, Matthew. 2016. "The Changing National and Political Role of Chinese Sports, 1949–2016." *Education about Asia* 21, no. 2: 49–53.

Hong Fan, Wu Ping, and Xiong Huan. 2005. "Beijing Ambitions: An Analysis of the Chinese Elite Sports System and Its Olympic Strategy for the 2008 Olympic Games." *International Journal of the History of Sport* 22, no. 4: 510–529.

Lee, Wing O. 1996. "The Cultural Context for Chinese Learners: Conceptions of Learning in the Confucian Tradition." In *The Chinese Learner*, edited by David A. Watkins and John B. Biggs, 25–41. Hong Kong: Comparative Education Research Centre and Australian Council for Educational Research.

Li, Cheng. 2010. "Introduction: The Rise of the Middle Class in the Middle Kingdom." In *China's Emerging Middle Class: Beyond Economic Transformation*, edited by Li Cheng, 3–31. Washington, DC: Brookings Institution Press.

Li, Chunling. 2010. "Characterizing China's Middle Class: Heterogeneous Composition and Multiple Identities." In *China's Emerging Middle Class: Beyond Economic Transformation*, edited by Li Cheng, 135–156. Washington, DC: Brookings Institution Press.

Lieberthal, Kenneth G. 2010. "Foreword." In *China's Emerging Middle Class: Beyond Economic Transformation*, edited by Li Cheng, xi–xiv. Washington, DC: Brookings Institution Press.

Louie, Kam. 2002. *Theorising Chinese Masculinity: Society and Gender in China*. Cambridge: Cambridge University Press.

Louie, Kam. 2015. *Chinese Masculinities in a Globalizing World*. London: Routledge.

Luo, Ping. 1995. "Political Influence on Physical Education and Sport in the People's Republic of China." *International Review for the Sociology of Sport* 30, no. 1: 47–60.

Miller, Toby. 1998. "Commodifying the Male Body, Problematizing 'Hegemonic Masculinity?'" *Journal of Sport and Social Issues* 22, no. 4: 431–446.

Nonini, Donald M. 2008. "Is China Becoming Neoliberal?" *Critique of Anthropology* 28, no. 2: 145–176.

Rossingh, Danielle. 2017a. "Li Na Land, Reality TV and Fashion: What China's Tennis Pioneer Did Next." *CNN*, 24 March 2017. www.cnn.com/2017/03/30/tennis/li-na-china-business-career/index.html.

Rossingh, Danielle. 2017b. "Why the Chinese Tennis Revolution Is Only Just Beginning." *Forbes*, 29 September 2017. www.forbes.com/sites/daniellerossingh/2017/09/29/why-the-chinese-tennis-revolution-is-only-just-beginning/#591a4b6a3f00.

Song, Jing, Erin Cavusgil, Jianping Li, and Ronghua Luo. 2016. "Social Stratification and Mobility among Chinese Middle Class Households: An Empirical Investigation." *International Business Review* 25, no. 3: 646–656.

State General Administration of Sport. 2015. "Guanyu jinyibu zuo hao tuiyi yundongyuan jiuye anzhi gongzuo de yijian" (Opinions on further improving the placement of retired athletes). State General Administration of Sport website, 13 May 2015. http://sports.people.com.cn/n/2015/0513/c22176-26996220.html.

Yin, Pumin. 2010. "A Rising Sport." *Beijing Review*, 10 November 2010. www.bjreview.com/print/txt/2010–11/01/content_308463.htm.

PART II

Reconstituting subjectivities

8

FIJIAN RUGBY WIVES AND THE GENDERING OF GLOBALLY MOBILE FAMILIES

Daniel Guinness and Xandra Hecht

Ani sat staring at the laptop screen waiting for Waqa, her husband, to appear online.[1] She took a sip of her hot sweet tea and thumbed through the pages of her well-worn Bible until she came to the previous day's reading. Their Skype conversations and Bible study in the cool of the Fijian morning had been the core of their marriage for the past two years. She would recount the daily events from their home near Suva, the capital of Fiji, he would tell her about the trials and tribulations of life as a professional rugby player in France. They would discuss plans, read verses from the Bible, and pray together that God would give them strength and guidance. Often their three children, aged between two and seven, would join the conversation after the prayers to greet their father. The virtual connection maintained the relationship, but also reminded her of the difficult marriage they were living at a distance.

Waqa had been contracted to European clubs since before they met, and they had lived together in England for the first five years of their marriage. This began to change three years ago when Waqa signed a contract with a French club. His salary was higher, but the family struggled to settle into the provincial French town where few people spoke English. Ani had become increasingly isolated at home with the children, unable to speak French, and with little support or friendship around her.

They also worried about their future. Waqa was in his thirties and his agent was already discussing "his final playing contract." After six months of prayer and deliberation, Ani took the family back to Fiji to use their savings to start businesses in Suva, where they calculated that their money would not dissipate meeting the endless requests for support from the famous player's extended family in the village.

But things had not been easy. The small taxi business she ran did not earn enough to pay their expenses in Fiji and the crops of *yaqona* (kava, a root that is pounded to make a popular traditional drink) and ginger were not ready for harvest from their gardens in the village. They continued to rely on his rugby salary. But rugby careers are uncertain and, after two years, Waqa's club did not renew his contract.

He was left without a job or salary, alone overseas, and unable to support his young family. He lived on the couch of a Fijian family in France, living off their generosity and the meals that former teammates would occasionally buy him. Ani cut back on household spending. They prayed every day that another contract would come soon. It had been a hard few months.

This morning, however, was different. She woke to find a text message that ignited all her hopes and fears at once. "Our faith has been rewarded. You can come back to France."

Waqa's face appeared on the Skype window. In his excitement he blurted out the news in a flurry of high-pitched exclamations incongruous with his gigantic 120 kg frame. The words released so great a wave of relief, excitement, and apprehension through her body that she had to ask him to repeat his story. "I have a new contract" he repeated, "They pay the house, and car, and [airline] tickets for the family. And they pay our debts in Fiji and France. The [club] president flew in today and signed a cheque for forty thousand euros."

Skype conversations, uncertainty, and absence are a frequent experience of many women in relationships with Fijian professional rugby players. These women experience a drastically different form of marriage from most other Fijian women. Ani spent many years apart from Waqa, caring for her young family and managing the household business interests in Fiji. During these periods, their marriage relied on virtual communication. Her life was for a long time defined by recurring collective decisions about whether to follow her husband's international career and leave Fiji or remain within the social world of Fiji but apart from her husband, a compromise between mobility and absence that is characteristic of transnational kinship in modern Fiji.

Women who marry or are in relationships with Fijian rugby players are often torn between seeing rugby as a blessing or a curse. Many women desire rugby players, who are physically fit men, emblematic of a prestigious form of Fijian masculinity, and part of one of the few industries that offers lucrative careers and pathways overseas (Presterudstuen 2010; Teaiwa 2005). The women who marry them are able to access resources and lifestyles rarely available otherwise. However, their lives and desires are often inhibited by their husbands' rugby aspirations, both those that are fulfilled and those that they pursue in vain. Many wives like Ani are left carrying on a life in Fiji with an absent husband. Others see household resources and a large part of their husband's time, energy, and hope gradually consumed by his pursuit of a rugby dream that is never realized.

Fijian rugby players see the possibilities of their careers as a source of national pride, for they show what they are capable of achieving on a global scale. Almost all prominent athletes are Indigenous Fijians or *i-Taukei* (currently 54% of the population of 875,000), and their success is regarded as part of the supposed naturalness of Indigenous Fijian moral and physical strength. Many understand successful migration as the result of a mixture of genetic endowment, God-given talent, and Fijian history, values, and communalism (Kanemasu and Molnar 2013a; Guinness

2018). Aspiring rugby players engage in multiyear projects of self-improvement, drawing on family structures and religious motivation (Besnier, Guinness, Hann, and Kovač 2018; Guinness 2018; Hann, this volume; Kovač, this volume). Since it was professionalized globally in 1995, rugby has taken on added significance as a source of employment and geographic and social mobility. This quickly led to increased opportunities for Fijian athletes to be paid, and there are now Fijian men playing at all levels of the sport's international hierarchy, from the top tiers occupied by Britain, Wales, France, and New Zealand to countries in the lower tiers, such as Japan, Romania, Sri Lanka, and the United States (Schieder 2014). Some athletes can earn upwards of €20,000 a month, over 30 times the average monthly income in Fiji of F$17,000 (€585). The most successful players are famous, wealthy, and respected as athletes, providers for families, and unofficial ambassadors of their villages and the Fijian nation (Guinness and Besnier 2016). However, like sport migrations in general (Besnier 2014; Besnier and Brownell 2012), rugby migration is gendered and contingent on careers that are fragile and ephemeral. In an industry increasingly driven by neoliberal logics of individual talent, and with information and opportunity asymmetries during contract negotiations, the reality is that the majority of would-be professionals are recruited to amateur clubs, rugby academies, or even high school teams for little or no pay, and may become unemployed at short notice, as was the case with Waqa.

Athletes' careers are often not individual projects, but rather the culmination of years of training supported materially and emotionally by extended kin. As is typical in global capitalist systems, athletes' wives and mothers are part of the (hidden) work of social reproduction that subsidizes the global rugby industry, shifting the risks and responsibilities for social reproduction on to families and particularly women (Kanemasu and Molnar 2014; Borenstein, this volume; more generally, Federici 1999). Many players' wives travel overseas with their partners, while others remain in Fiji to raise families or maintain local careers. Either way, their husbands' participation in the global rugby industry has consequences for the way they think about, practice, and experience kinship.

Even in the sporting industries that remain dominated by men, women can play central roles in supporting and guiding the efforts of their sons, brothers, and husbands. We draw upon data gathered during fieldwork by Guinness in multiple research projects on Fijian rugby since 2011 in Fiji, New Zealand, Australia, and France, and a series of interviews conducted by Hecht in Fiji. We refer to seven women directly, five of whom are *i-Taukei*, one of mixed *i-Taukei* and Indo-Fijian background, but raised in what she describes as *i-Taukei* family setting and values, and one French. We have predominantly focused on the experiences of the *i-Taukei* women whose husbands are playing in France. However, even among the *i-Taukei* women, there is significant variation, particularly in terms of educational attainment, career, position in chiefly hierarchies, and prior experience overseas. In addition, many are themselves engaged in projects to achieve something from the neoliberal system in which they and their athlete partners are immersed (whether this be a good family life, a happy marriage, a career, or other goals).

To understand the global rugby industry, we need to grasp how it combines with the social systems in which its athletes (and others) are enmeshed, in this case the Indigenous Fijian social structures, based on kinship, a variety of "traditional" and modern values, and the strong but changing influence of different Christian churches. Different ideologies, value systems, and social structures come together in ways that reinforce and support one another, as illustrated by the emotional solace that Christian faith and practices provide to Fijian athletes and families to persevere during difficult moments in careers, such as those faced by Ani and Waqa (Besnier, Guinness, Hann, and Kovač 2018; Guinness 2018; Hann, this volume; Kovač, this volume). Yet, these ideologies, values, and structures often also combine in ways that produce tensions and conflicting priorities, and through these contestations and ideological imperatives reshape kinship systems, religious communities, and global industries (Hossain, this volume; Calabrò, this volume). In that sense, rugby is part of a globalization process that has a profound effect on Fijian gender dynamics.

Indigenous Fijian kinship systems are adapting to the possibilities and restrictions of modernity. Increasing numbers of Fijians live away from the close-knit hierarchical village communities and communal economies that are at the core of many Indigenous conceptions of kinship. Individuals can benefit from the possibilities of salaried employment in regional centres, often sharing these resources with their families, villages, and churches, but also investing in their own houses, material possessions, and urban lifestyles. But these new lives are not independent of kinship relations, as homes can become staging points for relatives who visit the cities to seek employment or trade village goods, and those who eventually migrate to the city often settle in the same suburbs. But these new forms of employment and housing do afford different modes of interaction, more isolated from neighbours, with more possibilities for freedom from the observation of chiefs, extended families, and religious leaders.

The mobility of rugby players and families is also an expression of a migratory disposition that has emerged among Indigenous Fijians. In the late twentieth century, most emigrants were Indo-Fijians (the second largest ethnic group, currently 38% of the population), often for a mixture of economic, social, and political reasons tied to ongoing divisions in Fijian society with colonial antecedents (Voigt-Graf 2008).[2] It was only at the turn of the millennium that i-Taukei began to leave Fiji in increasingly large numbers, seeking opportunities in the global labour market (Mohanty 2006), in ways that parallel patterns extant in nearby Tonga and Samoa (Besnier 2011; Macpherson and Macpherson 2010; Lee 2009). These mobilities are "culturally informed, historically grounded responses to modernity and globalization" (Lilomaiava-Doktor 2009, 1). In Fiji, they are gendered, with Indigenous men largely moving as manual labourers (for instance as seasonal agricultural workers in Australia), while women are moving as educated professionals, particularly nurses and teachers. For i-Taukei men, rugby and the military represent rare avenues for both geographical and social mobility (Teaiwa 2008).

Transnationalism opens up possibilities for changes in social relations by enabling new social and economic structures for families. Transnational families are forming in ways that can both preserve and challenge traditional family structures. Migration flows create a family that may not experience many of the everyday practices and interactions (and tensions) of families in daily physical contact (Baldassar and Merla 2014). Relationships can now be maintained across international borders through virtual communication and remittances. However, when one member is physically absent, many forms of caring for kin rely upon physical proximity – preparing food, supervising children, and attending social functions – in ways that require a renegotiation of care in broader networks of kin (Wall and Bolzman 2014). For rugby families, these negotiations take place in ways that reveal the intersection of traditional norms with the social, political, and economic contexts of the transnational social field (Levitt and Glick Schiller 2004).

Rugby's construction of gendered spaces

Rugby is a national obsession in Fiji, but it is largely dominated by men. A growing number of women play rugby, but they remain marginalized in both the sport and society at large. However, women play a crucial role in facilitating Fijian success in the global rugby industry. They are the unseen workers preparing meals for husbands, sons, and their teammates, and the foundation of emotional support that enables husbands and sons to persevere through years without financial returns.

Rugby was originally introduced to Fiji by British colonial agents, including military officers, police commanders, and the schoolmasters of prestigious all-boys' schools. Today, it has been Indigenized by i-Taukei to such an extent that it now plays an important symbolic and social role in the performance and naturalization of a particular "Fijian" way of being. Fijians regard rugby as founded on and showcasing Indigenous values, particularly values of masculinity (Dewey 2014). As in neighbouring Tonga and Samoa (Besnier 2012; Clément 2014), village greens and urban spaces are the daily scene of impromptu and loosely structured games of touch rugby involving most boys and young men of the village; games that are important sites of gendered socialization in which younger boys learn what it means to be a man from their older brothers and cousins.

Even these casual games tend to be exclusively among men. Some girls participate in children's games, but very few carry it on later in life. Those who continued to play the sport are stereotyped as lesbians or transgender and subjected to widespread social scorn and occasional violence for violating gender norms (Kanemasu and Molnar 2013b, 2017). There are signs that these gender norms may be changing after a Fijian women's rugby 7s team competed in the 2016 Rio Olympics, supported through rugby promotion, academic conferences, and international NGO investment. However, without exception, the i-Taukei women discussed in this chapter regard rugby as a sport played by men.

Rugby is centred on two types of location, both almost exclusively occupied by men. The first are the training grounds, village greens, and beaches where men focus their passion on evening games and long hours of training to refine their skills and build their bodies. The second are the woven grass mats laid out on the living room floors and on the cement blocks of verandas of the senior players and coaches, where athletes discuss tactics, training, fundraising, professional matches, and their lives outside of rugby while taking turns drinking bowls of *yaqona*.

At the hard, dusty field where Guinness spent most of his time training while in Fiji, no women join the large games of touch rugby that draw boys and men from the neighbourhood. In fact, the entire space around the training ground was dominated by Indigenous men: young men training with coaches, a few older men watching from the edge of the pitch, men of all ages playing touch rugby at the end of the field, male security guards at a neighbouring building site, and young men gambling at the edge of the youth centre that overlooked the ground. Even the groups of Indo-Fijians who assembled outside the mosque situated near the field's southern end were predominantly men. On the only occasion that Guinness saw a woman engage with the training men, she tried to catch someone's attention by quietly calling out from alongside an electrical pole that stood about 30 metres from the field's furthest corner, rather than coming closer. Women do attend weekend matches and can be exuberant supporters, screaming support from the grandstands and jumping excitedly when their team performs well.

The second important activity for Fijian rugby is the informal *talanoa* (discussion, storytelling) that occurs daily in the living rooms and verandas of players' and managers' houses. It is in these informal discussions that plans are made for the on-field and off-field direction of the club and its players: conversations can cover training regiments and the performance of the coaching staff, fundraising plans for developments of the club or support of a family in need, negotiation of the social and political dynamics of the club, and, depending on who is present, a lot of jokes and stories. Often the *talanoa* carry on well into the night, accompanied by food, usually prepared by the host's wife, and generous servings of *yaqona*. On some occasions, women join in with the conversations, but this tends to be in closer family circles and small group settings. During these large group discussions, living rooms become male–dominated space, with the wives or other female relatives mainly entering the room in order to deliver the bowls of noodles or plates of cassava with curried meat that they prepare for the visiting men.

Providing for others, especially through the preparation of food, is a common expression of *loloma* (care, love, empathy) and according to traditional gender roles remains predominantly women's work. Fijians regard *loloma* as important and necessary to produce an individual's body, mind, character, and relationship with God. In villages, Fijians are taught to behave in ways that reflect positively on the family and community. For instance, in Vugalei village, elders stated that a complete person is expected to know how to perform custom (*na i-tovo vaka-vanua*), to appropriately cultivate relationships (*na veiwekani*) through food sharing, gift giving, and care, to be fluent in formal and informal local forms of the language (*na noda vosa vaka-Vugalei*), and to cultivate a relationship with God (*na veiwekani kei na Kalou*) (Nabobo-Baba 2006, 76–92). People praise characteristics such as *vakarokoroko* (respect), *yalomalua* (humility), *veiqaravi* (service), *dauloloma* (mutual compassion), *dauyalovinaka* (having a good heart), *dau talairawarawa* (dutiful, obedient), and *daugalu tu ga* (always having a quiet disposition). These same values and connections with village and family identities remain important for Fijians living in urban areas and even internationally.

Conceptions of traditional gender roles, themselves a partial invention of colonialism and missionization, promote the sense for women of their obligation both to husband and family and also to the church and broader community. In most families, whether in cities or rural settings, women do the bulk of domestic labour. Men, especially elders and those of high-ranking clans, are respected and deferred to in decisions about community because of their wisdom and spiritual power to maintain harmonious community (Toren 1990). These divisions are reinforced by most Christian denominations. In their sermons, Methodists encourage wifely submission and the sanctity of marriage, and Pentecostals and Catholics sanctifying male leadership (George 2015). Women are expected to be the backbone of the church, performing much of the work of organizing and preparing, but rarely occupy leadership positions or even sit in prominent positions within the church (Varani-Norton 2005, 240). Before church meetings or community gatherings, women prepare the food, gifts, and decorations and afterwards do most of the cleaning up.

Where women are working in market gardens or employed in the formal economy, they are expected to carry out these additional tasks without reducing either the quality or quantity of their domestic labour. They take great pride in this. In general, i-Taukei men have more time for *talanoa* over *yaqona* and are far more likely to have the free time available for recreational activities, such as playing rugby.

Successful men are regarded as being the products of families and communities in very direct ways and their success attributed to their inheritance from kin and the years of *loloma*. In the case of rugby players, it is widely believed that success comes from a combination of physical (e.g. size, strength, speed), mental (e.g. focus, good attitude, discipline, respect for coaches) and spiritual (e.g. faithfulness, being blessed by God with talents, good fortune) characteristics, all of which can be traced back to a good upbringing through community and faith, inheritance from kin and ancestors, and *loloma* (Guinness 2018). It is through *loloma* that mothers play such an important role in creating successful rugby athletes, although the bodies produced through *loloma* may be fatter than desired by professional rugby clubs, as is the case for the Ethiopian women runners and other elite athletes (Borenstein, this volume). Successful young men widely recognize and publicly celebrate the role that their mothers have had on creating opportunities for their success. This routinely resulted in athletes, particularly young unmarried men, sending large sums of their earnings to their mothers, who later distributes these remittances to other relatives or the local church, or invests them in village and family projects (Besnier, Calabrò, and Guinness, this volume). In this way, *loloma* and the related filial obligation to share resources among kin act mediate between the "traditional" gendered divisions of labour and the neoliberal rugby economy. Hence rugby provides an extension of gender roles, creating a highly visible and valued public sphere, where young men learn, refine, and demonstrate a neo-traditional masculinity, which women support through care and support.

The aspirations of rugby "wives"

> Back home I was an accountant and an office manager, I had a good career. I was good at it. Here, I tried for ten years to get work and never got a job. I didn't have papers, or I didn't speak enough French. It's like this for many women. They have the education and career in Fiji, while their husbands don't. But we come across to support our husbands and to make this sacrifice for our children. Not all women would do this. But Fijian women, we're like this. We make sacrifices for our children. (Mere, 35, speaking to Guinness in the south of France)

In a culture with clear formal and informal gender divisions of labour and social spaces, i-Taukei women take great pride and sense of responsibility for providing *loloma*. Yet, Mere notes that she and many other women had far more successful careers in Fiji than their husbands before their rugby contracts. And several of the women that we spoke to held strong career ambitions for themselves. Yet, Mere and her husband had made a series of decisions that saw them settling in France after he had finished his professional rugby career. Even at this point, ten years after leaving Fiji, she explicitly framed her life in terms of Indigenous ideals of a good life and a good wife.

The aspirations of young Fijians are influenced by the emergence of Fijian forms of modernity. As in other locations in the Pacific (Gewertz and Errington 1999; Besnier 2009), recent years have seen the rise of middle-class aspirations, evident in the shift from kinship-based gift exchange to a commodity based lifestyle, focused on connections with a global middle class. Many like Ani and Waqa are now starting up businesses rather than providing for poorer relatives. Changing aspirations can be linked to "incipient class divisions" in Fiji (Brison 2014, 18). These newer lifestyles also reflect an anxiety in Pacific modernities and feature an orientation to migration (Besnier 2011). It is far more likely that the rugby wives, many of whom belong to Pentecostal churches and had professional careers in Suva, will have these middle-class aspirations than their husbands.

There is a gendered aspect to the uptake of values of modernity. Parents encourage boys to connect with the local politics and dialects; in contrast, they guide girls, who after marriage will live outside of the community, to learn English and Bauan (the national standard dialect of Fijian) so they can succeed in education and the national labour market (Brison 2012). These early experiences shape divergent aspirations in adult life. Some Fijian girls become "modern women," often oriented to nonlocal employment and communities such as Pentecostal churches, which have English sermons and promote individual (rather than communal) relationships to God, and whose growing popularity can be partly attributed to the social spaces they provide outside of traditional chiefly hierarchies. These women "orient themselves to an imagined nation of Fiji where they can control their own lives and form friendships based on individual preferences rather than ethnic and kin ties" (Brison 2012, 93). This is rarely a complete departure from social norms and kinship systems and the level of individualistic aspirations in women's lives should not be exaggerated. Few women pass on the primary responsibility for domestic, reproductive, and caring labour to their husbands. Yet, the gendered nature of aspirations for modernity is reflected in the higher enrolment of women aged 19–21 in tertiary level education, and increased involvement of women in professions largely based in Suva, such as the civil service.

For some women, modern careers come with aspirations to study or work abroad. Members of the upper echelons of Fijian society have been studying overseas for the past century, primarily in Australia, New Zealand, and Britain. It is not uncommon for Suva-based families to have multiple links to Australia, North America, or New Zealand through university education, relatives involved in agricultural labour schemes (in New Zealand or Australia), and specific global labour markets, such as the armed services and nursing. Women who already have these connections may be looking for a chance to migrate overseas for work or other opportunities.

However, it is often the case that a husband's overseas employment leads to significant compromises between his career, his wife's career, and their extensive social lives and obligations in Fiji. For instance, one woman met her rugby-playing husband at the very time she won a highly competitive position in the medical sector in Fiji and elected to stay in Fiji throughout her husband's almost decade-long career. At the end of his career, she was in a position to support their young family while he slowly transitioned into a new farming life on the outskirts of Suva and struggled with a sense of loss of purpose and value. Guinness met several women who had to return to Fiji after a short stay with their husbands because they were not able to get a spousal visa and were thus dependent on his income or because they failed to assimilate to the foreign contexts. Other women emphasized their desire to remain in Fijian social networks so that their children could be raised with i-Taukei values and with family help. During early stages of an athlete's career, when the contracts are shorter and less remunerative, it is far more common for a wife to stay behind and pursue her own career or take care of their household business interests in Fiji.

Christian faith and sinful husbands

> (Laughing) Let me tell you what one of my aunts told me when I was still growing up. "NEVER EVER marry a police officer or a rugby player," and I asked her why. "Because he's a player – he'll be a player all along." I must say that young ladies, those that are not married or even those who have gotten to know these players – they see them as, I can use the word, "big time flirts."
> *(Va, 34, wife and daughter of rugby players, speaking in Suva)*

For many rugby marriages, whether located in Fiji or abroad, physical absence, trust, and emotional connectivity are tied together. Stories of husbands' flirtations in nightclubs drift back to their wives, often through gossip, which carry judgement along with information. Many of the women we spoke with brush these accusations aside as "coming with the territory" of dating a desirable man. In Fiji, women also partake in their own *talanoa* sessions, over *yaqona* or a cup of tea with biscuits or buns buttered with the local-favourite salted butter. The women see these informal support groups as essential to their wellbeing and sanity. With absent (at training or overseas) husbands, occasional rumours of infidelity and other household dramas, the *talanoa* sessions serve as an open space for rugby's women to vent, laugh, cry, and learn from the experience of other rugby partners. But they are also an avenue for gossip and the birthplace of rumours, for there is no explicit code of silence. Regardless, the women seem to understand that the benefits of a support group outweigh the downsides of sharing personal problems with outsiders.

For Laisiana, 27, living in Suva, rugby is something that she tolerates as part of the life of Vili, her husband, because it gives him such great happiness. However, it also tested their marriage. He had been playing throughout their four years together. She experienced his daily absence from home for training and *talanoa* as loneliness and found them frustrating at times. His rugby commitments meant that they spent almost no time at home together. In addition, she saw his involvement in the masculine spaces of rugby as a threat to their marriage. Vili's weekly rugby schedule involved drinking alcohol after games, and there were more frequent "grog sessions" around Christmas, when the players with jobs used their bonuses to pay for drinks for the whole team. These weekly binges normally culminated with the men venturing to Suva's nightclubs, where some continued to drink into the next day.

Laisiana saw rugby as an activity that drew her husband away from his commitments to her, the family, and the church. More than once, she went to the rugby clubhouse to bring him home. At times, she wouldn't be the only wife collecting her husband. Many women were anxious about rugby's potential to break up marriages. Divorce or even separation is rare for an Indigenous Fijian and is regarded by many churches as sinful and a source of disrespect for families. Rumours of discord in marriages spread quickly through close-knit communities and led to shame (*vei vakamaduataki*). To avoid being ostracized or to maintain convenient living situations, many couples remained in emotionally strained relationships. Laisiana and Vili separated once, when a woman from their neighbourhood claimed that he had fathered her child and he later admitted to having had an intimate relationship with her. At times she thought that rugby might offer a solution to her husband's long-term unemployment, whether through a professional contract or a local job opportunity via the social network. Nevertheless, Laisiana felt that she was sacrificing a lot for her husband's rugby aspirations. A steady household income, a house of their own, a stable marital relationship, and their own children were all part of the cost of rugby that she had accepted, or at least reluctantly acquiesced to.

Most women's worries about their husbands only increase when these men travel abroad for playing contracts. When their husbands are away for a prolonged period, many women worry about their husband's ability to resist temptation and to stay committed to faith, family, and values. For instance, Mili, 23, the wife of Peni, who was an athlete at the start of his career in France, believed that her husband's faith might have weakened because of the many challenges and "temptations" he faces while abroad, but she was unable to obtain a visa to join him:

> Since he's been there for long, um, for me I can tell, his relationship with God is a bit weak. A lot of times when we share, he's always talking about God and sometimes I ask him, do you even share with your friends and all? He doesn't say much … he thinks about what other people will say about him. … Yes, I sometimes feel that way (untrusting). Um, I've seen pictures on Facebook like this … and a lot of girls that fan Fiji players and all eh … like the way it is – girls that side [France], they don't care if the players are married or not, they go for them … he faces a lot of temptation there.

The challenges and temptations are real for young Fijian men based in France. Many struggle to meet the expectations of their employers, find French society difficult to navigate, and suffer from isolation from their social and emotional support networks. Peni arrived at his French club as one of the youngest players in the squad and one of only two men from Pacific Island nations. The French players and coaches tried to help him as much as possible but had little understanding of his home society. The other Pacific Island player and his wife became like a family to him, and he ate with them most evenings. However, he went home alone to an empty house to watch countless pirated American films as he struggled with the loneliness of being away. He began going to the nightclubs in a nearby city with other young athletes, but he ended up drinking for two days and resolved to avoid nightlife entirely.

Once, during his long Skype talk and prayer with Mili, Peni spoke to her of his inability to confide in her about his problems in France. She had noticed his reservation and described a rift between them as he struggled to deal with moral dilemmas on his own and distanced himself from his entire family. She understood the peer pressure from other young players to drink and mingle with rugby fans and explained to Hecht that she felt her husband sometimes struggled with accepting the reality that he was one of the very few married at his age.

In nightclubs, through friends, and at after-match functions, Fijian men regularly meet French women, some of whom are interested in sexual or romantic relationships. For some Fijian men, flirting and sleeping with these women can be an escape from the loneliness of being relatively isolated, a pleasure, and an assertion of masculinity. Some young Fijian men like to boast that their decisions and behaviours are not dictated by their spouses, a display of masculinity that is common in young male gatherings. All of this can lead to complicated domestic arrangements, with a few Fijians having children with French girlfriends while their wives look after their families in Fiji. At times, this is known and reluctantly accepted by spouses in Fiji, but is often kept hidden. The response of Fijian women to doubts they might have about an absent spouse is to return to the twin pillars of faith and kinship to provide strength to them and their partners and to act as a moral compass to guide their collective decisions.

Many Fijian men do remain faithful to both their marriages and their Fijian Christian values. There are strong alternative forms of athletic masculinity available to Fijian men, through the dual tropes of the dedicated professional fully committed to athletic subjectivity and the religious Fijian (promoted by many Fijian families). In contemporary Fiji, these tropes are considered to overlap and mutually reinforce, with dedication to godliness and prayer being regarded as essential parts of professional discipline (Guinness 2018). Group prayer and church services, especially those that are live-streamed from athletes' living rooms in France to fans and family watching via Facebook or other online platforms, can have performative value, whereby ties to family and faith are created and reinforced through their public performance.

Creating new communities in France

Fijians regularly form new communities when overseas. In the south of France, where rugby clubs are predominantly located in cities and towns scattered across the countryside, this has not resulted in the concentration of the Fijian population in a single settlement. During days off from training, many players and some women drive several hundred kilometres to visit other Fijians. They spend long hours in *talanoa* about life in Fiji, professional rugby prospects, and other Fijians in France while sharing *yaqona* if someone has brought some back from a recent trip to Fiji. In these small gatherings, the women will normally prepare the food, but more often sit with men to eat and discuss, enjoying the jokes about the lack of development of their respective villages, or about (minor) mistakes the men have made on the field, around the club house, or in navigating French society. There seems to be a partial redefinition of gendered spaces in these contexts, with Fijian women being more involved than they might be in similar contexts in Fiji. However, this does mirror practices in Suva when the gathering is smaller and consisting solely of close friends or family. In France, these gatherings are part of a larger social reconfiguration, where geographically isolated Fijian families and individuals link together to form new social units, meeting for meals, social outings, or prayer meetings.

The more established Fijian families house other Fijians who have economic difficulties (such as Waqa), often for extended periods. For instance, one Fijian family with three teenage children hosted a recently retired professional for six months while he tried to find work, a Fijian woman who left her Fijian athlete husband a year ago (they call her a cousin to save her from the embarrassment of separation), and five different younger Fijians for shorter periods. None of these guests pay for their accommodation, but all contribute to the household through regular domestic duties, taking the children to school, and providing meals and other resources when they are able.

In some ways, these networks mirror the Fijian communities that have formed in locations where there are many Fijian families living in the same town or city, particularly in Australia, the United Kingdom, the United States, and New Zealand. Elaborate social networks form replicate social structures from Fiji. For instance, in the United Kingdom, there are often as many as 50 Fijian families housed around military bases that have been major recruiters of Fijians. These population hubs have tended to replicate Fijian society, incorporating kinship, church, and chieftainship into the everyday lives of the transnational community there, in an attempt to live in accordance with "traditional" Fijian ways of life (*na ivakarau ni bula vakaviti*) (Hulkenberg 2015).

In France, the Fijian families showed great concern with the reproduction of social norms. For instance, Mere only spoke Fijian to her children, who communicated with each other in French and English. She made sure that they did Fijian-style duties and learnt Fijian customs and manners. When the French-based families organize Fijian-style meals and social events, they explicitly want to show their children how Fijian society functions because they believe this is important to raising their children properly. The women, who are at home more often and maintain links with relatives in Fiji, are important custodians and reproducers of culture.

However, in other ways, transnational Fijian families redefine life (Schieder and Presterudstuen 2014). In France, several Fijian families avoid large communal settings and are reluctant to contribute to *soli* (fundraising, tribute). In the United Kingdom, *soli* were frequent and came with such high expectations of families that they rendered several households unable to pay their utility bills. In France, many players were reluctant to contribute to the Fijian players' union that was founded to protect their interests and provide support for the young men who had recently arrived. The president of the association of Fijian players in France reported to Guinness that many people simply told him that they had decided that it is "better to keep the money for our own family." By comparison, Fijians in Japan constructed complex multi-ethnic networks among i-Taukei and Indo-Fijian migrants to the country (Schieder 2015), but the common narratives of cultural preservation were not matched by frequent communal meetings or resource sharing.

Family members in Fiji make frequent large financial demands of athletes' families, under the belief that all migrants are "millionaires" (Hulkenberg 2015), and because sporting success is associated with passion and talent rather than work (Besnier, Calabrò, and Guinness, this volume; Pietikäinen and Ojala, this volume; Calabrò, this volume). Couples learn to avoid certain social situations rather than being labelled as "greedy" (*mamaqi*), sometimes avoiding contact with relatives they feel request to much, channelling all requests via a single family member in Fiji. In many instances, it is the wife who is blamed for manipulating her husband to the detriment of his kin – a common tension in Fiji as married couples establish their own households independently of their parents, but greatly magnified by the vast differences in the earning potential between athletes and their kin, and the sheer amount of familial effort that has gone into some athletic migrations.

Several features of rugby careers and life in France influence these patterns. First, the geographical distribution of Fijians precludes community formation. Some towns might have a community of two families and a handful of single men, but this pales in comparison with the population hubs around army bases in the United Kingdom. Other players are sometimes incorporated into the groups, particularly other Pacific Island players, but even though the Pacific Island nations share many affinities with one another, the language barriers, perceived differences in character and behaviour, and differences in kinship structures and hierarchies hinder the creation of life "in the Fijian way." Second, rugby careers involve frequent movement, meaning that families must regularly re-establish themselves in new clubs, towns, and social circles. Third, rugby clubs contain their own dense systems of social relations, actively fostered by athletes and coaches alike. In some instances, these networks include strong support for the wives of players, but often Fijian women find it difficult to create friendships and connections. Finally, perhaps for these reasons, far fewer families than in the United Kingdom, Australia, or New Zealand hope to settle permanently in France after a husband's rugby career. Often, they discuss staying for part of their children's education or to receive the state pension upon retirement, but few want to stay for their whole lives.

These orientations reflect a shift in aspirations away from kinship-based worldviews and towards individualism. This is partly a direct result of Fijians engaging with the rugby system that implicitly encourages individualistic orientations in its players, through the contracting system and neoliberalized player management that reduces athletes to the quantifiable features of their physical bodies (Besnier, Guinness, Hann, and Kovač 2018). Several rugby clubs and player agents explicitly encourage players to put their money into personal savings, investments in property, and small businesses, rather than sending it all home as remittances. Clubs recruit financial planners to run financial management training focused on investing in nuclear family projects.

Women often have a significant life change when their husbands retire from rugby. Those who return from long periods overseas must re-enter Fijian society. Their husbands might experience a "social death" (Rosenberg 1984) as they shift from being a famous highly respected athlete to being an unskilled worker, often impaired by ongoing physical ailments as the result of rugby injuries. For some, this leads to a sense of shame, especially when their careers are not regarded as successful (Kanemasu and Molnar 2014) or when they have used up the finances accumulated during their playing days. The burden for caring for these men is largely handled within informal community and family support networks, which themselves are breaking down as the result of rural-urban migration, poverty, natural disasters, and social changes (Mohanty 2011). Drug and alcohol abuse can be severe problems for some men. In the worst-case scenarios, several women found themselves as the primary breadwinners, living in Suva away from family, responsible for domestic work, and caring for a depressed husband prone to violence.

Wives can have significant input into their husband's career decisions, an influence that might be in the direction of greater individualism or towards maintain social ties with Fijian. One player even joked that he was "just the muscle" while his wife was the brains behind his rugby career. Given that some women have superior educational and professional experience than their husbands, this is not surprising. Several women expressed frustration at their husbands' inability to negotiate better contracts with clubs.

Faith from the sidelines

Rugby has introduced new sets of values into the conjugal relations of rugby families. Men are encouraged to embrace an individualization focused on their professional career in a way that can have a profound impact on their relations with wife, children, and village kin. Women attempt to accommodate this in one of two ways, either by accepting a (sometimes isolated) life as homemaker in an overseas society or by consolidating their Fijian home and social life in the husband's absence. Either way is difficult and contrasts with the ability of many of these women in accommodating their professional lives with the wider obligations of church, kin, and community. While the women often grow in strength and resolve in these circumstances, their husbands struggle with a loss of personal strength, connectedness, and standing as their professional careers come to an end. This heaps pressure on their marriages. Overwhelmingly, women respond by returning to faith and Fijian values and attempting to draw their husbands into their project.

This is the unseen face of the Fijian rugby hero. Fijian women play a decisive role in achieving long-term success for their families through the rugby careers of their sons and husbands under neoliberal labour conditions. It acknowledges that the individual is always a social being, formed not just by long hours of training but by the bonds of family, marriage, *loloma*, *talanoa*, and *yaqona*, all of which give these men and women purpose and meaning. This is the unrecognized work that sustains the global sports economy, an economy in which the valuation of women's labour (and other unseen forms of labour) is not rewarded financially. This is the externalized and hidden work of producing athletes, who are then expected to be able to disentangle themselves from the bonds that built them and give them purpose, in order to move through the world as ideal neoliberal professionals.

In the contrast between women and their husbands, we see the different impact of "modernity" on men and women. Firstly, new professional spaces open new gender norms, notably employment for women, which does not necessarily nullify their care responsibilities, but does offer pathways to greater financial independence and control. Secondly, the already gendered global rugby industry has been integrated into modern Fiji in ways that celebrate and reproduce gender norms that are greatly influenced by received notions of tradition. Thirdly, transnational families continue to try to meet social expectations and resource obligations in Fiji but also create new constellations of community abroad. Finally, the gendered patterns of employment, mobility, and social norms that characterize this particular form of modernity have an impact on marriages, as wives and husbands struggle with absence, isolation, and rumours while trying to support each other in the pursuit of their mutual life projects.

Acknowledgements

This chapter is based on research conducted as part of Guinness' Ph.D. dissertation, funded by a Rhodes scholarship at the University of Oxford, and on research conducted by Guinness and Hecht as part of the project titled "Globalization, Sport, and the Precarity of Masculinity" (2012–17) funded by the European Research Council under the European Union's Seventh Framework Programme (Grant Agreement 295769). We thank our research participants in Fiji and elsewhere for the generous ways in which they shared their lives with us, as well as Niko Besnier, Patrick Guinness, Mark Hann, Uroš Kovač, Domenica Calabrò, Susan Brownell, and Yoko Kanemasu for their generous comments.

Notes

1 All names are pseudonyms.
2 Indo-Fijians, locally called "Indians," are largely descendants of indentured labourers who were brought to Fiji by the British as indentured sugarcane labourers in the latter part of the nineteenth and the beginning of the twentieth centuries, or migrated freely before the mid-twentieth century. Under British colonial rule, a system of social and economic segregation maintained divisions between Indo-Fijians and Indigenous Fijians.

References

Baldassar, Loretta, and Laura Merla. 2014. "Transnational Family Caregiving Through the Lens of Circulation." In *Transnational Families, Migration and the Circulation of Care*, edited by Loretta Baldassar and Laura Merla, 3–25. New York: Routledge.

Besnier, Niko. 2009. "Modernity, Cosmopolitanism, and the Emergence of Middle Classes in Tonga." *The Contemporary Pacific* 21, no. 2: 215–262.

Besnier, Niko. 2011. *On the Edge of the Global: Modern Anxieties in a Pacific Island Nation.* Stanford, CA: Stanford University Press.

Besnier, Niko. 2012. "The Athlete's Body and the Global Condition: Tongan Rugby Players in Japan." *American Ethnologist* 39, no. 3: 491–510.

Besnier, Niko. 2014. "Pacific Island Rugby: Histories, Mobilities, Comparisons." *Asia Pacific Journal of Sport and Social Science* 3, no. 3: 268–276.

Besnier, Niko, and Susan Brownell. 2012. "Sport, Modernity, and the Body." *Annual Review of Anthropology* 41: 443–459.

Besnier, Niko, Daniel Guinness, Mark Hann, and Uroš Kovač. 2018. "Rethinking Masculinity in the Neoliberal Order: Cameroonian Footballers, Fijian Rugby Players, and Senegalese Wrestlers." *Comparative Studies in Society and History* 60, no. 4: 839–872.

Brison, Karen. 2012. "Gendered Modernities among Rural Indigenous Fijian Children." In *Super Girls, Gangstas, Freeters, and Xenomaniacs: Gender and Modernity in Global Youth Culture*, edited by Karen J Brison and Susan Dewey, 85–103. Syracuse, NY: Syracuse University Press.

Brison, Karen. 2014. Children, Social Class, and Education. New York: Palgrave Macmillan.

Clément, Julien. 2014. *Cultures physiques: Le rugby de Samoa.* Paris: Éditions de la rue d'Ulm.

Dewey, Robert F., Jr. 2014. "Fiji and Pacific Rugby Research: The State of the Game." *Asia Pacific Journal of Sport and Social Science* 3, no. 3: 186–201.

Federici, Silvia. 1999. "Reproduction and Feminist Struggle in the New International Division of Labour." In *Women, Development and Labour of Reproduction: Struggles and Movements*, edited by Mariarosa Dalla Costa and Giovanna Franca Dalla Costa, 47–82. Asmara, Eritrea: Africa World Press.

George, Nicole. 2015. "'Starting with a Prayer': Women, Faith and Security in Fiji." *Oceania* 85, no. 1: 119–131.

Gewertz, Deborah, and Frederick Errington. 1999. *Emerging Class in Papua New Guinea: The Telling of Difference*. Cambridge: Cambridge University Press.

Guinness, Daniel. 2018. "Corporal Destinies: Faith, Ethno-Nationalism, and Raw Talent in Fijian Professional Rugby Aspirations." *HAU* 8, no. 1–2: 314–328.

Guinness, Daniel, and Niko Besnier. 2016. "Nation, Nationalism, and Sport: Fijian Rugby in the Local–Global Nexus." *Anthropological Quarterly* 89, no. 2: 1109–1141.

Hulkenberg, Jara. 2015. "The Cost of Being Fijian in the United Kingdom." *Anthropological Forum* 25, no. 2: 148–166.

Kanemasu, Yoko, and Gyozo Molnar. 2013a. "Pride of the People: Fijian Rugby Labour Migration and Collective Identity." *International Review for the Sociology of Sport* 48, no. 6: 706–719.

Kanemasu, Yoko, and Gyozo Molnar. 2013b. "Problematizing the Dominant: The Emergence of Alternative Cultural Voices in Fiji Rugby." *Asia Pacific Journal of Sport and Social Science* 2, no. 1: 14–30.

Kanemasu, Yoko, and Gyozo Molnar. 2014. "Life After Rugby: Issues of Being an 'Ex' in Fiji Rugby." *International Journal of the History of Sport* 31, no. 11: 1389–1405.

Kanemasu, Yoko, and Gyozo Molnar. 2017. "Double-Trouble: Negotiating Gender and Sexuality in Post-Colonial Women's Rugby in Fiji." *International Review of the Sociology of Sport* 52, no. 4: 430–446.

Lee, Helen. 2009. "Pacific Migration and Transnationalism: Historical Perspectives." In *Migration and Transnationalism: Pacific Perspectives*, edited by Helen Lee and Steve Tupai Francis, 7–42. Canberra: ANU E Press.

Levitt, Peggy, and Nina Glick Schiller. 2004. "Conceptualizing Simultaneity: A Transnational Social Field Perspective on Society." *International Migration Review* 38, no. 3: 1002–1039.

Lilomaiava-Doktor, Sailiemanu. 2009. "Beyond 'Migration': Samoan Population Movement (*Malaga*) and the Geography of Social Space (*Va*)." *Contemporary Pacific* 21, no. 1: 1–32.

Macpherson, Cluny, and La'avasa Macpherson. 2010. *The Warm Winds of Change: Globalisation in Contemporary Samoa*. Auckland: Auckland University Press.

Mohanty, Manoranjan. 2006. "Globalization, New Labour Migration and Development in Fiji." In *Globalization and Governance in the Pacific Islands*, edited by Stewart Firth, 107–120. Canberra: ANU E Press.

Mohanty, Manoranjan. 2011. "Informal Social Protection and Social Development in Pacific Island Countries." *Asia-Pacific Development Journal* 18, no. 2: 25–56.

Nabobo-Baba, Unaisi. 2006. *Knowing and Learning: An Indigenous Fijian Approach*. Suva: Institute of Pacific Studies, University of the South Pacific.

Presterudstuen, Geir Henning. 2010. "The Mimicry of Men: Rugby and Masculinities in Post-Colonial Fiji." *Global Studies* 3: 237–248.

Presterudstuen, Geir Henning. 2014. "Men Trapped in Women's Clothing: Homosexuality, Cross-dressing, and Masculinity in Fiji." In *Gender on the Edge: Transgender, Gay, and Other Pacific Islanders*, edited by Niko Besnier and Kalissa Alexeyeff, 162–183. Honolulu: University of Hawai'i Press.

Rosenberg, Edwin. 1984. "Athletic Retirement as Social Death: Concepts and Perspectives." In *Sport and the Sociological Imagination*, edited by Nancy Theberge and Peter Donnelly, 245–258. Dallas: Texas Christian University Press.

Schieder, Dominik. 2014. "Fiji Islander Rugby Union Players in Japan: Corporate Particularities and Migration Routes." *Asia-Pacific Journal of Sport and Social Science* 3: 250–267.

Schieder, Dominik. 2015. "Community Life and Discourses among Fiji Islanders in Kantō, Japan." *Anthropological Forum* 25, no. 1: 167–186.

Schieder, Dominik, and Geir Presterudstuen. 2014. "Sport Migration and Socio-cultural Transformation: The Case of Fijian Rugby Union Players in Japan." *International Journal of the History of Sport* 31, no. 11: 1359–1373.

Teaiwa, Teresia K. 2005. "Articulated Cultures: Militarism and Masculinities in Fiji during the Mid-1990s." *Fijian Studies* 3, no. 2: 201–222.

Teaiwa, Teresia K. 2008. "On Women and 'Indians': The Politics of Inclusion and Exclusion in Militarized Fiji." In *Security Disarmed: Gender, Race, and Militarization*, edited by Barbara Sutton, Sandra Morgen, and John Novkov, 111–135. New Brunswick, NJ: Rutgers University Press.

Toren, Christina. 1990. *Making Sense of Hierarchy: Cognition as Social Process in Fiji.* London: Athlone Press.

Varani-Norton, Eta. 2005. "The Church Versus Women's Push for Change: The Case of Fiji." *Fijian Studies* 3, no. 2: 223–247.

Voigt-Graf, Carmen. 2008. "Migration and Transnational Families in Fiji: Comparing Two Ethnic Groups." *International Migration* 46, no. 4: 15–40.

Wall, Karin, and Claudio Bolzman. 2014. "Mapping the New Plurality of Transnational Families: A Life Course Perspective." In *Transnational Families, Migration and the Circulation of Care*, edited by Loretta Baldassar and Laura Merla, 61–77. New York: Routledge.

9

THE GLOBAL WARRIOR

Māori, rugby, and diasporic Indigeneity

Domenica Gisella Calabrò

We were sitting in a wide semi-deserted park. Shahn's two little boys were having fun on a playground, not far from the premises of the New Zealand provincial rugby club where he played.[1] I was interested in his relationship to rugby and his past experience in Italy. Shahn spoke slowly and deliberately, occasionally falling silent. A poker face accentuated by a long black beard.

A Māori friend we had in common, Mat, had put us in touch. I first met Shahn at a gym where his team was holding an event. He did not speak much and soon after he had to leave. He offered to meet again in a city that was a two-hours' drive away. Two days later, we resumed the interview. He gave a few formal answers until it started raining, and we all moved to the rugby club. The interview stopped once again as his team began to crowd around us for a meeting. They were then playing the New Zealand Mitre 10 Cup, a tournament held over twelve weeks between August and November. Shahn asked me if I had any other questions. Before I could answer, he told me to wait, and disappeared in the meeting room with his kids. Half an hour later, we were back to the bench, and the recorder was on again.

Suddenly, his youngest son fell, bursting into tears. "You will excuse me," he said, calmly standing up. The two-year old looked tinier than he already was, folded around his father's very tall figure. "Do you have any more questions?" he asked once again. I smiled, "No, I think this is fine." I put my recorder into my jacket. The toddler calmed down and went back to his brother. "I'm actually happy you're from Italy," Shahn said staring at an indefinite point. "I really loved my time there," he added, smiling for the first time.

He suddenly started sharing anecdotes from his own time there, including episodes during which he had felt the object of special treatment. He then told me about his family's involvement in gangs and his grandfather expecting him to help his cousins get out of trouble; the help he would have liked to have at school, and his teenage fatherhood; his wife – the smart one of the couple, the one who was into Māori culture; the rugby game he loved, and the career he had nonetheless not dreamt of, but "aye, I did not have other skills"; his kids, whom he wanted to have a different life and hopefully go to university; his decision to go overseas, which was not an escape from responsibilities, but his desire to be responsible towards himself and his immediate family.

He had then turned 24 and wanted to see if there was still a chance for him in Aotearoa New Zealand. Shyly, he hinted that he hoped to be selected for the upcoming Māori All Blacks tour in November 2016. When his rugby time in New Zealand would be over, maybe within a few years, he hoped to go overseas again – "to France this time, my wife would love it."

Shahn was not selected for the Māori All Blacks. In May 2017, I heard he was packing to move to France. He told me he couldn't wait.

Mobile athletes, global warriors, and Indigenous men

Many Māori men today follow a career in rugby union to achieve a good life, tracing their trajectories as athletes and as men in a dynamic scenario of global mobility. Historically, Māori men have played a significant role in the illustrious New Zealand rugby (Mulholland 2009; Hokowhitu 2005; Ryan 1993). Their game has also contributed to restoring Māori's "depleted manhood" (Hokowhitu 2005, 90). In Māori settings, rugby has come to be associated with *mana* "spiritual prestige or authority," which makes players responsible towards their communities, and has become a privileged site for men to achieve recognition and leadership (Calabrò 2016). In 1995, the professionalization of international rugby added opportunities for socioeconomic progress. Since then, Māori older generations have been using the game's prestige and prospects to divert their youth away from lifepaths leading to criminality and suicide. Transnational mobility enables young men to showcase their individual and collective *mana* and pursue economic opportunities.

Overseas, Māori athletes become valuable as products of New Zealand rugby and as romanticized warriors. In response to the competitive and lucrative potentials of professional rugby, the All Blacks, New Zealand's national team, have turned their distinctive pre-match *haka*, which recalls the ritual dance that Māori ancestors performed prior to battle, into a highly successful marketing tool that casts contemporary Māori athletic prowess as the incarnation of an Indigenous warrior tradition (Calabrò 2014, 389). The image of the noble warrior nevertheless obscures its own role, in synergy with the rugby game, in naturalizing savagery and physicality as characteristics of Māori men (Hokowhitu 2003, 2004a, 2004b, 2008), thus transforming them into hyper-virile and emotionless bodies. When Shahn eventually managed to disclose the emotions and desires secreted in his athletic body, rugby emerged in its bare nature of space where history has tried to relegate Māori men's possibilities for recognition and socioeconomic inclusion, with gang membership looming as alternative destiny.

Some Māori thus view the warrior reference entailed in rugby as a reminder that their people, and men in particular, are still not sovereign over their lives, but rather inhabit a space of "coloniality" (Borrell 2015; Maldonado-Torres 2007; Mignolo 2007; Quijano 2000), where power differentials and violence outlive colonialism in all domains of life, shaping how descendants of colonial subjects perceive themselves and their possibilities. Others privilege an approach in which the image of the *toa* (warrior) rugby player is an expression of Māori men's worth and agency.

Māori masculinities share the colonial construct of the noble (yet violent) warrior with other Indigenous masculinities (McKegney 2014, 2011; Innes and Anderson 2015; Tengan 2002; Tengan and Markham 2009). Many Indigenous men embrace this image because it provides them with "relief from often untenable social conditions as well as a sense of masculine agency that colonization has rendered difficult to attain in other ways" (McKegney 2011, 258). Moreover, the warrior conjures an effort to withstand cultural, social, and political vulnerability, which characterizes the Indigenous condition as much as struggle does (Alfred and Corntassel 2005). If "invisibility and dehumanization are the primary expressions of the coloniality of being" (Maldonado-Torres 2007, 257), the warrior trope is simultaneously emblematic of the processes subtly controlling the self-image of Indigenous men and of their desires to be recognized as fully human. Within Māori rugby mobility, the warrior specifically evokes the global circulation of discourses and of life projects authenticating rugby flair as a feature of Indigenous Māori masculinities.

Rugby opens the door onto life-changing destinies for Māori men who show endurance and entrepreneurship. In contrast to Māori's collective claims to land, resources, and political recognition, which have been constituted by a neoliberal political economy that both honoured them and constrained their terms (McCormack 2011, 2012; Gershon 2008), Māori athletes' endeavours constitute an individual interaction with neoliberalism based on desires rather than claims. Yet, the international opportunities that rugby affords are also predicated on the athletes' geographical distance from their Indigenous context and the cultural alienation resulting from the commodification of the culture and individualism.

These are the questions I addressed during fieldwork I conducted in 2016–17 in Aotearoa New Zealand and in European locations that have welcomed Māori players and coaches, notably Italy, France, and the Netherlands.[2] As they leave *whenua* (land) and *tangata* (people) and engage with an international rugby industry interested in their warrior potential and charm, athletes experiment with alternative existences, as Shahn did. They rethink their lives, identities, and responsibilities. Still, they may experience new forms of invisibility away from the illustrious New Zealand rugby scene, their people, and the land where they hold special status, while being exoticized by the sport industries and audiences. Family members and Māori who prioritize collective interests may take pride in their achievements and suffer from their absence, idealize their life choices, or contest them.

The phenomenon highlights tensions about Indigeneity as a space defined by local and global strategies of regeneration in the context of histories of dispossession and present realities of structural marginalization. (Gomes 2013; Merlan 2009; de la Cadena and Starn 2007). The difficulties in defining Indigeneity have generated debates about its efficacy as a political and analytical category (Gagné and Salaün

2012; Kuper 2003; Béteille 1998). Meanwhile, its discourses have permeated the existences of those who inhabit its spaces. I thus understand diasporic Indigeneity as the (gendered) emotions, feelings, and desires nurtured within the politicized spaces of coloniality and resistance in which the athletes' existences are embedded (whether by self-identification or for being identified as Māori), which their sporting bodies carry all over the world, as well as the collective aspirations and fears attached to their global movements.

Indigenous groups and their members experience significant anxiety about discourses that challenge their identities and claims, which many internalize, adopting the oppressive lens of authenticity in the way they see each other and themselves (Gagné 2013; Hokowhitu 2015; Harrison, Carlson, and Poata-Smith 2013; Jolly 1992; Maddison 2013; Sissons 2005; Smith 1999). While many social actors and scholars have asserted that Indigenous identities are fluid and multifarious (McIntosh 2005), the notion of authenticity subtly resists by expecting groups and individuals to be resilient, which in the Indigenous discourse has become synonym of resistance (Lindroth and Sinevaara-Niskanen 2016). Māori narratives may actually portray rugby migration as an expression of resilience. The athletes' subjectivities rather disclose resentment towards structural disparities but also Indigenous dynamics, and their attempts at navigating both the ambivalence of rugby and collective expectations to break free from that feeling.

Voyages of resistance: Cultural continuity and adaptation

Ko te kai rapu, ko ia te kite.
The person who seeks will find.

★

Whakaki ki te maungatai ki te whenua: hoki ki te rangitai, ki te pukerunga.[3]
If we aim for the mountains, we're just going to hit the plains:
but if we aim for the sky, we'll hit the peaks.

★

He iti te kōpara ka rērere i te puhi o te kahikatea.[4]
Though the bellbird is small, it can reach the crown of the kahikatea.

★

E kore au e ngaro, he kākano i ruia mai i Rangiātea.
I will never be lost, for I am a seed sown in Rangiātea.[5]

These *whakatauki* (proverbs) exhort individuals to be proactive and take risks to fulfil their potential, in the understanding that they can improve their circumstances and that they will not get lost as long as they remember where they come from. Enacting these values may require voyaging. Māori mythology celebrates Polynesian ancestors whose adventurous pursuits brought knowledge to the collectivity, like the demi-god Māui, who travelled to the afterlife, and the navigator Kupe, who travelled the Pacific and eventually returned home to share what he had learned.

The latter's endeavours inspired the South-bound exodus of some Polynesians in times of struggle.

In their *whakapapa* (genealogy), Māori include the *waka* (canoe) which led their ancestors from Rangiātea to the shores of Aotearoa, and from which different *iwi* (tribes) were formed. In the same fashion, Māori history is replete with travels for sport, war, and other purposes, which have generated *mana,* and diasporic communities have formed in London and Australia. Māori rugby athletes' transnational mobility is thus culturally continuous with the mobility of their distant ancestors, who are frequently described as migratory (Hayes 1991; McCall and Connell 1993). Overseas, Māori rugby athletes easily connecting with Pacific Islander ones uphold the shared kinship.

Top-level Māori rugby players at the end of their careers began moving overseas in the early 2000s to play or take up coaching positions. Since then, an increasing number of athletes at various stages of their careers have been heading to Australia, Europe, North America, Japan and other parts of Asia. Some secondary-school graduates or university students use rugby for an "O.E.," the "overseas experience" that many New Zealanders embark on in their late teens or early twenties. Some move back and forth between Aotearoa New Zealand and overseas locations, while others settle overseas, particularly if they find a partner there. Thanks to their reputation and their skills, some Māori men who are overseas for other reasons become involved in the game as coaches and players.

These diverse patterns of mobility all share one commonality, namely the fact that they uphold a legacy of travels generating *mana,* and an image of Māori as curious, entrepreneurial, and adaptive. Parents of migrant athletes I met in Aotearoa New Zealand described their sons' experiences as enriching for everyone, and most athletes I spoke with said that they were motivated by a desire to discover the world. But this desire conflicts with discourses of authenticity that seek to anchor Indigenous people to the land from which they derive their special status. The movements of the Māori rugby athletes build on the "diasporic predicaments" of Indigenous existences in the Pacific region, and the "'commuting' (exchanging, changing, mitigating) they entail" (Clifford 2001, 474; see also Hauʻofa 1994). The normalization of the athletes' global mobility also positions them as men upholding ancestral values and practices rather than merely losing their culture to neoliberalism, following traditions of open-mindedness.

Defying negative representations, accusations of inauthenticity, and threats of cultural loss, those narratives validate a more contemporary discourse in which Indigenous people "are no longer officially perceived as 'savages.' Instead, they are represented, and represent themselves as resilient and adaptive agents" (Lindroth and Sinevaara-Niskanen 2014, 180). Their lives showcase adaptability, flexibility, and endurance in the face of adversities. They are able to handle multiple and complex relationships with non-Indigenous actors and institutions and with other Indigenous individuals and groups. These skills are similar to those praised in the neoliberal era, in which individuals are responsible for navigating risk and multiple alliances in a world defined by market principles of deregulation and privatization

(Gershon 2011; Gershon and Alexy 2011). Indigenous people have become the poster children of neoliberal subjectivity (Chandler and Reid 2016; Lindroth and Sinevaara-Niskanen 2018). Migrant Māori men then become perfect neoliberal subjects by virtue of their Indigenous status.

The discourse of resilience, however, operates as a form of biopower (Lindroth and Sinevaara-Niskanen 2014, 2016, 2018), trapping Indigenous people in a state in which "life is reduced to the celebration of mere survival … and [which] functions to discipline the indigenous themselves into performing their own resilience" (Chandler and Reid 2018, 262). From this perspective, the narrative that celebrates Māori athletes' migration as a form of sociocultural resistance may contribute to placing Māori men in an eternal present of struggling and coping as they search for a sovereign future. This resembles the effects of the promises that sport in the neoliberal era holds for many hopefuls all over the globe (Besnier, Calabrò, and Guinness, this volume).

Unlike Shahn, most athletes minimize the struggling and the coping by explaining that their careers and the associated migration are motivated by a desire to live their passion (compare Pietikäinen and Ojala, this volume). My interlocutors exhibited a neoliberal understanding of work, which is particularly evident in sport and encourages individuals to pursue what they like and show talent for, so that sacrifices become invisible (Besnier, Calabrò, and Guinness, this volume).

Behind the scene: Resentment and second chances

The emphasis on *mana* (and the resistance that it implies) deproblematizes a larger social process of relocation or dislocation of hope in the context of national political-socioeconomic dynamics that generate great inequalities (see Goss and Lindquist 2000, 398; Besnier 2011, 36–39). If New Zealand's socioeconomic standards and geopolitical profile situate it in the Global North, numerous negative statistics (unemployment, health problems, substance abuse, etc.) reveal Māori realities as more akin to those of the Global South. Frustration and bitterness often shape Māori lives as opportunities appear so close yet so elusive. While rugby affords some Indigenous men economic productivity and recognition, the New Zealand rugby industry can only offer employment to a few athletes, particularly as they have to compete for contracts with athletes of Pacific Island heritage, who present a formidable competition that also markets itself with its "warrior" qualities (Besnier 2015, 851).

Transnational mobility is often contingent on disappointment. Unlike other athletes, who are encouraged by their communities and work hard to migrate (Besnier, Calabrò, and Guinness, this volume; Guinness and Hecht, this volume; Hann, this volume; Kovač, this volume; Peters, this volume), leaving is a second choice for Māori athletes as they harbour the dream of wearing the prestigious All Blacks jersey and often aspire to be a Māori All Black for its symbolic value. To be eligible for the national teams, an athlete must have a contract with a club in the New Zealand top-level competition.

Sometimes, athletes set aside their dream of becoming an All Black because they prioritize seeking better lives for themselves and their families. For example, in 2016, Quentin, who had worn the Māori All Black jersey, accepted a three-year contract with Oyonnax Rugby, a club in the French Jura mountains, where I met him. Coming from a rugby family, his goal "used to be playing for higher honours in the family," and a six-month experience in Ireland had been the opportunity for him to see the world. His first-born changed his perspective. His wife was tired of changing location every six to eight months while he chased opportunities in different competitions, and with another child was on the way, he thought he "should" seize a "more secure opportunity … that pays better." In other instances, athletes decide to seek overseas contracts because they have been injured or involved in gangs. Overseas contracts potentially offer new beginnings and second chances. Gangs play a peculiar role in the way their direct or indirect presence interferes with opportunities to create different life paths, and resistance may mean athletes distancing themselves from an environment that hurts them.

Moving may also imply accepting to play and coach in countries where rugby occupies a peripheral position. For example, Jay, who played in Germany for five years before returning home in 2016, laughed as he remembered his shock when he met his new teammates, who were "mostly white haired, people who could have been my uncles." Players who played or had played rugby in Italy, Portugal, the Netherlands, Germany, or France joked about the level of rugby they sometimes had to put up with after being trained in New Zealand's very demanding game. Concurrently, they expressed annoyance as Indigenous men who had relied on rugby to claim a degree of visibility.

In the end, migration is not an easy way out either. Mat, a graduate in history, who is involved with his *hapū* (clan) and is an amateur player, contended that overseas rugby clubs, particularly in Europe, often prefer athletes from Pacific Island nations because the latter have the same rights to work and movement as E.U. citizens thanks to the economical agreements between Europe and African, Caribbean, Pacific countries. He lamented that, as citizens of a wealthy country with an advanced rugby industry, Māori athletes may not be given the same opportunities as people from poorer countries and their struggles may go unrecognized.

The Māori athletes are after all raised in a Global North rugby industry. Their powerful passport potentially enables them to easily visit a country and showcase their skills to a club; it makes young men eligible for a working holiday visa in several countries, which many actually use to obtain an overseas rugby experience, and it also enables their *whānau* to visit them. Some of the people I met had attended university and hoped to further or complete their studies in the future. Moving at the end of successful careers, some are already well-travelled and acquainted with the industry. A few use the game to get overseas life and work experience rather than going overseas for life-changing rugby career. The kind of expectations the athletes' families and people place on them also leave more space for them to negotiate their desires.

Mat realized that the primary obstacle was the disproportionate number of Māori boys and men investing themselves in a possible rugby career. Different Māori approaches to rugby mobility – from the overseas experience to the desire for a life change – actually form a continuum, as Māori boys and men have been using the same medium to reach their sky, as a result of authenticating rugby as an expression of their Indigeneity. In Māori contexts, the feelings associated with rugby opportunities that do not arrive, fail, or do not correspond to the athletes' dreams reveal forms of resentment. A sense of entitlement as Indigenous men, whose opportunities to reclaim their identity and honour their land, people, families, and themselves have been historically circumscribed to rugby and war, coexists with, and sometimes obfuscates, a realistic attitude to the logics of sport competition. Within this context, a rugby space that does not fulfil its promises or only partially fulfils them perpetuates non-recognition, generating a double exclusion.

The Māori athletes' attitude influences their access to opportunities overseas. In 2008, Caleb, a young man I had met in a university Māori language class, announced that he was going to temporarily stop university to seize a rugby opportunity in Australia. He then told me I would notice that most Māori prefer to act as "underdogs." In a similar way, while emphasizing his commitment to a career, Quentin added that "a lot of Māori boys do not like pressure ... and to keep working hard."

In fact, not so many passionate and talented Māori players are willing to seek out an overseas opportunity and perform their expected resilience as Indigenous men, Māori men, and neoliberal sportsmen. Contemporary Māori youth are often reluctant to leave their extended family (*whānau*) and friends, even in the context of unhealthy dynamics. They cling to their comfort zones in a broader national context – and world – that they often experience as hostile. As a result, few Māori play in European clubs, in contrast to their visible presence in Aotearoa New Zealand rugby.

For most athletes, the hardest part was actually finding the courage to leave families and friends. For example, Kelly, who had reached top levels in Italy and moved back to New Zealand because of injuries, smiled remembering,

> I just went there and knew nobody ... I was really nervous but ... sort of ... you need to get out of your comfort zone ... that's also why I was over there ... you need to get out of your comfort zone ... and pray for the best, I guess!

A neoliberal context that emphasizes that individuals are authors of their destinies may excite some, but is unbearable for those who have internalized a self-image as small birds, but have "forgotten" they can still reach the crown of the *kahikatea*, and not get lost.

Loss of human capital

On our first meeting in October 2008, the late Whetu Tipiwai, who was the *kaumatua* (elder, cultural and spiritual manager) of the Māori All Blacks, identified the overseas mobility of Māori athletes as a then-emerging phenomenon that benefited the athletes but affected Māori as a people (Calabrò 2014, 398–399). In his melancholic words, "we lose them." His use of "we" referred variously to Māori rugby, Māori people, the *iwi* (tribes), and families. In 2016, on a cold evening in Wellington, the cousin of an old friend became annoyed when she learned that I was researching athletes' transnational mobility. A woman in her fifties sporting the chin *moko* (tattoo) traditionally associated with women of *mana*, she contended that rugby was taking away Māori young men as the two world wars had, when Māori men had spontaneously organized an Indigenous battalion to show their loyalty to the country. "Will they come back?" the woman wondered. "And if they come back, will they be changed? What will they bring with them that can benefit us?"

In contrast to other contexts where communities depend on the remittances of migrant athletes for their basic survival (Guinness and Hecht, this volume; Peters, this volume; Besnier, Calabrò, and Guinness, this volume), many Māori see overseas opportunities as depriving the community of the athletes' human capital – their spiritual resources, their energy, their social skills (including the ability to navigate the rugby industry), and their potential leadership. As Shahn's experience illustrates, this capital can include guidance and support for more vulnerable members. In Indigenous terms, it is a loss of resilience – the qualities to positively respond to the struggles inherited from colonial history – at times where Māori are still working on cultural resurgence, social inclusion, and political empowerment. This perceived social and cultural drain extends to the athletes' children and partners.

This sense of loss also comes from an understanding of Māori identity as performative, whereby people of Māori descent construct full Māori identity by regularly enacting *whakawhanaungatanga* (creating the culture of the *whānau*, extended family) and engaging with people *kanohi ki te kanohi* (face-to-face). From a gendered perspective, this mirrors the feeling that Māori men's rugby prowess is not enough to gain recognition. As in the past, "demonstration of skills and prowess in warfare were among a number of ways to determine one's masculinity. However, masculinities were also based on generosity and the stability provided to the *iwi* (tribe) through leadership" (Borrel 2015, 167).

Many athletes do go back to Aotearoa New Zealand or plan to do so, but their return may still not appease collective anxiety and criticism. Some see professional rugby's demands, ethics, and money as corrosive, risking to turn Māori athletes away from Māori rugby (playing for the family, tribal groupings, and Māori people) and from the communities themselves (Calabrò 2016, 239–240). For instance, although Māori Television praised the global Māori rugby camps, some people were wary of overseas athletes commodifying Māori culture and rugby tradition. Beyond rugby, some Māori are unfamiliar or uncomfortable with conventional aspects of Māori culture (first and foremost the language) and disengage from the groups they are affiliated with by descent. When Mat connected me with his friends playing or having played overseas, he warned me that many of them were trying to reconnect with their *whakapapa*. Athletes see themselves as "authentic" Māori for their rugby skills, but often judge themselves as inadequate with respect to conventional definitions of Māoriness. Expecting to be judged by the researcher, a couple of overseas-based athletes appropriated the derogatory label "plastic Māori," used in both Māori and non-Indigenous contexts (Pearson 2015).

The concerns about the athletes' exodus consider the athletes in terms of *tātou*, the first-person inclusive personal pronoun in Māori, which refers to "we" as a collectivity, and view their mobility in relation to an Indigenous discourse of resistance. Nevertheless, the subjectivities of the athletes I encountered, regardless of the ways they formulated their Māori identity, presented going overseas as individual journeys of growth and learning in contexts (apparently) disconnected from their daily postcolonial dynamics. This divergence speaks to the tensions between Indigenous people as singular subjects and their desires on the one hand and Indigenous people as a collectivity and its needs on the other (Bellier 2011). Hence, the "relational definition of Indigeneity" is not solely determined by the opposition between Indigenous and non-Indigenous subjects (Merlan 2009), including the tensions among Indigenous subjects.

Becoming men

Justifying his departure, Shahn suggested that he could concretely do nothing to prevent his relatives from getting involved in the gangs, but he could benefit his immediate family. Quentin emphasized how "my parents were not too happy initially," for he was depriving them of their *moko* (grandchildren) and he would no longer play for the honour of the family. Although he could relate to their feelings, "it wasn't selfish," he repeated, "but [I was] putting my kids first." Bruce, whom I met in Bordeaux, has long played and coached in the United Kingdom and France. In 2000, he had played for the All Blacks. Two years later, he decided to leave temporarily, thinking he would not be selected again. His decision generated

> a lot of surprise … my family obviously did not want me to go, but understood why … for me, I was not going to stay there and say "I should have played more tests, I didn't. I could have played more tests, I didn't" … I did not want to be one of those people. For me it was like, I had achieved what I could.

His time in England soon turned into novel challenges and learnings, and a new collection of achievements. Yet, nobody understood his decision not to return on the basis of personal reasons, when he could have had another chance in the All Blacks.

Similarly, Hoani made the Māori All Blacks in 2007, but, one year later, he left for Italy. He was still in Europe, notably France, when we met. When I inquired whether his family had supported his decision, Hoani's voice went quiet "uhm … I think so." His Māori wife added, "well, they did not tell you not to go … they still talk to you!" We all laughed, but then the wife became serious. "No, they were fine. … They knew there was a big opportunity for him to take … so, who were they to stand in the way." Some Māori may indeed read the athletes' choice to go or stay overseas as egotistical. All athletes still operated within a frame of resistance, individually attempting to create alternative futures to resistance itself.

Athletes eventually disclosed difficulties like the precarity of contracts and benefits, the question of where to go next or whether one should stay, the linguistic barrier in non-English-speaking countries, cultural differences, and possible deceptions. A few players expressed rage and pain, recalling the social malaise they experienced in New Zealand. Mihaere, who briefly went to England as gang issues affected his domestic career, recalled his time away as the occasion to come to terms with his "anger against the white man," as he felt welcomed and respected overseas. While his second experience overseas turned out to be a false promise, he felt equipped to move on spiritually and work-wise, starting a new chapter in New Zealand, where he is now studying at a *whare wānanga* (Māori tertiary institution), and working with *rangatahi* (Māori youth) and as a cultural and spiritual mentor for Māori rugby. In this sense, the athletes' focus on their different lives or their children's multicultural upbringing emphasized the achievement of a life which felt more than surviving, in a context where many could relate to Jay, who, marvelling at his time in Germany, emphasized "growing up here, I thought I wouldn't go anywhere."

Unlike many athletes who seem not to consider the short-lived dimension of athletic careers (Besnier, Calabrò, and Guinness, this volume), the Māori athletes I met projected themselves in the long term. For many, moving to an overseas rugby contract is itself an end-of-career plan. Some overseas-based athletes had shifted into coaching.[6] Three athletes initiated businesses acknowledging the overseas fascination with the *haka* and tapping in their own rugby experience. Drawing on the purpose of the *haka* to bring a team together, Storm, based in the Netherlands, developed a "haka authentic experience" for local companies. Starting in Italy and progressively expanding to other parts of Europe and Asia, the Middle East, and North and South America, Regan and Troy organized rugby camps for youth that incorporate aspects of Māori culture like the *haka, waiata* (songs), ancestral stories, the *pōwhiri,* the Māori welcome ritual to welcome participants and, on match day, their families, and the *hakari,* the closing feast.

Re-enacting *whānaungatanga* and *manaakitanga* (hospitality) in foreign settings, the rugby camps encouraged participating Māori athletes to become more self-aware and appreciative of their culture. It also made them more responsible, leading them to perform the role of *kaitiaki* (guardians) of their culture and history. This guardianship also emerged with other athletes. For instance, Storm formulated the *haka* experience business as a response to the many foreigners "distorting" and "mimicking" it, and to the fact that people who are not Māori are "using it" for their own gain. Other players were protective towards the *haka* when asked by locals to perform it.

Overseas, athletes generated new ways of engaging with their kin. While endeavouring to find their place in the world, some have emphasized their attempts to honour their family's work ethic and in some cases rugby achievements. Many were proud to provide their parents and other family members the opportunity to see the world. In turn, parents rejoiced in those opportunities. A few athletes had learned the languages of the host countries and yet, they ironically highlighted, they could not speak their own language. This generated the desire to study Māori, but also the feeling that they had the ability to learn it.

In the stories and mobility patterns I came across, multiple desires intertwined to transform into a vital force which encouraged the athletes to leave their (some-times uncomfortable) comfort zones and open themselves to the possibility of new trajectories and relations. All their aspirations could be summarized as an attempt to honour their desire for the world, which is not simply "seeing the world" as mere travellers, but rather existing beyond a state of resilience. As the athletes migrate, or even before when they envisage their migration, their masculine subjectivities recall the notion of *becoming* as conceptualized by Gilles Deleuze and Felix Guattari (Parr 2005), which captures the process whereby individuals generate new ways of being as they try to fulfil their desires (Biehl and Locke 2010).[7] From this perspective, the expression "plastic Māori" could lose its derogatory connotation, for "in facing and stretching their limits, people exercise various degrees of plasticity" (Biehl and Locke 2010, 349). Plasticity may still recall adaptability. It nonetheless refers to the capacity to mould into something new, or, in a neurological understanding of the term, to re-wire, in contrast to resilience, a term which hard science coined to define materials' ability to maintain (or return to) their position after stress.

Invisible journeys towards recognition

On 25 March 2000, the *Phnom Penh Post* announced that Cambodia's rugby national team would travel to Hong Kong for their first international match ever. A Māori expatriate, Hawea, captained the team. Together with other expatriates, he had introduced the game to the region. His cousin shared a copy of the newspaper article and recommended that I talk with him. Hawea enthusiastically told many anecdotes, stressing how the initiative he was part of contributed to introducing the sport in schools and changed many young men's lives. But hardly anybody knew about his achievements because they were not there to see it. When I asked him why he would not share the stories, silence was his answer. In discussions about *mana,* I was often reminded of another *whakatauki,* who told me that the *kumara* (sweet potato) does not say how sweet it is. Yet legendary figures like Kupe and Māui as well as the soldiers from the Māori battalion had seemingly shared what they saw, did, and learned.

Different players were happy with the way they were or had been contributing to rugby in the host countries, sharing their skills as well as their comradery and leadership. This was particularly evident in coaching, as athletes often led teams to success. Some were happy to be sharing parts of their culture, like how to perform a "proper" *haka.* Athletes were open to reciprocating to the people and countries that had given them an opportunity, welcomed them into their worlds, and helped them grow as individuals. But as my questions prompted reflections on Māori rec-ognition of their journeys, the athletes' responses revealed a latent angst about not being seen. Just as the power of masculinities is contextual in a general way (Besnier, Guinness, Hann, and Kovač 2018), in overseas rugby contexts Māori men may find themselves in a distinct hierarchy in their own country, but their distance from the families, friends and country, whose recognition they have long sought for, reinstates their vulnerability.

The lively discussion with three members of Oyonnax Rugby – Benjamin, Hoani with his wife, and the coach Lipi, who was hosting the gathering – sometimes accompanied by Benjamin's guitar, slid into silence when we touched on issues of *mana* and the recognition of what they were doing in France, until Hoani shared the uncomfortable feeling that people at home did not show much interest in either their achievements or difficulties. He later added that nobody had ever asked him how he felt about his experience, which was the reason why he had not faced his own emotions about recognition.

The athletes' movements demand a re-examination of giving. In describing their engagement with rugby and people overseas, the athletes used the language of reciprocity. Similarly, they framed their relationship with their distant families as a matter of reciprocity in that they endeavoured to respect themselves, strove to create good futures for their offspring, offered their families opportunities to join them, and attempted to provide a positive image of Māori. But silence and distance contributed to misrecognition even overseas.

Quentin was supposed to be part of the group discussion in Oyonnax, but having arrived just before it was over, we eventually had a one-to-one interview. The coach Lipi was still trying to figure out the player who had only recently joined the team and seemed silent and reserved. Lipi saw Quentin's delayed arrival as a sign of self-centredness. But, after overhearing our conversation from the kitchen, he deemed important to tell me he had misread Quentin and now realized that he was in fact focused and responsible.

Māori discourse idealizes its ancient history of voyages, but may forget to create space for the athletes' stories, as had happened in the case of the men who fought in the two world wars. Concurrently, the athletes' silence echoes processes that have historically reduced Māori men to bodies (Hokowhitu 2007), to the extent that they forget how to communicate. Many Māori having internalized negative definitions of themselves, athletes may also fear to come across as *whakaiti* (conceited) or avoid sharing experiences that could confirm negative images. In our conversations, they struggled to share their vulnerability, but more easily brought that to the fore when accused of self-centredness for leaving the family behind or capitalizing on Māori culture.

Eventually, the separations produced by the Māori athletes' transnational mobility potentially trigger ancestral grief as well as collective and individual fears of losing oneself in a sea of non-recognition, which includes both the possibility of not being "seen" and thus being left behind, and of not recognizing what one has or can *become*, as a sociocultural group and an individual.

Overseas, recognition reveals ambiguity as it often borders with processes that maintain Māori out of the human realm. The (resilient) warrior image contributes to Māori athletes' appeal to the international rugby industry, media, and audiences, which often fetishizes them, as they fetishize Pacific Island rugby men (Besnier 2014; Grainger 2009; Hawkes 2018). However, when the warrior's magical powers become ineffective because of injury or a poor performance, the player is likely to fall into oblivion and be easily replaced, causing further scarring.

A Dutch rugby club manager highlighted the importance of having players like Māori on the squad, "naturally gifted" and better performing than "white New Zealanders," and therefore paying them well, even though they may be a bit lazy. A similar comment reproduced the naturalization and racialization of Māori skills ingrained in colonial discourse, which camouflages itself in the guise of *flair*, with the old corollary of laziness negating the sacrifices that athletes make on and off the field. With overseas recruiters ascribing the warrior rugby athletes' performance to a racialized natural talent, one might wonder if the global rugby industry will lose interest in Māori men, who are increasingly fair-skinned and diversely built.

At the rugby camps in Italy, children were particularly intrigued by the athletes' tattoos, which some longed to touch and others desired on their own bodies. A mature Italian woman affiliated with a club that was hosting a Māori rugby camp referred to the athletes as "gods," but she equally recounted having perceived the first Māori man she ever met as "strange and intimidating," evoking the fear that the warrior provokes. The little knowledge that people overseas have of the athletes' Indigenous condition gave rise to subtle forms of dehumanization.

However, "if you get to know him," the Italian woman added, "he has a kind heart, and if you get to know his culture, then you can understand him." Unaware of the negative stereotypes of which Māori men are the object in New Zealand, she came to see the man as ordinary. Many camp participants, particularly the teenagers, switched from revering the athletes to being fond of the men who, in the course of the camp, encouraged them to take responsibility, respect each other, respect the game, be disciplined, and remember to laugh. Similarly, the camp's participants appreciated having learned stories about the *haka* and Māori myths and history, and I caught many of them sharing what they had learned with their parents, such as correcting them for having got the *hongi* (greeting) wrong by pressing their foreheads rather than their noses, and thus missing out on the exchange of vital force that is central to the *hongi*.

This last scenario contrasts with many situations in New Zealand, where prejudice and fear often prevent non-Indigenous New Zealanders and Māori from connecting with one another, and rob Māori men of self-confidence, whereas – as many Māori remind me whenever I visit New Zealand – foreigners seem to be much more appreciative and respectful of them. Overseas, athletes' political anonymity enabled athletes to forget, if only briefly, the baggage of Indigeneity, which would pop up again when questions elicited old insecurities about their identities, memories revived pain, and whenever they realized that, even though they might remember where they came from, their own people might forget or not recognize them. Overall, the athletes' attempts to create new existential trajectories through transnational mobility remain situated in the realm of precarious resilience, for the very fact that they still operate within their assigned and embodied identities as athletes, warriors, and Indigenous men.

The precarity of becoming

Indigenous masculinities are often entangled with references to warriorhood in the presence of an enemy. Neoliberal sport has contributed to this entanglement, as the warrior is full of qualities that the sport industries long for. My ethnography has led me to a notion of warriorhood as it is generated within the contemporary moment: one that is suffused with resilience, where the Indigenous discourse and the neoliberal discourse meet and part. Being resilient has become a new condition to authenticate Indigenous people. While neoliberalism may praise and reinforce Indigenous resilience, it obscures structural inequalities and constructs a field in which warriors are needed. But this process becomes a form of resilience to resilience. More importantly, resilience does not address the resentment which silently intoxicates Indigenous men's perceptions of themselves and their social relations in the context of unsolved inherited trauma.

Rather than warriors, the athletes I encountered came across as navigators trying to reminisce about a time when they were free to fulfil their potential as people, and to remember that their ancestors were able to navigate the Pacific. For them, the rugby industry, its overseas opportunities, neoliberal dynamics, and Indigeneity itself are the new Ocean to navigate. The latter notion "holds the promise of rearticulating and reframing questions of place, space, movement, and belonging" (Byrd and Rothberg 2011, 3). However, its demands may repress individual desires of generating new forms of being and may obscure its corresponding journeys. Moreover, collective narratives and (attempted) performances of resistance may overshadow people's struggles, which include the crystallization of a resilient existence. Eventually, Indigeneity's imperatives and dynamics seem to only allow limited space to face deeper issues of ancestral trauma and healing and thus produce ontological decoloniality.

Acknowledgements

Some of the research reported herein received funding from the European Research Council (grant agreement no. 295769) for the project titled "Globalization, Sport and the Precarity of Masculinity" (GLOBALSPORT) based at the University of Amsterdam. I am grateful to the athletes, their families, and other people I encountered on the field for sharing their stories, opinions, and emotions, and for their warm welcome and hospitality. Special thanks to Mat Mullany and Daniel Arthur for connecting me with a number of rugby players. The GLOBALSPORT team and Susan Brownell offered useful comments. Thanks to my coeditors Niko Besnier and Daniel Guinness. Thank you to my colleague and friend Sara Amin for encouragement and feedback. My deep gratitude to my sister Laura for her support in completing this chapter. This is to the loving memory of my father Candeloro, who, despite his illness, encouraged me to stay focused on this research.

Notes

1 My interlocutors wanted their identity to be disclosed and thus I am not using pseudonyms.
2 In New Zealand, I attended the Auckland region Māori Rugby tournaments held over three weekends in October 2016. I interviewed men who had played or coached overseas, and professional athletes who considered playing overseas. I interacted with parents and other kin of athletes who were or had been overseas. In Europe, I attended three *haka* rugby camps in Italy and one in the Netherlands, which gathered a few players based on the continent; and I visited the French cities of Oyonnax, Albi, and Bordeaux to meet locally based coaches and players. This research draws on doctoral fieldwork I conducted in New Zealand in 2008–09 and 2010, investigating the connection between rugby and Māori identity.
3 This proverb features in the haka composed for the Māori All Blacks (Calabrò 2016, 232).
4 The *kahikatea* is a tree endemic to New Zealand.
5 By *Rangiātea*, Māori refer to a group of islands in the Pacific Ocean from which their ancestors moved to New Zealand, and therefore to their ancient homeland.
6 When I started research in Māori contexts, coaching opportunities in New Zealand were virtually inaccessible beyond Māori rugby, whereas overseas rugby contexts, particularly emerging ones, have long shown an interest in their skills and leadership as warriors of yesteryear.
7 The applicability of Deleuze and Guattari's work to Indigenous contexts is beyond this chapter's scope. However, it could be useful to do so with regards to the analysis of individual desires and the worlds they may produce, particularly as a counterpoint to the tendency in Indigenous Studies to endorse Foucault and his analysis of power.

References

Alfred, Taiake, and Jeff Corntassel. 2005. "Being Indigenous: Resurgences against Contemporary Colonialism." *Government and Opposition* 40, no. 4: 597–614.
Bellier, Irène. 2011. "L'anthropologie, l'indigène et les peuples autochtones." 19ème Conférence Robert Hertz à l'invitation de l'Association pour la recherche en anthropologie sociale, Juin 2011, Paris.
Besnier, Niko. 2011. *On the Edge of the Global: Modern Anxieties in a Pacific Island Nation.* Stanford, CA: Stanford University Press.
Besnier, Niko. 2014. "Pacific Island Rugby: Histories, Mobilities, Comparisons." *Asia-Pacific Journal of Sport and Social Science* 3: 268–276.
Besnier, Niko. 2015. "Sports Mobilities Across Borders: Postcolonial Perspectives." *International Journal of the History of Sport* 32, no. 7: 849–861.
Besnier, Niko, Daniel Guinness, Mark Hann, and Uroš Kovač. 2018. "Rethinking Masculinity in the Neoliberal Order: Cameroonian Footballers, Fijian Rugby Players, and Senegalese Wrestlers." *Comparative Studies in Society and History* 60, no. 4: 839–872.
Béteille, André. 1998. "The Idea of Indigenous People." *Current Anthropology* 39, no. 2: 187–192.
Biehl, João, and Peter Locke. 2010. "Deleuze and the Anthropology of Becoming." *Current Anthropology* 51, no. 3: 317–351.

Borrell, Phillip. 2015. "Patriotic Games: Boundaries and Masculinity in New Zealand Sport." In *Indigenous Men and Masculinities: Legacies, Identities, Regeneration*, edited by Robert Alexander Innes and Kim Anderson, 165–180. Winnipeg: University of Manitoba Press.

Byrd, Jody A., and Michael Rothberg. 2011. "Between Subalternity and Indigeneity: Critical Categories for Postcolonial Studies." *Interventions* 13, no. 1: 1–12.

de la Cadena, Marisol, and Orin Starn. 2007. "Introduction." In *Indigenous Experience Today*, edited by Marisol de la Cadena and Orin Starn, 1–30. Oxford: Berg.

Calabrò, Domenica Gisella. 2014. "Beyond the All Blacks Representations: The Dialectic between the Indigenization of Rugby and Postcolonial Strategies to Control Māori." *The Contemporary Pacific* 26, no. 2: 389–408.

Calabrò, Domenica Gisella. 2016. "Once Were Warriors, Now Are Rugby Players? Control and Agency in the Historical Trajectory of the Māori Formulations of Masculinity in Rugby." *Asia-Pacific Journal of Anthropology* 17, no. 3–4: 231–249.

Chandler, David, and Julian Reid. 2016. *The Neoliberal Subject: Resilience, Adaptation and Vulnerability*. London: Rowman & Littlefield.

Chandler, David, and Julian Reid. 2018. "'Being in Being': Contesting the Ontopolitics of Indigeneity." *The European Legacy* 23, no. 3: 251–268.

Clifford, James. 2001. "Indigenous Articulations." *The Contemporary Pacific* 13, no. 2: 468–490.

Gagné, Natacha. 2013. *Being Māori in the City: Indigenous Everyday Life in Auckland*. Toronto: University of Toronto Press.

Gagné, Natacha, and Marie Salaün. 2012. "Appeals to Indigeneity: Insights from Oceania," *Social Identities* 18, no. 4: 381–398.

Gershon, Ilana. 2008. "Being Explicit about Culture: Māori, Neoliberalism, and the New Zealand Parliament." *American Anthropologist* 110, no. 4: 422–431.

Gershon, Ilana. 2011. "Neoliberal Agency." *Current Anthropology* 52, no. 4: 537–555.

Gershon, Ilana, and Allison Alexy. 2011. "The Ethics of Disconnection in a Neoliberal Age." *Anthropological Quarterly* 84, no. 4: 799–808.

Gomes, Alberto. 2013. "Anthropology and the Politics of Indigeneity." *Anthropological Forum* 23, no. 1: 5–15.

Goss, John, and Bruce Lindquist. 2000. "Placing Movers: An Overview of the Asian-Pacific Migration." *The Contemporary Pacific* 12, no. 2: 385–414.

Grainger, Andrew. 2009. "Rugby Island Style: Paradise, Pacific People, and the Racialisation of Athletic Performance." *Junctures* 12:45–63.

Harris, Michelle, Bronwyn Carlson, and Evan Te Ahu Poata-Smith. 2013. "Indigenous Identities and the Politics of Authenticity." In *The Politics of Identity: Emerging Indigeneity*, edited by Bronwyn Carlson, Michelle Harris, and Martin Nakata, 1–9. Sydney: UTS ePress.

Hau'ofa, Epeli. 1994. "Our Sea of Islands." *The Contemporary Pacific* 6, no. 1: 147–161.

Hawkes, Gina Louise. 2018. "Indigenous Masculinity in Sport: The Power and Pitfalls of Rugby League for Australia's Pacific Island Diaspora." *Leisure Studies* 37, no. 3: 318–330.

Hayes, Geoffrey. 1991. "Migration, Metascience, and Development Policy in Island Polynesia." *The Contemporary Pacific* 3, no. 1: 1–58.

Hokowhitu, Brendan. 2003. "Race Tactics: The Racialised Athletic Body." *Junctures* 1:21–34.

Hokowhitu, Brendan. 2004a. "Tackling Māori Masculinity: A Colonial Genealogy of Savagery and Sport." *The Contemporary Pacific* 16, no. 2: 259–284.

Hokowhitu, Brendan. 2004b. "Physical Beings: Stereotypes, Sport and the 'Physical Education' of New Zealand Māori." *Ethnicity, Sport, Identity: Struggles for Status*, edited by J.A. Mangan and Andrew Ritchie, 19–218. London: Frank Cass.

Hokowhitu, Brendan. 2005. "Rugby and *Tino Rangatiratanga*: Early Māori Rugby and the Formation of Māori Masculinity." *Sporting Traditions* 21, no. 2: 75–95.

Hokowhitu, Brendan. 2007. "The Silencing of Māori Men." *New Zealand Journal of Counselling* 27, no. 2: 63–76.

Hokowhitu, Brendan. 2008. "Authenticating Māori Physicality: Translations of 'Games' and 'Pastimes' by Early Travellers and Missionaries to New Zealand." *International Journal of the History of Sport* 25, no. 10: 1355–1373.

Hokowhitu, Brendan. 2015. "Taxonomies of Indigeneity: Indigenous Heterosexual Patriarchal Masculinity." In *Indigenous Men and Masculinities: Legacies, Identities, Regeneration*, edited by Robert Alexander Innes and Kim Anderson, 80–95. Winnipeg: University of Manitoba Press.

Innes, Robert Alexander, and Kim Anderson. 2015. *Indigenous Men and Masculinities: Legacies, Identities, Regeneration*. Winnipeg: University of Manitoba Press.

Jolly, Margaret. 1992. "Specters of Inauthenticity." *The Contemporary Pacific* 4, no. 1: 49–72.

Kuper, Adam. 2003. "The Return of the Native." *Current Anthropology* 44, no. 3: 389–402.

Lindroth, Marjo, and Heidi Sinevaara-Niskanen. 2014. "Adapt or Die? The Biopolitics of Indigeneity – From the Civilising Mission to the Need for Adaptation." *Global Society* 28, no. 2: 180–194.

Lindroth, Marjo, and Heidi Sinevaara-Niskanen. 2016. "The Biopolitics of Resilient Indigeneity and the Radical Gamble of Resistance." *Resilience* 4, no. 2: 130–145.

Lindroth, Marjo, and Heidi Sinevaara-Niskanen. 2018. *Global Politics and Its Violent Care for Indigeneity: Sequels to Colonialism*. London: Palgrave Macmillan.

Maddison, Sarah. 2013. "Indigenous Identity, 'Authenticity' and the Structural Violence of Settler Colonialism." *Identities* 20, no. 3: 288–303.

Maldonado-Torres, Nelson. 2007. "On the Coloniality of Being: Contributions to the Development of a Concept." *Cultural Studies* 21, no. 2–3: 240–270.

McCall, Grant, and John Connell. 1993. "Pacific Islander Migration: Context and Prospects." In *A World Perspective on Pacific Islander Migration: Australia, New Zealand and the USA*, edited by Grant McCall and John Connell, 1–16. Kensington, NSW: Centre for South Pacific Studies, University of New South Wales.

McCormack, Fiona. 2011. "Levels of Indigeneity: The Maori and Neoliberalism." *Journal of the Royal Anthropological Institute* 17, no. 2: 281–300.

McCormack, Fiona. 2012. "Indigeneity as Process: Māori Claims and Neoliberalism." *Social Identities* 18, no. 4: 417–434.

McKegney, Sam. 2011. "Warrior, Healers, Lovers, and Leaders: Colonial Impositions on Indigenous Male Roles and Responsibilities." In *Canadian Perspectives on Men and Masculinities: An Interdisciplinary Reader*, edited by Jason A. Laker, 241–268. Toronto: Oxford University Press.

McKegney, Sam. 2014. *Masculindians: Conversations about Indigenous Manhood*. Winnipeg: University of Manitoba Press.

McIntosh, Tracey. 2005. "Maori Identities: Fixed, Fluid, Forced." In *New Zealand Identities: Departures and Destinations*, edited by James H Liu, Tim McCreanor, Tracey McIntosh, and Teresia Teaiwa, 38–51. Wellington: Victoria University Press.

Merlan, Francesca. 2009. "Indigeneity: Global and Local." *Current Anthropology* 50, no. 3: 303–333.

Mignolo, Walter D. 2007. "Introduction: Coloniality of power and de-colonial thinking." *Cultural Studies* 21, no. 2–3: 155–167.

Mulholland, Malcolm. 2009. *Beneath the Māori Moon: An Illustrated History of Māori Rugby*. Wellington: Huia.

Parr, Adrian. 2005. *The Deleuze Dictionary*. Edinburgh: Edinburgh University Press.

Pearson, Sarina. 2015. "Romanticism and Reality on the GC: Transnational Māori on the Gold Coast." *Pacific Studies* 38, nos. 1–2: 253–271.

Quijano, Aníbal. 2000. "Coloniality of Power and Eurocentrism in Latin America." *International Sociology* 15, no. 2: 215–232.

Ryan, Greg. 1993. *Forerunners of the All Blacks*. Christchurch: Canterbury University Press.

Sissons, Jeffrey. 2005. *First Peoples: Indigenous Cultures and Their Futures*. London: Reaktion.

Smith, Linda Tuhiwai. 1999. *Decolonizing Methodologies: Research and Indigenous Peoples*. London: Zed.

Tengan, Ty P. Kāwika. 2002. "(En)gendering Colonialism: Masculinities in Hawai'i and Aotearoa." *Cultural Values* 6, no. 3: 229–238.

Tengan, Ty P. Kāwika, and Jesse Makani Markham. 2009. "Performing Polynesian Masculinities in American Football: From 'Rainbows to Warriors.'" *International Journal of the History of Sport* 26, no. 16: 2412–2431.

10

BEING "THE BEST EVER"

Contradictions of immobility and aspiration for boxers in Accra, Ghana

Leo Hopkinson

Floyd Mayweather is an unbeaten and hugely wealthy African American boxer with a carefully curated public image of global mobility and opulent wealth. He is widely known by the self-selected moniker T.B.E. "The Best Ever." Although now retired, during my fieldwork with boxers in Accra between 2014 and 2016, Mayweather was the most lauded boxing icon among my interlocutors. They watched Mayweather's fights avidly, but they were equally dedicated to the images and video clips circulating on social media, in which Mayweather appeared in lavish clothing and surrounded by huge material wealth (e.g., cars, houses, private jets), handling large sums of cash. This proliferation of images represents a new aspect of the "media of compression" that make global connection and vast material wealth so tantalizing and seemingly accessible for young people (Weiss 2009, 8), and that shape athletes' aspiration to participate in global sporting industries (Besnier 2015). Yet, most aspiring athletes never realize these aspirations.

"T.B.E." is also the nickname (or "guy name," as Accra boxers say) that Daniel, a boxer who trained at the Attoh Quarshie boxing gym where I conducted much of my fieldwork, chose for himself.[1] Daniel has boxed for eight years, but unlike Mayweather he is viewed by other boxers and coaches as relatively unskilled and unlikely to ever become globally mobile or wealthy through the sport. Although Daniel regularly professes his commitment to becoming "a champ" or "the best," he is aware of his technical shortcomings. Yet he is well respected in the gym. His guy name is acknowledged even by more skilled boxers who are globally mobile and have achieved financial success. Rather than encouraging him to temper his claims, Daniel's coaches and fellow boxers laud his ambition and commitment to training.

Daniel is not exceptional. Many boxers in Accra nurture aspirations that far exceed their skills and choose similarly ostentatious guy names, but are still accepted and respected by their peers. As a paradigm of seemingly hopeless aspirations, Daniel's claim to being "The Best Ever" raises two questions: *why* is the claim accepted despite Daniel's limitations, and *what* is being recognized by this acceptance, if it is clearly not Daniel's skill in the ring? Daniel's appropriation of "T.B.E." is a public commitment to the gendered success that Mayweather represents for boxers in Accra and to ambition in the face of limited opportunity. For the many athletes like Daniel who find themselves on the periphery of global sporting industries with little hope of fulfilling their ambitions, performing aspiration rather than embodying sporting prowess is central to their gendered identity.

Aspiration and fantasy in global sporting industries

As other authors in this volume argue, aspirations to sporting success on a global scale have become since the 1990s a feature of gendered experience in many countries of the Global South. Increasing global connection and economic integration since the 1980s has led to new forms of marginality and exclusion for many in the Global South (Weiss 2009; Geschiere and Nyamnjoh 2000; Comaroff and Comaroff 1999). Against this backdrop, young men who find forms of social adulthood increasingly difficult to achieve through conventional gendered roles have turned to sport as a route to social mobility (Besnier 2015; Besnier, Calabrò, and Guinness, this volume). The neoliberal economic reforms that Ghana underwent in the late 1980s and early 1990s were typical of this moment and resulted in changes to labour markets that saw forms of employment previously associated with masculinity and social adulthood in Ghana (such as government or state-industry employment) become inaccessible to many young men (Esson 2013). Changes like these precipitated a situation in Ghana and across Africa wherein young men increasingly found employment in "feminine" roles, such as market trading and hawking, and consequently sought to express their masculinity in ways other than employment (Esson 2015; Weiss 2009). During this period, Ghanaians' hopes of participating in global sporting industries were fuelled by increasingly available images of sporting migrants' success in the wealthy leagues and competitions of Europe and North America. Sport as a route to financial wealth and social mobility has thus become an attractive pursuit for many young Ghanaians in much the same way as it has for young men across the Global South.

Ambitions to participate in global sporting markets come hand in hand with projects of global mobility and transnational migration (Besnier, Guinness, Hann, and Kovač 2018). However, the extreme competitiveness of sporting industries means far fewer aspiring athletes realize dreams of global mobility and engagement than hold them, leaving the question of how athletes deal with the discrepancy between their aspirations and their immobility. In Accra, the presence of a relatively high number of globally mobile athletes contributes to a sense that engagement in a global industry is a real possibility for ambitious boxers. Yet, there are far more aspiring but immobile boxers like Daniel than boxers who have led successful international careers. For many, the juxtaposition of global engagement and exclusion illustrates the conditions of millennial capitalism as a space of simultaneous opportunity and exclusion (Comaroff and Comaroff 2001). While some athletes labour under the sincere belief that they can realize grand sporting ambitions, many others realize the limits of their dreams. In Accra, performing aspiration is central to the masculinity of immobile athletes. These performances reveal Accra boxers' critical perspective on the global boxing industry, which promises them much but often does not deliver. Daniel's participation in boxing shows how aspirant athletes simultaneously engage with and are critical of neoliberal sporting markets, rather than blindly participating despite the odds of success being stacked against them.

Under neoliberal economic reforms like those implemented in Ghana since the 1980s, the self becomes conceptualized as a business or bundle of skills and network connections, which must be reflexively self-governing and constantly seek self-improvement. West Africa athletes implement intense programmes of bodily discipline, spiritual commitment, and magico-religious practices in the pursuit of participation in global sporting industries (Kovač 2018; Hann 2018a). The "athlete self" is thus constantly engaged in corporeal and spiritual bettering and in social networking in the service of future sporting success (Hann 2018b). Yet, many of my interlocutors in Accra were well aware of their limited futures in the transnational boxing industry. Athletes like Daniel, who recognize their limitations yet continue to publicly perform aspirations to success, show that the athlete self's focus on self-improvement is not the only goal of training and competing. Daniel participates in the sport neither in the blind hope of success nor because he sees improving his athletic ability as a route to social mobility. Instead, performing aspiration is central to the gendered self-making of involuntarily immobile athletes like Daniel.

While Daniel often talks publicly of "taking his chance" and "getting lucky," discourses characteristic of neoliberal capitalist logics, he is also a realist who leverages resources and skills to present himself as an ideal masculine subject despite recognising his athletic shortcomings and immobility. To do so, he reframes market trading from a feminine form of work dominated by women (Esson 2013, 88; Overå 2007; Thiel and Stasic 2016) to one that facilitates and supports his masculinity. Like youth in Kinshasa (De Boeck and Plissart 2004, 48–49), he constantly reframes his experiences of connection and marginality to articulate a sense of agency while simultaneously recognising his exclusion from an imagined world of capitalist modernity and boundless consumption. Daniel's life can be read as a criticism of the rags-to-riches myths and millennial capitalist ethos that proliferate in the Global South. His immobility and lack of skill as an aspiring boxer challenge the assumption that sporting aspiration is necessarily an index of reflexive self-improvement in the mould of an idealised neoliberal subjectivity (Gershon 2011). Instead, aspiration itself is central to gendered selfhood for athletes in Accra.

Boxing in Accra: Migration and mobility

In Ghanaian popular consciousness, boxing is associated with the Ga ethnic group and the neighbourhood of Ga Mashie in central Accra. The sport is understood as a contemporary continuation of the historic Ga pugilistic practice of *Asafo Atwele*, itself a marker of masculinity in Ga Society (Akyeampong 2002; Dunzendorfer 2014). During my fieldwork, there were 41 boxing gyms in Accra, of which 25 were in Ga Mashie; no other neighbourhood had more than four gyms. The network of gyms in Ga Mashie are the nodes around which the sport is structured both socially and spatially.

During my fieldwork, I followed an established tradition of foregrounding bodily praxis and embodied experience in ethnographic research (Jackson 1989; Bourdieu 1977; Stoller 1989; Wacquant 2004). I was affiliated principally with the Attoh Quarshie gym, a relatively large gym with a membership of over 40 boxers, of which around 20 train together on any afternoon. I trained there three to five times a week. Depending on the schedule of upcoming fights, I joined other members on morning runs and I controlled my diet and sleep prior to bouts as my interlocutors did. Boxers' strict regimen is reminiscent of the reflexive practices of self-improvement associated with athletes attempting to enter neoliberal global sporting industries across West Africa (Hann 2018b; Kovač 2018). However, athletes like Daniel follow these regimens while also recognising their immobility, and ground their participation in a sense of gendered selfhood in a subtly different way.

The Accra boxing family (the collective term that my interlocutors used) includes women in all the various roles involved in the sport – as boxers, coaches, referees, judges, promoters, and managers (Figure 10.1). While spaces were often largely male dominated and only a few women boxed actively, women were not excluded from training, competing, organizing, or promoting boxing. None of the coaches or referees I spoke to opposed women training at their gyms or competing, despite the fact that the sport has historically been a male domain. Indeed, several of the most experienced, globally successful, and well-travelled boxers at the Attoh Quarshie were women.

Accra boxers are strikingly mobile globally and actively engaged in the global boxing industry. During my fieldwork, boxers and coaches travelled across six continents to ply their trade, and over the last 40 years Ghana has produced nine world champions, the most recent in February 2019. Most boxers who travel overseas to fight return to Ghana within a week of competing, often the very next day after a bout. A small number of athletes migrate semi-permanently to work with coaches and promoters based abroad. There were also rumours of irregular migration involving overstaying short-term visas granted for single bouts, often in Western Europe and the United States. However, more prominent than these rumours was a widespread sense that foreign consulates were so paranoid about boxers absconding while abroad that they were reluctant to issue Ghanaian boxers visas, and thus limited boxers' ability to work abroad despite legitimate offers of employment.[2] Coaches and boxers often spoke of building up a reliable travel record by leaving destination countries prior to visa expiration as a strategy to increase the likelihood of being granted visas in future.

On their travels, boxers and coaches participated at the highest levels of the sport – several challenged for professional world titles or competed

FIGURE 10.1 A coach watches boxers train in a gym, Accra, Ghana, 2015. (Source: Leo Hopkinson)

in the Olympic Games, pan-African championships, and amateur world championships. However, many more travelled for less prestigious competitions, titles, and bouts. The mobility of African boxers who train in Accra is facilitated by pervasive racialized stereotypes in the global boxing industry of Ghanaians as inherently "tough" and physically "durable" – able to withstand much physical attrition during a bout. These stereotypes are reminiscent of the racialized profiling of sporting communities around the world, for example the emphasis on African footballers' strength and physicality (Yeku 2018) and the profiling of Pacific Islanders in the international rugby industry as large, muscular, and athletic (Besnier 2015). Although toughness and durability are stereotypes attached to Ghanaian boxers, they were readily applied to black African boxers from across West Africa who trained in Accra. As a result, boxers who train in Accra are sought-after opponents in the centres of the global boxing industry in North America and Western Europe. European and American managers and matchmakers have established links to the Accra boxing community, often by way of the Ghanaian diaspora, through which they recruit Accra boxers to fight abroad. In recognition of this, several of my interlocutors from neighbouring countries chose to identify as Ghanaian for the purpose of their boxing records in the hope of increasing their global mobility.

While Ga Mashie provides a migratory starting point for some boxers, it is also a destination for boxers from across the world. During my fieldwork, boxers from the United States, Britain, Lebanon, Kazakhstan, Nigeria, Benin, Kenya, Uganda, South Africa, Namibia, Cameroon, South Korea, Argentina, and Mexico (and no doubt other countries I was unaware of) came to live, train, and compete in Accra. Most came for short periods of up to two weeks for a single professional bout, but a few came to train for longer periods and a number of boxers from Nigeria and Benin had migrated permanently to Accra in the hope of furthering their careers. In addition to leveraging the racialized stereotype of the Ghanaian boxer to increase their chances of getting lucrative fights abroad, these athletes cited as reasons to migrate the high quality of coaching, sparring, and training available in Accra. This constitutes a twist on the image of mobile athletes invariably moving from the Global South to the Global North.

Further complicating the idea of Accra as a peripheral source of sporting labour in the global boxing industry, several of the more successful Ghanaian boxers I worked with chose to base their careers in Accra rather than migrating overseas permanently despite having the resources to do so. Many had trained and fought abroad for long periods, often in the United States or Britain, where large Ghanaian migrant communities facilitate their arrival and employment. Yet several chose to relocate to Accra as they too felt that training there, specifically in Ga Mashie, was better for their careers. However, these athletes still successfully sought well-paid fights abroad in the boxing hubs of Western Europe, North America, and elsewhere. These complex patterns of migrant labour complicate the paradigm of sub-Saharan countries as sources of sporting labour and migratory starting points, as well as the idea that permanent migration is central to sporting aspirations. For many boxers in Accra, temporary global mobility anchored in a life in Ghana is a central feature of ambitions to success in the sport (Figure 10.2).

Accra is better understood as a hub of global mobility linking West Africa to the global boxing industry than as a starting point for migration (compare Crawley, this volume, on Ethiopian runners). The complex dynamics of mobility through which boxers engage with the industry are not encapsulated by a paradigm that contrasts the Global South as source of labour with the Global North as a consumer of labour. In Ga Mashie, former world champions, world-title challengers, and African champions are regularly found training alongside novices and boxers of much inferior skill. Only a small proportion of Accra boxers are globally mobile and fewer still maintain this mobility during their entire careers. However, those who are globally mobile are a tangible and celebrated presence in the city. If global mobility and immobility are generally experienced at the same time (Salazar and Smart 2011; Jónsson 2012), athletes like Daniel experience their immobility particularly acutely in contrast to their mobile peers. Yet, globally recognized and mobile athletes' presence in Ga Mashie helps maintain a sense of possibility and potential for immobile athletes. Boxers understand Accra as a globally connected node, which allows immobile athletes like Daniel to position themselves as actively engaged with a global industry rather than being immobile, peripheral, and marginal.

FIGURE 10.2 Boxers jump rope outside the gym, Accra, Ghana, 2015. (Source: Leo Hopkinson)

Constructing masculinities

Understanding boxing as the quintessential "manly art" (Oates 1987; Wacquant 2004, 37) belies the ways that gendered experience is contextually contingent and constantly in the process of being redefined (Butler 1990; Connell and Messerschmidt 2005). For Accra boxers, this re-making draws on both globally prevalent discourses of masculinity and gender roles grounded specifically in central Accra. Boxers' masculinities and the gendering of the sport are therefore not static but constantly remade in response to shifting gender norms and discourses at both the global and local scale. Daniel's participation in the sport is one such moment of re-making in relation to the contemporary icon of Floyd Mayweather.

For boxers in Accra, "being a man" is not a given but requires careful planning and effort. For example, over the Easter weekend of 2015, I spent several days with Idris, an aspiring light-heavyweight from the Attoh Quarshie, who was a mechanic by trade and ran his own business north of Ga Mashie. We had been given the long weekend off from training and many boxers took the time to relax, party, and socialise. Idris and I spent a day at a packed beach in central Accra. He told me about his life; growing up close to the border with Burkina Faso, moving to Accra as an 18-year-old and eventually beginning training aged 29 at the Attoh Quarshie, just over a year before. He was an amateur at the time, but like many who enter the sport he wanted to turn professional, "win titles" and "get big fights abroad." As we talked, Idris reflected on the place of gender in his experience; beginning his sentences with phrases like "if you want to be a man" or "to be a man you have to," he narrated his life to me as an ongoing project of gendered self-making (Smith 2017).

In the evening, we left the beach and headed back to his shop on a quiet side street, which consisted of a cramped passage where he keeps his tools, some stacked chairs, a table, cooking equipment, clothes, and an awning. He erects the awning on the side of the street and works under it during the day. We washed at a nearby public bathroom, cleaning the sand off our legs, hands, and faces, before laying out the chairs and the table in the street. Idris sent his apprentice away to buy food, and when he returned we sat down to eat. As we ate, Idris stopped abruptly, looked into the middle distance and said, "It's hard to be a man."

Across the table, the apprentice sighed deeply and nodded. Surprised by the immediacy of his reflection, I asked why. As a man, he explained, you have to plan your future because nobody will do it for you. As a 17-year-old in the northern region of Ghana, he had planned to come to Accra, become a mechanic and establish his business before becoming a boxer. Boxing was what he had wanted to do since he was young, but first he had to "make means" for himself – create financial security to support himself as he trained. He described how he now plans to travel and fight abroad before retiring and returning to Ghana, building a house and adding car import to his already successful business. Being a man – not just being male – requires work and a plan. Idris' words also reference the common theme of self-improvement that ran through many boxers' discussions of gendered experience, and reflect understandings of neoliberal selfhood as a process of reflexive self-development (Gershon 2011). Although Idris' plan was unique, the fact that he had one was not. Of course, his aspirations to become a particular type of man reflect a concern with becoming adult that go beyond gender. In one form or another, boxing figures centrally in my interlocutors' aspirations to become the men they want to be, but it is never coterminous with gender (Figure 10.3).

In a similar vein, the sport played a varying role in women's gendered sense of self. Some women boxers I knew trained and boxed sporadically, while others were regular amateur competitors and boxed on the national amateur team, and one world-title challenger migrated from Nigeria to Accra to further her career before migrating to the United States through the sport. Like men who box, women boxers held ambitions of global mobility and financial wealth, but these aspirations were shaped by different gendered expectations outside the gym. In a context where childcare and retail businesses such as provisions shops and market stalls are considered women's labour, women boxers at times spoke of the conflict between their training regimes and their responsibilities as businesswomen or parents, often sacrificing the former for the latter (compare Borenstein, this volume, on women runners in Ethiopia). By contrast, many male boxers proudly justified leaving workplaces in the afternoon to train because for them the latter was a "job," irrespective of whether they received any payment for boxing. Sarah, the world-title

FIGURE 10.3 A boxer between rounds in training, Accra, Ghana, 2016. (Source: Leo Hopkinson)

challenger who subsequently moved to the United States, told me she was waiting until her boxing career ended to have children and start a business, as she did not think it possible to attend to both at the same time.

The gendered possibilities of a boxing life are clearly different and although women's experiences in the sport are certainly worth exploring, the relatively small amount of data I have on women boxers limits my capacity to analyse their gendered experience. From here on, I focus on how male boxers construct masculinity in relation to the sport, without taking for granted that there is something inherently masculine about the male boxing body or experience.

Masculinity and generosity

In the Attoh Quarshie, boxers often reference iconic Ghanaian and foreign boxers by talking about them, appropriating famous boxers' ring-names as "guy names," imitating others' style of movement in the ring, and carefully choosing attire reminiscent of iconic boxers. First among icons during my time in Accra was Floyd Mayweather. Mayweather personified boxers' ambitions of global mobility, material wealth, and a winning record. His popularity peaked when he fought Manny Pacquiao for the world welterweight titles in May 2015, in what was at the time the richest bout in history. In Accra, the fight was hotly anticipated. Boxers wore caps and clothes branded with "T.B.E." and "T.M.T." ("The Money Team"), Mayweather's own brand of clothing and also the name of his entourage. Boxers shouted "T.M.T." and "T.B.E." around the gym as they trained, and spoke of their allegiance to T.B.E. and lauded Mayweather's defensive skills and tactically astute style. The countless men's clothing boutiques around Ga Mashie and Kantamanto market, the city's largest clothing market, were awash with garments printed with T.M.T. and T.B.E. many boxers enjoyed wearing the gear. Many boxers and coaches predicted that Pacquiao would lose and most openly supported Mayweather.

The fight itself was a masterclass in defensive boxing from Mayweather, who beat Pacquiao convincingly on points over 12 rounds. Few in Accra were surprised. I asked a boxer called Abraham a few days after the fight why he liked Mayweather so much: "T.B.E.! Floyd. The. Money. Mayweather." He went on: "I like the way he fights, and I like his business. He works hard in training and he gets money. Floyd respects himself."

Although Mayweather's opulent wealth and global success make him a distant figure for the majority of boxers in Accra, he remains tangible in some respects because several Ghanaian boxers have worked for him as sparring partners, most recently Bastie Samir. Following the 2008 Beijing Olympics Games, Bastie was signed on as a professional by a major U.S.-based promoter. He moved to the United States for three years, during which time he worked as a sparring partner for Mayweather and others. Since then, Bastie has returned to Ghana to pursue his professional career. He is widely known, regularly spars at gyms around Accra, and is often seen around Ga Mashie. Other high-profile Ghanaian boxers such Ike Quartey and Joshua Clottey have shared a ring with former Mayweather opponents, including Oscar De La Hoya and Manny Pacquiao, Mayweather's two highest profile opponents before 2015. Even the youngest and least experienced boxers in Accra are likely to have watched YouTube videos of Ghanaians sharing a ring with these international icons in Las Vegas or New York. Simultaneously, they see these Ghanaians around Ga Mashie, in gyms or at fights, and likely will have spoken to them, trained alongside them, and perhaps even sparred with them. Joshua, Ike, and Bastie among others are a tangible link between the Accra boxing family and the world that Mayweather occupies and symbolizes. The presence of these athletes lends to Ga Mashie a sense of being connected to a global industry.

Mayweather's lavish consumer lifestyle and seemingly vast amounts of cash reflect boxers' desire for a disposable income as a marker of masculinity, as possessing material wealth and being in a position to be generous is widely understood as a masculine trope in Ghana, particularly among young men (Esson 2013; cf. Besnier 2015, 853; Newell 2012). As a man, one should be able to give freely to others in a public way. Discussing their aspirations in the sport one afternoon, two professional boxers made this clear:

> *David:* I will get a house there and here, and I will get a nice car, top car [David and Nana playfully imitate cruising with one arm out of the window, and turning the steering wheel with the other] and I will get nice clothes, plenty. Then I will be able to give small things to people.
>
> *Nana:* Yeah, I will have money and be like [mimes shuffling paper bills out of his palm into the air].
>
> *Leo:* But if you give away all your money you will have none left.
>
> *David:* No, if you give things to people it is good, because they will respect you. You will never want.

As David's and Nana's conversation illustrates, a self-respecting man has the capacity to give material goods and cash generously. Respect (*bu* in Ga) is a reflexive concept; one can only respect other persons who are perceived to respect themselves. *Bu* is a relationship constituted between subjects rather than given from one subject to another. Performing self-respect demands respect from others and in this sense attention to the self is also attention to one's relationships with others. As a reflexive and relational concept, *bu* helps illuminate Abraham's earlier statement about Mayweather – Abraham respects Mayweather because Mayweather demonstrates self-respect through his skill in the ring *and* his accumulation of wealth as a successful businessman. Generosity and the capacity to give freely generates respect between subjects that is clearly gendered, as Nana went on to explain:

> If you start boxing and stop your job, your girlfriend has to be happy with you because you can make plenty of money and then you can give her things. You can buy things for her, so it is good to become a boxer as a man.

Aside from gift giving, self-respect is demonstrated materially through stylish and clean clothing, conspicuous displays of material wealth including cars and jewellery, and careful and graceful bodily comportment (Newell 2012; Shipley 2009). This was clearly apparent when coaches reprimanded boxers dressing in dirty or dishevelled training gear and described them as disrespectful. Boxers invest significant time and effort in dressing to a particular aesthetic reminiscent of contemporary U.S. hip-hop stars and Floyd Mayweather's public image. Opulent wealth in this form is reminiscent of the "X-way," the "hegemonic ideal of masculinity associated with a footballer's lifestyle" in Ghana (Esson 2013, 89). For my interlocutors, Mayweather's displays of wealth demand respect from others and demonstrate his self-respect. Like aspiring footballers (Esson 2013), boxers in Accra see accruing money and material wealth as a way to articulate masculinity through the capacity to give to others and dress well. By doing so, one demands respect as a visibly self-respecting man; becoming a respected man requires cultivating relationships of generosity.

Although boxing is locally associated with wealth and opulence, many professional boxers supported families on around 300 cedi (US$70) a month, a lower-end income. Many found seeking respect through gift giving difficult. Yet they continued to desire to be seen as publicly generous and were socially expected to do so. The irony of the situation is not lost on boxers like Nana, who bemoan the disjuncture between expectations and realities.

Virile masculinity: Giving and getting

Boxers also associated gift giving and global mobility with virile heterosexual masculinity.[3] A neighbour of mine who boxed at the Attoh Quarshie often described the capacity to give material goods or cash away to sexual partners, implicitly women, as an important part of "being a man." As an amateur, he made little money through the sport, often only earning when he trained with the national team or competed in international competitions. Consequently, he found it difficult to realize the heterosexual masculinity to which he aspired, as he explained when reflecting on coaches' criticisms of him:

> People say I like girls too much, that I am always with girls, coach is always saying this. But I don't have money, so I can't get them things, so instead I talk to them a bit and give them some words instead, and then see if they want to come [have sex] with me. ... Like this one girl I was talking to [earlier that day]. But then she didn't want to, I can't give her anything.

Many of my interlocutors saw transactional sex as a benefit of the vast wealth that sporting icons like Mayweather possessed, although transactional sex is by no means the only form of sexual activity that they engaged in. Gift giving is therefore a route to both gendered respect (*bu*) and heterosexual virility. Similarly, travel and global mobility contributed to aspirations of heterosexual virility. A favourite call-and-response chant of one Attoh Quarshie boxer beginning to travel as a professional articulated this succinctly: "*Ke ote abroji* [if you go abroad], fuck the *yoyo* [women]! *Ke ote abroji*, fuck the pussy!" Boxers found sexual encounters with women while abroad particularly desirable and often publicly recounted such encounters, whether true or fictional, in the gym. In this sense, travel was an opportunity to realize and recount a globally engaged, heterosexual masculinity.[4]

The boxer as a virile, heterosexual man is a commonly held stereotype within the sport and among members of the Ghanaian public. At a meeting of the Ghanaian Coaches' Association, when the issue of the possibility of disease transmission through exposure to bodily fluids in the sport was broached, an experienced coach noted with a wry smile, "As we know, the boxers like to fuck all those women in Bukom [a neighbourhood in Ga Mashie particularly strongly associated with boxing]." The statement was a double entendre. Meant to comment on bloodborne STI transmission, it was delivered with an air of self-satisfaction and met with quiet chuckles around the room, highlighting the expectation that boxers are virile sexual actors. The coach both affirmed and problematized boxers' heterosexual virility, recalling the ambivalence of the concept of "African men" when used as a naturalized category of sexual actor. Although clearly socially constructed, the idea of "African men" as a specific group of actors shapes men's understanding of masculinity and experience of sexual encounters (Spronk 2014). Similarly, although boxers reflect critically on stereotypes about them, these stereotype still shape their gendered experience, aspirations, and sense of self.

Being virile and highly sexually active is particularly problematic for boxers when juxtaposed to the regimented lifestyle that they are expected to maintain, particularly when travelling abroad and preparing for bouts. Prior to a fight, boxers are supposed to remain celibate to improve their "focus," strength, and "condition," as sex is understood to diminish these attributes significantly.[5] The paradox that boxers should be sexually active and abstinent at the same time resonates with analyses of the contradictory forms of selfhood engendered by neoliberal market conditions (Gershon 2011; Besnier 2015). Given the value that boxers place on sexual encounters abroad and the limited time that boxers spend aboard when travelling to fight (no more than two weeks prior to a fight), the strain of this paradox is heightened when boxers travel. Male boxers found sexual encounters aboard highly desirable, yet having sex abroad reduces a boxer's "condition" and his likelihood of performing well in a bout, and undermines his relationship of trust with his coach.[6] Different aspects of gendered aspiration are pitted against one another when boxers become globally mobile.

As a globally mobile, unbeaten, skilled, and extremely wealthy boxer, Mayweather is an icon of a masculinity grounded in gender roles, idioms, and ideals specific to Accra. However, boxers like Daniel who are neither globally mobile nor wealthy remain widely respected members of the boxing family. The details of Daniel's participation in the sport, which I explore in the following section, reveal how he performs an iconic masculinity despite his immobility, and answers the question of why Daniel is recognized as "T.B.E." despite his paucity of skill in the ring.

Daniel, "T.B.E."

Daniel is a 31-year-old welterweight (69 kg) amateur boxer at the Attoh Quarshie, where he has been training for eight years. He wears a polished bald scalp and sometimes sports a carefully styled Marvin Hagler-like handlebar moustache.[7] Daniel is also a trader at Kantamanto, the large clothing market close to Accra railway station, which spills onto the tracks once the one-train-a-day leaves the station each morning. He trades primarily in clothing inspired by the style of U.S. and West African hip-hop artists, which is popular among young men, particularly boxers. Brands such as October's Very Own (or OVO – Drake's record label), YMCMB (Young Money Cash Money Billionaires, the brand of the Young Money hip-hop crew), T.M.T. (Mayweather's brand), and Jordan AIR (after the basketball player Michael Jordan) cover his shop in the market. At the market, he is known as a boxer and takes pride in conspicuously leaving work every afternoon to train.

At the gym, Daniel sports carefully assembled attires branded with major sportswear labels and basketball and football-team logos. Branded sportswear is popular in the gym, and boxers and coaches carefully choose, wash, and prepare their gear prior to training each day. Daniel's attire is among the most varied, flamboyant, and carefully selected in the gym. His aesthetics resemble those of wealthy sporting icons and he revels in his outfits being obviously matched and prepared, all of which other boxers and coaches described as commanding their respect (*bu*). It was no surprise, when one day Daniel emerged from the changing room in bright white shorts and a top with gold trim, the letters "T.B.E." emblazoned in gold across the shoulders, white trainers with gold trim, and a pair of gold boxing gloves by Title, a popular U.S. brand. As he walked out of the changing room, he was greeted with shouts of "T.B.E." and "FLOYD!," to which he responded "T.B.E.! THE. MONEY. TEAM." He was clearly pleased with the recognition that the outfit garnered from his gym-mates.

Despite his ostentatious dress sense and frequent references to Mayweather, Daniel understands that he is not a skilled boxer relative to others in the gym. This became most apparent during the many informal meetings that took place after training, when boxers were told to rank themselves "by level." "Level" is a relative measure of skill and experience commonly used in the Attoh Quarshie and beyond. As boxers formed a single line in front of the coaches, Daniel would self-identify among the boxers of a low level. Yet, he would also candidly speak about his desire to be a "champion" and "The Best Ever." Following a fight night on the outskirts of Accra, I asked Daniel how his bout went. He told me that he lost on points and explained with a deliberately American accent, "I gotta' keep trainin'. You gotta' train to be the best, to be a champion, man!"

His commitment to becoming "the best" was also embodied in the way that he mimicked, much to the chagrin of the coaches, a movement known as a shoulder roll; this involves dropping the lead hand low and sandwiching the chin between the rear hand and forward shoulder, and is characteristic of Mayweather's defensive style in the ring. However, successful execution of a shoulder-roll defence requires a high level of skill that Daniel does not have, and the technique is specifically not taught by the Attoh Quarshie coaches for this reason. Hence the coaches' annoyance when Daniel deliberately performed this ineffective defensive technique rather than striving to develop effective boxing skills.

Although Daniel regularly spoke about travelling to the United States to fight, he had never boxed outside Accra. His coaches made it clear to me that he would likely never box overseas and that he knew it. Despite the gulf between his aspirations and the possibility of realising them, Daniel remained a valued member of the gym. He was often chosen to represent the gym at public events to which it sent representatives, such as funerals or weddings. The coaches liked Daniel and described him as a "good boy" who "respected" because he trained hard and regularly, and contributed generously to the gym by helping with maintenance, representing the gym at events, and giving generously for repairs, collections, and new equipment. Other boxers described how Daniel was a "good person" who "respected himself," citing how he regularly gave clothing and small amounts of cash to other boxers, paid for drinks and taxi rides, and helped boxers and coaches to source rare and sought-after clothing and equipment from the market. Daniel's generosity and commitment to the gym, combined with his recognized lack of skill, was understood as a sign of humility, which coaches and other boxers respected. Outside the gym, Daniel also had a reputation for having lots of sex and many girlfriends, and some described how his sense of style, generosity, and self-respect made him attractive to women.

Daniel's veneration of Floyd Mayweather operates on several levels: materially in his clothing, verbally in his references to Mayweather's nicknames and brands, physically as he appropriates Mayweather's boxing style at the expense of developing effective boxing skills, ideologically in his commitment to becoming "the best," and socially in his generosity and reputation for heterosexual virility.

Despite lacking technical prowess, Daniel achieves a sense of gendered respect as a "good man" by skilfully performing aspiration. His work and skill as a market trader, traditionally feminine work in Ghana, supports his masculine performance of aspiration and generosity. He trades exclusively in clothes that reference the iconic masculinity to which he and others aspire, and uses his access to these materials to perform a material commitment to aspiration impeccably and dress in a highly respectable manner. Few others at the gym would have had the resources, knowledge, and opportunity to put together the "T.B.E." outfit that he wore with such pride. In particular, the skills and connections to have the vest printed with "T.B.E.," alongside the cash to buy the full matching outfit, would have been beyond the means of many. His relatively successful business at the market also enables him to give generously and position himself as a respectable, respected, and virile man. Whether the rumours of his popularity with women are true or not, his virility and self-respect are confirmed by his generosity. Daniel's skill in fashioning a masculine aesthetic is not lost on his gym-mates, many of who ask him for advice and help in acquiring particular items and putting together outfits of their own.

Despite his grand ambitions, Daniel is not naïve enough to ignore the fact that he does not participate in the global boxing industry and remains involuntarily immobile.[8] He uses his skill and success in the market, and his refined sense of the aesthetics of aspiration, to invoke the figure of the aspirant athlete and become an ideal moral subject – a good man – in locally specific terms. Daniel demonstrates that technical boxing skills are not the only way of articulating oneself in the mould of an iconic masculinity. Rather, Daniel's skill in commodifying aspirations to global success in locally legible terms makes him "T.B.E."

Aspiration, masculinity, and (im)mobility

Pursuing success in global sporting industries is an increasingly attractive option for young men in the Global South seeking work and social adulthood (Besnier, Guinness, Hann, and Kovač 2018). In response to the demands of neoliberal sporting industries, the "athlete self" emerges as a reflexive and self-governing individual, constantly in pursuit of self-improvement through networking, training, and enlisting spiritual powers to enhance their athletic prowess and potential for global mobility (Kovač 2018; Hann 2018b). Athletes like Daniel complicate this model since they recognise their athletic limitations and instead are invested in performing aspirations to success. This is perhaps most evident in how Daniel stylistically embodies Mayweather's boxing techniques, despite the fact that they do not improve his technical ability, and claims to be "T.B.E." despite his lack of skill in the ring. Performing aspiration is as important to masculinity as projects of athletic self-improvement and networking, and for some athletes who recognise their own immobility, it may even become more important. For those like Daniel, aspiration is not the state that precedes gendered selfhood, but a gendered form of being itself.

Daniel can articulate himself as a man of global connection because Accra is a global hub of boxing rather than a migratory starting point. In Accra, he rubs shoulders with globally mobile and recognized athletes, lending to his experience a sense of global connection and allowing him to claim participation in a global industry despite his immobility.

Young people in Africa and across the Global South are increasingly concerned with bending chance, fate, and fortune to secure a prosperous future in response to the social and economic marginality of neoliberal economic reforms (Cooper and Pratten 2015; Gaibazzi and Gardini 2015; van Wyk 2012). For athletes, this work often involves strict training, spiritual regimens, and magico-religious practices designed to increase athletes' chances of becoming globally mobile and successful (Besnier, Guinness, Hann, and Kovač 2018; Guinness 2018). Daniel's efforts stand apart from these regimens and technologies of manipulating chance because they are not calculated to improve his likelihood of sporting success and fortune. He consciously performs a rhetorical commitment to sporting aspiration as a state of being, but becomes the man he wants to be by carefully manipulating his skills and resources outside boxing.

Were Daniel to commit his efforts to taking a chance on success as a professional boxer, as many of his peers do, he knows he would likely never become the man he wants to be. Daniel's participation in boxing can be read as a criticism of the neoliberal logics that encourage investment in chance and fate, logics that animate young men's participation in sporting industries in Accra and across the Global South. Daniel's commitment to the gym and the boxing family is sincere; he is not a cynic. Yet, he is also critical of an industry that promises much but often fails to deliver.

Although boxers like Daniel problematize the concept of the "athlete self" and do not engage with the logic of chance that pervades neoliberal sporting industries, they are not totally disengaged from neoliberal selfhood. Performing aspiration, or in Daniel's terms, "hustling to be the best," means constantly working to articulate himself as the man he wants to be despite his exclusion. Daniel is "The Best Ever" because he embodies a form of aspirant masculinity more effectively than those who, ironically, are often closer to realising ambitions of global sporting success and mobility than he is.

Acknowledgements

This research was carried out with the generous support of the United Kingdom Economic and Social Research Council. Thanks to Niko Besnier for involving me in this project and for all his feedback on my research in Ghana and on this chapter. Thanks also to Domenica Gisella Calabrò and Daniel Guinness for their help developing the chapter and to Luke Heslop, Benjamin Hegarty, and Mark Hann for their always generous and insightful discussion. My research would not have been possible without the guidance and support of all my friends, gym-mates and acquaintances in the Accra boxing family, particularly the membership of the Attoh Quarshie. I am eternally grateful to all of you for allowing me to be a part of your lives and spaces. Thanks in particular to Washington for feedback on this chapter and so many other aspects of my work. Finally, thank you to Daniel for being a generous, gracious, and kind friend, teacher, and gym-mate.

Notes

1 I use pseudonyms throughout unless my interlocutors specifically asked me not to. I refer to globally active boxers by their real names when their identity is relevant to my argument and is public knowledge.
2 This contrasts with accounts of Senegalese wrestlers' migration patterns (Hann 2018b; this volume).
3 While my interlocutors were critical of non-heterosexual sexualities and none claimed to have had any such sexual encounters, everyone I asked claimed to know people who have had same-sex experiences. There is an LGBT+ community in Accra, yet non-heterosexual people, and gay men in particular, are systematically marginalized in Ghana, where homosexuality remains a crime. In the gym, the physical intimacy of boxing was never openly sexualized and none of my interlocutors reflected in private on this intimacy as sexual.
4 Being a heterosexual man will have shaped my data here. Although I challenged homophobic and transphobic opinions whenever possible, my interlocutors often refused to engage in dialogue on non-heterosexual sexualities and diverse gender experiences. The exception were several middle-aged women I lived with who explained that intimate and sexual relationships between women were more permissible than between men.
5 "Condition" is the readiness to fight and results from boxers' proper adherence to training ideologies, hierarchies, and concepts of bodily constitution. Runners in Ethiopia have a similar concept (Crawley, this volume; Borenstein, this volume).
6 For women boxers, sex before a bout is also seen as reducing condition and breaching the trust between coach and boxer. However, the women boxers I knew showed little interest in sexual encounters abroad so travel did not represent the same clash of ideals for them as it did for men.
7 Hagler is a former middleweight champion from the United States who wore a polished bald scalp and handlebar moustache throughout his career in the 1970s and 1980s. The iconic combination of stylistic details is often an overt reference to Hagler, particularly when boxers sport it.
8 My argument here supports de Haas's (2014) assertion that the lives and strategies of those who wish to travel but cannot, the involuntarily immobile, should be a central concern of migration studies.

References

Akyeampong, Emmanuel. 2002. "Bukom and the Social History of Boxing in Accra: Warfare and Citizenship in Precolonial Ga Society." *International Journal of African Historical Studies* 35, no. 1: 39–60.

Besnier, Niko. 2015. "Sports Mobilities Across Borders: Postcolonial Perspectives." *International Journal of the History of Sport* 32, no. 7: 849–861.

Besnier, Niko, Daniel Guinness, Mark Hann, and Uroš Kovač. 2018. "Rethinking Masculinity in the Neoliberal Order: Cameroonian Footballers, Fijian Rugby Players, and Senegalese Wrestlers." *Comparative Studies in Society and History* 60, no. 4: 839–872.

Bourdieu, Pierre. 1977. *Outline of a Theory of Practice*. Translated by Richard Nice. Cambridge: Cambridge University Press.

Butler, Judith. 1990. *Gender Trouble: Feminism and the Subversion of Identity*. Abingdon, UK: Routledge.

Comaroff, Jean, and John L. Comaroff. 1999. "Occult Economies and the Violence of Abstraction: Notes from the South African Postcolony." *American Ethnologist* 26, no. 2: 279–303.

Comaroff, Jean, and John L. Comaroff, eds. 2001. *Millennial Capitalism and the Culture of Neoliberalism*. Durham, NC: Duke University Press.

Connell, Robert W., and James W. Messerschmidt. 2005 "Hegemonic Masculinity: Rethinking the Concept." *Gender & Society* 19, no. 6: 829–859.

Cooper, Elizabeth, and David Pratten, eds. 2015. *Ethnographies of Uncertainty in Africa*. Basingstoke, UK: Palgrave Macmillan.

De Boeck, Filip, and Marie-Françoise Plissart. 2004. *Kinshasa: Tales of the Invisible City*. Leuven: Leuven University Press.

de Haas, Hein. 2014. *Migration Theory: Quo Vadis?* International Migration Institute Working Paper Series, 100. Oxford: International Migration Institute, University of Oxford.

Dunzendorfer, Jan. 2014. "Ethnicized Boxing: The Tale of Ghana's Boxing Roots in a Local Martial Art." *Sport in Society* 17, no. 8: 1015–1029.

Esson, James. 2013. "A Body and a Dream at a Vital Conjuncture: Ghanaian Youth, Uncertainty and the Allure of Football." *Geoforum* 47: 84–92.

Esson, James. 2015. "Better Off at Home? Rethinking Responses to Trafficked West African Footballers." *Journal of Ethnic and Migration Studies* 41, no. 3: 512–530.

Gaibazzi, Paolo, and Marco Gardini. 2015. "The Work of Fate and Fortune in Africa." *Critical African Studies* 7, no. 3: 203–209.

Gershon, Ilana. 2011. "Neoliberal Agency." *Current Anthropology* 52, no. 4: 537–555.

Gershon, Ilana. 2018. "Employing the CEO of Me, Inc.: US Corporate Hiring in a Neoliberal Age." *American Ethnologist* 45, no. 2: 173–185.

Geschiere, Peter, and Francis B. Nyamnjoh. 2000. "Capitalism and Autochthony: The Seesaw of Mobility and Belonging." *Public Culture* 12, no. 2: 423–452.

Guinness, Daniel. 2018. "Corporal Destinies: Faith, Ethno-Nationalism, and Raw Talent in Fijian Professional Rugby Aspirations." *HAU* 8, no. 1–2: 314–328.

Hann, Mark. 2018a. "Senegalese Football's Impossible Dream." *Anthropology News* 59, no. 4: e202–e207.

Hann, Mark. 2018b. "Sporting Aspirations: Football, Wrestling, and Neoliberal Subjectivity in Urban Senegal." Ph.D. Dissertation, Amsterdam Institute for Social Science Research, University of Amsterdam.

Jackson, Michael. 1989. *Paths Towards a Clearing: Radical Empiricism and Ethnographic Inquiry*. Bloomington: Indiana University Press.

Jónsson, Gunvor. 2012. "Migration, Identity and Immobility in a Malian Soninke Village." In *The Global Horizon: Expectations of Migration in Africa and the Middle East*, edited by Knut Graw and Samuli Schielke, 105–120. Leuven: Leuven University Press.

Kovač, Uroš. 2018. "The Precarity of Masculinity: Football, Pentecostalism, and Transnational Aspirations in Cameroon." Ph.D. dissertation, Amsterdam Institute for Social Science Research, University of Amsterdam.

Newell, Sasha. 2012. *The Modernity Bluff: Crime, Consumption, and Citizenship in Côte D'Ivoire*. Chicago: University of Chicago Press.

Oates, Joyce Carol. 1987. *On Boxing*. Garden City, NY: Dolphin/Doubleday.

Överå, Ragnhild. 2007. "When Men Do Women's Work: Structural Adjustment, Unemployment and Changing Gender Relations in the Informal Economy of Accra, Ghana." *Journal of Modern African Studies* 45, no. 4: 539–563.

Salazar, Noel B., and Alan Smart. 2011. "Anthropological Takes on (Im)Mobility." *Identities* 18, no. 6: i–ix.

Shipley, Jesse Weaver. 2009. "Aesthetic of the Entrepreneur: Afro-cosmopolitan Rap and Moral Circulation in Accra, Ghana." *Anthropological Quarterly* 82, no. 3: 631–668.

Smith, Daniel Jordan. 2017. *To Be a Man Is not a One-day Job: Masculinity, Money, and Intimacy in Nigeria*. Chicago: University of Chicago Press.

Spronk, Rachel. 2014. "The Idea of African Men: Dealing with the Cultural Contradictions of Sex in Academia and in Kenya." *Culture, Health & Sexuality* 16, no. 5: 504–517.

Stoller, Paul. 1989. *The Taste of Ethnographic Things: The Senses in Anthropology*. Philadelphia: University of Pennsylvania Press.

Thiel, Alena, and Michael Stasik. 2016. "Market Men and Station Women: Changing Significations of Gendered Space in Accra, Ghana." *Journal of Contemporary African Studies* 34, no. 4: 459–478.

Van Wyk, Ilana. 2012. "'Tata Ma Chance': On Contingency and the Lottery in Post-Apartheid South Africa." *Africa* 82, no. 1: 41–68.

Wacquant, Loïc. 2004. *Body & Soul: Notebooks of an Apprentice Boxer*. Oxford: Oxford University Press.

Weiss, Brad. 2009. *Street Dreams and Hip-Hop Barbers Shops: Global Fantasy in Urban Tanzania*. Bloomington: Indiana University Press.

Yeku, James. 2018. "The Racist Myth of the 'Physical' African Football Team." *Al Jazeera*, 27 June 2018. www.aljazeera.com/indepth/opinion/racist-myth-physical-african-football-team-180625130343810.html.

11

THE DREAM IS TO LEAVE

Imagining migration and mobility through sport in Senegal

Mark Hann

If you stay here, if you live here, you train and you want to recover, [your friend] says come and see this girl, you go, you don't recover. But in the United States or England, when training is finished, you can rest, you can sleep. You recuperate. You're not tired. There's no stress. But if you're in Senegal, you will have stress. The people, the supporters, the fans. They come and tire you out, there's no rest. And over there, there are better materials and vitamins that you can drink.

(Modou, wrestler, Dakar, Senegal)

The dream is to leave. To go to Europe, and play for one of the big teams. Barcelona, Real Madrid, Manchester United. Especially in the English league. In 2009, in my neighbourhood, people called me Tevez. Because they saw that I fought like [Argentine football star Carlos] Tevez on the pitch. At the time, I didn't even know Tevez. But I started watching him on TV. That's what gave me the idea to go to England.

(Pape, footballer, Dakar, Senegal)

Like many other young Senegalese men, both Pape and Modou frequently expressed a strong desire to leave Senegal. However, they did so through the lens of their respective sports.[1] Each of these young aspiring athletes articulated their vision of the future by invoking images, practices, and conventions of the particular sport industry that they sought to become part of. In modelling his style of play on that of the Argentine player Carlos Tevez, Pape imagined himself playing at the major clubs in England, Spain, or Italy that he followed on television. Modou, meanwhile, envisioned a future in which he could benefit from superior training conditions and nutritional supplements in the United States, following in the footsteps of his wrestling idols such as Modou Lô and Balla Gaye 2.

Pape and Modou are not alone in their aspirations to become mobile athletes. Their ambition is shared by thousands of other young men in Dakar, West Africa, and other locations across the Global South. With the increasing commoditization and liberalization of sports markets (Andrews and Silk 2012; Miller et al. 2001; Scherer and Jackson 2010) and the ensuing expansion of athletic recruitment to the Global South (Lanfranchi and Taylor 2001; Carter 2013; Klein 2014), sport has become a vector of hope for young men seeking to monetize their physical prowess in the global sport industries (Besnier, Calabrò, and Guinness, this volume). While patterns of recruitment and athletic mobility are complex and vary from sport to sport, the general trend sees the movement of young men from locations in the Global South towards the lucrative leagues in the Global North. These include footballers from Latin America and West Africa moving to leagues in Europe; Pacific Island rugby players to Australia, New Zealand, the United Kingdom, and France; and baseball players from the Dominican Republic who aspire to play in American Major League Baseball. Although the reality of such mobilities is often more circuitous than commonly assumed (Besnier 2012), broadly speaking athletic mobility runs from South to North or periphery to centre.

The case of Senegal, therefore, poses an intriguing challenge to the paradigm of athletic mobility as it is usually presented. Unlike in most other countries in which many young men strive to make it in the world of professional sports, the sporting landscape in Senegal is contested by two enormously popular and potentially lucrative disciplines: football and traditional wrestling with punches. While football is firmly oriented towards a career abroad, and preferably in the prestigious European leagues, wrestling is celebrated as national heritage and takes place within the borders of Senegal.

The presence of two aspirational sporting trajectories that are at first glance diametrically opposed in their positioning vis-à-vis the global serves to complicate narratives around athletic mobilities and desires of mobility more generally (compare Hopkinson, this volume, on boxers in Ghana; Crawley, this volume, on runners in Ethiopia). The hope of a sports career engenders rich and textured imaginations and future-oriented practices of an elsewhere in the daily lives of young men in Dakar. Migration and mobility are thus imagined and produced through the lens of the two sports in question, wrestling and football. The migration aspirations (and in some cases, actual experiences) of my interlocutors reveal some of the different ways in which the fantasy of migration emerges in each sport, the tensions and discourses involved, and the realities that underpin this fantasy. The neoliberal sports industries therefore produce millennial fantasies of successful and lucrative sport migration. Despite their many differences, both wrestling and football in Senegal are embedded in global economic structures that may be described as neoliberal. Neoliberalism in this context refers to a set of ideologies and dispositions characterized by entrepreneurialism, self-discipline, responsibility, and optimization of the self (Besnier, and Calabrò, and Guinness, this volume). Both wrestlers and football players may be understood as "entrepreneurs of the self" (Foucault 2008), and striving towards migration is a constitutive part of these neoliberal "athlete-selves" (Hann 2018).

The mobilities envisioned by young Senegalese athletes are not necessarily driven by a desperation to "leave at any cost," but are instead highly specific and curated projects. Moreover, athletic mobilities are frequently the subject of much contestation and debate by prospective migrants, their families, and those within the two sports. Sport migrations are embedded in familial structures as well as being the subject of much contestation by families and peers. The dream of a sports career can also have a significant impact on the lives of would-be athletes and their families, in terms of financial planning, education and work choices, and marriage.

Finally, the relationship between the category of athletic mobility and other forms of migration and mobility is complex and shifting, as the popular dream of athletic migration among young Senegalese men is embedded within a broader context of migratory ambitions and dispositions. While the former is sometimes treated as a distinct category of elite labour circulation, my ethnographic research shows that the lines between the two are often blurred and that presenting oneself as a mobile athlete can be a creative strategy of legitimization (compare Hopkinson, this volume). Athletic migration might therefore be broadened to include "informal" projects of migration in which the sporting component is largely a product of "cruel optimism."

Sport, hope, and the everyday production of the "future elsewhere"

When young men in Dakar dream of the future, they often imagine the need to move overseas in order to find success. They may experience staying in Dakar as forced immobility (Prothmann 2018) or "killing time" (Ralph 2008) – an experience that mirrors accounts of boredom (Mains 2007; Masquelier 2013) and "waithood" (Honwana 2012) of young people in other locations in Africa. Young men in Dakar often live at the family home for a long period of time because finding gainful employment is difficult or because they are following prolonged university education. As a result, they are unable to meet the expectation that they marry and become the head of a household until later in life – often in their 30s or 40s, if at all. The years spent in a state of "waithood" at the family home are a frustrating prolonged adolescence, in which young men may have to share rooms with brothers or cousins, look after younger siblings, and carry out domestic chores. Both migration and sport can appear to be a shortcut, cutting down or even completely bypassing this unsatisfying life stage – and a combination of the two is a particularly attractive proposition.

In recent decades, sport, and football in particular, has emerged as a privileged site through which young men pursue the desire to be mobile. As growing media coverage of European football via satellite television has enabled African audiences to participate in the spectacle of the global game (Akindes 2011, 201; Figure 11.1), an increasing number of young men seek to transform their ability and passion for

FIGURE 11.1 Young boys in Dakar wearing replica football shirts of European clubs Bayern Munich and Manchester City, May 2015.
(Source: Mark Hann)

the sport into a lucrative international career. This fantasy is fuelled by the images of African stars such as Didier Drogba, Samuel Eto'o, or Michael Essien, whose success at the highest level of the European game inspires millennial fantasies (Besnier and Brownell 2012) among those who hope to emulate them. The proliferation of elite football academies in West Africa – notably Ghana, Côte d'Ivoire, Cameroon, and Senegal – serves to satisfy European clubs' desire to recruit cheap talented players (Darby 2007, 2013), but also to attract resourceful young men who see sport as an entrepreneurial means towards mobility (Esson 2013, 2015a, 2015b, 2015c). In Senegal, this is not limited to football; wrestling, as we shall see, is also tied to imagining oneself being elsewhere.

In a country where remittances form a significant part of family income and migration is seen as indicative of successful masculinity (Melly 2011), such "imaginaries of exile" (Piot 2010) proliferate. However, it is perhaps to limit these imaginaries simply to projects of migration. People can also engage with global cultural forces as strategies of extraversion (Fouquet 2007; Mbodj-Pouye 2012), in which the desire of an "imagined elsewhere" (Fouquet 2008) becomes a mode of subjectivation.

Exile is imagined in terms of not only its spatial conditions, but also a temporal orientation to the future. Globalization is often described as a reworking of space and time, and it is unsurprising that youth are particularly disposed to future-oriented practices (Cole and Durham 2008). Young athletes often articulate their expectations of a better future in terms of hope. Although the concept of hope is sometimes understood as more or less a subordination to external factors (Crapanzano 2003), it can also be viewed as an "active and even agentive modality" (Cole and Durham 2008, 15) or a "labor of hope" (Elliot 2016). It is perhaps a combination of both of these understandings which best captures how the hopeful fantasies of Senegalese athletes are actively produced through their daily practices.

Stuck in Dakar: An immobile footballer

> I have to go to Europe. There is nothing for me here.
>
> *(Pape)*

Many of the young football players I met in Dakar shared Pape's attitude. They effectively lived in a state of permanent hope or fantasy, projecting themselves into an imagined future away from Senegal, preferably playing football in a top European league. This dream, as Pape's story illustrates, seems close enough to appear within grasp, but remains remote and improbable for most players. Many young men invest years towards the pursuit of an international football career, only to find themselves with little to show for it at the end.

When I first met Pape, I was introduced as a researcher who was interested in football. In the mixture of French and rudimentary (in my case) Wolof we spoke in, perhaps something got lost in translation. As was often the case when I showed up at football matches or training sessions, I was initially taken for a scout or agent of some sort, someone who could facilitate a transfer to, or at least a trial at, a European football club. I later found out that this was no mere fantasy on Pape's part. He trained at a football school called Étoile, where some of the most talented players in the Senegalese capital hoped to gain professional contracts. In the world of football academies and schools in Dakar, white men did periodically descend upon Dakar and spirit young players away for a trial at a provincial French second division club. In fact, nearly all of the white men I encountered on football pitches during my fieldwork were in some way involved in the business of moving talented young players to Europe, so there was little reason for Pape to think I was interested in anything else. Quite soon, however, my dishevelled appearance, propensity to take public transport, and attempts to learn the local language seemed to convince him that I was not part of the glamorous football business.

Pape's mode of living may be described as taking place in an imagined elsewhere, in an imagined future. Although he attended a vocational school, as required by the rules of his football school which sought to promote educational goals, he did not invest much effort into his scholarly duties. Instead, he openly stated that he only did it because he had to; it was a necessary hurdle which he had to overcome on his path towards reaching his destiny as a football player. He saw little point in building up a future in Dakar, and his only motivation for taking on odd jobs was to earn money to sustain himself as he struggled to achieve what he saw as his inevitable departure. It seemed to me that he framed all of his activities and relationships towards his eventual goal of a career abroad; almost nothing was presented in terms of its value in and of itself for his present-day life in Dakar.

Pape was first acknowledged as an exceptional talent among his age group when representing his neighbourhood in a football tournament, and was swiftly invited to trial at the country's most prestigious football academy, Diambars, located some 80 kilometres south of Dakar in the tourist resort of Saly. Over the course of the trial, over one hundred candidates were whittled down to select just three players for one of the highly coveted places at the football school (Figure 11.2). Pape made it to the last ten but did not make the final cut, even though many of the coaches and players present were certain he would make it. Despite this setback, his reputation was such that he was quickly taken on by another well-known football school which had contacts abroad and was able to send a number of players abroad for trials or sport scholarships. Pape was convinced that he would be the next one to go. At the beginning of my fieldwork in 2014, he already had one foot out of the country. "They're going to come and take me with them," he assured me. This was why, he told me, there was little point in him taking his studies seriously or finding a part-time job. In his mind, he had already left Senegal.

However, the scholarships and trials on offer at prestigious schools and football clubs outside Senegal were for players aged 16 and 17; at this point, Pape was already 19 according to his official documents, and in reality significantly older. Although this was rarely commented on explicitly, it was clear to me from my interactions with his coaches and managers that a career in the local leagues was

FIGURE 11.2 Footballer during a training match in Dakar, October 2014. (Source: Mark Hann)

the best he could hope for. Pape was aware of this, and acted with the urgency of someone who knew he was running out of time. Although he initially gave off the impression of someone who had already packed his bags and was on the way to the airport, his optimism faltered as the season progressed. He became increasingly critical in his assessment of the football school, claiming that they had let him down and disappointed him. He could no longer sit around and wait for them to help him; he had to take matters into his own hands. Pape asked me to take pictures and videos with my DSLR camera, with the intention that I would then edit YouTube clips that he could send to his contacts in France. He had a couple of friends who lived in Europe (primarily in France), who he said would show his videos to agents and clubs there. Despite my scepticism, Pape told me story after story about various agents, scouts, and club representatives who needed only to see his video before booking him on to the next flight to France. He refused to listen when I told him that I was not able to shoot and edit a film of suitable quality, or that no club would recruit a player based only on video footage. And even if he did succeed in arranging a trial at a French club, what would he do if the club decided against signing him on a contract? Pape smiled evasively, and said he would take a bus to where his friends lived, and find work on the black market. It would be better to live as an undocumented migrant in France, he believed, than to stay in Senegal. He was desperate to forge a career as a football player – but equally, he was prepared to jettison the project of football migration for a precarious life on the margins of society, as long as he could get to Europe.

As futile as the whole enterprise seemed to me, I nonetheless agreed to film him during training and matches, eventually putting together a modest highlights reel. Unsurprisingly, nothing came of this attempt, and Pape became increasingly despondent. He carried on training and playing at Étoile, but his performances and motivation seemed to decline. Meanwhile, he resolved to get a job in order to make money, eventually finding work at a restaurant thanks to a family connection. I first assumed that it was a pragmatic decision, and that he was preparing for the eventuality of a life after football in which he would need to make ends meet. However, he was in fact hatching a plan. "If they [Étoile] don't help me leave, there are others who will," he told me, cryptically. As the weeks progressed, he began dropping more and more hints in a similar vein, suggesting that he was preparing something big, expressing doubts that he would be around for my birthday in a few months, and asking me about what it was like to fly in an aeroplane. Whenever I pushed him for more information, he told me that he could not reveal his plans to me yet, as this would bring bad luck. "I will tell you when it's the right moment."

The right moment arrived in early July. It turned out that Pape had been liaising through Facebook with a former coach of his who had worked with him earlier in his career. The coach, a Frenchman by the name of Pierre who had worked extensively in Senegal and was currently based at a small lower division club in France, had been something of a mentor to Pape, and had "always believed in me." Pierre was offering Pape a trial at his club, with the stipulation that Pape should pay a percentage of the airfare himself. Once Pape transferred the money and the correct paperwork, Pierre would take care of buying the tickets and arranging the visa. Pape had already put together most of the money through various odd jobs and a loan from an aunt. I was to provide the money to accelerate his passport application. Having heard many stories about fake agents cheating would-be players and their families out of large sums of money with promises of trials abroad, I was somewhat alarmed at this story and initially unwilling to get involved. Pape insisted that he knew Pierre well, that he trusted him, and that he would never cheat him. I spoke to Pierre on the phone, and his story was consistent with what Pape had told me. Furthermore, an internet search confirmed that he was indeed a coach at the team in question, and, as a former player in the French championship, he even had a Wikipedia page dedicated to his career. I was still puzzled by the story, but it seemed unlikely that a seemingly established figure in French football whose identity could be easily verified would be attempting to swindle young Senegalese men out of relatively small sums of money. I gave Pape the money for his passport, while fighting a sense of guilt that I was enabling a risky endeavour. When I asked him what he would do if the trials were not successful, he told me that he had it all planned out: he would "escape" from the football club, take a bus to a nearby town where a friend of his lived, and find work on the black market.

When we said goodbye before my departure from Senegal in summer 2015, Pape assured me with a confident smile that we would meet in Europe in just a few weeks' time. However, months later, the situation remained unchanged. Pape was still waiting for one document or another, the dates of the trials had changed, or the flights had to be rebooked. For a while, I was asked to send more money for new plane tickets, new papers, or bribes at the visa office. However, when I returned to Dakar at the end of the year, Pape was still stuck there.

Pape ended up staying in Dakar, and it seemed that he would have to abandon his dream of a professional career. He was fortunate to find employment in the catering industry, but the years – almost a decade – that he had spent pursuing the elusive football contract now counted against him. His commitment to football had prevented him from building a more stable working life through school, apprenticeships, or vocational training, incurring both a loss of earnings and delaying his working life in the process. The social repercussions of an unfulfilled football career can therefore be experienced as a delay of adulthood – or in other cases I encountered, long-term unemployment or substance abuse. Pape's story illustrates the powerful draw which the sport industries exert over young men, and the great lengths to which some will go in order to pursue the dream. His trajectory also demonstrates the profound socio-economic impact of the global sports fantasy.

Wrestling with mobility

The aspirations and dreams of migration and/or mobility emerge in vastly different ways in wrestling and in football. The affinity between football and the desire to migrate is an obvious one. Because of Senegal's marginal position in a global industry, young football players' dreams of professional careers are automatically

FIGURE 11.3 Wrestlers training in a suburb of Dakar, February 2017.
(Source: Mark Hann)

and inextricably linked to hopes of achieving mobility. As a sport which is largely contained within the borders of the nation, wrestling provides a wholly different context (Figure 11.3). Despite this, in recent years, wrestling too has become associated with mobility both within Senegal, and, increasingly, internationally. Generally speaking, footballers aspire to more permanent forms of mobility in the sense of a transfer to a destination country with a high-status league competition, or at least trials abroad, which may allow them to sign a contract. In contrast, wrestlers aspire to a different type of mobility: the ability to travel back and forth between competing in Senegal and training in prestigious destination countries such as France, Italy, and the United States. This simplified division corresponds roughly to distinctions made between settlers and sojourners (Rouse 1992), or similar typologies of migrant athletes (Agergaard, Botelho, and Tiesler 2014). Both wrestlers and football players therefore share an aspiration to become transnational (Glick Schiller, Basch, and Blanc 1995), although the ideal type of transnational mobility aspired towards varies.

Like many young Senegalese men, Modou hoped to travel abroad. As a wrestler, he framed his desired type of mobility in line with the overseas trips of his wrestling heroes. In 2015, I asked him if he wanted to leave Senegal:

> Senegal is nice but abroad is also nice. If you stay here you have to help yourself. That's why you have to leave. That's why I want to go to England or USA. But if you stay here and work a lot, you don't have to leave.

At this stage, his ambitions of leaving Senegal were vague, and the destination unclear. His selection of England as a destination was purely for my benefit, as our further conversations revealed that he did not know a great deal about the country besides its best football teams. The United States is firmly established as a land of milk and honey among Senegalese youth – specifically in the context of wrestling. Since Mohamed Ndao Tyson emerged as a revolutionary force in the wrestling arena in the 1990s brandishing the stars and stripes, the United States has been considered the preferred destination of high profile wrestling stars. Many of the arena's biggest names, including Gris Bordeaux, Balla Gaye 2, and Modou's idol and namesake Modou Lô, spend several months a year in the United States, ostensibly working on their form and fitness ahead of a combat. The local wrestling daily *Sunu Lamb* eagerly reports the departure of wrestlers to the United States, as well as their arrival in Dakar upon their return. However, information on their activities, and even their precise whereabouts, in the United States is largely shrouded in mystery, and the subject of much rumour and gossip.

In interviews, wrestlers emphasize the "good conditions" for training available in the United States, where they make use of professionally equipped gyms and solicit the services of specialist coaches in areas such as nutrition, conditioning, weight training, boxing, or judo. "Good conditions" also refers to the peaceful tranquillity and relative anonymity under which they can supposedly focus on training (compare Crawley, this volume; Borenstein, this volume) – unlike in Dakar, where prominent wrestlers are the subject of constant attention and scrutiny. Wagging tongues also suggest that the availability and quality of various performance-enhancing substances such as anabolic steroids attracts wrestlers to prepare their fights abroad – something which is strenuously denied by those involved, but sometimes painfully obvious in the altered physiology of certain wrestlers upon their return to Senegal. Indeed, it seemed likely to me that Modou's mention of "vitamins" was a veiled reference to the abundance of performance-enhancing substances, both legal and illegal, which he believed could be freely obtained abroad.

Modou's ambitions to travel to the United States were therefore framed in terms of a popular narrative according to which wrestlers use mobility as a means of self-improvement. While the exact nature of this self-improvement was contested and subject to much debate, its overall benefits were accepted within the wrestling world. International mobility, in particular to prestigious destinations such as the United States and Europe, was a marker of success, associated with the possibility of participating in otherwise hard-to-access markets in training equipment, supplements, and fitness culture. This type of travel stood for the improvement of the individual, the cult of the individual celebrity, and the removal of the wrestler from his training association or *écurie* for long periods of time.

"Fake wrestlers," visas, and *anciennes gloires*

Modou's desire to move abroad was embedded in the ideas and discourses which surround the trips abroad undertaken by famous celebrity wrestlers such as his hero and namesake Modou Lô. However, the ideal of a luxury training camp in top-class professional conditions is only available to those at the very top of the sport, namely those wrestlers who have sufficient earnings, sponsorship money, or patronage of wealthy supporters. In the early 2000s, only the two biggest stars of that era travelled to the United States, Mohamed Ndao "Tyson" and Yahya Diop "Yékini." Following in their footsteps, the current generation of wrestlers are regularly seen entering and leaving the premises of the U.S. embassy in Dakar applying for visas of varying duration, from three months up to ten years. Popular wisdom holds that recognized wrestlers' visa applications are looked upon favourably by consular officials, and that some are even able to acquire visas for close kin. Indeed, wrestlers are often granted visas upon being able to produce official documentation from promoters and the sport's governing body, the Comité national de gestion de la lutte (CNGL), which confirms that they are going abroad to prepare for a combat, and that they are cer- tain to return within the terms of the visa. The documentation, usually in the form of a contract between the promoter and the CNGL, thus acts as a guarantee that the wrestler will not overstay the visa.

A friend of mine told me, with just a hint of bitterness, that wrestlers were so much at an advantage in the opaque and arbitrary process of obtaining a visa that people would pose as wrestlers in order to better their chances. While this claim initially seemed somewhat implausible to me due to the fact that a genuine wrestler would be easily verifiable through his media presence alone, it did under- line the fact that wrestling is a profession which allows considerable mobility, or at least that people perceive it as such. Wrestling is therefore considered to be a legitimate means of accessing much-desired transnational mobility, with the most famous and successful wrestlers regularly travelling abroad to train in superior conditions. Even wrestlers of lower rank are often able to translate their status as competing athletes into trips abroad, often financed by fans in the diaspora or politicians, or through their association with other, more famous wrestlers. And migration to Europe or elsewhere is also a viable option for post- career wrestlers.

Modou's departure

The last time I saw Modou was in February 2017. I had returned to Dakar for a short fieldwork visit, and I received a mysterious call from him. He wanted to meet me urgently, but I wasn't to tell any other friends or family members. He was unable to tell me what he wanted to speak to me about, but he said he would visit me at my apartment later that evening. At around 10 P.M., my phone rang. It was Modou. We are by the Oilibya gas station, he told me. Do you want to come and meet us? He clearly did not want to be seen. I told them to come towards the house, but that I would meet them halfway. I went downstairs a minute later, just in time to see two broad silhouettes coming around the corner. In the unlit street, the light of the moon and a flickering television from a neighbouring house were enough to reveal the beaming smiles of Modou and his friend Mbaye as they approached. After greeting me in whispered tones, they looked furtively down the street to make sure no one was watching. Apart from a local marabout hunched over his smartphone a few houses down, the street was empty. We sneaked into the house undetected, and quickly made our way to my room on the first floor.

It turned out that they planned to travel to Morocco the following day, having purchased discounted plane tickets with the help of Mbaye's elder sister, a trader who frequently travelled back and forth between the two countries. With her help, they would travel to Casablanca, where they planned to stay for two months. They didn't require a visa or any other official documents; just the plane ticket and a specified amount of "pocket money" (*argent de poche*). The two men had spent the last few days and weeks visiting relatives, friends, and acquaintances, trying to raise the necessary funds. These amounted to approximately CFA 150,000 (roughly €230) for the plane ticket, and an additional CFA 80,000 (€120) "pocket money." Mbaye was ready to go, Modou was still missing CFA 30,000 (€45), which is where I came in. I agreed to give him the money, although I expressed my misgivings as to whether the arrangement was legitimate and trustworthy.

I was particularly concerned about the CFA 80,000 fee that appeared to have been imposed by the intermediaries arranging the passage, as well as the role of a man named Ali, with whom Modou told me he had spoken on Facebook. Ali was in Morocco, and he owned a gym; he was apparently going to help Modou train for a fight. The cloak-and-dagger secrecy surrounding the whole enterprise and the somewhat informal-sounding financial arrangements reminded me of the countless stories I had heard about unscrupulous traffickers who took families' entire life savings, leaving prospective migrants stranded at various points along the route. However, my concerns were met with laughter. They reassured me that everything was legitimate and reliable, pointing to the fact that it had been arranged by Mbaye's sister and that their friend Cheikh had already reached Casablanca by the same means. I tried to ask for further details about the trip, but it was clear that they were in a hurry to get home and pack their bags. We said our goodbyes before they slipped silently out of the house, careful to avoid being seen by anyone.

A few days later, I received a notification on my phone: "Modou has sent you a photo." I opened it up to see a photo of Modou, smartly dressed in a leather jacket, fashionably ripped jeans, and Adidas shoes, sitting on a bench outside a Burger King on a palm-lined boulevard. This was followed by a selfie of Modou, Mbaye, and Cheikh sitting around a large plate of food. They had made it to Casablanca, Morocco.

The story did not end there. I continued to text Modou and Mbaye in Morocco. The latter was not a big user of social media (other than sharing religious videos of the *Tijjaniyah* brotherhood), and I only heard from him sporadically. He would simply tell me that he was fine and politely enquire after my own wellbeing. Modou was a little more forthcoming. Aware of my interest in photography and my habit of posting photos on my Facebook page, Modou started to send me images of Morocco which he had taken with his phone. These included a forested mountainous landscape, supporting his written claim that "*Maroc mungi nekh rekk*" (Morocco is simply nice). On one occasion, he told me that he was training in Morocco and that he would return to Senegal if he had a combat. A few weeks later, he told me that his gym membership had expired (*sama inscription dafa jekh depuis 2 semaines*) and that he didn't have enough money to renew it. And later still, he told me that I should come to Casablanca to see all of the Africans on the beach, desperate to get to Spain. I asked him if he wanted to go to Spain as well. He answered in the affirmative.

A few months after this exchange, I spoke to Mbaye's older brother Ahmed. He was deeply critical of his brother's decision to migrate to Morocco and especially of the manner in which he did it. When I mentioned that Mbaye and Modou were in Morocco, he rolled his eyes in exasperation and disapproval. "There's nothing in Morocco," he said. "Why did he go there? They think they aren't Africans, and they treat black people like slaves. Now Mbaye knows this, and he realizes he made a bad decision." Ahmed went on to tell me that Mbaye, Modou, and their friend Cheikh were living together in a tiny room. They had found employment at a local bakery, where they were promised wages at the end of each month. However, after two or three months, they still hadn't been paid. They had run out of money, and had to rely on Western Union transfers from one of Mbaye's sisters who lived in France in order to pay the rent. According to Ahmed, they had not informed anyone of their plan to leave, only telling Mbaye's father one day before the flight, so that he could not prevent them from going.

Ahmed blamed Mbaye's sister, who had helped them to book the plane tickets and encouraged them with their plans, but he also blamed Mbaye for being impatient. The family – specifically, Ahmed and Mbaye's father – had only recently invested in new premises for their bakery business in Dakar. With their father now well into his seventies, and Mbaye's older brothers no longer living in Dakar, the young man clearly had good prospects of gaining a senior role in the family business. According to Ahmed, though, Mbaye did not show a particularly strong work ethic, showing up to work late, and clocking off early to join his friends in the gym. He was uninterested in pursuing his role at the bakery, where he had worked regularly since his teens. He frequently mentioned vague plans to migrate, but Ahmed never took them seriously. Now he was in Morocco, and there was a sense that he had let his family down, disappointed them, even betrayed them. "He had everything in Senegal," Ahmed told me. "Why would he give that up? He will be back within three months, I'm sure of it." What about his friend, Modou? – I asked. "You mean the wrestler? Well for him it's different. He was just doing the wrestling."

Mbaye and Modou's secretive project of migration to Morocco, their communication after arriving in Casablanca, and the response of Mbaye's family are parts of a puzzle which only fully reveals itself when pieced together. Taken individually, each of these perspectives tells a very different story. When I initially heard about their plans in the shadowy room in Dakar, my response was one of apprehension and worry; it sounded like an ill-prepared trip into the unknown. Had I taken at face value their messages and photographs from Casablanca, I would have been reassured that they did in fact know what they were doing, and that they were having a productive time. Finally, the conversation with an exasperated Ahmed in London suggested that they were beginning to question and even regret their decision. Together, these different perspectives point towards the contested nature of such migration projects, and the complex tensions which inform and motivate them. The story of Mbaye and Modou's journey to Morocco further illustrates how mobility is embedded in family and relational networks. In Modou's case, it also offers a glimpse of how the imagination of a sporting career intersects with the project of migration, blurring the lines between what is considered as "sport migration" and what is not.

Athletic migration as entrepreneurial practice

Both in football and in wrestling, aspiring young athletes desire mobility. The form that mobility takes varies significantly both between and within the sports. In football, young men's aspired form of mobility is transnational migration, although this can take multiple forms: FIFA-sanctioned transfers between clubs, sports scholarships as in the case of the Étoile players, or more informal projects of mobility devised by players, their families, and various middlemen. There is a relatively short window of opportunity for young men to migrate through football, although this can be extended by altering one's official age. Transnational mobility is often preceded by other forms of mobility within Senegal, in particular from rural areas or provincial cities to Dakar or Mbour where the major clubs, academies, and football schools are located. Players may be recruited by clubs organizing trials in rural areas or they might move to stay with relatives in Dakar in order to attempt to make a career in football. While there are opportunities to play football professionally within Senegal, notably in the national and inter-district championships, these are generally poorly remunerated.

In wrestling, Dakar exerts a similar pull on athletes from around the country. Here, unlike in the case of football however, Dakar is not just a node on the way to an international market, but the centre of the industry itself. The vast majority of wrestling associations, known as *écuries* (French for "stables") are located in the capital, and practically all wrestlers of note both live and train in the capital. Despite this, the relationship to rural areas is vital and maintained through frequent visits. Of the three main types of wrestling practised in Senegal, two offer athletes the opportunity to compete internationally. *Lutte traditionnelle sans frappe* (traditional wrestling without punches) is essentially similar to the discipline of traditional African wrestling, the rules of which were elaborated prior to the first Economic Community of West African States (CEDEAO/ECOWAS) championships in 1995. The discipline is also prominent at the *Jeux de la Francophonie* (Francophonie Games); in both tournaments, Senegalese wrestlers dominate. In addition, both male and female wrestlers are considered to be the likeliest candidates to add to Senegal's current Olympic record of just one silver medal. The third and by far most lucrative form of wrestling, *lutte avec frappe*, does not offer international competition beyond the one-off novelty fight between Bombardier and Baboye in 2013 at the Bercy arena in Paris, aimed at the Senegalese diaspora. Nonetheless, its protagonists are increasingly mobile. Virtually every major wrestler completes a significant portion of their training abroad, with the United States the preferred destination. Beyond training, many wrestlers spend much of their time abroad, where they are frequently involved in business. Increasing numbers of non-elite wrestlers also travel abroad to train and work. Being a wrestler is thought to be advantageous in terms of acquiring visas and forging business contacts within the Senegalese diaspora; likewise, being internationally mobile bolsters one's reputation and opportunities (both within the sport and beyond) in Senegal.

Football and wrestling are therefore strongly associated with different forms of mobility, notably transnational migration – although they are articulated in different ways. Success in either sport is closely connected to the ability to travel abroad to play (in football) or train (in wrestling). This is perhaps unsurprising in the case of football, where the dominant and financially superior leagues, particularly in the Global North, have long recruited the best players from other parts of the world. In wrestling, it is a more recent development, although the process has accelerated and intensified in both sports. One significant result of this is that the two – sport and international mobility – have become indelibly linked to one another in the imaginations and aspirations of young men. To dream of becoming a footballer or a wrestler is equally to dream of leaving the country and having a prosperous career abroad. The line between the two has become blurred.

This has consequences for how young men such as Pape and Modou think about the future and set about chasing their goals. Their respective stories demonstrate that the existence of discrete categories such as "sport migration" or "athletic mobility" must be called into question. While in some rare cases football players may be plucked from an academy to pursue a professional career in Europe or elsewhere, this is more the exception than the rule. More typically, the direct route is inaccessible, leading young men to take matters into their own hands. They may do so by mobilizing agents, coaches, friends, family members, or even strangers on Facebook. They are aware that such projects of migration may not lead directly to the career they envisage. In Pape's case, he bet everything he owned and pooled all the financial resources he could to raise money for a trial at a lower division French club, but he was prepared to abandon the dream once in Europe if it didn't work out and become a *sans papier*. In Modou's case, a similar pattern emerged. What started off as an expressed desire to access improved training conditions in Morocco gradually morphed into exactly the sort of desperate Mediterranean migration project which has dominated headlines as the "refugee crisis" in recent years.

The distinction applies equally to athletes at the other end of their career, such as Malal Ndiaye, Modou's mentor, and a wrestler of considerable renown throughout the country. Malal was very mobile as he pursued less popular types of wrestling, notably Olympic wrestling in which he represented Senegal at the 2012 Olympic Games. Despite this, his "athletic mobility" did not return dividends, in that he did not earn a great deal of money from his career on the global scene, despite the symbolic weight of representing Senegal internationally. Instead, he was able to mobilize his social capital acquired as a wrestler to move to Italy, where he found employment as a bouncer. How athletes become mobile are thus varied, and not always the direct result of their sporting endeavours. Indeed, the post-career activities of athletes are often eclectic and not necessarily connected to sport. Of course, this can work both ways: at the height of media and political debates surrounding migration in 2015–16, heartwarming stories emerged about migrants and refugees who "became" professional football players, notably the Gambian players Bakery Jatta and Ousmane Manneh, who were offered contracts at the German clubs Hamburger SV and Werder Bremen respectively.

This calls into question the notion that global sports systems produce a discrete category of migration with the aim of moving elite athletes to elite clubs. Instead, my fieldwork shows that the processes described as "athletic migration" are in fact a messy collection of highly individual projects characterized by the agency and aspirations of athletes themselves. In this sense, we can understand athletic migration not only as a system of exchange and circulation, but also as a highly entrepreneurial practice. Young men such as Pape and Modou essentially became athletic migrants by declaring themselves as such, and subsequently mobilizing a range of resources to put their plans into effect. Athletic migration as practice is thus rooted in individual and collective agency, and may be considered as a further manifestation of neoliberal personhood in action. Initially, mobility manifests itself as a dream or a fantasy which permeates everyday life. But in many cases, the fantasy may turn into action using sometimes desperate means. By embarking upon risky and self-driven projects of mobility, the "athlete self" navigates the precarious interstices of the global sports industry. For every athlete that makes it, there are many more who fall through the cracks.

Acknowledgements

The research reported herein received funding from the European Research Council under Grant Agreement 295769 for a project entitled "Globalization, Sport and the Precarity of Masculinity" (GLOBALSPORT). I would like to thank the following in no particular order for their valuable feedback, support, and inspiration in writing this chapter: Niko Besnier, Peter Geschiere, Daniel Guinness, Domenica Gisella Calabrò, Susan Brownell, Cheikh Tidiane Wane, Dominique Chevé, Agnes Hann, Mamadou Khouma Gueye. Thanks also to Ross Ludlam who edited an earlier version of this paper. I would also like to thank all of my friends and interlocutors in Senegal who shared their knowledge, ideas, and personal stories with me.

Note

1 All names used in the article are pseudonyms, and some details have been changed in order to protect the anonymity of my interlocutors. Exceptions to this are prominent athletes and other well-known figures whose celebrity precludes anonymization.

References

Agergaard, Sine, Vera Lucia Botelho, and Nina Clara Tiesler. 2014. "The Typology of Athletic Migrants Revisited." In *Women, Soccer and Transnational Migration*, edited by Sine Agergaard and Nina Clara Tiesler, 191–216. London: Routledge.

Akindes, Gerard A. 2011. "Football Bars: Urban Sub-Saharan Africa's Trans-Local 'Stadiums.'" *International Journal of the History of Sport* 28, no. 15: 2176–2190.

Andrews, David L, and Michael L Silk. 2012. *Sport and Neoliberalism: Politics, Consumption, and Culture.* Philadelphia: Temple University Press.

Besnier, Niko. 2012. "The Athlete's Body and the Global Condition: Tongan Rugby Players in Japan." *American Ethnologist* 39, no. 3: 491–510.

Besnier, Niko, and Susan Brownell. 2012. "Sport, Modernity, and the Body." *Annual Review of Anthropology* 41: 443–459.

Carter, Thomas. 2013. "Re-Placing Sport Migrants: Moving beyond the Institutional Structures Informing International Sport Migration." *International Review for the Sociology of Sport* 48, no. 1: 66–82.

Cole, Jennifer, and Deborah Durham. 2008. "Figuring the Future: Children, Youth, and Globalization." In *Figuring the Future: Children, Youth, and Globalization*, edited by Jennifer Cole and Deborah Durham, 3–23. Santa Fe, NM: School for Advanced Research Press.

Crapanzano, Vincent. 2003. "Reflections on Hope as a Category of Social and Psychological Analysis." *Cultural Anthropology* 18, no. 1: 3–32.

Darby, Paul. 2007. "Out of Africa: The Exodus of Elite African Football Talent to Europe." *Journal of Labor and Society* 10, no. 4: 443–456.

Darby, Paul. 2013. "Moving Players, Traversing Perspectives: Global Value Chains, Production Networks and Ghanaian Football Labour Migration." *Geoforum* 50: 43–53.

Elliot, Alice. 2016. "The Makeup of Destiny: Predestination and the Labor of Hope in a Moroccan Emigrant Town." *American Ethnologist* 43, no. 3: 488–499.

Esson, James. 2013. "A Body and a Dream at a Vital Conjuncture: Ghanaian Youth, Uncertainty and the Allure of Football." *Geoforum* 47 (June): 84–92.

Esson, James. 2015a. "Better off at Home? Rethinking Responses to Trafficked West African Footballers in Europe." *Journal of Ethnic and Migration Studies* 41, no. 3: 512–530.

Esson, James. 2015b. "Escape to Victory: Development, Youth Entrepreneurship and the Migration of Ghanaian Footballers." *Geoforum* 64 (August): 47–55.

Esson, James. 2015c. "You Have to Try Your Luck: Male Ghanaian Youth and the Uncertainty of Football Migration." *Environment and Planning* A 47, no. 6: 1383–1397.

Foucault, Michel. 2008. *The Birth of Biopolitics: Lectures at the Collège de France, 1978–1979*, translated by G. Burchell. New York: Picador.

Fouquet, Thomas. 2007. "De la prostitution clandestine aux désirs de l'Ailleurs: Une 'ethnographie de l'extraversion' à Dakar." *Politique africaine* 10, no. 3: 102–123.

Fouquet, Thomas. 2008. "Migrations et 'glocalisation' dakaroises." In *Le Sénégal des migrations: Mobilités, identités, sociétés*, edited by Momar Coumba Diop, 241–276. Paris: Karthala.

Glick Schiller, Nina, Linda Basch, and Cristina Szanton Blanc. 1995. "From Immigrant to Transmigration: Theorizing Transnational Migration." *Anthropological Quarterly* 6, no. 1: 48–63.

Hann, Mark. 2018. "La lutte précaire: Un sport de combat sénégalais à l'ère du néolibéralisme." *Corps* 16: 99–109.

Honwana, Alcinda Manuel. 2012. *The Time of Youth: Work, Social Change, and Politics in Africa.* Sterling, UK: Kumarian Press.

Klein, Alan. 2014. *Dominican Baseball: New Pride, Old Prejudice.* Philadelphia: Temple University Press.

Lanfranchi, Pierre, and Matthew Taylor. 2001. *Moving with the Ball: The Migration of Professional Footballers*. Oxford: Berg.

Mains, Daniel. 2007. "Neoliberal Times: Progress, Boredom, and Shame among Young Men in Urban Ethiopia." *American Ethnologist* 34, no. 4: 659–673.

Masquelier, Adeline. 2013. "Teatime: Boredom and the Temporalities of Young Men in Niger." *Africa* 83, no. 3: 470–491.

Mbodj-Pouye, Aïssatou. 2012. "Literacy, Locality, and Mobility: Writing Practices and 'Cultural Extraversion' in Rural Mali." In *The Global Horizon: Expectations of Migration in Africa and the Middle East*, edited by Knut Graw and Samuli Schielke, 155–174. Leuven, Belgium: Leuven University Press.

Melly, Caroline. 2011. "Titanic Tales of Missing Men: Reconfigurations of National Identity and Gendered Presence in Dakar, Senegal." *American Ethnologist* 38, no. 2: 361–376.

Miller, Toby, Geoffrey A. Lawrence, Jim McKay, and David Rowe. 2001. *Globalization and Sport: Playing the World*. London: Sage.

Piot, Charles. 2010. *Nostalgia for the Future: West Africa after the Cold War*. Chicago: University of Chicago Press.

Prothmann, Sebastian. 2018. "Migration, Masculinity and Social Class: Insights from Pikine, Senegal." *International Migration* 56, no. 4: 96–108.

Ralph, Michael. 2008. "Killing Time." *Social Text* 26, no. 4: 1–29.

Rouse, Roger. 1992. "Making Sense of Settlement: Class Transformation, Cultural Struggle, and Transnationalism among Mexican Migrants in the United States." *Annals of the New York Academy of Sciences* 645, no. 1: 25–52.

Scherer, Jay, and Steven J Jackson. 2010. *Globalization, Sport and Corporate Nationalism: The New Cultural Economy of the New Zealand All Blacks*. Bern, Switzerland: Peter Lang.

12

"THIS IS A BUSINESS, NOT A CHARITY"

Football academies, political economy, and masculinity in Cameroon

Uroš Kovač

In Buea, the capital of the Southwest Region of Cameroon, home to 130,000 Anglophone Cameroonians, the importance of football to everyday life is hard to escape.[1] Every morning before 6:00 A.M., as the owners of grocery shops, boutiques, hair salons, restaurants, and bars prepare for the workday, young men jog up and down the main road that connects the town's landmarks, including the bus station, the university campus, the stadium, the council building, and old Buea Town. Many run for fun, perhaps towards a small field where they will play "santé," a casual game of football played with friends before the workday begins. Others head towards the stadium, which will soon overflow with football clubs and academies training for the next local competition, or for the next trial designed to select the most promising young footballers and sell them to clubs overseas.

Football clubs and academies are deeply embedded in Cameroon's politics and economy (Vidacs 2010).[2] Their development reflects the country's specific colonial experience, the nature of the postcolonial state since its 1961 independence, the economic shifts that have shaped the country's economy since the early 1990s, and the transformations of the global football market in the 1990s and 2000s. The last two points, economic changes and global football, are particularly relevant. Since its introduction by the colonial powers in the early twentieth century, football in Cameroon has always been immersed in transnational processes. These processes became particularly important in the 1990s with the expansion of the global market for football players and the commercialization of global football. At the same time, young Cameroonian men began seeing football as a way to migrate overseas and earn a living. The idea of playing football for a living has increasingly appealed to young men, mainly from poorer backgrounds, although not exclusively, who found themselves navigating increasing economic uncertainty that resulted from the economic crises in the 1980s and the failure of the neoliberal structural adjustment programmes that followed. In this context, the commercialization of football as a global sport and the expanding market for players that increasingly looked to West African countries for talented young men, fuelled the emergence of football academies that focused on commodifying young men and preparing them for attractive but precarious transnational careers.

Here I am concerned with these football academies as mediators between the globalized football market and young Cameroonians' masculine aspirations and expectations. During my fieldwork in the Southwest Region of Cameroon in 2014–15, a reputable and successful academy in coastal Limbe (an hour's drive from the regional capital Buea) was losing its most valuable players. Yet Unisport Limbe FC had an enviable infrastructure for training and lodging footballers, and the team participated in Elite One, Cameroon's top division.[3] Young footballers were flocking instead to Buea Young Star FC, a small ad hoc lower-level football academy in Buea.

At first, I was puzzled as to why footballers would leave a well-established club that provided them with the experience of top-level football matches, high-level training, and a salary (albeit sporadic) to join a small club that was barely organized, competed only in minor regional competitions, and provided no income. They gave me a straightforward reason: Buea Young Star FC focused on cultivating individual talented footballers and selling them to wealthy clubs in Europe. An opportunity to migrate, however elusive, attracted young footballers who dreamed of playing abroad for a living. This opportunity promised to fulfil their aspirations to participate in the globalized imagery of masculine success embodied by famous elite athletes, and a solution to the growing demands of their families to begin fulfilling their masculine roles as providers. Young men's aspirations helped shape the football academies, and the academies in turn sought to cultivate young men willing to embrace the precarity of a transnational athletic career.

By focusing on football academies, I seek to capture how "global and local economic policies, institutions, activities, and processes of valuation produce cultural meanings with which people engage" (Adebanwi 2017, 4). In a West African setting, economic and political activities are constitutive of a political economy that is defined by "negotiability, flexibility, resilience, innovation, and entrepreneurship … alongside the dangers of extraction and marginality in the global economy" (Guyer 2004, 6). In the neoliberal post-structural-adjustment period, the future, however uncertain, takes precedence over the present and the past, and people are willing to submit themselves to new forms of disciplinary power that promise inclusion in transnational circuits (Piot 2010). This development is especially pertinent to football academies, given the sport's global commercialization and the expansion of a transnational market for football players grounded in neoliberal ideas of free enterprise.

Football academies in Cameroon play a crucial role in selecting and cultivating young men as subjects willing to embrace new forms of precarity. In the academies, the value of "suffering" for the sake of an uncertain future emerges as central. My emphasis on "suffering" may be surprising in the context of a recent call in anthropology to move "beyond the suffering subject" (Robbins 2013) and to consider subjects of anthropological inquiry as more than people who merely suffer. However, here I am concerned with how football academies produce and cultivate a "suffering subject" specific to the demands of the expanding global market. While young footballers in Cameroon routinely, as they say, "suffer" on the football fields, especially when they have to train and play without compensation, academy managers insist that they need to be taught a new form of "suffering," one that asks them to disregard their current needs and obligations and orient themselves to future success in a globalized market, however uncertain this success might be. The academies seek to reframe the obligations placed on young men as male adult providers, and to teach them to embrace the precarity that is inherent in the globalized market.

Economic transformations on a global scale since the 1980s have destabilized previously predictable ways in which men around the world used to perform adult masculinity, especially through economic productivity (Besnier, Guinness, Hann, and Kovač 2018; Cole and Durham 2007; Cornwall, Karioris, and Lindisfarne 2016). This has prompted some commentators to remark that a "crisis of masculinity" is ongoing (e.g. Comaroff and Comaroff 2000, 307; Perry 2005). However, the idea that masculinity is in crisis often emerges as an ideological construct that can obscure structural conditions such as the restructuring of the economy (Yang 2010), attributing social problems to masculinity and pathologizing men (Smith 2017). In other interpretations, the "crisis of masculinity" is attributed to the decrease of men's economic and political power in relation to women, while in fact men still control most domains of life (Morrell 2002).

Scholars have also discussed masculinity by focusing on how people assert some forms of masculinity as "hegemonic." The core of the notion of "hegemonic masculinity" (Connell 1987; Connell and Messerschmidt 2005) is useful because it not only captures the fact that people construct masculinity differently in various contexts and histories, but also recognizes that different forms of masculinity are hierarchically ordered. Yet, the concept is of limited value because it assumes that masculinity is a coherent entity and that a single form of masculinity emerges as hegemonic in a particular context (Besnier, Guinness, Hann, and Kovač 2018).

Instead of discussing masculinity as inherently hegemonic or in a crisis, here I address how political economy shapes gendered subjects, and in turn how gendered aspirations shape the political economy. Masculinity is a production inextricable from the political economy, and is grounded in gendered aspirations and disciplining regimes specific to a given political and economic moment. Cameroonian footballers' aspirations and economic hardships show that the performance of masculinity in the contemporary post-structural-adjustment moment is intertwined with the economic uncertainty that haunts young men, but also with the proliferation of attractive but elusive opportunities of enrichment that come with the globalization of images and markets. Football academies play a key role in catering to young men's gendered aspirations and in shaping masculine subjects.

Cameroon, football, and migration aspirations

Since the mid-1990s, young Cameroonians have increasingly seen overseas migration as the only way to deal with economic hardships, and football has become an attractive way for young men in particular to attempt to leave. Young men's aspirations to migrate through football have been driven by global transformations grounded in neoliberal ideology of deregulation (Besnier, Calabrò, and Guinness, this volume).

In the early 1990s, global television corporations started injecting millions into elite European football leagues, and through the decade the leagues became thoroughly commercialized. In the same period, the number of television sets grew throughout Africa (Akyeampong and Ambler 2002, 15) and satellite broadcasting blossomed. People all over the continent could now watch European football leagues and many preferred watching European football on television screens to national league matches on football fields (Akindes 2011). Young men idolized successful international African footballers like Samuel Eto'o and Didier Drogba. The possibility of making a football career abroad began looming large in the imaginations of young men on the continent.

Meanwhile, many European clubs began scouting West Africa (as well as Latin America) for inexpensive young players (Alegi 2010, 98). A number of legal developments, such as the 1995 Bosman ruling and the 2000 Cotonou Agreement, which allowed skilled workers (including footballers) to cross borders more easily (at least in theory), helped the migration of footballers from Africa to increase (Poli 2006; Poli, Ravenel, and Besson 2015). As Europeans "discovered" Africa as a pool of inexpensive talent, and as young people across Africa "discovered" the expanding football market, European and African entrepreneurs and organizations opened football academies in or near African capital cities, mainly for the purpose of selecting players for the international football market (Darby, Akindes, and Kirwin 2007; Darby 2013; Esson 2015). Young men flocked to these academies, seeing them as gateways to migrating overseas.

A story from Anglophone Cameroon is a case in point. In 2004, a newly formed football academy assembled and trained a young team of under-21 players and, in coordination with partners in Europe, arranged for the team to take part in a youth competition in Italy. The team's performance at the tournament was mediocre at best, but they reportedly attracted the attention of Italian football scouts. When the time came for the team to leave for the airport and return to Cameroon, half the team went missing, no fewer than ten players having decided to try their luck individually in Europe. Despite their undocumented status, two of them made it all the way to clubs in the top tier of Italian football and at least three signed contracts in Finland, Switzerland, and Greece. This "incident," which happens frequently (Okeowo 2016), has become a cautionary tale for the region's football coaches and managers. For the young footballers with whom I trained in 2014 and 2015, the story confirmed their belief that opportunities await in Europe and elsewhere, and that football academies are a way to seize them (Figure 12.1).

FIGURE 12.1 First division football match in Limbe.
(Source: Uroš Kovač)

The largest football academy, École de football Brasseries du Cameroun, had already been running in the Francophone economic hub Douala since 1989. Today, it prides and markets itself as a producer of world-class footballers. The Anglophone Southwest Region joined the game somewhat later, and academies have emerged since 2000. In 2015, I identified 27 football clubs and academies in the region. Some profiled themselves as academies aimed at nurturing young generations of footballers, while others were football clubs competing in divisional, regional, and national competitions. Almost every one of the hundreds of young men training at one of the clubs dreamt of landing a contract with a wealthy club overseas.

In reality, it is extraordinarily difficult to stand out as an exceptional footballer. For example, in 2015, the École de football Brasseries du Cameroun selected a cohort of eighteen 13-year-olds from 3,584 hopefuls who took part in trials throughout the country (Nonos 2015). Considering that this is only one academy, and that a new cohort of 13-year-olds participates every year, it is clear that many boys and young men harbour dreams of a career in football even though only very few will succeed in playing professionally. Moreover, to have a crack at signing a contract with a club overseas, Cameroonian footballers need to be between 18 and 21 (at least on paper), so the window of time for success is narrow. Many projects of becoming a professional athlete amount to "cruel optimism" (Berlant 2011), in which dreams appear close, achievable, and meaningful, yet beyond one's grasp.

The context of footballers' desire to migrate overseas is Cameroon's protracted economic crisis. In the 1990s, as the transnational football market was expanding, young Cameroonians were suffering from the consequences of austerity measures imposed by the International Monetary Fund and the World Bank and the disappointments of the "good governance" model of democratization. As in many other countries in Africa (Ferguson 2006; Harrison 2010), neoliberal reforms had failed to deliver on the prosperity they had promised. The country's GDP continued to plummet: between 1986 and 1994, it decreased by 42.4%. With austerity measures and the dismantling of the public sector, many civil servants were demoted or laid off. The figure of the *fonctionnaire*, a person who used academic qualifications to obtain desirable positions in the public sector, became increasingly elusive (Geschiere 2013, 56). At the same time, the neopatrimonial state rallied around the long-standing president, the ruling political party did not relinquish power despite calls for democratization, and state resources remained out of reach for most young Cameroonians. Finally, the devaluation of the currency by 50% in January 1994 dealt a severe blow to many Cameroonian household budgets.[4] Facing a lack of opportunities at home, many Cameroonians turned their attention to migration (Alpes 2012; Nyamnjoh 2011).

Cameroonian young men in particular faced diminishing opportunities to fulfil the masculine role of provider for their families. For them, football has emerged as a new way to imagine a future abroad, a particularly masculine aspiration that seeks not only income, but also glory and recognition. As elsewhere in West Africa (Engh and Agergaard 2015), women in Cameroon also watch and play football, and some manage to migrate and make a living from playing. But it is overwhelmingly young men who dream of opportunities to play overseas and who see football academies as a way to fulfil their aspirations to migrate.

"This is a business, not a charity": Buea Young Star FC

Buea Yong Star FC is a good example how new academies flourish on young men's desire to migrate, and how a business ideology has penetrated football in Cameroon. Founded in 2010, the academy quickly gained popularity among aspiring footballers in the Southwest Region. Its founder and president, Kelvin, is an aspiring entrepreneur in his late 20s. He was born in Buea to a father from the Grassfields and a mother from the West Region, most likely Bamileke, both ethnic groups known for their "spirit of entrepreneurship" (Warnier 1993). A former footballer and a football fan, he was keen to develop young talented footballers from poor backgrounds and help them sign contracts with clubs abroad and to develop a profitable business based on selling them. He founded the club with the help of two German partners, a football agent in his late 30s and a youth football coach. Kelvin also maintained a relationship with a Nigerian football agent based in Eastern Europe. In the club's 2011 promotional video, the German agent described the club's mission as follows:

Always think of where you are coming from and where you want to go. You have to do all that you are able to do to realize your dream. With probably our support, we can realize for some of you the dream to go to Europe.

"Dream" and "Europe," terms that frequently go together in an industry that feeds on hope, figured prominently in the aspirations of young footballers, many of whom had seen some of their friends travel abroad to play football and earn money (Figure 12.2). Buea Young Star FC promised to cater to this aspiration.

Kelvin maintained good relationships with his foreign partners. Every year, the coach from Germany spent two weeks with the team, trained them, selected 25 players who were to train with the team for the upcoming year, and, most important, made a selection of the most talented candidates for trials abroad. Kelvin paid for his accommodation in an upscale hotel in Buea. A key purpose of this expensive exercise was a performance of meritocracy: a demonstration that an external "unbiased" person objectively observed the footballers and selected the most promising. In practice, this was not always the case, but to a certain extent the performance worked to circumvent the common Cameroonian accusation that club presidents chose footballers not based on merit but personal connections, kinship ties, and ethnic affiliations.[5]

For Kelvin, football was "a business, not a charity." Alongside his proclaimed desire to help young poor Cameroonians reach their dreams of playing in Europe, profit (financial or otherwise) was his main goal. Although I was unable to find exact information about sales and profits, a sketch of what went into selling a player,

FIGURE 12.2 A billboard in downtown Buea announcing the beginning of selection for a prominent football academy, Buea, Cameroon, June 2015.
(Source: Uroš Kovač)

and some assessments of financial profits and the general economy of the process, provides a rough picture.

After identifying a player with potential, Kelvin would invite him to sign a contract. If the player was under 18, Kelvin would seek his parents' permission. These were usually long-term contracts, from five to ten years, and could be extended. The contract stated that Kelvin would receive a percentage of the player's salary if he was signed up with a club and, each time the player was transferred, a percentage of the fee that the receiving club paid to the source club. Occasionally, Kelvin would help record a video of the player in action to present to clubs and managers abroad and write up a basic C.V. that listed the player's age, weight, height, position, and transfer history.[6] He would then arrange for and contribute to the cost of the player's passports, visas, and airline ticket. Occasionally, he acted less as the head of a football club and more as a *doki-man*, a migration broker (Alpes 2017): arranging invitation letters from his European partners, a key requirement for visa applications; organizing visa appointments at European embassies; and producing passports that lowered the player's age.

Having organized the documents, Kelvin would send the player to his business partner, the Nigerian football manager based in Eastern Europe, who would find a club for him to train in, usually in a third or fourth division. In the first year, Kelvin would not expect the foreign club to pay the player. This would be a period for the player to develop his skills in a European setting and try to obtain a residence permit. The expectation was that the player would be bought by another club, and Kelvin would profit from the sale.

During my 12-month fieldwork, Kelvin arranged trials and documents for ten players. For five of them, the document procedures failed or were deemed too expensive and protracted, or the players left the club for a different reason. The other five travelled to various destinations in Europe, including Portugal, Germany, Bosnia and Herzegovina, Poland, Latvia, Estonia, and Slovakia. Most visited at least two countries, following Kelvin's instructions. Some returned to Cameroon, either briefly or indefinitely. Three players found salaried positions in clubs in Eastern Europe.

Even when a player was sold, it was not clear that the sale was financially profitable for Kelvin. For instance, he sold one player to a small club in Eastern Europe, where the player earned €350 a month. Kelvin took 20% (€70), which he then shared with the other participants in the production chain: his two partners in Germany and his partner in Eastern Europe. Considering what he had invested in the player, it is difficult to see how this sale could be cost-effective. In another case, however, Kelvin sold one player to a first division club in Eastern Europe, and the player even went on to perform for the Cameroonian national team, which won the 2017 Africa Cup of Nations. In 2017, a widely used website that archives information about transfers in football estimated the player's market value at €250,000.[7] It is difficult to know what Kelvin collected (or is still collecting years after the sale), but the case shows that sending outstanding individual players abroad can potentially be lucrative for both the manager and the player.

Importantly, footballers did not see themselves as being exploited by the transnational industry or by club presidents such as Kelvin. From their point of view, as with young athletes from poor backgrounds elsewhere (Klein 2008), commodification was an opportunity to migrate abroad and earn a living by playing the beautiful game. Migrating abroad, even for a short period of time, could bring much more financial and social capital to the young men than playing in Cameroonian clubs, most of which were dependent on the financial whims of Cameroonian investors and notorious for not paying salaries regularly. Footballers were aware that opportunities for signing contracts with clubs abroad were also notoriously fickle, yet for most of them the commodification that led to migration meant progress and a better chance for a livelihood.

Over time, Buea Young Star FC developed a reputation of a promising new academy, based on a few stories of footballers who travelled overseas for trials and contracts. Most of all, the academy relied on young footballers' zeal to leave Cameroon.

Producing "suffering" subjects

However, young men's aspirations to migrate were not enough to successfully run a football academy. Kelvin needed to make sure that the footballers were disciplined, committed to training hard despite difficult conditions and uncertain outcomes, prepared to deal with the challenging (and sometimes exploitative) conditions they would encounter overseas, and ready to submit to his guidance and leadership. He played a crucial role in preparing young men for the precarity of a transnational athletic career.

As an entrepreneur and a gatekeeper of young footballers' access to the global market, Kelvin was less focused on managing Buea Young Star FC as a football team than on identifying talented individual players and managing their entry into transnational markets. He sought to develop close relationships and methods of supervision of individual promising players. He claimed that the psychology classes he had attended at university allowed him to assess not only football skills but more crucially the character of each individual player. On many occasions, he discussed with me a player's individual characteristics: who was "stubborn" and who was "focused," who had a "zeal," and who was "disciplined." He was particularly critical of *stronghed* (stubborn) footballers who were not willing to follow instructions, especially concerning migration. He complained about the two most common transgressions of footballers who eventually manage to leave Cameroon: "running away," namely hiding from the manager and the authorities, looking for other employment opportunities abroad, and staying in Europe illegally; and being defeated by the often deplorable living conditions in the destination country and flying back to Cameroon without the manager's permission. Kelvin demanded from the footballers to submit to his guidance and trust his decision making, rather than acting on their own accord.

The consequences of Kelvin's priority to train individual footballers, rather than the team as a whole, became clear to me during a meeting between the coach, the team captain, and Kelvin himself. In 2015, Buea Young Star FC competed in the regional (third) division against teams of the Southwest Region. The players sometimes referred to it as the "devil league," because club presidents were not required by the Fédération camerounaise de football (FECAFOOT), Cameroon's football governing body, to pay their players or provide them with daily or weekly training bonuses. At the time of the meeting, the club was not performing well. We all sat around the table, opposite a television set that was broadcasting a rerun of an English Premier League match between Arsenal FC and West Bromwich Albion FC. The coach argued that the main reason for the club's low performance was that the footballers had not received any kind of compensation for more than three months:

> Most of these players that are in the club now, they are not small children. They are big people, and all of them have some [financial] responsibilities. Now, players did not receive training bonuses for two or three months, and this affects the results. That is the main problem. ... For this [low] level of football, or let me say for these players in Buea, if you want to see the results you must give them training bonuses.

Kelvin disagreed, arguing that most players were not eligible for training bonuses and that giving bonuses to everyone was not an effective business model. Moreover, it clashed with his key objectives for the academy:

> The objective for the club is not to win the league. The objective is to train people who have potential, and then select the best and send them out of the country. For this season, for me, I only don't want the team to be last. So this does not bother me too much. I only worry about the performance of individual people that we need to select and prepare to travel abroad.

The focus on preparing individual players for the transnational market is clear. Not winning a league competition did not indicate a lack of ambition. An important incentive for Kelvin to remain in the regional "devil league" was the fact that the administrative rules were much looser. While first division teams had to follow FECAFOOT's administrative instructions in order to play, in the "devil league" there was more space to manipulate players' documents and tamper with their official age. Engagement with global markets seemed to work better from the grey areas of unregulated spaces in Cameroonian football.

Furthermore, Kelvin's focus on developing individual players led him to a model of allocating club finances that was strikingly different from other clubs in the Southwest Region. Kelvin continued:

> I will not invest in every man equally. I can only put down money for something that is marketable, for something that has a prospect for future. I will

put down money for something that will give me profit later. So I must concentrate on people that have some prospect.

Again, the commodification of players is grounded in assessment of future value: which players are likely to bring profit in the future.

Moreover, in Buea Young Star FC, commodification led to the nurturing of young men who were equally oriented to the future and willing to "suffer" for the sake of success in football. Kelvin continued:

> [The players] need to suffer today so they will see the results tomorrow. Not ask [for money] now, but understand that you need to put your best into your training, so you can have the results later. … Also, there are match bonuses, if you win the match, you get [CFA] 3,000. In my own ideology, that is better. If I come to the training and do not receive a training bonus, but I know that I will get 3,000 if I win a match, I will do what? I will fight to win, I will give my best!

Finally, Kelvin framed "suffering" for the sake of the future as a sign of maturity and adulthood:

> Not every man in Buea can play this professional football! [Points to the Premier League match on the television set] Only *one-one* [i.e. "very few"]. … And they are not children, they are growing a beard! They know what they want to do in life, so they need to do it.

Importantly, Kelvin framed focus and determination as signs of adulthood. His definition of adult masculinity is strikingly different from the coach's definition. Knowledgeable of local football and of the needs of young men, the coach worried about the footballers' obligations to provide for their families. Meanwhile, for Kelvin, the gatekeeper to transnational markets (and the one who had the last word), the markers of adult masculinity were grounded in qualities that allowed young men (who were "growing a beard") to compete in transnational markets, namely the capacity to suffer for the sake of future success. Needless to say, it was highly uncertain whether that future would bring success in the form of contracts.

Here we see how a football academy operates on the fact that young men are on the brink of becoming adult male providers and how an individual who runs an academy as a business seeks to shape them to comply with the demands of the market and his own business interests. Disciplining subjects for participation in transnational markets turns out to be strikingly gendered: the disciplining process seeks to shape young men as gendered subjects. Gendered expectations and aspirations inform the logic of business and commodification, and in turn the logic of business and commodification penetrates gender ideology.

Finally, Kelvin's evocation of "suffering" demands attention. "We are suffering" is a common refrain among Anglophone Cameroonians. Just like Nigerians (Larkin 2017, 48–49), Cameroonians speak of "suffering" during times of economic hardship and when their hard work fails to deliver. Cameroonian footballers in the "devil league" often "suffer" – when they are forced to train on badly maintained pitches that are conducive to injuries, when they are asked to play demanding matches on empty stomachs, and when their efforts result in meagre (if any) financial returns. And yet the president of a prominent football academy insisted that young men needed to be taught the value of "suffering," a value that they seemed to be lacking.

It is clear that Kelvin sought from footballers a specific kind of "suffering," one that was oriented towards success that was elsewhere and in the future. While previously the footballers would "suffer" on bad training pitches for the sake of representing a club, achieving local glory, and earning a small income, club presidents like Kelvin trained young men to "suffer" in order to qualify for moving abroad and competing in transnational markets. The capacity for this kind of "suffering" would become important once footballers migrated abroad and were confronted with the arduous and sometimes exploitative conditions in foreign clubs.

It turns out, then, that the subject with the capacity to suffer for the sake of an uncertain future is not a given among young African men who aspire to migrate. Instead, it is produced in academies such as Buea Young Star FC. In other words, the suffering subject, the subject in economic distress prepared to suffer for a better future, is not simply "there" for the global markets to use, but needs to be produced and nurtured.

From "social development" to near bankruptcy: Unisport Limbe FC

The changing political economy of football in Cameroon is illustrated in the example of another academy in the Southwest Region, one that was based on a different ideology. Unisport Limbe FC was founded in 2000 in Limbe by a prominent political figure, who told me that the primary aim of the academy was humanitarian: it focused on, in his words, "social development" by "helping disadvantaged children through sports." The club made no profit, but the founder had "good connections" with wealthy men who invested significant amounts of money in the club.

In 2014–15, Unisport Limbe FC had one of the most developed infrastructures in the Southwest Region. The campus included two full-sized football fields, one grass and one sand; three dormitory blocks with bunk beds that could house about 60 children or adults; a large dining room with a bar and television sets; a large conference room with tables, chairs, and a blackboard; a small leisure room with a television set and a ping-pong table; a large administration office decorated with trophies; and a sumptuously furnished office for the president. The dormitories had a regular supply of water in barrels and electricity worked most of the time. The academy owned two buses, one that could transport a team of 25 and one to transport children between the campus and the schools they attended in Limbe. The academy employed a technical director, four coaches, an administration assistant, a secretary, a doctor, two cooks, several drivers, and a groundskeeper.

The Unisport Limbe FC men's team competed in the Elite One first-division league and the academy trained boys aged 12 to 18. In July of each year, boys were selected in football trials and in September approximately 35 moved to the campus. The boys' parents paid yearly fees between CFA 800,000 and 1.3 million (€1,225–1,990), which covered food, lodging, training, and tuition fees for schools (in comparison, government schools charge CFA 50,000 and some private schools CFA 150,000). In addition, about 30 day students attended but lived with their families in Limbe. These students only paid symbolic fees.

Unisport Limbe FC was the only academy in the region that insisted on students performing well academically. All boarding students were registered in Limbe schools. The bus would take the boys to their respective schools every morning and collect them at the end of the day. They had to keep their school uniforms neat and clean. The staff often complained that some boys were only interested in playing football and neglected their studies. The club president insisted that the boys needed to pass with acceptable grades and planned to develop a policy that the men's team recruit only footballers with secondary school diplomas. The strong emphasis on education, unique among academies in the region, was grounded in an understanding that sport was an unpredictable field. The academy's website explains:

> While football has grown to become arguably the most popular and most played sports on the planet, with its top professionals being amongst the best paid athletes in the world, there is however no guarantee that being hyper-talented and undergoing a rigorous and efficient training program will lead to becoming a successful professional football player. ... Ensuring the basic and secondary education of our trainees serves not only as a backup in case of a failed football career but also serves as a fundamental tool which will be beneficial to them during their football careers and even after their playing days.

This way of addressing the uncertainty of success in professional football was strikingly different to that of the Buea Young Star FC's president. While the latter argued for single-minded determination and focus on the sport as a solution to the vagaries of an athletic career, the Limbe club emphasized education as an alternative and addition to a future in football.

The Limbe club president was critical of how regional football had changed under the influence of the expanding transnational market of football players. He was clearly shaken by the emergence of new small academies, clubs, and entrepreneurs that focused almost exclusively on selling players to overseas clubs and by young footballers' attraction to them. In January 2015, I asked him about this as we were sitting together watching a friendly match between Unisport Limbe FC and Buea Young Star FC. He became visibly irritated:

> We are a professional team, not some amateur team that is only after selling players! If the players want to travel, they can go with their own traveling program, if their contract with us is over. We are here to build a team and play. … Also the kids at the academy, we have to first build up quality players, we cannot just sell them like that.

In spite of its noble aim to protect young men from the vagaries of the transnational football market, Unisport Limbe FC's reputation was sliding in 2014. The president had become widely seen as unapproachable, arrogant, and brash, lacking a clear vision, and most of all financially incompetent. These rumours mostly focused on the men's team, which was losing matches and was stuck at the bottom of the table, with a relegation to second division looming.

In 2015, the club president complained to me that the wealthy businessmen, influential political figures, and corporations that had supported the club in the past were no longer willing to do so. Financing the men's team had become difficult. According to FECAFOOT officials, professional football clubs in Cameroon are required to pay their players at least CFA 100,000 a month. In the wealthiest clubs in 2015, such as Coton sport FC de Garoua, footballers could receive up to CFA 400,000.[8] In addition, most Elite One clubs would pay their footballers additional amounts for their meals or when they won. Normally, Unisport Limbe FC paid their players CFA 5,000 a week and CFA 25,000 when they won (which in 2015 rarely happened), occasionally fed the players, and paid their travel expenses to away matches. But almost all Unisport Limbe FC footballers complained that they had not received their salaries for months. Players frequently grumbled that they were "hungry" and could not meet the demands that their families placed on them. Coaches complained that the club was in a horrendous financial state. They blamed the president, accusing him of being deaf to the needs of his subordinates and disengaged from the Cameroonian elites who could finance the club.

Most importantly, the footballers were angry that the president was reluctant to sell them to overseas clubs. They saw him as hindering their ambition to "reach a higher level." They considered his reluctance to throw young men into the uncertain waters of the transnational circulation of footballers as close-minded and deaf to the rapid changes of the global football business. This is why they flocked to Buea Young Star FC, which contributed to the demise of the academy that claimed to protect them from the uncertainties of transnational markets.

This demise shows that football academies are under pressure to adapt to the changing political economy of football. The pressure comes from different sources: the emerging business-savvy football academies, but also from the young footballers themselves, who have become certain that their masculine aspirations and the growing demands of provider masculinity can only be fulfilled through academies that are responsive to the sport's global commodification. The neoliberalization of football academies thus also happens "from below." Crucially, it takes place in an economic and political context in which there are few options for young men to fulfil their roles in the local economy and in which migration aspirations and globalized imagery of spectacular success have come to occupy their minds.

Football academies: Between aspirations and economic transformations

The active participation of African economic agents in the global circulation of people and goods is not new: politics and economy in Africa has a long history of "extraversion," namely "mobilizing resources derived from their (possibly unequal) relationship with the external environment" (Bayart 2000, 218). But football academies like Buea Young Star FC are new in the Southwest Region of Cameroon and they clearly are a response to the expansion of the transnational market for football players driven by global economic changes, as well as by young men's own aspirations.

In these academies, young men are taught to prioritize "suffering" for the sake of the future, however uncertain, over present needs and obligations – a value that they, from the point of view of academy leaders, seem to lack. Academies like Buea Young Star FC formulate this value as a sign of adulthood and maturity that needs to be inculcated. Young men thus need to be taught to embrace a new form of precarity, one that comes with the expansion of the global market for football players. Global markets thus rely on the willingness of young men to "suffer" for the sake of an uncertain future.

A perspective that moves away from an exclusive focus on aspiring migrants on to the organizations that shape them allows us to move beyond seeing migrants from Africa as victims of large-scale processes beyond their control or, in contrast, as active agents who willingly dive head-first into the vagaries of migration. The young men I worked with are indeed driven to leave. But football academies such as Buea Young Star FC play a key role. The academies do not simply find and "harvest" desperate young men willing to suffer. Instead, they seek to produce migrants willing to engage with globalized precarity. This process is a concrete example of how transnational migrants are produced at the intersection of neoliberal transformations.

Likewise, this perspective helps us to move away from limited approaches to masculinity that rely on representations of men as either victims of contemporary global transformations or as powerful agents who reproduce the hegemony of certain forms of masculinity. We see instead how organizations like football academies play a key role in the way that large scale changes grounded in neoliberalism shape gendered subjects, in this case young men captivated by enticing but volatile opportunities for mobility who face economic hardships in post-structural-adjustment Africa.

Acknowledgements

The research reported herein has received funding from the European Research Council under Grant Agreement 295769 for a project entitled "Globalization, Sport and the Precarity of Masculinity" (GLOBALSPORT). I am grateful to Cameroonian footballers and their families for their warm friendships and insightful conversations, and to the academies' presidents, coaches, and staff members for participating in the research. I am thankful to Niko Besnier, Daniel Guinness, and Domenica Gisella Calabrò for constructive feedback on this chapter. I also thank Peter Geschiere, who commented on numerous previous versions. This chapter is a revised version of a chapter in my PhD thesis titled "The Precarity of Masculinity: Football, Pentecostalism, and Transnational Aspirations in Cameroon," defended in December 2018 at the University of Amsterdam.

Notes

1 Cameroon comprises a large and politically dominant Francophone area and a smaller and marginalized Anglophone area, the result of different colonial histories.
2 Throughout this chapter, I use the terms "club" and "academy" interchangeably. Technically, they are not the same: clubs are teams that compete in national and regional leagues and academies are football schools that train boys and young men under the age of 18. In practice, however, the two overlap: some of the most successful clubs in national competitions call themselves "academies," and some football schools maintain teams with older players and compete in national and regional leagues.
3 All names of clubs and people are pseudonyms. I have slightly altered some minor details in order to protect my interlocutors' anonymity.
4 For a review of the economic and social impact of neoliberal reforms in Africa and Cameroon, see Konings (2011, 2–6).
5 During football matches at all levels (from small regional leagues to national team matches), when a footballer clearly underperformed, Cameroonian spectators often labeled him a "coach's player" or "president's player," indicating that he was on the team not thanks to his skills but to a close relationship with the team's decision makers. There was much talk of club presidents and coaches taking bribes for fielding certain footballers.
6 Footballers would often make these videos themselves to show to potential managers.
7 http://www.transfermarkt.de.
8 For the sake of comparison, teachers in government schools earn around CFA 100,000; however, in some private schools, teachers' wages could be as low as CFA 25,000. A secretary at Unisport Limbe FC earned CFA 60,000. Some civil servants, such as programmers employed by the General Certificate of Education board, would earn up to CFA 500,000. The official national minimum wage in 2014 was CFA 36,270, well below the demands of the workers' unions for a CFA 62,000 minimum wage (Business in Cameroon 2014).

References

Adebanwi, Wale. 2017. "Approaching the Political Economy of Everyday Life: An Introduction." In *The Political Economy of Everyday Life in Africa: Beyond the Margins*, edited by Wale Adebanwi, 1–32. Woodbridge, UK: Boydell and Brewer.

Akindes, Gerard A. 2011. "Football Bars: Urban Sub-Saharan Africa's Trans-local 'Stadiums.'" *International Journal of the History of Sport* 28, no. 15: 2176–2190.

Akyeampong, Emmanuel, and Charles Ambler. 2002. "Leisure in African History: An Introduction." *International Journal of African Historical Studies* 35, no. 1: 1–16.

Alegi, Peter. 2010. *African Soccerscapes: How a Continent Changed the World's Game*. Athens: Ohio University Press.

Alpes, Maybritt Jill. 2012. "Bushfalling at All Cost: The Economy of Migratory Knowledge in Anglophone Cameroon." *African Diaspora* 5, no. 1: 90–115.

Alpes, Maybritt Jill. 2017. "Why Aspiring Migrants Trust Migration Brokers: The Moral Economy of Departure in Anglophone Cameroon." *Africa* 87, no. 2: 304–321.

Bayart, Jean-François. 2000. "Africa in the World: A History of Extraversion." *African Affairs* 99 (April): 217–267.

Berlant, Lauren. 2011. *Cruel Optimism*. Durham, NC: Duke University Press.

Besnier, Niko, Daniel Guinness, Mark Hann, and Uroš Kovač. 2018. "Rethinking Masculinity in the Neoliberal Order: Cameroonian Footballers, Fijian Rugby Players, and Senegalese Wrestlers." *Comparative Studies in Society and History* 60, no. 4: 839–872.

Business in Cameroon. 2014. "Cameroon to Increase Minimum Wage From 28,000 to 36,270 FCFA." *Business in Cameroon*, 22 July 2014. www.businessincameroon.com/public-management/2207-4959-cameroon-to-increase-minimum-wage-from-de-28-000-to-36-270-fcfa.

Cole, Jennifer, and Deborah Durham. 2007. "Introduction: Age, Regeneration, and the Intimate Politics of Globalization." In *Generations and Globalization: Youth, Age, and Family in the New World Economy*, edited by Jennifer Cole and Deborah Durham, 1–28. Bloomington: Indiana University Press.

Comaroff, Jean, and John L. Comaroff. 2000. "Millennial Capitalism: First Thoughts on a Second Coming." *Public Culture* 12, no. 2: 291–343.

Connell, R.W. 1987. *Gender and Power*. Sydney: Allen and Unwin.

Connell, R.W., and J.W. Messerschmidt. 2005. "Hegemonic Masculinity: Rethinking the Concept." *Gender and Society* 19, no. 6: 829–859.

Cornwall, Andrea, Frank Karioris, and Nancy Lindisfarne, eds. 2016. *Masculinities under Neoliberalism*. London: Zed.

Darby, Paul. 2013. "Moving Players, Traversing Perspectives: Global Value Chains, Production Networks and Ghanaian Football Labour Migration." *Geoforum* 50: 43–53.

Darby, Paul, Gerard Akindes, and Matthew Kirwin. 2007. "Football Academies and the Migration of African Football Labor to Europe." *Journal of Sport & Social Issues* 31, no. 2: 143–161.

Engh, Mari Haugaa, and Sine Agergaard. 2015. "Producing Mobility Through Locality and Visibility: Developing a Transnational Perspective on Sports Labour Migration." *International Review for the Sociology of Sport* 50, no. 8: 974–992.

Esson, James. 2015. "Escape to Victory: Development, Youth Entrepreneurship and the Migration of Ghanaian Footballers." *Geoforum* 64: 47–55.

Ferguson, James. 2006. *Global Shadows: Africa in the Neoliberal World Order*. Durham, NC: Duke University Press.

Geschiere, Peter. 2013. *Witchcraft, Intimacy, and Trust: Africa in Comparison*. Chicago: University of Chicago Press.

Guyer, Jane. 2004. *Marginal Gains: Monetary Transactions in Atlantic Africa*. Chicago: University of Chicago Press.

Harrison, Graham. 2010. *Neoliberal Africa: The Impact of Global Social Engineering*. London: Zed.

Klein, Alan M. 2008. "Progressive Ethnocentrism: Ideology and Understanding in Dominican Baseball." *Journal of Sport and Social Issues* 32, no. 2: 121–138.

Konings, Piet. 2011. *The Politics of Neoliberal Reforms in Africa: State and Civil Society in Cameroon*. Leiden: African Studies Centre.

Larkin, Brian. 2017. "The Form of Crisis and the Affect of Modernization." In *African Futures: Essays on Crisis, Emergence, and Possibility*, edited by Brian Goldstone and Juan Obarrio, 39–50. Chicago: University of Chicago Press.

Morrell, Robert. 2002. "Men, Movements, and Gender Transformation in South Africa." *Journal of Men's Studies* 10, no. 3: 309–27.

Nonos, Frédéric. 2015. "Coupe Top 2015: 18 jeunes intègrent l'Efbc." *Camfoot.com*, 9 August 2015. www.camfoot.com/actualites/coupe-top-2015-18-jeunes-integrent%2C21958.html.

Nyamnjoh, Francis. 2011. "Cameroonian Bushfalling: Negotiation of Identity and Belonging in Fiction and Ethnography." *American Ethnologist* 38, no. 4: 701–713.

Okeowo, Alexis. 2016. "The Soccer-Star Refugees of Eritrea." *New Yorker*, 12 December 2016. www.newyorker.com/magazine/2016/12/12/the-soccer-star-refugees-of-eritrea.

Perry, Donna L. 2005. "Wolof Women, Economic Liberalization, and the Crisis of Masculinity in Rural Senegal." *Ethnography* 44, no. 3: 207–226.

Piot, Charles. 2010. *Nostalgia for the Future: West Africa after the Cold War*. Chicago: University of Chicago Press.

Poli, Raffaele. 2006. "Migration and Trade of African Football Players: Historic, Geographical, and Cultural Aspects." *Africa Spectrum* 41, no. 3: 393–414.

Poli, Raffaele, Loïc Ravenel, and Roger Besson. 2015. "Exporting Countries in World Football." *CIES Football Observatory Monthly Report* 8, October 2015. https://football-observatory.com/Montly-Report-issue-8-Exporting-countries-in.

Robbins, Joel. 2013. "Beyond the Suffering Subject: Toward an Anthropology of the Good." *Journal of the Royal Anthropological Institute* 19, no. 3: 447–462.

Smith, Daniel Jordan. 2017. *To Be a Man Is Not a One-Day Job: Masculinity, Money, and Intimacy in Nigeria*. Chicago: University of Chicago Press.

Vidacs, Bea. 2010. *Visions of a Better World: Football in the Cameroonian Social Imagination*. Münster: Lit Verlag.

Warnier, Jean-Pierre. 1993. *L'esprit d'entreprise au Cameroun*. Paris: Karthala.

Yang, Jie. 2010. "The Crisis of Masculinity: Class, Gender, and Kindly Power in Post-Mao China." *American Ethnologist* 37, no. 3: 550–562.

13

SKATING ON THIN ICE

Young Finnish male hockey players' hopes in the neoliberal age

Sari Pietikäinen and Anna-Liisa Ojala

Whatever it takes!

Eighteen-year-old Finnish ice hockey player Mikko, who participated in our collaborative ethnographic project about aspiring hockey professionals, sent us the photo of a flipboard in his team's dressing room after performing at a junior (under-20-year-old or U20) team's tryout. The dressing room of an elite league youth team in Finland is home base for players from different parts of the country. The flipboard was covered with slogans: *Whatever it takes; The only option is winning; All in; Together; No pain; All day, every day; Ollaan yhdessä pommikoneita!* (Let's be bombers together!); *Winning is inevitable, Halu ratkaisee* (You've got to have the will); *Hyvällä flowlla* (With good flow); *Have fun.* Although the entire team is Finnish speaking, the slogans were written in both English and Finnish, reflecting the role of English as the lingua franca of global sports and global youth culture.

The player told us that the slogans had been written by another player to cheer the new team on. The team consisted of 30 aspiring professionals aiming high in competitive hockey, both as individuals and as a team. Each player was committed to playing and practicing hockey every week and often several times a day, but without any guarantee that this investment would carry him to the top. The slogans reflect the mindset a young player must subscribe to in order to succeed on the ice. The hope of one day becoming a hockey professional calls for commitment, discipline, and flexibility, including readiness to move between local, national, and international teams. "Whatever it takes!" the whiteboard slogan declares.

Since the 1960s, ice hockey has been transformed from a local sport practiced in a limited number of countries into a global industry with over one million registered players in 72 countries. This shift has turned it into a hotspot of economic investment, a subject of ideological interest, and source of professional aspirations on a global scale. The largest professional league is the North American Hockey League (NHL), which is made up of 30 teams in the United States and Canada and has revenues between US$99 million and 219 million (Ozanian 2016); in comparison, the Finnish league, Liiga, is comprised of 15 teams, with revenues in the US$4.2–12.5 million range (Vehviläinen 2016).

Finland is known internationally as a "hockey nation." Hockey is the second most popular team sport after soccer (Szerovay 2018, 34; Lämsä and Rautakorpi 2015). But hockey is highly gendered: in 2018, over 90% of under 20-year-old practitioners in Finland were male (Suomen Jääkiekkoliitto 2017; Mononen, Blomqvist, Koski, and Kokko 2016, 28). Men have the legitimate hockey bodies, skills, and potential career opportunities, whereas women have very few opportunities to pursue a professional career and, in the Finnish public sphere, they are always talked about in comparison to men (Herrala 2015, 14–15).

Despite the sport's global reach, Finnish ice hockey is firmly rooted in regional towns and dependent on both public and private support. Most ice arenas are multipurpose spaces, built and owned by the local municipality, and sports teams can rent them at relatively low cost. However, running a professional hockey club requires considerable resources. The hockey club covers, among other things, equipment, the salaries of various professionals, and the cost of travel between regional towns across the country. As a result, clubs invest time and money to convince sponsors to support the team and its players. Ideally, local enterprises support local teams with long-lasting sponsorship contracts and regional municipalities with subsidies and facilities. But, in recent years, many Finnish hockey teams have been in crisis. In many regions, the economy has stagnated because of changes in the global economy. Declining public financial support, shrinking ticket revenue, and hockey professionals' demands for better salaries have made local Finnish hockey teams struggle. Even when hockey is just a hobby, it requires considerable financial investment from the player's family who foot the bill of licences, equipment, and tournaments. Hockey relies on considerable voluntary work. A hockey team's tight finances will increase competition and reduce players' chances of pursuing a professional career. Many Finnish boys and men who harbour hopes of working as professional hockey players are skating on thin ice.

The route to professional rinks begins with non-profit organizations run by local sports clubs and continues with semi-professional and professional hockey teams. The most promising players are first offered spots in in the junior league and later in a professional league. Subsequently, they can aspire to join hockey's transnational labour flows.

Professional hockey players are mobile. In fact, mobility has become a form of capital for players, since their economic and symbolic values are interchangeable: they move "up" or "down" the network of teams and leagues of different ranks in national and global hockey spaces. For example, some former NHL players have landed contracts in the Finnish national league worth between €250,000 and

€320,000 a season. This is paltry compared to the NHL, where the average salary is €2.6 million and top salaries are as high as €12.4 million for Jonathan Toews of the Chicago Blackhawks or €9 million for Sidney Crosby of the Pittsburgh Penguins, in addition to endorsements (Ozanian 2016).

In Finland, mobility has become part of aspiring professionals' imagination, with an ultimate goal of "moving up" from local and national teams to the NHL. This mobility has turned some hockey leagues into professional and economic dreams-come-true spaces, while turning others into cooling-off spaces where professionals past their prime continue playing on good salaries and hold on to professional status (da Silva and Pietikäinen 2018). Some hockey teams have opted for a dual role: developing young talent in a reservoir for the elite leagues and offering opportunities to play the game at a decent professional level. The Finnish elite teams belong to the latter category.

Many young Finnish men hoping to become professionals know that the chances of success are slim and competition is fierce. In the high-performance U20 league, players have the opportunity to display their potential as professionals. The league consists of 18 teams with a total of between 450 and 550 players, depending on the time in the season. While displaying their hockey skills, they must also show their readiness to be mobile and flexible for the precarious yet potentially lucrative hockey markets.

The ethnographic materials we discuss in this chapter were part of a larger project, Cold Rush, which was concerned with language and identity in expanding Arctic economies, including winter sports. The ethnography focused on an elite Finnish U20 hockey team and its players, who were about to either succeed or fail as professionals. Finding themselves at a turning point in their life trajectory, they faced the transition from promising amateur to aspiring professional, with various potential career routes ahead of them. Our key participants were four current players and one former player during the 2016–18 hockey seasons. They were between 18 and 20 years old, white, and from middle-class families.

We used various data-collection methods in our research, including interviews and the observation of games, training sessions, and other events. We also asked the players to take notes on their practice routines and to photograph their daily activities with their phone cameras and send the images to us via WhatsApp. Anna-Liisa Ojala held regular interviews and discussions with the players about their experiences and aspirations for their hockey careers. This collaborative ethnography – a research design where researchers and participant produce data together (Heller, Pietikäinen, and Pujolar 2018) – amounted to 33 interviews with the players, 22 observation days or events, and 1,859 photographs and video clips taken by the players. We focus on their experiences and perceptions of hockey mobility, including the hopes and the risks they see before them. We pay particular attention to the routes and crossroads that the players consider valuable or harmful to their potential hockey careers and to the development of their hockey talent.

Neoliberal configurations on ice

Today, competitive sport is one of many fields in which the logic of neoliberalism is at work, the product of the deregulation of markets and the economization of social life (Brown 2015; Kelly 2013). Neoliberalism has brought about a number of related transformations, including the privatization and economization of many social domains such as work, education, health care, the family, and the care of the body. Market rationality has become the organizing principle of human activity, including its governance (Brown 2015). In this market-ordered world, subjects must develop "entrepreneurial selves" (Foucault 2004) by becoming flexible, ready to manage and better themselves to succeed in contexts characterized by constant competition, rankings, and ratings (Gershon 2018, 173). In the neoliberal age, sport is understood as the complex conjuncture of professionalized, competitive, privatized, and commercial activities (Andrews and Silk 2012; Dubal 2010). Under these conditions, the most promising athletes are traded as commodities.

One way of thinking about the juncture of sports and neoliberalism, especially from young aspiring professionals' perspective, is through the lens of a Foucauldian understanding of neoliberalism as an "art of government" and a modality of self-governance (Foucault 2004, 131; Brown 2015; Gershon 2018). For Foucault (1977, 2004), neoliberalism produces subjectivities that are constantly under surveillance but often in subtle and invisible ways, so that aspiring athletes normalize and accept this surveillance, making it their own project. Here, power does not work through force but through promise and desire. The body and the self become sites of regulation, control, investment, and hope. Foucault uses the notion of *docile body* to illustrate how individuals within their bodies are subjected, used, transformed, and improved under neoliberal conditions (Foucault 1973).

Under neoliberalism, a complex network of practices, discourses, and experiences shapes what we do to ourselves (Kelly 2013). The neoliberal self is produced through *technologies of the self*. As Foucault argues, technologies of the self:

> permit individuals to effect by their own means or with the help of others a certain number of operations on their own bodies and souls, thoughts, conducts and way of beings, so as to transform themselves in order to attain a certain state of happiness, purity, wisdom, perfection or immortality.
>
> *(1988, 18)*

Technologies of the self define what is true or false, what is permitted or forbidden, and desirable or undesirable (Rose 1990). With technologies of the self, individuals make themselves the object of their own technical practices, such as subjecting behaviour to norms, regulating movements, and self-surveilling, but also potentially resisting norms (Besley 2005; Jokinen 2016; Markkula 2003). While the self is the outcome of a dynamic interplay of forces and strategies, technologies of the self are discursive configurations of these effects, shaped by structures of power (Behrent 2013, 76–79; Gershon 2018, 174–175).

The entrepreneurial self seizes any opportunity for profit and is constantly ready to compete (Martin Rojo 2018, 4), but it must remain flexible, shifting to meet market demands by means of constant self-work and self-improvement. All activities are opportunities for production and investment subject to a cost calculation (Martin Rojo 2018, 7). Navigating and managing the contradictions of the neoliberal logics, neoliberal subjects must become "the CEO of me, Inc.," as Gershon describes it, "seeing oneself as a bundle of skills, assets, qualities, experiences and relationships, a bundle that must be consciously managed and constantly enhanced" (2018, 175).

One of the central claims of neoliberalism is that it not only frees individuals from over-protective or limiting control, but also shapes them into moral and responsible human beings, since they shoulder the risks of the decisions they make (Brown 2015). In these circumstances, success requires producing a new kind of self that is responsible for his or her actions, displaying individual entrepreneurism and assuming responsibility in every domain. In this process, the individual becomes doubly responsibilized: he or she is expected to fend for him- or herself, can be blamed for any failure to thrive, and is expected to act for the wellbeing of the economy, but can also be blamed for its problems (Brown 2015, 134). The most successful "CEO of me" uses communication, marketing, and development strategies without losing sight of risks and potentialities (Gershon 2018). In the case of the young aspiring hockey players, mobility between teams is a key strategy for career advancement. It also increases the need to learn to navigate the contradictions of neoliberal logic that characterize competitive hockey markets. These include tensions between individual success and the success of the team, between valuing skills and valuing reputation, and between taking care of one's body and playing for success.

Investing in hockey mobilities: Local, national, and global routes

For young aspiring players, hockey mobility creates a familiar neoliberal dilemma as it presents them with various possibilities, each valid but often mutually exclusive and always entailing some risks. Moreover, players and managers have overlapping but different professional, economic, and affective *investments* in hockey mobilities. This creates different expectations and interests; for example, what managers or coaches see as best for the team can differ from what an individual player considers best for his career development.

Figure 13.1 illustrates possible routes that were open to young aspiring hockey players in 2017. In Finland, there were 15 professional elite league teams (Liiga), marked by pucks in the figure. They were the only teams that could provide players and staff a fully professional working environment. These teams are located in major cities, mostly in the southern or central parts of the country. Semi-professional or first-division teams (Mestis), marked with skates in the figure, are located in smaller towns but in the same regions as Liiga teams. Mestis teams are feeder teams for the

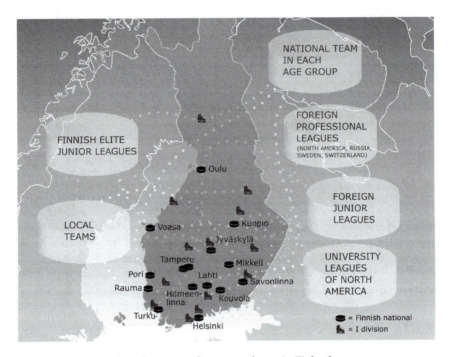

FIGURE 13.1 Potential hockey routes for young players in Finland.
(Source: Cold Rush Project)

Liiga; they have signed contracts with at least one Liiga team that enables the latter
to send their former their surplus of players to practise and play. Mestis teams have
lower budgets and smaller arenas, but they can play an important role in the towns
where they are located by providing sorely needed entertainment. Together, these
two leagues, Liiga and Mestis, constitute the centre of gravity of Finnish hockey
mobility, offering a professional career or the hope of achieving one.

The teams all foster junior talent and career development. Liiga clubs have a
high-performance junior team. The media often refers to these as mills that grind
out player material for the national and international professional leagues. In the
U20 team, the oldest junior players' abilities are put to the test. They can aspire to
join junior and professional leagues or university leagues in North America, which
may lead to contracts with NHL teams. But moving overseas can involve emotional
stress. In some countries, it is also restricted by regulations that limit the number
of non-citizen players that a team is able to recruit (Allain 2008). For example,
teams that belong to the United States Hockey League, the top junior league in the
country, may only recruit six non-citizen players at any given time if at least two
are Canadians.

The players who participated in our fieldwork were all pursuing hockey careers
that began in smaller clubs before they transferred to a high-performance club in
their early teens or mid-teens. Three had remained in their home town, a large

national hockey hub with high-performance junior teams, while the other two had moved to this town to pursue their career aspirations. One of them, Joonas, had moved 300 kilometres from his home town because in his home town he was not considered to have enough potential.[1] He did not want to give up hope for a professional career and thus decided to move by himself, at age 15, to the next closest elite-level team that accepted him.

The trajectories that the five players had followed is typical of players in their age group. In their own estimations, 15 of their 28 teammates were considered local (within a radius of 50 kilometres) while the others had moved in their teens from other districts. This move from home at an early age is in stark contrast to trends in the general population: in Finland, young people leave their parents' home at the average age of 21.9 (men earlier than women) and in European Union member states, at the age of 27.1 (Eurostat 2017).

Joonas's route to a professional career from a small peripheral town to a larger city is typical. As in neighbouring hockey country Sweden (Bruner, Macdonald, Pickett, and Coté 2011), in Finland players from small towns (10,000–30,000 inhabitants) are over-represented in U20 teams. While local teams in small towns export junior players, large hockey hubs accumulate them for the professional market. Players also move locally between teams of the same network. Within a network, Liiga and Mestis teams can trade players. The temporality of these local mobilities is unpredictable: depending on how well the player performs and the skill and team position a club requires, a player can be moved between teams with only a day's warning, even if for a single game.

An aspiring professional player considers any geographical location attractive if it has a successful hockey team or a team that might advance his career, even if the town has little else to offer, such as movie theatres, restaurants, or cultural events. For example, in April 2017, Anna-Liisa Ojala took a one-hour car trip with three players to explore a town that had the closest Mestis team and hockey arena. For the players, playing on that team represented a step up in their career development. However, the town is much smaller than the hockey hub where they lived and practiced, offered declining services, and had rising unemployment. The main street featured a church, one grocery store, and a few bars and restaurants. Many shop fronts were boarded up and only a few people could be seen walking or driving.

During the trip, the players weighed the pros and cons of moving to the town. The researcher asked if the players could imagine living in the town. Mika thought it would be hard and Mikko found the place ugly and old-fashioned. Yet the town sported a partly publicly run successful hockey team, even though the facilities at the arena were basic. This made the players reconsider what they required of where they lived. Despite the town's limited services, they were ready to move there if the team offered them a contract. They saw the move as an opportunity for their career and thought that, because hockey work is intensive, they should move to the town instead of commuting there, even though it was only a one-hour drive from home.

Hockey careers require players to be ready to move to economic and cultural peripheries. For example, of the 15 Liiga teams in the 2016–17 season, only one was located in a city whose population had declined in the past 30 years, whereas 6 out of 13 Mestis teams were located in such towns, mostly in rural Finland. In other words, Liiga team cities are economic and cultural hubs that attract hockey players as well as other inhabitants, whereas Mestis hockey often takes place in towns that had been left behind by the country's rural-to-urban flight. The players' willingness to move to these smaller towns, from which other young people yearn to leave, suggests that all that counts for them is hockey.

In similar fashion, a town, large or small, can become unattractive in the eyes of players if its hockey team falters. Anna-Liisa Ojala asked players to list towns that would not be attractive for hockey mobility. One midsize Liiga team city kept coming up in the answers; the players explained that the team was not doing well in the league. The players saw mobility between teams as a move in their career that they needed to weigh carefully. They consider mobility, even to peripheral places, as part of the game, helping or hindering their career. The players did not weigh the necessity of moving against the cost of losing social networks and educational opportunities.

To find out more about the past and future mobilities of the players, we asked the players to map out their trajectories to date as well as their ideal career path. The route they typically identified took them straight through the local elite sports development system, from a local junior team to a high-performance U20 team in the same city, then to mandatory military or civilian service at the end of their U20 team eligibility, on to semi-professional or professional teams, and finally, to a professional hockey team. Three players had already embarked on this trajectory. Looking back at their development, they said that the team where they spent their childhood and early teenage years didn't matter as long as they could move to a high-performance club in their later teens. Sometimes this requires moving from their home town to another hockey district, which was the case of Mika, an 18-year-old goalie. He thought that the time he spent playing in his home town was unimportant but considered the time he spent in the professional hockey organization's youth team from the age of 15 as significant. This move had allowed him to develop his skills to near-professional level. In future, he hopes to play on a Mestis team after he turns 20 and move to a professional hockey team. Instead of aspiring to move internationally, Mika saw his future in Finland.

Hockey mobilities: Moving up, holding on, and moving out

Anticipation and speculation are fundamental ways in which players related to their future: how much ice time they will have in the next game, will they be selected to play in the next season, will they be scouted for a new team, and ultimately will they make it as professional players? One strategy for self-governance available for them is to discipline their bodies. They worked almost everyday to increase their physical strength, bodily capital that they hope would convert to hockey capital. While a contract with a Mestis team would signify a successful capital conversion, they did not expect it to happen right away.

The player's trajectory hinges on how coaches, scouts, agents, and sport managers assess his potential. As one NHL scout explained to us, the high status of a national team or a Liiga team trickles down to the players. Also, when a highly valued team gives a player a lot of ice time and responsibility in the rink, it increases his value and attracts the positive attention of scouts and coaches. Hockey mobility is produced by both individual success and team success.

Among our research participants, career trajectories centred on three types of mobility, which we term "moving up," "holding on," and "moving out" to describe the direction of the mobility and its desirability for the players' aspirations. The first type of mobility, moving up, is attractive because it takes the player to a better team and thus increases his career chances. In contrast, if a player holds on, he stays on the same team and on the same path, but he can still hold on to the hope to eventually join a better team. Moving out means abandoning career aspirations and opting for a different life. Moving between teams of different statuses helps players build a network of professional hope and risk. Instability and unpredictability are part-and-parcel of hockey markets, where, similarly to other professional sport markets, many experience a mismatch between expectations and opportunities (Besnier, Brownell, and Carter 2018). Figure 13.2 illustrates the various local hockey mobility routes for the players in the Finnish elite sports development system.

The players have three options, which they value differently. The best possible option is to play on the professional Liiga teams, at the top of the figure. The second best is to play on a Liiga feeder team, in the middle of the figure. The last option is to play on recreational teams in the second division, at the bottom of the figure.

Since only high-performing athletes can play and sign contracts in one of the Liiga clubs' U20 teams, to be contracted by one of these teams indicates, the player must be recognized as one of the best in his age group. He is on track to become a professional. This was the case of four of our research participants. If a player does not get an offer from a Liiga club's U20 team, the local Mestis junior team was the next best option, as it provides opportunities for a player to be observed and developed. If he succeeds in this environment, he still stands a chance to be chosen for a Liiga club's U20 team. Local recreational Mestis teams do not sign collaboration contracts with professional hockey teams and do not compete for the same players and resources. Our five players had a clear idea of what each kind of team could offer.

Mika the goalie thought that his transition from his home town's team to the Liiga club's U20 team had been an important step in his career. He did not question the economic, social, and emotional costs of this move that it had involved, but rather kept his eye on his career trajectory: moving up in the hierarchy of Finnish hockey toward professionalism. Moving up in the hierarchy of local teams strengthens his identity as a potential professional and provides better conditions for talent development.

The path to professional hockey pushes the players to develop an entrepreneurial self who uses its skills and body as a bargaining chip, looks after himself financially, and negotiates the best possible contract. One manifestation of this entrepreneurial

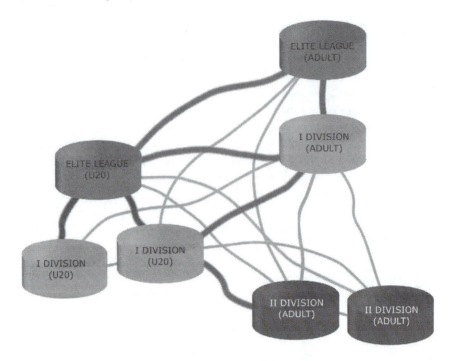

FIGURE 13.2 Local hockey mobility possibilities in Finland.
(Source: Cold Rush Project)

approach was contracting a professional agent to help with contract negotiations, which two of our five research participants had already done. Joonas, a promising player who was about to break into a professional team, had hired an agent during several weeks of negotiations over his first junior contract. Weighing whether to move from a junior hockey track to the professional team, he carefully calculated the financial aspects of these options. This first experience of financial negotiations was emotionally draining and he felt a sense of relief when he was finally offered a contract.

Although his new contract only earned him a modest salary, it was econom- ically important for him because he lived alone and was not otherwise employed. His parents helped him financially, but pro-level skates, sticks, and other equipment represent a significant investment for most people of his age. Symbolically, signing a contract was also an important milestone in that it indicated that the club was willing to invest in him. This placed him in a strategic position in the hockey market. It also gave some tangible hope that he would fulfil his dream of becoming professional. Joonas was on his way to move up.

Holding on represents a different experience. Two of our research participants, Jere and Mikko, were in that position, as they were unable to secure a contract with a youth team. They were instead focused on continuing to play at their current level, and in order to do so, they were prepared to work selflessly for the club, obeying coaches to the letter and internalizing the organizations' logic to remain on the roster. In Foucault's (1977) terms, they needed to become docile bodies that are used, transformed, and improved to fit to the demands of the organization and the market. Emotionally, Jere and Mikko prepared themselves for a second-best career. 18-year-old Jere talked about his future as "having a few adventures," since "you don't get to the Liiga that easily." He is ready to be geographically flexible and willing to move to other parts of Finland or abroad, but he is not in a position to plan his hockey future in detail. This flexibility and tolerance for insecurity are hallmarks of neoliberal logics on ice.

As in other sports, the global hockey industry needs large numbers of players to develop a few elite players. High-performance hockey teams are organized around competition and exclusivity but also need players who are willing to submit to the commercial logic of hockey even if they are not headed for a lucrative professional career (Ojala 2020). In Finland, the welfare system provides a safety net for players who do not make it, mitigating risk (Andersson and Carlsson 2009). In contrast to many other places (e.g., Guinness and Besnier 2016), Finland offers alternatives for geographical and social mobility to athletes who do not succeed. Education and health care are free and unemployment and social security benefits are available to everyone during and after a sports career, making it possible for players to think of hockey as an adventure rather than a career, as Jere did.

Sometimes, players can hold on to their dreams of a career by moving to a farm team or a new team at the same level if they are pushed out of their current team when new players are recruited at the start of the season. Liiga U20 team players do not think of farm-team players as serious competitors on the hockey markets. Our five research participants saw Mestis farm teams as a place where any player from an elite-level team could play if they wanted. Nonetheless, moving to the farm team or being left out of the next season's U20 team while still eligible was an undesirable way to end the season.

The young men had grown accustomed to players who were not selected for the team and considered this fate to be part of the game. Joonas light-heartedly commented that this outcome was a personal hell for the player, but that it wasn't his problem. For him, not being selected was a routine event in a high-performance team sport. His comment echoes a neoliberal logic in which the individual is responsible for his own fate and relationships between individuals can easily turn friendships into competitions (Beslay 2005; Brown 2015). Of course, competition is always central to professional sports, but the contrast between talk of commitment to the team and the absence of this talk the moment a player fails to be selected is remarkable. The same logic applies at the institutional level: no official on the team cared for the players' emotional wellbeing once they were not selected. When it came to winning games and developing talent, officials helped players manage their feelings and expectations, but this care work stopped when it came to player's career and personal life.

Moving out, the last mobility strategy available to players, consists in giving up on a career and opting to play hockey recreationally and valuing the sport as lifestyle. A player may move out either because he is unable to continue along the old path or because he decides not to. For example, Aaron decided to move out of the professional track at the age of 20. In the week that followed his decision, he was resentful of his former coach, feeling that he hadn't been assigned the position he felt he deserved. His new team held practices at a basic ice arena, which had no dressing room or storage facilities, and the training programme was not well organized. Practice was very different from practice at the goal-oriented teams for which he had previously played: the players did not push themselves, took their time to gather around the coach when he summoned them, and observed lax discipline. However, after three months, Aaron had incorporated this new hockey rationale and described his season as follows: "I had quite a lot of fun there. I was given a lot of ice time and I was playing for fun." He was still the same player with the same skills, but now he no longer subscribed to the rationale of high-performance sports and didn't conduct himself as a disciplined athlete. His approach now aligned with that of his new teammates, emphasizing sport-for-all and collective wellbeing. He had become a recreational hockey player.

Conclusion: Malleable and mobile hockey hopes

To be an aspiring hockey player means becoming a docile, disciplined, yet flexible sport subject. Malleability and mobility are part of hockey life. Junior players who aim high must be willing to move from hockey peripheries to hockey hubs, and from one team or division to another. The best hockey organizations offer high-performance junior curricula and opportunities to move up in the business, and eventually a contract and a consequential move to a new town and team. Whether a player lives up to expectations is a measure of his value in a competitive hockey market. Players whose performance does not live up to expectations have two options: either they hang on to their current status and train to turn their talents into valued hockey skills, securing a contract in the next round; or they move out from the professional field, foregoing their aspirations to go professional player and opting for recreational hockey.

The logic of neoliberalism on ice has reconfigured the relationship among talent, skills, the player's bodies, and success. From early on, aspiring hockey players learn to consider their bodies and skills as commodities that can be exchanged for a contract, mobility, and time on the ice. At the same time, the player is alone responsible for any setback he may face during his career. To manage these risks, some players hire agents. The logic of neoliberalism encourages them to view themselves, their bodies, skills, and careers as a business.

The hope of becoming a professional player is powered by the success of other young Finnish players: for example, in 2019, Finland won gold at the 43rd Ice Hockey World Junior Championship in Vancouver, for the third time in six years, and a few months later, Finland won the gold medal at the 2019 International Ice Hockey Federation World Championship, hosted by Slovakia, with a team that was younger than ever before. Playing on both winning teams was Kaapo Kakko, who had just turned 18 and who was drafted a month later as the number two pick by the NHL team New York Rangers. Each of the last four years has been "the year of the Finn" in the annual NHL event, with young Finnish players being drafted. The *New York Times* remarked on this phenomenon with the February 2019 headline "In the N.H.L., Finland Is Now Here, There, and Everywhere" (Knoll 2019). Since Finland is the least populous of the major hockey nations, the success of young players in international hockey markets is taken as evidence that no other country does a better job than Finland in developing hockey talent, using the practices and career routes that the five players with whom we did our research did. Even though the players themselves are aware that they might never make it to the NHL, the success of other players of the same age and with similar training feeds speculative hockey hopes.

Acknowledgements

This chapter is based on research conducted in the context of the Cold Rush project (2016–21), funded by the Academy of Finland. We thank Niko Besnier for his unfailing support and insightful comments, which greatly improved the chapter.

References

Allain, Kristi A. 2008. "Real Fast and Tough: The Construction of Canadian Hockey Masculinity." *Sociology of Sport Journal* 25, no. 4: 462–481.

Andersson, Torbjörn, and Bo Carlsson. 2009. "Football in Scandinavia: A Fusion of Welfare Policy and the Market." *Soccer & Society* 10, no. 3–4: 299–304.

Andrews, David L., and Michael L. Silk. 2012. "Sport and the Neoliberal Conjuncture: Complicating the Consensus." In *Sport and Neoliberalism: Politics, Consumption, and Culture*, edited by David L. Andrews and Michael L. Silk, 1–19. Philadelphia: Temple University Press.

Behrent, Michael. 2013. "Foucault and Technology." *History and Technology* 29, no. 1: 54–104.

Besley, Tina. 2005. "Foucault, Truth Telling and Technologies of the Self in Schools." *Journal of Educational Enquiry* 6, no. 1: 76–89.

Besnier, Niko, Susan Brownell, and Thomas F. Carter. 2018. *The Anthropology of Sport: Bodies, Borders, and Biopolitics*. Oakland: University of California Press.

Brown, Wendy. 2015. *Undoing the Demos: Neoliberalism's Stealth Revolution*. New York: Zone.

Bruner, Mark W., Dany J. Macdonald, William Pickett, and Jean Côté. 2011. "Examination of Birthplace and Birthdate in World Junior Ice Hockey Players." *Journal of Sports Sciences* 29, no. 12: 1337–1344.

da Silva, Emanuel, and Sari Pietikäinen. 2018. "Foreign Captains in Elite Hockey Markets: Mediatized Discourses of Professionalization between Routes and Roots." *Sport in Society* 21, no. 11: 1795–1816.

Dubal, Sam. 2010. "The Neoliberalization of Football: Rethinking Neoliberalism through the Commercialization of the Beautiful Game." *International Review for the Sociology of Sport* 45, no. 2: 123–146.

Eurostat. 2017. "When Are They Ready to Leave the Nest?" Eurostat: Your Key to European Statistics, 3 May 2017. http://ec.europa.eu/eurostat/en/web/products-eurostat-news/-/EDN-20170503-1.

Foucault, Michel. 1973. *The Order of Things: An Archaeology of the Human Sciences.* Translated by Alan Sheridan. New York: Vintage. (First published 1966.)

Foucault, Michel. 1977. *Discipline and Punish: The Birth of the Prison.* Translated by Alan Sheridan. New York: Pantheon. (First published 1975.)

Foucault, Michel. 1988. "Technologies of the Self." In *Technologies of the Self: A Seminar with Michel Foucault*, edited by Luther H. Martin, Huck Gutman, and Patrick H. Hutton, 16–49. London: Tavistock.

Foucault, Michel. 2004. *The Birth of Biopolitics: Lectures at the Collège de France, 1978—79.* Translated by Graham Burchell. New York: Picador.

Gershon, Ilana. 2018. "Employing the CEO of Me, Inc.: US Corporate Hiring in a Neoliberal Age." *American Ethnologist* 45, no. 2: 173–185.

Guinness, Daniel, and Niko Besnier. 2016. "Nation, Nationalism, and Sport: Fijian Rugby in the Local-Global Nexus." *Anthropological Quarterly* 89, no. 4: 1109–1142.

Heller, Monica, Sari Pietikäinen, and Joan Pujolar. 2018. *Critical Sociolinguistic Research Methods: Studying Language Issues that Matter.* London: Routledge.

Herrala, Helena. 2015. "Tytöt kaukalossa: Etnografinen tutkimus tyttöjen jääkiekkoharrastuksesta." Ph.D. thesis, University of Lapland.

Jokinen, Eeva. 2016. "Precarious Everyday Agency." *European Journal of Cultural Studies* 19, no. 1: 85–99.

Kelly, Mark G. R. 2013. "Foucault, Subjectivity, and the Technologies of the Self." In *A Companion to Foucault*, edited by Christopher Falzon, Timothy O'Leary, and Jana Sawicki, 510–27. Malden, MA: Wiley Blackwell.

Knoll, Andrew. 2019. "In the N.H.L., Finland Is Now Here, There, and Everywhere." *New York Times*, 13 February 2019. www.nytimes.com/2019/02/13/sports/rantanen-laine-finland.html.

Lämsä, Jari, and Jukka Rautakorpi. 2015. "Joukkuelajit – suurin liikuttaja?" Online presentation by Research Institute for Olympic Sports and the Finnish Olympic Committee. https://docplayer.fi/18410705-Joukkuelajit-suurin-liikuttaja.html.

Markkula, Pirkko. 2003. "The Technologies of the Self: Sport, Feminism, and Foucault." *Sociology of Sport Journal* 22, no. 1: 87–107.

Martin Rojo, Luisa. 2018. "Neoliberalism and Linguistic Governmentality." In *The Oxford Handbook of Language Policy and Planning*, edited by James W. Tollefson and Miguel Pérez-Milans, 1–26. Oxford Handbooks Online, DOI:10.1093/oxfordhb/9780190458898.013.28.

Mononen, Kaisu, Minna Blomqvist, Pasi Koski, and Sami Kokko. 2016. "Urheilu ja seuraharrastaminen." In *Lasten ja nuorten liikuntakäyttäytyminen Suomessa: Liitu-tutkimuksen tuloksia 2016*, edited by Sami Kokko and Anette Mehtälä, 27–35. Helsinki: Valtion liikuntaneuvosto.

Ojala, Anna-Liisa. 2020. "Being an Athlete and Being a Young Person: Technologies of the Self in Managing an Athletic Career in Youth Ice Hockey in Finland." *International Review for the Sociology of Sport* 55, no. 3: 310–326.

Ozanian, Mike. 2016. "The NHL's Most Valuable Teams." *Forbes*, 30 November 2016. www.forbes.com/sites/mikeozanian/2016/11/30/the-nhls-most-valuable-teams-3/#52935ac17eff.

Rose, Nikolas. 1990. *Governing the Soul: The Shaping of the Private Self.* London: Routledge.

Suomen Jääkiekkoliitto Ry. n.d. Website of the Finnish Ice Hockey Association. Accessed 17 May 2017. www.finhockey.fi/index.php/info.

Szerovay, Mihaly. 2018. "Global and Local Interactions in Football: Comparing the Development Paths of Finland and Hungary." Ph.D. thesis, University of Jyväskylä. http://urn.fi/URN:ISBN:978-951-39-7314-8.

Vehviläinen, Maija. 2016. "Liigajoukkueiden taloudessa huimia eroja." *Kauppalehti*, 16 August 2016. www.kauppalehti.fi/uutiset/liigajoukkueiden-taloudessa-huimia-eroja-kauppalehti-kokosi-joukkueiden-tulokset/524a6f85-ccdd-3f8d-ae8d-3a05ba2242ac.

Epilogue

14

NEOLIBERALISM, THE GIFT ECONOMY, AND GENDER

Susan Brownell

The analysis of the interconnection of sport, migration, and gender in the contemporary era provides novel insights into the ascendance of neoliberalism as the dominant organizing ideology of the global market economy, a process that began in the early 1980s and peaked with the collapse of socialism in the late 1980s. While neoliberalism has been much discussed by academics, sport migration illuminates unexplored corners and sheds light on surprising aspects of its modes of operation as both ideology and practice. The scholarship collected in this volume not only reveals that beneath the broad label of neoliberalism lurks a diverse reality, but also shows how the local reality in turn complicates, reshapes, and contradicts the principles and practices of neoliberalism.

Crossing the Global North–South divide

Neoliberal ideology conceptualized the global economy as divided into two halves, the wealthy "Global North" and impoverished "Global South," categories originally proposed by West German Chancellor Willy Brandt (Independent Commission on International Development Issues 1980) in a manifesto for building "sustainable prosperity based on equitably shared resources" (124) – a promise that, as the contributors to this volume show, remains far from being fulfilled, in large part because the neoliberal assumptions about how to create prosperity were fundamentally flawed. In the world of sport, instead of shifting resources from North to South in order to reverse the exploitative colonial relationships of the previous centuries (as advocated by Brandt), since the 1990s there has been an escalating drain of athletic talent from the postcolonies to the same European and North American global cities that were the metropoles of nineteenth- and early-twentieth-century colonialism and imperialism. Seemingly repeating the colonial pattern, the transnational migration of athletes from the Global South to the Global North reinforces the simplistic dichotomy of an impoverished South and a wealthy North when athletes migrate in search of a better life than the one available in their homelands. Indeed, the volume describes the stories of many Global South–North settlers, including Fijian rugby players moving to France, Britain, Wales, Australia, New Zealand, or the United States; and Cameroonian and Senegalese footballers moving to Western Europe.

However, the greater portion of the volume describes migration patterns that do not follow this conventional pattern. For one thing, the trajectory of migrations is shaped by the economic infrastructure of particular sports. In general, professional team sports require that migrants are "settlers" – permanent or long-term residents – because these sports are more place-bound. Because football has been the focus of much of the scholarship and media coverage on sport migration, this is probably the pattern that commonly comes to mind. But this volume reminds us that athletes in individual sports may be "sojourners" who take short-term trips to matches, meets, or tournaments, or stay for a longer but not indefinite period of time in sport academies, high schools, or universities. Like the settlers, many of the sojourners also move from South to North because those same global cities are the locations of major tournaments, matches, and races – such as Ethiopian runners travelling to compete in marathons and road races in the United Kingdom, Western Europe, Japan, and the United States; Senegalese wrestlers travelling to France, Italy, and the United States; or Ghanaian boxers travelling to Britain or the United States. However, the flexibility of individual sports reduces the absolute imperative to make a long-term move with all the obstacles that entails (visas, try-outs, contracts, etc.), and many of these athletes are content to remain in their homelands to live and train. Moreover, without the geographical restrictions of the team sports, some individual sports develop training epicentres outside the North. Ghanaian boxing has such a strong international reputation that, during Leo Hopkinson's fieldwork, the neighbourhood of Ga Mashie in Accra attracted boxers who mostly came for a single professional bout and occasionally for longer periods of training and competing, from numerous sub-Saharan nations as well as the United States, Britain, Lebanon, Kazakhstan, South Korea, Argentina, and Mexico. Some boxers from Nigeria and Benin had migrated permanently. These were just the countries represented during his fieldwork; there may have been others.

While many Ethiopian runners move to Europe, Japan, or North America to train, many others remain in their homeland and aim to gain contracts for appearances at major road races without permanently emigrating. High-altitude Ethiopian training camps attract both professional elite athletes and recreational marathoners from the Global North. While these sports offer a degree of optimism, in contrast with the depressing desperation of too many would-be emigrant footballers and rugby players, the fact remains that the six most prestigious marathons, the Abbott World Marathon Majors, take place in Tokyo, London, Berlin, Boston, Chicago, and New York City. Individual sports are also not characterized by the intense male domination that prevails in almost all professional team sports. Marathoning attracts both male and female athletes, and Hannah Borenstein's chapter on Ethiopian female runners is the only one in this collection about sportswomen.

Thus, a large segment of global sport migration may look like a new form of colonial extraction by the same old colonial-era powers, an impression strengthened by the intensified recruiting of athletes in the Global South and establishment of feeder academies by professional European and North American teams as a result of the turn to neoliberalism described in this book. This resource extraction is largely gendered male, as if male athletic labour is the only resource worthy of exploitation.

However, the world has changed since the collapse of colonial empires; it is just that the biggest change has not occurred in the relationship between Global North and Global South. Perhaps the most important way in which today's global economic order does not resemble the colonial order is in the rise of what some scholars, observing the inadequacies of the North–South binary, have proposed to call the "Global East":

> all those societies that fall somewhere between North and South – too rich to be in the South, too poor to be in the North. And this is no small black hole: it encompasses those societies that took part in what was the most momentous global experiment of the twentieth century: to create communism.
>
> *(Müller 2020, 1)*

The region is often ignored in the sources that discuss global inequality. The Global East is liminal; it is not-quite-North and not-quite-South. On the map, it stretches across the middle of Eurasia between the North and South. An important contribution of this volume is to describe how a number of countries are playing a role in the global economy of sports that does not fit the North–South dichotomy.

By 1980, Japan was the only non-Western nation on the northern side of the Brandt line. In colonial history, Japan occupies a controversial position as a non-Western nation that sought to challenge Western colonialism by establishing an Eastern empire. Like the former European colonial powers, it is today a major destination for football and rugby players. At the same time, it contributes interesting non-Western cultural twists to global sport (Japanese-style baseball and sumo, for example), one of which is the *ekiden,* a distinctive mode of long-distance relay road racing reflecting the Japanese cultural context. A developed professional *ekiden* system is not found elsewhere in the world, although races have been organized outside Japan in increasing numbers in the last decade. As Michael Peters describes, the economic resources of the *ekiden,* which generate substantial corporate sponsorship and television revenues, attract long-distance runners to Japan to essentially become professional athletes who are not members of professional teams, but who instead represent high schools, universities, and, for the select few, corporations. The *ekiden* have created a pipeline for Kenyan and Ethiopian long-distance runners who move to Japan. Unlike the male domination that prevails in most Western sports, *ekiden* teams employ both men and women and some of the relays are mixed-sex relays – which is even more remarkable by contrast with the rigid stance against mixed-sex sports in the Western-dominated international sport system, which does not even recognize records set by women marathoners in mixed-sex races (Besnier, Brownell, and Carter 2018, 141–143).

Many chapters in this volume illustrate the distinctive position in transnational flows of migrants that is occupied by countries that do not fit well the North–South binary. The liminal position between North and South that Eastern Europe and Turkey occupy is evident in the chapters by John McManus and Uroš Kovač. Sport migrants are attracted to this region in the first place because it offers better opportunities than they have at home, but in the second place because they see these countries as a steppingstone to a professional contract in the Global North. Like Cameroonian footballers moving to Eastern Europe, sub-Saharan African footballers moving to Turkey aspire to move on to Western Europe, as do Fijian and Tongan rugby players moving to Romania.

China is also taking on the role of a sporting bridge between South and North, as well as being a node in a regional circulation of Eastern European, Chinese, and South Korean athletes – and to a lesser extent Japanese and North Korean athletes. The Chinese Super League is becoming a destination for African footballers, along with players from all regions of the world – with a comparatively large proportion (relative to their national populations) coming from Eastern European countries and South Korea. China is a desirable stop on the marathon circuit for Ethiopian runners (Crawley, this volume). Chinese athletes also aspire to migrate to Western Europe and North America, and large numbers of retired top athletes in many sports are now living and coaching in the United States. In Chinese tennis, ambitious would-be sojourner athletes see training in either privately run academies or the state-run sport system, or a combination of both, as a launching pad for achieving international rankings or gaining an athletics scholarship at a U.S. university (Haugen, this volume).

It is impossible to talk about postcolonial sport without discussing cricket, that most quintessential sport of the British Empire. In some ways it is now the most decolonized sport. Beside Ghanaian boxing, West Indies cricket is the only other example in this volume of a sports epicentre located within the Global South, and Guyanese cricketers who aspire to move to Trinidad are the only other example of migration within the Global South. Of course, the pinnacle of global cricket is now located in India, a particularly interesting example of the reversal of the old colonial cricket hierarchy focused on Britain (Hossain, this volume).

Crossing borders

For all migrants, whether sporting or not, one of the major obstacles to migration is the visa. Mark Hann's chapter about Senegalese footballers paints a painful portrait of the obstacles that migrants face and the tribulations that they endure in trying to obtain a visa, a thread that runs throughout many of the chapters. This is despite the fact that one of the attractions of sports is that athletes have easier access to visas than other manual labourers. A unique situation exists in China, where an internal visa system is essentially in place, known as the "residence permit" (*hukou*) system, which prevents people with a rural *hukou* from legally moving to cities; undocumented rural–urban migrants do not have full rights of citizenship in cities, such as access to free healthcare or public education for their children. Thus, the first aspiration of rural athletes is to be able to move to the city where the provincial team is located and acquire a permanent urban *hukou*. The golden apple is a Beijing *hukou* (Haugen, this volume).

This volume demonstrates that the limited access to sports epicentres in itself structures an entire industry of agents and academies, with a detrimental effect on the lives of many athletes. The chapters raise the question of what global sports in a world without national borders would look like. Why, in this age of global fandoms and televised and online sport, do these old geographic obstacles still limit the opportunities of aspiring athletes in parts of the world? While the old colonial order might have undergone some shifts, it seems that some of the even longer-term structures of the Westphalian order of nation-states remain largely unchanged and continue to serve the interests of the conventional powers. It is not just that nation-states restrict immigration; they also structure access to opportunity within their borders through hierarchies of class, race, indigeneity, and gender.

In many countries with strong domestic professional opportunities, the main goal may simply be to be selected for the national team. Ice hockey players hope to make it to the top of the Finnish system as a steppingstone to North America's National Hockey League. In comparison with the other groups discussed in this volume, those white, working- or middle-class ice hockey players seem better prepared to make the jump into the global sports system because they have already been trained in the "technologies of the self" required to fully function as a neoliberal subject (Pietikäinen and Ojala, this volume). For most of the other athletes discussed in this volume, the pursuit of a sporting dream is motivated by their lack of privilege and limited opportunities in their homeland. Even those who manage to migrate to the Global North may still end up working in menial jobs or running small businesses after retirement.

Being selected for the All Blacks of New Zealand is the first choice of Māori players, whereas moving to Europe, Japan, and North America means they have abandoned this dream. However, within their home nation, they feel that they have not fully left behind their colonial status and do not possess sovereignty over their lives (Calabrò, this volume). Māori men may be considered particularly well-suited for rugby because of their "warrior" culture, but many consider the All-Blacks' performance of the pre-match *haka* ritual as a reminder that they are marketable because of the exotic appeal of their indigeneity.

It is worth pointing out that as great as obstacles of location, race, class, and ethnicity may be, gender everywhere poses the biggest obstacle to would-be athletes. Even when they have the opportunity to participate in sports, the gravitational field of the family pulls even more strongly on women than men, making it difficult for them to fully escape into the orbit of market principles that revolves around professional road races, as is true of Ethiopian female runners, among others (Borenstein, this volume).

Neoliberalism

A central theme of the chapters is the ascendancy of neoliberal ideology and policy in the Global North starting in the 1980s and its impact on the shape of the global sports world. The triumph of the free market and individualism when the Soviet bloc collapsed was a major turning point that led to the historical moment captured in these chapters. Contrary to expectations in the West, the Chinese Communist Party did not fall after 1989 and China never fully abandoned socialism, but instead flourished economically under "socialism with Chinese characteristics." Today China has a unique hybrid economy in which state-owned enterprises (central, provincial, and local government-owned) contribute about 30 per cent of the national GDP. Reforms to reduce the number of enterprises that are wholly state-owned have been implemented ever since the market reforms began in 1978, but the process has been very slow because the Party has chosen to prioritize "social stability" over economic productivity. The continued existence of a vast government bureaucracy and huge civil service has also helped to mitigate the instability resulting from the shift toward neoliberal ideology and preserve the respect for education that went along with the thousand-year-old tradition of choosing civil servants through a written examination. And so China did not suffer the negative effects of the downsizing of the civil service suffered elsewhere in the Global South, where the North pressed neoliberal reforms upon countries as a condition for aid packages, eliminating the large numbers of stable government jobs that had previously represented the most sought-after career options. By contrast, in China most sports are still state-supported despite forty years of policies aimed at weaning sports off of government support. Tennis is one of the first sports in which new, market-oriented institutions have emerged. However, athletes and their families make strategic choices about whether to seek positions within the state-supported system or "fly solo" at their own expense in the private academies. If they have the option, most prefer a hybrid strategy of remaining within the government system for security and only leaving it behind when the athlete is good enough that the risk is minimal and the rewards worth it (Haugen, this volume).

People in China continue to firmly believe that education is the path to social mobility, which poses obstacles for the sports system because parents are reluctant to allow their children to be recruited into sports boarding schools, where they receive a subpar education that will likely prevent them from testing into a university. Only when it is obvious that children are not strong students will parents consider sports as an alternative path, which may guarantee admission into a top university if they are particularly talented athletically. After they retire, a small number of top-level athletes are hired to work in the government sports system and some may eventually become civil servants, but the vast majority are cast out onto the job market.

The situation in China is very different from that of countries in the Global South where governments were eviscerated by austerity programmes and household farming destroyed by economic restructuring. With limited replacement options, sports stepped in to fill the gap, but as an anchor for the local economy, sports careers are a poor substitute for civil service because they are precarious and short-lived. They also do not require a high educational level as government jobs did, contributing to a devaluation of education in society at large. This situation contrasts with China, which controlled its own fate and has been downsizing on its own schedule rather than one imposed by more powerful neoliberal states; there, state-supported institutions provide security and, in the larger picture, social stability in the midst of a transition to a risky market economy. On the surface, China's situation is unlike the cases in the Global South, but at a deeper level in both situations there was a conflict between the state and the market, which the state lost; the only difference was the pace at which the triumph of the market proceeded. Ultimately, the global economy is inescapable. There is no alternative and in order to take part, everyone has to play by the neoliberal rules of the game. Haugen's chapter is useful for capturing this transitional moment in China that has already passed in other parts of the world where, as many chapters in this book demonstrate, many of the old social institutions partly or fully collapsed but were never replaced by a fully developed neoliberal economy.

It may seem that the athletes who succeed in obtaining that international visa or internal *hukou* and professional contract have done an end run around the hierarchies built into the neoliberal economy. But let us recall that it was precisely the neoliberal privatization of television networks in the 1980s and the 1990s that offered up images of sporting celebrity and wealth to global consumers. That a select few can end up as celebrities on television reinforces the hierarchy by maintaining the neoliberal fiction that hard work, discipline, and talent will give anyone access to the capitalist good life. Neoliberalism proves to be inescapable. Professional athletes are both exceptional and ordinary: exceptional in that the top athletes make a huge amount of money, including migrants (which is not the case for manual workers of other kinds); but they are ordinary in being like any other neoliberal workers at this historical moment. Like the work of low-status manual labourers, their labour is characterized by precarity, brevity, and work-life imbalance, and they face all of the key dilemmas that are embedded in how neoliberalism defines work.

The market cannot do without the gift economy and gender

This volume's focus on the social lives of athletes reveals that they are thoroughly embedded in gift economies centred on kinship. While most of the world's professional athletes are men, many of the chapters reveal that these men would not be where they are if not for a support network of women – wives, mothers, and sisters – who maintain the households in the home communities that not only define these men as men, but also serve as the fallback when their careers come to an end. The chapter on Fijian rugby wives by Guinness and Hecht in particular details how this "hidden economy" operates in tandem with the neoliberal calculations and practices that athletes are compelled to master. In many instances, players and agents may perceive the claims of kin as a counterproductive drain of financial resources and mental energy that distracts from the goal of sporting success. One wonders why the players continue to respond to requests from relatives and send remittances from far away. The easy answer is that gift giving reflects the values they were raised with and that their identities are still strongly embedded in these communities, especially where racism and anti-immigrant sentiment work against a sense of belonging in their host country. If they cut themselves off from the gift economy, they do so at a cost, cutting off more than just the flow of money; they also cut off a part of themselves. It is only the very successful athletes happily settled in the host country who have enough financial and social independence to refuse to bow to the imperatives of the gift economy.

All of the athletes described in this volume are would-be neoliberal subjects still embedded in gift economies. They may counterbalance the claims of reciprocity through religion, justifying their seeming individualism with Pentecostalism or Islamic devotion, but they are still pulled back into an economy that is dominated by reciprocity, responsibility, and debt. It is because of this pull that gender is so problematic for these athletes. They are expected to act like neoliberal individuals, but because they are not free of the gift economy, they are not free of the gender expectations that go along with it. If they successfully follow the rules of the gift economy, they will be recognized as masculine men by their kin and home community, a recognition that most of them seem to crave. (The logic operates differently for women, whose responsibility to the household trumps the responsibility to have a lucrative job.) The market does not offer an alternative system of values and masculine identity, and so athletes can escape neither the economic logic of the market economy nor the value system of the gift economy.

The topic of gender might seem like an "add-on" to the weightier topics of migration and neoliberalism, but one of this volume's novel contributions is to suggest that the global market economy, or at least the global sports economy, cannot do without the gift economy and the constructions of gender that underpin it. It is in the realm of family, household, village, and neighbourhood that athletes are constructed as men and occasionally as women, and it is those situated identities that motivate them to make the sacrifices they do in order to pursue sports as a profession. Without the often intense pressure generated by those bonds and obligations, one suspects that the risk and precarity of that path might lose some of its appeal.

References

Besnier, Niko, Susan Brownell, and Thomas F. Carter. 2018. *The Anthropology of Sport: Bodies, Borders, Biopolitics*. Oakland: University of California Press.

Independent Commission on International Development Issues. 1980. *North-South: A Programme for Survival: A Report of the Independent Commission on International Development Issues*. Cambridge, MA: MIT Press.

Müller, Martin. 2020. "In Search of the Global East: Thinking between North and South." *Geopolitics* 25, no. 3: 734–755.

INDEX